This collection of essays, four of which are published in English for the first time, represents the life's work of the historian Tim Mason, one of the most original and perceptive scholars of National Socialism. Mason pioneered the social and labour history of National Socialism, and was the author of the groundbreaking book *Social Policy in the Third Reich* (1977). Mason was probably best known, however, for a series of brilliant, provocative articles and essays, written between 1964 and 1990, whose combination of empirical rigour and theoretical astuteness secured his reputation as one of the most respected historians of his generation. Many of these essays were landmarks in the definition and elaboration of major debates in the historiography of National Socialism, including the domestic origins of the Second World War, the role of Hitler in the Nazi system of rule, the class character of the regime, and the problem of working-class resistance. The ten essays selected here include Mason's most significant writings on these themes, as well as his pathbreaking study of women under National Socialism, and examples of the comparative work on fascism and Nazism to which he had turned shortly before his death. A complete bibliography of his publications is also appended.

D1089476

NAZISM, FASCISM AND THE WORKING CLASS

ESSAYS BY TIM MASON

NAZISM, FASCISM
AND THE
WORKING CLASS

TIM MASON
Late Fellow of St Peter's College, Oxford

EDITED BY
JANE CAPLAN
Professor of History, Bryn Mawr College

Published by the Press Syndicate of the University of Cambridge
The Pitt Building, Trumpington Street, Cambridge CB2 IRP
40 West 20th Street, New York, NY 10011–4211, USA
10 Stamford Road, Oakleigh, Melbourne 3166, Australia

First published 1995

Printed in Great Britain by Bell and Bain Ltd, Glasgow

A catalogue record for this book is available from the British Library

Library of Congress cataloguing in publication data
Mason, Timothy W., 1940–90
Nazism, fascism and the working class / Tim Mason; edited by Jane Caplan.
p.   cm.
Includes bibliographical references and index.
ISBN 0 521 43212 X. – ISBN 0 521 43787 3 (pbk)
1. Working class–Germany–History–20th century.   2. Labor policy–Germany–History.
3. National socialism–Germany–History.   4. Fascism–Germany–History–20th century.
5. Germany–Social conditions–1933–1945.
6. Germany–Politics and government–1933–1945.   I. Caplan, Jane.   II. Title.
HD8450.M3715   1995   94–9513
305.5′62′09430904–dc20   CIP

ISBN 0 521 43212 x hardback
ISBN 0 521 43787 3 paperback

CONTENTS

vii

ACKNOWLEDGEMENTS

THIS VOLUME emerged from discussions among a group of friends and colleagues whom Tim Mason had designated his literary executors shortly before his death in March 1990. The group (Raphael Samuel, Simonetta Piccone Stella, Ursula Vogel and myself) decided to pay tribute to Tim's life and work in a series of publications and events, and an edition of his major essays seemed to us to deserve a central place in this project of celebration and commemoration. I took on this work in the name of these friends of Tim's, and their advice and friendship has been indispensable at every stage. I am grateful to Simonetta Piccone Stella, Geoff Eley and Molly Nolan for reading an early version of the Introduction and offering me thoughtful comments and suggestions. Victoria de Grazia came to the rescue at short notice by sorting out some knotty textual and historical problems in the Italian text. I owe thanks to Lorraine Kirschner for much-needed help with typing, and to Jessica Reynolds for assistance in the complex task of assembling the composite Bibliography of works cited. Richard Fisher commissioned this volume on behalf of Cambridge University Press, and has been patient and supportive throughout its prolonged passage into print. Finally, thanks to the generous hospitality of Philip and Naomi Lavori, and with the support and friendship of Natalie Sacks, I was able to complete much of my work on this volume in the tranquillity and solitude of the White Mountains of New Hampshire. This healing environment eased the sometimes painful task of preparing this tribute to a dear friend whose loss I still mourn.

ORIGINAL TITLES AND SOURCES OF ESSAYS

'Some Origins of the Second World War', *Past and Present*, no. 29 (December 1964), pp. 67–87.
'The Primacy of Politics. Politics and Economics in National Socialist Germany', in S. J. Woolf (ed.), *The Nature of Fascism* (London 1968), pp. 165–95.

'Zur Entstehung des Gesetzes zur Ordnung der nationalen Arbeit vom 20. Januar 1934. Ein Versuch über das Verhältnis "archaischer" und "moderner" Momente in der neuesten deutschen Geschichte', in Hans Mommsen, Dietmar Petzina and Bernd Weisbrod (eds.), *Industrielles System und politische Entwicklung in der Weimarer Republik* (Düsseldorf 1974), pp. 322–51.

'Innere Krise und Angriffskrieg 1938/1939', in F. Forstmeier and H.-E. Volkmann (eds.), *Wirtschaft und Rüstung am Vorabend des Zweiten Weltkriegs* (Düsseldorf 1975), pp. 155–88.

'Women in Germany, Family, Welfare and Work, 1925–1940, Part I' and 'Women in Germany, Part II', *History Workshop Journal* no. 1 (spring 1976), pp. 74–113; and no. 2 (autumn 1976), pp. 5–32.

'Intention and Explanation. A Current Controversy about the Interpretation of National Socialism', in Gerhard Hirschfeld and Lothar Kettenacker (eds.), *Der 'Führerstaat'. Mythos und Realität/The 'Führer State'. Myth and Reality* (Stuttgart 1981), pp. 23–42.

'Die Bändigung der Arbeiterklasse im nationalsozialistischen Deutschland', in Carola Sachse et al., *Angst, Belohnung, Zucht und Ordnung. Herrschaftsmechanismen im Nationalsozialismus* (Opladen 1982), pp. 11–53.

'Gli scioperi di Torino del Marzo 1943', in F. F. Tosi, G. Grasso and M. Legnani (eds.), *L'Italia nella seconda guerra mondiale e nella resistenza* (Milan 1988), pp. 399–422.

'The Domestic Dynamics of Nazi Conquests. A Response to Critics', in Thomas Childers and Jane Caplan (eds.), *Reevaluating the Third Reich* (New York 1993), pp. 161–89.

'Whatever Happened to "Fascism"?', *Radical History Review*, no. 49 (winter 1991), pp. 89–98.

ABBREVIATIONS

ACS	Archivio Centrale dello Stato
ADAP	*Akten zur deutschen auswärtigen Politik*
ADGB	Allgemeiner deutscher Gewerkschaftsbund
AEG	Allgemeine Elektrizitätsgemeinschaft
AGR	*Affari generale e riservati*
AM-Apparat	Antimilitarisches Apparat
AOG	Arbeitsordnungsgesetz
Aski	Ausländersonderkontern für Inlands-Zahlungen
BA/MA	Bundesarchiv/Militärarchiv
BDM	Bund Deutscher Mädel
DAF	Deutscher Arbeitsfront
DINTA	Deutsches Institut für technische Arbeitsschulung
DRA	*Deutscher Reichsanzeiger*
DZA	Deutsches Zentralarchiv
Gestapo	Geheimes Staatspolizei
GPSA	Geheimes Preussisches Staatsarchiv
IMT	International Military Tribunal, Nuremberg
KdF	Kraft durch Freude
KPD	Kommunistische Partei Deutschlands
MI	Ministero dell'Interno
NSBO	Nationalsozialistische Betriebszellenorganisation
NSDAP	Nationalsozialistische Deutsche Arbeiterpartei
NSV	Nationalsozialistische Volkswohlfahrt
PCI	Partito comunista d'Italia
RAM	Reichsarbeitsministerium
RArbBl	*Reichsarbeitsblatt*
RGBl	*Reichsgesetzblatt*
RM	Reichsmark
RWM	Reichswirtschaftsministerium
SA	Sturmabteilung der NSDAP
SD	Sicherheitsdienst des SS
SS	Schutzstaffel
SPD	Sozialdemokratische Partei Deutschlands
WHW	Winterhilfswerk

INTRODUCTION

Jane Caplan

I

THE TEN essays collected here span the scholarly career of Timothy Mason, from the first article he published at the age of twenty-four to one of the last pieces he wrote shortly before his death in 1990. Between that precocious critique of A. J. P. Taylor in 1964 and the final response to critics of his own mature work, Mason's essays on National Socialism and fascism defined or reinterpreted many of the controversies that preoccupied historians during a period of continuous debate. He had long been urged by colleagues to publish a collection of these writings, scattered as they were through a quarter-century of publication in periodicals, edited volumes and conference proceedings. This edition, appearing now five years after Mason's death, has something of the character of a *Gedenkschrift*, but it is not simply a pious memorial to a talented historian who died too young. Mason's work on the history of Nazi Germany was pathbreaking, and his influence as a teacher and writer has had a profound effect on the shape and direction of research into National Socialism. An easily accessible edition of his major essays is certainly long overdue. It is offered here with the confidence that it will be valued equally by readers familiar with Mason's work and by those discovering it for the first time.

The purpose of this Introduction is to offer a critical context for reading these essays, not a biography of their author or a personal memoir. Readers who want to know more about Mason's personal qualities as teacher, colleague and friend should turn to the eloquent and loving memoirs of his life published in *History Workshop Journal* in 1990.[1] Still, it would do less than justice to the character of his achievement not to say a few words about the man as well as his work. Raphael Samuel, a fellow founding-editor of *History Workshop* and a friend for thirty years, has described him as 'the stormy petrel of

---

[1] 'Tim Mason. A Memorial', *History Workshop Journal*, no. 30 (autumn 1990), pp. 151–84.

historical scholarship, a man passionately engaged not only in the
minutiae of research...but...above all in its moralities...he thrived on
polemic [and] pushed himself to extremes'.[2] Something of this quality of
intellectual, political and moral passion is legible in the writings reproduced
here – and not only in the style and content of the individual essays, but
even more in Mason's choice of his life's work as a historian. His decision
to study National Socialism was among other things a self-imposed
assumption of what he repeatedly described as a 'moral and political
obligation': an obligation the historian owed 'to the millions who were
shot, gassed, crippled, tortured, imprisoned, uprooted' as a consequence
of the Nazi regime,[3] an obligation to approach this history with utter
seriousness, to struggle to understand and explain it, to communicate as
clearly as possible whatever quantum of explanation could be distilled
from the appalling evidence. Mason would certainly not have claimed
this as his unique burden. It is shouldered by anyone who elects to study
this desolate period of Europe's recent past, and he had the utmost
admiration for those few of his colleagues who in his view had managed to
bear it without buckling under the moral weight. We cannot know
whether some ultimately intolerable accumulation of that burden figured
in Mason's decision in March 1990 (and a decision it was) to take his own
life. What is certain, though, is that in his work he neither compromised
nor evaded the moral challenge he had taken upon himself.

   Tim Mason belonged to a generation of European historians of
National Socialism, trained in the 1960s and early 1970s, who were the
beneficiaries of a tremendously fertile intellectual conjuncture. On the
one hand, there was the opening-up of the immense archival deposits left
by the Nazi regime, which began to be reassembled, catalogued and made
available to researchers in the early 1960s; on the other, this period saw a
revival of intellectual and political interest, especially on the left, in the
theoretical dimensions of fascism. Mason's particular strength was that
he combined a sturdy respect for the documentary evidence with a critical
interest in the marxist conceptual armoury of capitalism, fascism and
class relations. His unflagging dedication to the archival record was
doubtless due in part to the traditionalist training he received as an
undergraduate at Oxford, where the climax of three years in the history
school was the final reverential encounter with 'the documents' in the
Special Subject paper. His writing is peppered with references to the lack
of research on some particular subject, gaps in the documentary record,

---

[2] Ibid., pp. 180 f.
[3] Timothy W. Mason, *Social Policy in the Third Reich. The Working Class and the National
   Community* (Oxford/Providence 1993), p. 4. This is a translation and expansion of
   Mason's revised doctoral dissertation, first published as *Sozialpolitik im Dritten Reich.
   Arbeiterklasse und Volksgemeinschaft* (Opladen 1977).

frustrations about the deficient state of knowledge and so on; he was deeply critical of work that was cavalier with the sources, or neglectful or ignorant of what could be found; his first book, indeed, was an immense compilation of source documents on Nazi labour and social policy.[4] But he contrived to combine his own zealous immersion in the sources with an equally robust enthusiasm for the 'big questions' which saved him from the interpretive timidity and pedantic narrowness of vision that have all too often been the product of that venerative Oxford training. For Mason, the 'big questions' were above all political and moral: about power, and about its effects on people, those who wielded it and, especially, those who suffered from it.

Mason worked from a critical marxist perspective, and his chosen exemplars were the Englishman Edward Thompson and the German Franz Neumann, two scholars from different strands in the marxist tradition to whom his work makes repeated reference. Thompson's *The Making of the English Working Class*, published in 1963 as Mason was embarking on his own career, offered a passionate, heroic model for telling a story about class that was primarily a story about the people by and for whom 'class' was made. From Thompson he drew a plastic notion of class not as an abstraction or a thing, but as a relationship among real people, a 'lived experience'. When Mason asserted that 'class relations are the constitutive element in the history of industrialized capitalist states',[5] he meant not some theoretical reification, but the real, fractured struggles by working men and women to wrest lives and meanings out of the careless and brutal indignities of daily existence in a capitalist economy, fascist or otherwise. If Thompson offered a moving interpretation of class as a living social relation, Franz Neumann's 1942 study of the Nazi regime, Behemoth, which drew on the intellectual and political resources of the Frankfurt school, provided Mason with a different kind of analytic paradigm. Here marxist resources were applied undogmatically and with moral urgency to the analysis of a barbaric and tyrannical system of rule, whose intricacies defied reduction to simplistic formulas.[6] Neumann's brilliant account of the structure and functioning of the Third Reich gave due weight to the special significance of the economy and of class, but did not press ideology and politics into a vulgar marxist straitjacket. It was precisely because Neumann's work was 'theoretically modest',[7] and

---

[4] *Arbeiterklasse und Volksgemeinschaft. Dokumente und Materialien zur deutschen Arbeiterpolitik 1936–1939* (Opladen 1975); its lengthy introduction, based on his doctoral dissertation, was subsequently expanded and published independently (see note 3 above).

[5] Mason, *Social Policy in the Third Reich*, p. xxi.

[6] Franz Neumann, *Behemoth. The Structure and Practice of National Socialism* (London 1942). For a contextual discussion of this work, see Martin Jay, *The Dialectical Imagination* (Boston/Toronto 1973), pp. 161–5.

[7] *Social Policy in the Third Reich*, p. 284, n. 16.

because it offered a political analysis of the Nazi regime that did not lose
sight of capitalism and class relations, that Mason continued to regard
Behemoth as 'the best single work on the Third Reich'.[8]

It may seem something of a paradox that Mason's early publications
were devoted more to matters of interpretation and high politics than to
social history and working-class life. In part this reflected the state of
research when he began his work. In the 1960s and 1970s, historians were
engaged above all in exploring the institutional structure of the Third
Reich, drawn to the opportunities for its reconstruction which were then
being offered by the newly available archival resources – reams of
documentation from ministries, government agencies, the NSDAP
(National Socialist German Workers' Party) and its satellites.[9] Like some
of his contemporaries – among them Martin Broszat, Hans Mommsen,
Lutz Niethammer – Mason worked first at this level before turning to the
field of social history, which, starting in the mid-1970s, was to become
generally more prominent in British and German research. As so often in
the development of historical enquiry, it was the questions thrown up by
the initial research, and the inadequacy of one kind of approach or one
genre of sources to answer them, that prompted this shift in direction.
This change also coincided with the coming to maturity of a generation of
historians schooled in the political culture of the late 1960s, which among
young West Germans prompted an intense and painful interrogation of
the older generation's social relations and individual conduct under
National Socialism. Mason himself contributed to this, especially through
his work on women and on the workers' opposition, which set the
research agenda for the next twenty years. But, along with his commitment
to class as a register of political experience, agency and analysis, Mason
remained deeply and unapologetically interested in understanding the
structure and functioning of the political institutions themselves. The
Third Reich, after all, was not only a perverse kind of social organism, but
also represented an unparalleled accumulation of power deployed for
utterly unprecedented purposes: no history of it can be adequate which
does not take account of this overwhelming fact of power.

Mason repeatedly insisted that Nazi Germany remained a class society,
though of a peculiar kind, and his most sustained efforts were devoted to
explicating the response of the working class to this monstrously
oppressive regime. But he struggled throughout his career with the

[8] 'The Primacy of Politics. Politics and Economics in National Socialist Germany' p. 53, n.
2, below.
[9] The development of this historiography is examined in Ian Kershaw, *The Nazi
Dictatorship. Problems and Perspectives of Interpretation* (London 1989); see also Jane
Caplan, 'The Historiography of National Socialism', in Michael Bentley (ed.), *The
Writing of History. An International Guide to Classical and Current Historiography*,
(London, forthcoming).

conundrum of how to depict the exact calibration of class and politics in the Nazi regime, a struggle which also expressed some of his conflicted relationship with marxist theory. The story of working-class insubordination he told in his book *Social Policy in the Third Reich* and in some of the essays reprinted here oscillates between depicting it as the quasi-spontaneous expression of economic class conflict on the one hand, and, on the other, as the muted echo of working-class traditions of political militancy which even the Nazis were unable to stamp out until the intensified terror of the wartime regime. The regime itself he saw as having subsumed at least some of the functions of capital in the conduct of class conflict; indeed, Mason contended that '*social and economic history is always about the state*'.[10] And when forced to choose between class conflict and politics as the ultimate determinants of Nazi projects, he finally opted for the political over the social, arguing that 'there is no clear path that can be traced from class conflict to the fundamental projects of the Third Reich', that the 'constitutive element' in the Third Reich was not capitalism but the Nazi regime itself.[11]

Over his lifetime, Mason published two books, more than two dozen major essays and articles, and numerous shorter pieces and book reviews.[12] The choice of essays for this edition (made by Raphael Samuel, Simonetta Piccone Stella, Ursula Vogel and myself) involved lengthy discussions about what to cull from this long list of publications, but was eventually guided by a number of criteria. In the first place, we decided that this collection should be devoted to Mason's primary achievement as a historian of National Socialism and fascism, even though this meant passing over some of his most eloquent writing and narrowing the range of his historical voice. This was a decision reached with some reluctance, but was made in the interests of this book's coherence as well as for more pragmatic considerations of its length. We have therefore included most of the major essays on National Socialism, and have excluded only a number of shorter pieces, and others that are already incorporated in his book *Social Policy in the Third Reich*, or that are basically alternative versions of the same essay.[13] Second, we wanted to make available in

[10] Mason, 'The Making of the English Working Class', *History Workshop Journal*, no. 7 (1979), p. 224.
[11] *Social Policy in the Third Reich*, pp. 285, 294; see also the discussion of his essay 'The Primacy of Politics', below.
[12] See Bibliography for a complete list of Mason's publications.
[13] *Social Policy in the Third Reich*, Chapter 1, 'The Legacy of 1918 for National Socialism', was based on a previously published essay; Chapter 2, 'National Socialism and the Working Class, 1925 to May 1933', was published in English shortly after the original German publication of the book. For this collection, we chose to include 'Internal Crisis and War of Aggression 1938/1939' (translation of the 1975 essay 'Innere Krise und Angriffskrise 1938/1939'), on the grounds that it summarizes the argument presented in

English translation the most important of the essays previously published only in German or Italian. Third, and overlapping the other criteria, we have tried to ensure that our selection will illuminate Mason's special strengths as a historian: his capacity to break the mould of a congealed argument, to crystallize the shape of some still indistinct debate, to synthesize empirical and interpretive scholarship with a characteristic combination of precision and daring. Finally, by selecting essays written throughout Mason's career, we wanted to show how his historical interests evolved and expanded, while remaining pivoted on the axis of a few insistent, overriding themes: the relationship between politics and class, the sources and limits of individual and collective agency, the ferocity and destructiveness of Nazi power, and, most controversially, the domestic sources of Nazi aggression in 1939.

The essays are reprinted here in chronological order of first publication, but looked at thematically they can be divided into three reasonably logical groupings. First, there are three essays ('Some Origins of the Second World War', 'Internal Crisis and War of Aggression' and 'The Domestic Dynamics of Nazi Conquests') that directly address Mason's most controversial thesis about the domestic and social sources of the German decision for war in 1939. Then there are four essays ('The Primacy of Politics', 'Intention and Explanation', 'The Containment of the Working Class' and 'Whatever Happened to "Fascism"?') that can all be seen as primarily interpretive or theoretical in content. Finally, the three remaining essays in this collection ('The Origins of the Law on the Organization of National Labour', 'Women in Germany' and 'The Turin Strikes of 1943') are case studies in the social history of National Socialism and fascism. There is inevitably an arbitrary element in this classification, since all the essays address the interlocking themes already identified in this Introduction. However, by adopting this division here I hope that the place of Mason's work in the historiography of National Socialism will emerge more clearly.

II

The origins, timing and nature of the war that began in 1939 lay at the heart of Mason's research project, and it is his arguments on this issue that have roused the greatest controversy. The essays published here take us from the first embryonic statement of his arguments, couched in the

Social Policy in the Third Reich; and 'The Domestic Dynamics of Nazi Conquests. A Response to Critics', which appears in an expanded version in the same book, because it was among Mason's final compositions and brings full circle the issues raised in his first publication (Chapter 9 below). Chapters 4, 7 and 8 in the present collection exist in a number of versions; we chose the most authoritative text in each case.

form of a critique of A. J. P. Taylor's heterodox interpretation of the origins of the Second World War; through a 1975 essay in which Mason summarized the arguments he had by then developed more fully in his doctoral dissertation; and finally to a late essay in which he replied to the criticisms of his arguments that had by then accumulated. In a nutshell, his thesis was 'that the accelerating dynamic of Nazi aggression in 1938 and 1939 was strongly conditioned by the *internal* problems of the regime, problems that progressively narrowed the margins for foreign policy choices and made it increasingly difficult for the regime to wait for the right moment to launch its wars of conquest'.[14] Mason took it as axiomatic that an expansionist war was the *ultima ratio* of Nazism, and Hitler's overriding objective; what lay in need of explanation was the *specific timing and the character* of the war that began in 1939, neither of which, he argued, could be seen as the outcome of freely chosen policy decisions. In Mason's view the timing of the war and its character as a *Blitzkrieg* could not be adequately explained by reference to Hitler's intentions alone or from the record of foreign policy and diplomatic decisions, nor was it the consequence of the purely economic circumstances of the rearmament programme, even if all these played some part. The key to explaining the timing and character of the war of 1939 was a domestic social crisis provoked by the contradiction between the economic consequences of rearmament on the one hand, and the Nazi regime's fear of popular political unrest on the other. This contradiction reflected the heart of the Nazi project, or more specifically Hitler's vision of it. On the one hand, there was the core commitment to a war of expansion; on the other hand, the belief that for this purpose Germany must and could be converted into a coherent, harmonious, organic social community, a community solid enough to participate in this imperialist project without the risk of social disintegration. Hitler in particular was convinced that Germany's defeat in 1918 had been the consequence of a massive working-class defection from the imperial state, provoked by the heavy material sacrifices imposed upon workers who were also the targets of deliberate leftist subversion. This aggravated version of the stab-in-the-back legend was, Mason suggested, the crucial 'legacy of 1918' for the Nazi leadership;[15] he argued that it played an absolutely critical role in the policy-making circumstances of the mid-1930s.

By 1936/7, according to this hypothesis, the Nazi regime was caught in an insoluble dilemma of its own making. The forced pace of rearmament was not only exhausting Germany's available material resources (raw

[14] P. 296, below.
[15] See his essay, 'The Legacy of 1918 for National Socialism', in A. J. Nicholls and E. Matthias (eds.), *German Democracy and the Triumph of Hitler* (London 1971), pp. 15–39; incorporated into *Social Policy in the Third Reich*, Chapter 2.

materials, food supply, foreign exchange) and straining the relationship between the production of armaments, capital goods and consumer goods, but had also created a crisis of full employment. This reversed the conditions of 1933, when the Nazi regime had been able to take advantage of the disastrous conditions of depression and mass unemployment by smashing the organizations of the working class, destroying its political leadership, and subjugating it to Nazi rule. 'In a vital respect', Mason wrote, 'the repression of the working class began in the labour market'; and, by the same token, 'full employment...formed the basic condition for the emergence of the workers' opposition' to the regime.[16] As we shall see, Mason also contended that the forms of working-class insubordination that emerged after 1937 – the pressure for pay hikes, the job-changing, the relaxation of productive effort, the widespread rejection of workplace discipline in general – were not simply manifestations of spontaneous economic class conflict, but expressed the vestiges of a political class consciousness that the Nazi regime had been unable to erase completely, and which it could not now risk meeting by political repression alone.[17] At any rate, whatever its precise character this situation of widespread worker indiscipline played havoc with the regime's objectives, posing serious challenges to its economic policy and vision of social peace alike. These manifestations of working-class recalcitrance exposed the fact that the much-trumpeted 'national community' (*Volksgemeinschaft*) was no more than a self-interested myth propagated by the Nazi leadership. The image of a classless nation pulling together in pursuit of common goals was, on this reading of the evidence, an ideological fiction that had little concrete purchase among the mass of German workers (or, for that matter, among their social superiors and political masters). The reality consisted, at best, of apathy, and at worst, of a militant if fragmented rejection by workers of their conditions of life under dictatorship.

To contain the potentially disastrous effects of the overheated economy and overstretched labour market, the regime would have had to intervene with rigorous measures to reimpose labour discipline, raise taxes and curb consumer spending. But the Nazi leadership, chiefly Hitler, was unwilling to risk the further erosion of its popular security by imposing either material sacrifices or further regimentation on the working class. The fortunate conjuncture of 1933 was past; the conditions of the late 1930s presented the regime with risk rather than opportunity. Moreover, such voices as were raised within the government on behalf of a serious war economy were smothered under the confusion of a regime that Mason described as 'a jungle of competing and overlapping economic

[16] Tim Mason, 'The Workers' Opposition in Nazi Germany', *History Workshop Journal*, no. 11 (spring 1981), p. 122.   [17] See pp. 22–3 below.

organizations, interest groups and authorities, which was essential for preserving the political power of the Nazi leadership, but which precluded effective economic planning and administration'.[18]

These interlocking economic and social pressures amounted by 1938/9 to 'a comprehensive politico-economic crisis of the whole system of government',[19] which massively reduced the government's room for manoeuvre, and robbed it of the choice of timing its military decisions to best advantage. It must be noted that Mason consistently emphasized that his thesis was intended to explain the *timing* of the war – 1939, as against Hitler's original calculation of 1943 – and its specific *character* as a *Blitzkrieg*, a quick campaign that would not involve protracted military and economic mobilization. In other words, this was an argument 'not . . . that Hitler was "forced to go to war" in the sense of not wanting to, but rather that the wars which the Third Reich actually fought bore very little relation to the wars which [Hitler] appears to have wanted to fight'.[20] Mason believed the German rearmament economy could not have survived until 1943 without the imposition of the repressive workplace discipline that Hitler shied away from; hence the 1939 decision was a dangerous *Flucht nach vorn*, an oxymoronic 'flight forwards' into a risk-laden war of expansion as a substitute for even more risky domestic repression. Its goal was not just the territorial imperialism long announced by Nazi ideology, but the imposition of a new dialectic of discipline and solidarity on the German people, and the systematic, ruthless plunder of conquered resources of materials, plant and labour so that the German population could be spared from excessive privation and launched into a bright new future of racial dominance on the continent of Europe. But, as Mason went on to argue, the solution attempted in 1939 itself became imprisoned in a fatal logic. If war initially 'became necessary in order for rearmament to be continued at a high level, [f]ollowing from this, and subsequently in time, war became in every sense an end in itself for the regime . . . For Nazism, wars basically served the prosecution of further wars'.[21] This was, then, a momentous reversal of the primordial ideological premise of Nazi imperialism: '*Lebensraum* . . . originally a design for a timeless barbaric empire . . . was transformed by Nazi practice into the wartime political economy of hit and run, of living off the land, of nihilism'.[22]

The component parts of this complex argument, not all of them

[18] P. 50 below.   [19] P. 114 below.   [20] P. 229 below.
[21] Pp. 318–19 below; see also p. 125. Already in 1964 Mason had quoted with approval Taylor's own observation that 'Germany needed the prizes of war solely in order to make war more successfully': p. 51 below.
[22] Tim Mason, 'Debate. Germany, "Domestic Crisis" and War. Comment 2', *Past and Present*, no. 122 (February 1989), p. 218.

original to Mason, have found a varying degree of acceptance among historians of the Nazi period. Thus the regime's and Hitler's commitment to war as an ultimate objective has not been seriously contested since Taylor's unsuccessful attempt in 1960 to show Hitler as the victim of diplomatic circumstances. The originality of Mason's own critique of Taylor, which was part of a barrage of criticism levelled at him in the 1960s, lay in its application of an embryonic form of his thesis about the domestic context of the policy-making in the later 1930s.[23] There is also widespread agreement that the years 1937/8 marked a rupture in the history of the Third Reich, a point at which the regime's policies accelerated and radicalized. Historians disagree, though, whether this was the intended result of a deliberate turn of the policy screw, or (as Mason argued) the indirect effect of increasingly confusing conditions of decision-making that undermined the regime's capacity for rational policy-making.[24] More mixed, as we shall see below, has been the fate of his contention that a cohesive *Volksgemeinschaft* was unable to overcome the divisions of class, the symptoms of which Mason identified in the residual socio-political solidarity of the organized working class after 1933 and in the endemic economic class conflict that accompanied the persistence of capitalism under the Nazis. Although the degree of acceptance varied, each of these individual points in Mason's argument enjoyed wide circulation so that they have become a familiar feature of the historiographical landscape in the past twenty-five years.

By contrast, what never found broad support was Mason's full-fledged, culminating argument that there was 'a causal connection between the social and economic crisis in Germany and the acceleration of military expansionist policies towards war in 1938-9'.[25] Critics have protested that Mason exaggerated the evidence of crisis by over-interpreting sparse documentary evidence, especially on the extent of working-class disaffection, and that he ignored or discounted other potential explanations for Hitler's decisions in 1938/9. On the specific issue of the conduct of German foreign policy in the late 1930s, a number of historians, among them Joachim Fest and Jost Dülffer, faulted Mason for ignoring other components of Hitler's strategic thinking in 1939 than simply his caution about popular unrest: notably, his miscalculation of British strategic interests, his fear that Germany was losing its edge in the international arms race, his propensity to reach for radical, confrontational solutions in situations of impasse. In his response, Mason did not dismiss these

---

[23] For the 'Taylor debate', see Esmonde M. Robertson (ed.), *The Origins of the Second World War* (London 1963), and Gordon Martel (ed.), *The Origins of the Second World War Reconsidered. The A. J. P. Taylor Debate after Twenty-Five Years* (London 1986).

[24] See the discussion of 'Intention and Explanation. A Current Controversy about the Explanation of National Socialism', pp. 18–19 below, and references in the essay itself.

[25] *Social Policy in the Third Reich*, p. 294.

criticisms outright – the evidence for them is too compelling – but
basically tried to incorporate them in his own overarching thesis about
systemic crisis.[26]

The hypothesis of systemic crisis, though, remained the keystone of
Mason's interpretation, and it was to criticisms of this – advanced
especially by Ludolf Herbst and Richard Overy – that he primarily
devoted his attention. Herbst disputed the appropriateness of the claim
of crisis by arguing, on the basis of systems theory, that the term has a
very precise set of definitional conditions which the pre-war situation in
Germany did not meet. He pointed out, for example, that the economy,
where the signs of crisis were most clear, was not 'the system' as such, but
only a sub-system; that the regime still had reserves of power with which
to meet events in 1939; and that there is precious little evidence that
either the Nazi leaders or ordinary Germans were ever conscious that a
'crisis' existed.[27] Overy similarly rejected the substance of Mason's
interpretation, criticizing his excessively pessimistic account of the state
of the German economy in the later 1930s, his exaggerated estimate of
the threat posed to the regime by the working class, and his neglect of
foreign policy and diplomatic relations in the run-up to September
1939.[28] He argued that the German economy had shown 'no real signs of
crisis' in the later 1930s, but only the 'frictions' in the distribution of
resources that were common to all industrial economies. Contemporary
assertions that the German economy was in crisis in the 1930s were, he
suggested, mainly the expression of German conservatives' wishful
thinking, which was readily picked up by foreigners eager to hear that
Nazi Germany was a paper tiger; it was not until 1941/2 that anything
deserving the name of crisis surfaced, and then only as a result of the war
itself. In Overy's estimation, 'Hitler's decision to solve the Polish
question in 1939 stemmed not from domestic considerations but from
diplomatic and military':[29] he took a calculated foreign-policy gamble
and lost, owing to French and British intransigence. The appropriate
explanatory scenario was, therefore, not the alleged pressure of German
domestic circumstances, but Hitler's own 'obsessive historical vision'
together with 'the disintegration of the established international power
constellation during the 1930s'.[30]

---

[26] Pp. 300–1 below.
[27] Ludolf Herbst, 'Die Krise des nationalsozialistischen Regimes am Vorabend des
Zweiten Weltkrieges und die forcierte Aufrüstung', *Vierteljahrshefte für Zeitgeschichte*,
vol. 26, no. 3 (July 1983), pp. 347–91.
[28] For Overy's main critique, see 'Germany, "Domestic Crisis" and War in 1939', *Past and
Present*, no. 116 (August 1987), pp. 138–68; see also his 'Hitler's War and the German
Economy. A Reinterpretation', *Economic History Review*, 2nd ser., vol. 35, no. 2 (1982),
pp. 272–91, and his *War and Economy in the Third Reich* (Oxford 1994).
[29] Overy, 'Germany, "Domestic Crisis" and War', p. 164.   [30] Ibid., p. 167.

In his responses to these criticisms, Mason was particularly brisk with Overy, whom he accused of having 'thrown the argument [about the origins of the war] back by over a decade'.[31] Overy, he asserted, had ignored the historiographical consensus about the essential incoherence of the Nazi regime, and he did not command knowledge of the German archival sources that supplied the evidence of crisis. Conversely, he was irritated by Overy's claim that Hitler's thinking in 1938/9 could be readily reconstructed from documentary sources: Mason believed that, on the contrary, the written evidence was so sparse and delphic that no hypothesis about Hitler's views could be definitively confirmed or refuted.[32] Any argument based primarily on the interpretation of Hitler's motivations would therefore be inherently inconclusive. As well as these criticisms on the grounds of evidence, Mason identified two interpretative weaknesses in Overy's interpretation: he had exaggerated the smoothness of Germany's economic recovery in the 1930s, and he had no explanation for the shift in the character of the war from territorial imperialism to opportunistic plunder.

Mason's resistance to Overy's critique was due, I think, partly to his belief that Overy had misidentified his own analysis as history 'from below', when in fact Mason was no less concerned than was Overy with the dynamics of state power and decision-making at the top;[33] and partly to Overy's use of somewhat limited documentary sources, a provocative point for Mason for reasons I have already indicated. With his other critics, Mason was less impatient in tone, even where their arguments overlapped with some of Overy's. In 'The Domestic Dynamics' he admitted that the majority of historians did not agree with him; he appeared willing to take their criticisms seriously and to modify his position in response. He conceded a particularly telling point to them by allowing that there was no 'incipient general breakdown of the whole system of rule' in 1938/9, and proposing instead a more restricted concept of *economic* crisis alone.[34] Still, the nub of his older argument survived in his contention that this economic crisis carried with it insoluble political and military consequences; and in that sense he was still articulating a belief that the economic sphere is not just one among the other spheres of public life, but is in some way determinant of the others. Thus he argued

[31] Mason's response to Overy was published as 'Comment 2' in the debate 'Germany, "Domestic Crisis" and War', *Past and Present*, no. 122 (February 1989), pp. 205–21; quotation here from p. 206. A critical response by David Kaiser was published in the same issue ('Comment 1', pp. 200–5), together with Overy's reply to both comments, pp. 221–40. Because he had already responded to Overy in this comment, Mason excluded him from consideration in 'The Domestic Dynamics of Nazi Conquests'; hence the extended discussion here.

[32] On the antinomies of Mason's use of documentary evidence and its silences, see below p. 21.

[33] See Mason, *Social Policy in the Third Reich*, p. 290.   [34] P. 312 below.

that 'the regime was splitting at the top and disintegrating openly at the base'[35] at the beginning of the war, and that by 1939/40 it was locked into the fatal cycle of war for the sake of plunder and plunder for the sake of war.

Ultimately a good part of these disagreements comes down to the question of how to weight the multiple factors that make up the explanation of complex events. No participant was proposing a crudely monocausal explanation for the war; no one was arguing for the irrelevance of Hitler, or denying that Germany was in an irreducible sense responsible for the war, or that it came perilously close to victory before 1941; no one was disputing the Nazi regime's formidable capacity for ruthess violence. The problem is partly a matter of emphasis, or as Mason put it, 'a basic dilemma of perception'. Echoing a widely held view, he pointed to the

great sense of incompatibility between the Third Reich that, on the one hand, we know to have mobilized such terrifying destructive energies, to have unfolded such sustained and violent bureaucratic and military power, to have resisted until the very end of the war; and, on the other hand, the Third Reich [as] a regime whose leadership was increasingly entrapped in economic and political contradictions largely of its own making and that sought escape or resolution or maintenance of its distinctive identity through a series of sudden lurches in policy and through ever more explosive risk-taking.[36]

In suggesting that the basic problem is one of emphasis or perception, however, I am not saying that the choice of approach or of answer is a trivial matter of preference – far from it. Implicit in the various possible choices are profound differences of interpretation, differences that express deeply held and sometimes fundamentally conflicting beliefs about the historical meaning of the Third Reich, and that have therefore provoked acrimonious academic debates. Mason himself was not shy of engaging in polemical argument with those whose views were different from his own; his fervour could sometimes tip over into impatience or irritation if he suspected an opponent of political obtuseness or scholarly shortcomings. Yet his motivations were not factious or self-serving, nor was his insistence on the sovereignty of historical truth disingenuous. Rather, I think his occasionally polemical tone bore witness to the strain of combining his high standards for empirical research with his equally powerful commitment to a particular version of political morality. Moreover, Mason took on some of the most challenging problems in the history of National Socialism and fascism, exploring and in some cases defining a number of major interpretative controversies in the field. These more discursive essays are not so much attempts at coherent theorizing – that was not Mason's primary concern. The essays reprinted

---

[35] P. 315 below.   [36] P. 320 below.

here can perhaps better be seen as a set of meditations that turn on concrete instances of contradiction: between politics and economics in Nazi Germany, between the aims and achievements of the Third Reich, between working-class hostility to Nazism before 1933 and its apparent passivity under Nazi rule, and between Nazi Germany and Fascist Italy.

The concept of contradiction has a long pedigree in dialectical theory, whether marxist or not. Mason's use of this concept was strictly undogmatic, and perhaps only at times did it carry a specifically marxist inflection. Nevertheless, he did draw his basic understanding of the term from marxism, and it pervaded his understanding of Nazism, perhaps even of the historical process in general. Following marxist orthodoxy, he identified class conflict as the paramount form of contradiction, and the economy, the sphere in which class interests clashed head-on, as the determining element in any social formation. More loosely, he saw the large-scale structures with which historians deal – states, societies, governments, economies – as complicated articulations of multiple parts that are not inherently harmonious, but achieve only occasional, temporary stability. These principles informed two of his basic propositions about National Socialist Germany. First, 'class conflict remained endemic in Nazi Germany',[37] despite the regime's efforts to install a classless *Volksgemeinschaft*. Second, the Nazi system never achieved even a provisional stability. This was because its project of forced social transformation precluded the kind of negotiated compromise between working-class and business interests that it is the function of 'normal' pluralist-democratic politics to produce; and because the absence of normative politics and aims in Nazism left the regime to accelerate into a kind of objectless mobilization which became increasingly radicalized, improvisatory and brutal. The ultimate contradiction within National Socialism could be seen as the tendency towards implosive self-destruction on the part of a regime that seemed bent on its own explosive enlargement.

These conclusions are present in the essays on the origins of the war, but are addressed most explicitly in those I have identified as more directly theoretical – 'The Primacy of Politics', 'Intention and Explanation', 'The Containment of the Working Class' and 'Whatever Happened to "Fascism"?' The first two essays in this list deserve particular attention here, because they were undoubtedly the most original and influential of all Mason's publications. 'The Primacy of Politics' was an early contribution – the first by a British scholar – to the burgeoning debate in West and East Germany in the 1960s on marxist approaches to the history of fascism.[38]

[37] *Social Policy in the Third Reich*, p. 285.
[38] However, it should be noted that Mason deliberately avoided the generic term 'fascism'; he confined his attention to National Socialism alone, leaving the issue of fascism in abeyance until his late essay 'Whatever Happened to "Fascism"?'

The essay was originally published in 1966 in a West Berlin marxist periodical, *Das Argument*, which had devoted a sequence of issues to discussions of fascism theory.[39] Working from the standard marxist premise that the political sphere was connected to the economic by the relationship of (determined) superstructure to (determining) base, Mason nevertheless rejected the conventional conclusion enshrined in orthodox marxist–leninist (i.e. Third International) theory since the 1930s, that is, that fascism was 'the open, terroristic dictatorship of the most reactionary, most chauvinistic and most imperialist elements of finance capital'.[40] He contended instead that after 1936 the National Socialist government was extraordinary in the degree to which it became detached from, and even antagonistic to, the economic interests it would normally be expected to represent. This inversion of the normal relationship proposed by marxist theory was, he suggested, 'unique in the history of modern bourgeois society'; such a 'primacy of politics' could only have been established if there had been 'far-reaching structural changes . . . both in the economy and society' after 1933.[41]

Here Mason was addressing not so much an abstract point about the structural relationship between the economy and politics in marxist theory, but rather the concrete historical relationship between capitalism and fascism, or more specifically the connection between big business and the Nazi government. Marxist intellectuals and Communist Party ideologists throughout Europe had debated this relationship since the rise of fascism in the 1920s, but by the 1960s much of this earlier literature had been forgotten or marginalized in both orthodox marxist–leninist and liberal scholarship. But the 1960s and 1970s saw the rediscovery of dissident marxist writings on fascism that had been buried since the 1930s, as part of a vast movement of textual reclamation and reinterpretation within the Western European left, which was eventually to result in a

---

[39] 'Der Primat der Politik. Politik und Wirtschaft im Nationalsozialismus', *Das Argument. Berliner Hefte für Probleme der Gesellschaft*, no. 41 (December 1966), pp. 473–94. The other volumes in the *Das Argument* fascism series were nos. 30 (February 1964), 32 (February 1965), 33 (May 1965), and 47 (July 1968). The *Das Argument* debate also involved East German historians for whom the economic logic of National Socialism as the agent of monopoly capital was an article of political as well as historiographical faith; issue no. 47 included critiques of Mason's article by the East German scholar Eberhard Czichon ('Der Primat der Industrie im Kartell der nationalsozialistischen Macht', pp. 168–92), a response by Tim Mason ('Primat der Industrie? Eine Erwiderung', pp. 193–209), and a further comment by East German historians Dietrich Eichholtz and Kurt Gossweiler ('Noch einmal. Politik und Wirtschaft 1933–1945', pp. 210–27). Kershaw, *The Nazi Dictatorship*, Chapter 3, especially pp. 44–50, is an informative discussion of this literature and its broader context.

[40] This is the conventionally quoted core of the lengthy 1935 Comintern document on fascism that remained canonical for marxist–leninist scholarship into the 1960s and beyond; see Georgi Dmitrov, *Report to the 7th Congress Communist International* (London n.d. (1935)), p. 40.   [41] P. 54 below.

major transformation of the political landscape. The question of fascism was only one among numerous currents in this leftist project of cultural reinvention, but it was a prominent one, since it was widely argued that the possibility of fascism lurked permanently in the shadows behind capitalism, to which it was available as a repressive resource in times of crisis. The sense of fascism as a threat in the present thus stimulated the study of its political history, especially among West Germans conscious of their nation's particular historical burden.

Mason's contribution to this project drew on the concept of bonapartism, which was then undergoing something of a renaissance among West German marxists.[42] Originally 'bonapartism' had been Marx's term for the stalemate of class forces in France after 1848 which had allowed Louis Napoleon to seize the political initiative in 1851 and maintain it by means of a plebiscitary democracy that substituted for a class politics. Engels had used a version of the same idea in his analysis of Bismarck's authoritarian parliamentarism in the 1880s.[43] It had then been taken up again in the 1930s and applied to fascism by marxists such as Leon Trotsky, the Austrian social democrat Otto Bauer and the dissident German communist August Thalheimer, who presented various versions of the basic proposition that the fascist regimes were beneficiaries of a paralysis of class forces that had simultaneously prevented the ruling class from holding onto power and the working class from seizing it.[44] Bonapartist theories were appealing to neo-marxists in the 1960s and 1970s because they opened up the space between the economic and the political which had been sealed shut by orthodox marxist–leninist theories of 'state monopoly capitalism' and fascism. Marxist intellectuals began to rethink the role of politics and ideology in capitalist societies, and this led to criticism of the reductive base/superstructure model of economic and political relationships. More sophisticated models were proposed to capture the complex ways in which the interests of social classes are expressed at the level of politics and government, and more

[42] As his footnote references in Das Argument to Marx's Class Struggles in France and The 18th Brumaire of Louis Bonaparte indicate; interestingly, these references to Marx were omitted in the English version. Another of the articles in the same issue of Das Argument was R. Griepenburg and K. H. Tjaden's study of August Thalheimer's bonapartist fascism theory, 'Faschismus und Bonapartismus', pp. 461–72.

[43] Friedrich Engels, 'The Role of Force in History' (1887), in Karl Marx and Friedrich Engels, Collected Works, vol. XXVI (London 1990), pp. 455–510.

[44] See Otto Bauer, 'Der Faschismus', and August Thalheimer, 'Über den Faschismus', in Otto Bauer, Herbert Marcuse and August Thalheimer, Faschismus und Kapitalismus. Theorien über die soziale Ursprünge und die Funktion des Faschismus, ed. Wolfgang Abendroth (Frankfurt am Main 1967); Leon Trotsky, The Struggle Against Fascism in Germany (1930–40) (New York 1971); Martin Kitchen, 'August Thalheimer's Theory of Fascism', Journal of the History of Ideas, vol. 34, no. 1 (1973), pp. 67–78; Jost Dülffer, 'Bonapartism, Fascism and National Socialism', Journal of Contemporary History, vol. 11, no. 4 (October 1976), pp. 109–28.

elaborate concepts of class representation, mediation and ideology were articulated.[45] Mason took no direct part in this debate after his original 1966 article, but his concept of the 'primacy of politics' in National Socialism was influential among both liberal historians and those who were attracted, like him, to the explanatory power of marxism while remaining sceptical of its claims to theoretical self-sufficiency.[46]

Mason's approach, as already suggested, was unusual in bridging what was otherwise a rather impermeable division between empirical and theoretical scholarship. On the whole, the 1960s/70s fascism debates were internal to the left, and then not always cordial; most academic historians were either critical of their abstraction or their alleged political distortions, or else simply ignored them.[47] Critics of marxism could also object that the kind of conclusion reached by Mason or Poulantzas pointed more to the difficulty marxism had in sustaining its untenable theory of economic determinism than to any substantive advance in the understanding of National Socialism. However, the marxists were in a sense in good company. Liberal scholarship also had room to recognize the Nazi regime as anomalous, irrational, a disruption of the expected norms of development in modern industrial society. Where marxists saw capitalism itself as inherently contradictory and fascism as an extreme expression of this essential irrationality, liberals were likely to see capitalism as rational or at least salvageable, and fascism as the irrational aberration from this norm. Liberals had always tended to see Nazi ideology as irrational and utopian; but now evidence of the incoherent character of the Nazi regime as such was beginning to accumulate as research in the West and East German archives yielded a much more richly detailed history of the National Socialist movement and regime than had hitherto been available. This research was especially strong in

[45] For a survey of stamocap theory and its critics, see Bob Jessop, *The Capitalist State. Marxist Theories and Methods* (New York 1982).

[46] To some extent Mason's propositions about the primacy of politics and the uniqueness of the Nazi state 'in the history of bourgeois society' coincided with the concepts of the 'relative autonomy of politics' and the 'exceptional state' put forward in Nicos Poulantzas, *Fascism and Dictatorship. The Third International and the Problem of Fascism* (London 1974). Poulantzas distinguished, however, between bonapartism and fascism as types of 'exceptional' regime, and repudiated bonapartist theories of fascism as such, including Mason's: see pp. 59–62, 85 n. For Poulantzas' concepts of bonapartism and 'relative autonomy' in general, see idem, *Political Power and Social Classes* (London 1973). See also Jane Caplan, 'Theories of Fascism. Nicos Poulantzas as Historian', *History Workshop Journal*, no. 3 (spring 1977), pp. 83–100, and Ian Kershaw, 'The Nazi State. An Exceptional State?', *New Left Review*, no. 176 (July–August 1989), pp. 47–67.

[47] Exemplary of Mason's unusual position was the inclusion of 'The Primacy of Politics' in a collection of essays on Nazism and fascism edited by the anti-marxist historian of modern Germany Henry A. Turner, Jr, *Nazism and the Third Reich* (New York 1972), pp. 175–200; for Turner's view that both 'orthodox' and 'non-orthodox' marxist scholarship on fascism was worthless, see Turner (ed.), *Reappraisals of Fascism* (New York 1975), p. x.

the political field – the Nazi seizure of power, the structure of the Nazi state, the role of state, party and police bureaucracies after 1933, military and foreign policy, and so on – and in studies of Hitler's role. By the later 1970s it had generated an interpretative controversy about the sources of Nazi terrorism that had nothing to learn from the left in point of intensity or animosity.

In what was perhaps his most influential essay, it was Mason who managed to pin down the historical shape and moral implications of this debate. This essay, 'Intention and Explanation', was first presented at an important conference on Nazi Germany, held in England in 1979, which brought together an unprecedently broad and disunited group of historians, mainly from West Germany and Britain. The event was unusual for the bitter tone of its arguments, and for their prolongation beyond the conference and its published proceedings into a sharp published exchange among West German participants.[48] The most divisive argument was about how to explain the most heinous policies of the Nazi regime – the spiral of domestic repression, military aggression, imperialism and exploitation, ultimately the genocidal war against Europe's Jews. Behind this lay a moral issue: whether some kinds of explanation amounted to a 'trivialization' (*Verharmlosung*) of National Socialism – not exactly an apologia for the regime, but a way of understanding it that tended to minimize or relativize its worst evils. The division here was not so much between marxists and liberals, but 'between two different schools of *liberal* thought about historical work and about the responsibility of the historian'.[49] These opposing schools had already been identified by other historians and labelled 'functionalism' and 'intentionalism', but it was Mason's essay that put these terms into wider currency by summarizing what they meant and by exploring the contrasts between them.

Representative of the functionalist approach was the work of Hans Mommsen and Martin Broszat, two leading West German historians whose research had disclosed the extraordinary political intricacy of the Nazi system of rule, and provided solid evidence that the regime did not merit its popular image as a mechanically efficient dictatorship ruled by an omnipotent tyrant. Their findings led these and other historians to see the increasingly radical and violent acts of the regime 'not as the work of a

---

[48] See Klaus Hildebrand, 'Nationalsozialismus ohne Hitler?', *Geschichte in Wissenschaft und Unterricht*, vol. 31 (1980) pp. 298–305, and see the subsequent article by Wolfgang Mommsen in vol. 32 as well as Hildebrand's reply and a further contribution by Karl Dietrich Erdmann; also the anonymous rebuttal of Hildebrand by another conference participant, in *Geschichtsdidaktik*, vols. 5 and 6 (1980/1); full details in Kershaw, *The Nazi Dictatorship*, Chapter 4, which also examines the interpretive issues outlined here.

[49] P. 213 below. The argument could also be seen as an analogue to the debate about economic determinism among marxists, since for liberals the relationship between ideas and political action is equivalent in significance to the relationship between the economy and politics for marxists.

deliberate dictatorial will, but rather as the consequences of the way in which the Nazi leadership conceived of political power and of the way in which political power was organised in the Third Reich'.[50] The hyper-political, personally competitive, inherently unstable character of the regime produced either 'non-policies or evasions' or else 'sudden and drastic decisions', both of which gave further twists to the spiral of instability and radicalism. In this scenario, Hitler appeared more as 'the beneficiary . . . than the architect' of the enormous powers that fell to him as Führer. But the sedulous cult of popularity that surrounded him had a paradoxically constraining effect: it became virtually impossible for Hitler to risk the image on which his legitimacy depended by sanctioning patently unpopular policies.[51] In this analysis too, Nazi ideology was not the origin of specific, calculable policy goals, but the source of a restless, aimless dynamism that further undermined the vestiges of institutional stability, and propelled the descent into extremes of violence that were essentially without rational purpose. In other words, the dynamic of the Nazis' most heinous policies could not be attributed straightforwardly to Hitler's intentions or to the dictates of the Nazis' ideological programme, but had to be seen as the indirect effect or function of the regime's structure and *modus operandi*.

By contrast with this picture of a regime determined by its own structural incoherence, and of Hitler as a 'weak dictator' (Mommsen's description), 'intentionalist' historians such as Karl Dietrich Bracher and Klaus Hildebrand saw the power and ideology of Hitler as the decisive political motor.[52] They explained Nazi policies as the wilful effects of Hitler's political ideology and intentions, principally his overriding project of imperialist, genocidal war. Although they saw these goals as no less irrational and utopian than did the functionalists, they argued that Nazi policies bore the clear stamp of Hitler's ideology and did not need to be explained by complex structural accounts that gave such a negligible role to the man, his will and his beliefs. It was, the intentionalists claimed, a trivialization of National Socialism's truly barbaric essence to see the crimes of Nazism as less than fully intended, as if they were merely the side-effect of something else.

---

[50] Quotations here and in the rest of this paragraph are from p. 214 below. Representative works by the authors cited include Hans Mommsen, *Beamtentum im Dritten Reich* (Stuttgart 1966); and idem 'National Socialism. Continuity and Change', in Walter Laqueur (ed.), *Fascism. A Reader's Guide* (Harmondsworth 1976), pp. 179–210; Martin Broszat, 'Soziale Motivation und Führer-Bindung des Nationalsozialismus', *Vierteljahrshefte für Zeitgeschichte*, vol. 18, no. 4 (1970), pp. 329–65; idem, *The Hitler State. The Foundation and Development of the Internal Structure of the Third Reich* (London 1981).

[51] Ian Kershaw has explored this in detail in *The Hitler Myth. Image and Reality in the Third Reich* (Oxford 1987).

[52] For representative works by Bracher and Hildebrand, see Mason's citations, pp. 212 and 218 below.

On the face of it, these might not necessarily be entirely incompatible accounts of the dynamic of the Third Reich, which obviously embraced not only Hitler and his ideology but also the specific and disorganized context of policy-making under the Nazis. Mason's characterization of the dispute as intellectual rather than political may also suggest that there was room for the kind of compromise that was virtually impossible between marxists and liberals. But the charge of trivializing National Socialism, which had originally been made by Bracher, was a calumny that could scarcely be taken lightly. Moreover, as Mason pointed out, the argument had deep roots in German historiography, though he perhaps underplayed the inflammatory power of this tradition. Intentionalism owed a lot to the kind of reductive historicism that had dominated German historiography since the midnineteeth century: like this historicism, intentionalism too emphasized the primacy of foreign policy, the significance of the individual statesman, the transparency of the documentary record to the trained reader, the authority of narrative over explanatory history.[53] Characteristically, Mason was especially outraged by what he saw as the moral fraudulence of the intentionalists, their implication that the moral duty to hate Hitler overrode the historical obligation to explain National Socialism – as if those who moved beyond Hitler in their attempt to explain somehow failed the moral test. Mason insisted that this was a false dichotomy, just as neither the person of Hitler nor the structure of the Nazi regime could be left out of any realistic attempt to understand the policies of the Third Reich. Epigrammatically, he pointed out that 'the monstrous will and administrative dilettantism were . . . necessary to each other'.[54]

'Intention and Explanation' is perhaps the richest of Mason's essays, and one of the most passionate in tone. It was an opportunity to meditate on the perplexing relationship between structure and agency in history, which was also a trope for Mason's concern about the relationship between politics and morality. These are troublesome issues for any historian or social scientist, but perhaps especially for someone schooled in the marxist tradition, who wanted to find 'concepts for the analysis of National Socialism, which *both* capture objective processes (capital accumulation, institutional darwinism, expansionism) *and* also relate clearly to the self-consciousness of the political actors'.[55] Mason suggested as a bridging concept the notion of 'struggle' – a term which encapsulated Hitler's social darwinism, and connoted the competition inherent in the capitalist economy as well as the physical conflict of war. He outlined a kind of hierarchy of competitive struggle in the epoch of capitalism, culminating in genocide, 'the most distinctively nazi, the most terrible

---

[53] Mason had already implicitly criticized historicism without actually naming it as such: see p. 34 below, and also p. 300.   [54] P. 224 below.   [55] P. 229 below.

part of an over-arching politics of struggle.' Explaining this relationship between capitalism and genocide, between the politics of class and the politics of race, was a fundamental obligation, and the largest zone of failure in marxist historiography. [56]

Although the essay did help to solidify a debate that was to focus especially on the origins of the genocide of the European Jews, this debate addressed not the relationship between genocide and capitalism, but another of the issues which Mason also discussed: the problem of sources and their interpretation. He had insisted that the documents of the Nazi regime were neither complete nor transparent enough to yield to the kind of literal reading he accused the intentionalists of fostering. Going somewhat beyond the conventions of critical source evaluation, he argued that historians of National Socialism needed to allow for metaphorical, symbolic, hidden and contradictory meanings in the utterances of their authors.[57] Though he referred loosely to literary criticism as a source for this notion, this was not an embrace of the strategies of deconstructive reading, which had not yet begun to attract much attention among historians (and when they did, Mason professed perplexity and unease at the tendency). Yet the documentary record of genocide is an archetype of the undecidable text, a tangle of metaphors, gaps and silences at the crux of the Third Reich which has made it difficult to reconstruct the exact process of policy-making, let alone to demonstrate that the 'Final Solution' was in any meaningful sense the culmination of a series of deliberate political steps. In Mason's lifetime this co-existence of infamy and uncertainty had already led to a process of deeply reflective argument among historians about the empirically verifiable sources and development of the Nazi regime's anti-Semitic policies.[58] Subsequently, it has prompted a handful of historians to join in the debates about interpreting the 'holocaust' which began to crystallize following the turn towards the problematics of text and representation among some members of the discipline.[59] Mason himself had taken little part in the 1970s/80s debates

[56] See Tim Mason, 'Open Questions on Nazism', in Raphael Samuel (ed.), *People's History and Socialist Theory* (London 1981), pp. 205–10. Mason referred repeatedly to the notion of struggle in his writings; see e.g. pp. 36, 248, 299 below.

[57] Characteristically, Mason saw this as an issue not of theory but of empirical research: 'This deficiency in giving an account of intentions and actions is a weakness in marxist work on fascism; but the weakness is not in the theory as such, for the challenge can be met by further research along the lines of the various non-literal ways of reading sources referred to above' (p. 227 below).

[58] This literature is vast and defies brief citation here; for an introduction to the issues and further references, see Kershaw, *The Nazi Dictatorship*, Chapters 5 and 8.

[59] This development has taken place since Mason's death, and to date largely among US academics; it thus is not strictly relevant here, but given the intrinsic importance of the issue a brief comment may be in order. It should be remembered that attempts to interpret rather than historically reconstruct and narrate the Nazi genocide are not in themselves new, but have long been pursued by artists, writers, philosophers and

about Nazi genocide; he admitted that he was psychologically incapable
of dealing with the record of inhumanity and suffering generated by Nazi
anti-Semitism, and subjecting it to the kind of critical analysis that he
believed was the only path to historical comprehension.[60] Still, some of
his own most salient, and controversial, propositions about the origins of
the war of 1939 depended on a creative reading of textual absences,
ambiguities and discontinuities, especially in some of Hitler's statements.[61]
Even more obviously, his writing about the relationship of the working
class to National Socialism not only required imaginative inference and
conjecture to fill out sparse documentary evidence, but also turned
precariously on a historical absence: why was there not more concerted
working-class resistance to National Socialism after 1933?

The question is posed in this counter-factual form in 'The Containment
of the Working Class', one of several essays devoted to a problem that was
central to Mason's understanding of Nazi Germany. If, as most historians
agree, the NSDAP had been unable before 1933 to seduce organized
workers from their allegiance to the parties of the left, and if the Nazis
smashed the working-class movement – parties, trade unions, cultural
organizations – as soon as they came to power, why was there no evidence
of working-class revolt after 1933? 'Why did that class in German society
which suffered greater disenfranchisement, greater persecution and
greater oppression than any other not mount at least one major challenge
to the regime? . . . Why did the Nazi regime, which abused a large part of
its subjects in such an unexampled way, survive through the last year of a
war which it was obviously losing *without any major mass challenge to its
power?*'[62] The choice of words here is important. Mason had argued that
there was widespread and continuing evidence that workers were never

cultural critics. New since the 1980s, however, is the scale of these efforts, and the more
direct engagement of historians, drawn not only by autonomous intellectual movements
within the discipline, but also by the inevitable recession of the 'holocaust' into historical
memory and the connected revival of extreme 'revisionism', i.e. the politically motivated
anti-Semitic denial of the historicity of the Nazi genocide. Among publications testifying
to the shift of intellectual paradigms among historians, see especially Saul Friedlander
(ed.), *Probing the Limits of Representation. Nazism and the 'Final Solution'* (Cambridge,
MA 1992), which reprints papers from an interdisciplinary conference devoted to
exploring the relationship between representation, interpretation and historical truth;
Geoffrey Hartman (ed.), *Holocaust Remembrance. The Shapes of Memory* (Oxford 1993);
and Saul Friedlander, *Memory, History, and the Extermination of the Jews of Europe*
(Bloomington, IN 1993). For a survey of cultural representations, see James Young,
Writing and Rewriting the Holocaust. Narrative and the Consequences of Interpretation
(Bloomington, IN 1988). For the problem of denial, see Pierre Vidal-Naquet, *Assassins of
Memory. Essays on the Denial of the Holocaust* (New York 1992) and Deborah Lipstadt,
Denying the Holocaust. The Growing Assault on Truth and Memory (New York 1993).

[60] *Social Policy in the Third Reich*, pp. 282 f.: 'my historical imagination kept on failing me:
facts which I could not face, and therefore could not understand and not give a proper
place to'. Mason's 'Open Questions', brief as it is, is the only example of his writing
devoted to the subject.

[61] See e.g. p. 298 below, and *Social Policy in the Third Reich*, pp. 262–6.

[62] Pp. 234 and 236 below.

successfully integrated into the Nazi *Volksgemeinschaft*, and that their alienation from the Nazi regime was expressed in countless acts of workplace indiscipline and insubordination – absenteeism, sabotage, small-scale strikes, pressure on pay and conditions, job-changing. The acts of resistance that interested him most were those that revealed some elements of collective consciousness and organization; but he also believed that superficially 'spontaneous' and individual acts could disguise deeper motives. Crucially, Mason wanted to see this repertoire of worker resistance as ultimately not economic but political in character, as being aimed not against employers but against the regime itself (indeed, he suggested that employers' and workers' self-interest could coincide and result in collusive decisions – for example, buying labour-force stability by granting higher wages – that jeopardized the regime's political priorities). As we have already seen, this interpretation was integral to his larger argument that the Nazis' failure to integrate the workers fully left the regime vulnerable to its own fear of working-class revolt, and that this played a precise, if indirect, part in the regime's decision to go to war in September 1939.[63] The question is, then, why the workers' opposition, if it really was an expression of vestigial class consciousness, never climaxed into something more organized, open and strategic. To answer that the regime's concessions to the workers were sufficient to forestall such a revolt would not be consistent with Mason's larger thesis, since this would amount to conceding that the regime did, in the end, manage to integrate the working class. The alternative – that the regime was successful in coercing the working class into submission – is equally unacceptable, since it would cast doubt on the other side of Mason's thesis, that the Nazis' fear of working-class disaffection set limits to the regime's willingness to use force.

Mason thus saddled himself with a complicated balancing act, which once again registered that oscillation between political and social interpretations of class to which I have already alluded. He had to explain, in effect, why working-class opposition to the Nazi regime was just enough to fuel Hitler's paranoia about 1918, yet not quite enough to challenge the regime openly; why it was political but not organized. It was no wonder that the issue of resistance continued to vex him, driving him finally, as we will see, to explore the very different experience of the working class under Italian fascism, in the hope that it would help solve the conundrum. Yet although his commitment to treating the working class primarily as a class may have led him to formulate his questions somewhat awkwardly, in the end he reached what is surely the best way of broaching the issue: as a question not about the quantity of resistance (as if that could possibly be computed), or even about its measurable effects,

[63] P. 9 above.

but about its form and its quality. The most successful parts of 'Containment' are those that conjure up the complex, contradictory, disorienting world of (mainly male) workers under the grotesque sign of the Third Reich: the experience of 'a forty-year old male metal worker, ex-union member, who got a wage increase the month after his brother had been stuck in a concentration camp, then found his eldest son called up for Labour Service' etc. etc.[64] To my mind, the entire essay is best read as a brilliant evocation of the seductions and terrors of life under Nazism (its 'fears, rewards, disciplines, routines'),[65] as a meditation on the hidden injuries of tyranny as well as its blatant oppressions. If it is more successful as this than as an answer to the possibly unanswerable question with which it begins, that surely makes the essay no less valuable.

Though counter-factual questions are often evidence of interpretative embarrassment, it would be unfair, I think, to regard Mason's perplexity in 'Containment of the Working Class' as redundant or self-inflicted. One does not need to subscribe to his overarching thesis to recognize that there is a puzzle about the scope of organized resistance to the Nazis, from not only the working class, but the military, the political elites and the churches as well. Most historians have approached this question precisely as Mason did – counter-factually, as a problem of explaining why there was not more opposition, even from these social leadership groups, and why what did take place was so sporadic and unsuccessful. Mason's own earlier work, notably his book *Social Policy in the Third Reich*, in fact gave the critical stimulus to West German research in the later 1970s and 1980s into the problem of 'popular' resistance to National Socialism and everyday life under the regime.[66] Historians following Mason's lead encountered the same basic dilemmas: what merits the label 'resistance' if

---

[64] P. 238 below.

[65] *Angst, Belohnung, Zucht und Ordnung. Herrschaftsmechanismen im Nationalsozialismus* (Opladen 1982), – the German title of the book in which the essay first appeared.

[66] Research into working-class resistance and compliance includes not only the volume *Angst, Belohnung, Zucht und Ordnung*, with essays by Carola Sachse, Tilla Siegel, Hasso Spode, and Wolfgang Spohn, but also and pre-eminently the following selected titles: the collective oral history project *Lebensgeschichte und Sozialkultur im Ruhrgebiet 1930 bis 1960 (LUSIR)*, ed. Lutz Niethammer (Bonn 1983), 3 vols.; Detlev Peukert and Jürgen Reulecke (eds.), *Die Reihen fast geschlossen. Beiträge zur Geschichte des Alltags unterm Nationalsozialismus* (Wuppertal 1981); Alf Lüdtke, '"Formierung der Massen": oder Mitmachen und Hinnehmen? "Alltagsgeschichte" und Faschismusanalyse', in Heide Gerstenberger and Dorothea Schmidt (eds.), *Normalität oder Normalisierung? Geschichtswerkstätten und Faschismusanalyse* (Münster 1987), pp. 15–34; idem, 'Wo blieb die "rote Glut"?', in Lüdtke (ed.), *Alltagsgeschichte. Zur Rekonstruktion historischer Erfahrungen und Lebensweisen* (Frankfurt am Main 1989), pp. 224–82; idem, '"Ehre der Arbeit"? Industriearbeiter und Macht der Symbole. Zur Reichsweite symbolischer Orientierungen im Nationalsozialismus', in Klaus Tenfelde (ed.), *Arbeiter im 20. Jahrhundert* (Stuttgart 1991), pp. 343–92; Detlev Peukert, *Inside Nazi Germany. Conformity, Opposition and Racism in Everyday Life* (London 1987) – to name only a few. On everyday opposition and compliance in general, the counterpart to the *LUSIR* project is Martin Broszat (ed.), *Bayern in der NS-Zeit* (Munich 1977–83), 6 vols.; also Ian Kershaw, *Popular Opinion and Political Dissent in the Third Reich. Bavaria 1933–1945* (Oxford 1983).

not exclusively self-conscious, deliberate and public acts of political opposition; what counts as consent or compliance, especially in conditions of police terror? The attempt to answer these questions, as well as to explain the weakness of organized resistance, gave rise to the first social histories of Nazi Germany; and these showed that the conventional image of social atomization plus totalitarian regimentation was inadequate as a description of the intricacies and ambiguities of everyday life under Nazism. Later, historians began to draw on concepts of dispersed power and conflicting subjectivities which are probably most familiar from the work of Foucault, but which also derive from the literatures of feminism and cultural criticism. These cumulative shifts in interpretation and research have resulted in far more nuanced accounts of the pressures and compensations of ordinary life and the meaning of everyday 'experience' (including the experience of institutionalized racism), accounts which also revise or cross the boundaries between work and home, public and private, political and personal.[67]

Despite his perceptive vision of fractured working-class consciousness, quoted above, Mason did not really follow these new extensions of the scope of investigation beyond the factory wall: his own work remained largely focused on the workplace, and for him the private sphere, narrowly understood as the family, remained largely a site of depoliticization and withdrawal. Responding to the most pertinent early examples of this research, he went about as far as he could, without risking his overarching thesis, in conceding that if the regime could not risk ruling by coercion alone, it must have ruled at some level by consent. He accepted that the regime was able to exercise some powers of 'political seduction' which did lead to a partial integration of the working class, though he was still inclined to give greater weight to what he called the 'neutralization' of the working class by the destruction of its political solidarity, its organizations and leadership in 1933. Although he was willing to distinguish between expressly political resistance and what he called a 'workers' opposition' that was not strictly political, he also continued to insist that most of the opposition expressed on the shop-floor had the regime, not the employers, as its ultimate target.[68] However, research on the experience of German workers after 1939 convinced him that the war brought qualitatively new pressures on working-class consciousness. At first the regime was able to

[67] See Geoff Eley, 'Wie denken wir über Politik? Alltagsgeschichte und die Kategorie des Politischen', Berliner Geschichtswerkstatt (ed.), *Alltagsgeschichte, Subjektivität und Geschichte. Zur Theorie und Praxis von Alltagsgeschichte* (Münster forthcoming). I am grateful to the author for allowing me to see this essay in manuscript.
[68] 'Containment of the Working Class' itself represented an extension and revision of Mason's thinking beyond the arguments first set forth or implied in his essay 'Labour in the Third Reich', *Past and Present*, no. 33 (April 1966), pp. 112–41, and in *Social Policy in the Third Reich*; see also 'The Workers' Opposition in Nazi Germany', and the epilogue to *Social Policy in the Third Reich*, pp. 284–94.

continue its policy of 'the light hand' in newly seductive and corrupting ways: by offering initially 'cheap' victories; plundering conquered territories for material goods; using the slave labour of 'inferior' races to exempt German women from conscription, to relieve German workers of much heavy labour, and at the same time to flatter Germans' sense of superiority and racial pride. Ultimately, however, the exigencies of the war both obliged and enabled the Nazis to impose upon workers the militarized political discipline and economic exploitation that the regime had shied away from before 1939. Yet through all this Mason continued to assert his original, fundamental premise: the Nazis' claim that they would replace class society with a genuinely new social order was a sham. Nazi 'egalitarianism' remained opportunistic, demagogic and superficial to the end; class itself survived the mutilations and corruptions of class consciousness.[69]

In 'Containment of the Working Class', Mason struggled with the question of an appropriate comparative context for evaluating the German opposition. He suggested that historians should not be misled by the superficial universality of human experience under different regimes of oppression and injustice: more important were the specific local histories, traditions and environments in which repression and resistance were enacted. Two of his final essays explored further aspects of this question, though incompletely. 'Whatever Happened to "Fascism"?' is a brief reflection on the shifts in research interests and the new intellectual and political alignments that had transformed the historiographical scene in the 1980s. The older paradigm of fascism had by then virtually vanished from scholarly discourse as a result of these changes: the dissolution of the 1960s/70s conjuncture on the left, the assertion of new feminist political and intellectual perspectives, intensive research into Nazi genocide, and the rise of a new debate, the so-called *Historikerstreit*, about the place of National Socialism in German history.[70] Historians of Nazism no longer referred their work to a wider concept of fascism, but were concentrating on issues and themes that were specifically pertinent to Germany, especially racial policy.

[69] See *Social Policy in the Third Reich*, pp. 331–69. The main texts to which Mason was responding here were Ulrich Herbert, *Fremdarbeiter. Politik und Praxis des 'Ausländer-Einsatzes' in der Kriegswirtschaft des Dritten Reiches* (Berlin/Bonn 1985), and Wolfgang Franz Werner, *'Bleib übrig!' Deutsche Arbeiter in der nationalsozialistischen Kriegswirtschaft* (Düsseldorf 1983).

[70] This was Mason's only published comment on the *Historikerstreit*. This voluminous debate among West German historians can be sampled (in translation) in Peter Baldwin (ed.), *Reworking the Past. Hitler, the Holocaust, and the Historians' Debate* (Boston 1990); and trans. James Knowlton and Truett Cates, *Forever in the Shadow of Hitler? Original Documents of the Historikerstreit* (Atlantic Highlands, NJ, 1993). For surveys and commentary, see Richard Evans, *In Hitler's Shadow. West German Historians and the Attempt to Escape from the Nazi Past* (New York 1989); Charles Maier, *The Unmasterable Past. History, Holocaust and German National Identity* (Cambridge, MA 1988); Geoff Eley, 'Nazism, Politics and the Image of the Past', *Past and Present*, no. 121 (November 1988), pp. 171–208; and Kershaw, *The Nazi Dictatorship*, Chapter 8.

Although Mason's reflections on this sea-change retain his characteristic clarity of thought and forthrightness of expression, he was unable to develop his ideas fully or to resolve his somewhat paradoxical reactions to the new situation. His old reservations about the abstractions of fascism theory were nevertheless coupled with unease at its disappearance from historical discourse; he expressed interest in the new concept of 'biopolitics' which had emerged from innovative research on women and on Nazi racism, yet also puzzlement that this seemed to echo some of the conservative tones of the intentionalists.[71] But if Mason himself could not press these questions any further, he was certainly accurate in identifying a widely shared sense of intellectual impasse in the 1980s. Political and intellectual changes on the largest scale had already obscured many of the familiar landmarks of the left, and this loss of orientation has become even more complicated since then, with the stunning political reversals across Russia and Europe since 1989, and the climacteric of postmodernism in academic discourse. An academic Rip Van Winkle who fell asleep in, say, 1970, would have found the whole field of 'theory' virtually unrecognizable twenty years later: familiar concepts and questions banished, class theory in retreat, the problem of the 'text' elevated to a new epistemological significance, the entire relationship between object and knowledge in history intellectually transformed.

It is pointless to speculate how Mason might have faced these challenges. In the last years of his life, his own intellectual strategy was clear: to begin the comparative empirical research on Italian fascism which he had come to see as the best way to pursue the questions about class, power and resistance which were always the most compelling for him. In the essay from this last period of work which is reprinted here, 'The Turin Strikes', Mason appears somewhat self-conscious about his tactic of close reading and critical evaluation of the documents, and tentative in his conclusions. Whether to see this as a case of *reculer pour mieux sauter* or a certain kind of retreat is perhaps a matter for the individual reader's temperament. Some of his hesitancy may have been due to the fact that this was a new field for him, and one already beset by intricate political mythologies. Yet this was also its allure: 'Decisive events, wholly inadequate sources and interpretations loaded with burning political implications'[72] – this epitomizes Mason's sense of his raw materials, of the challenge they present. The historian's task is to

---

[71] The link here is intricate, but basically stems from the argument made by Bracher, Hillgruber and others that it was Hitler's anti-Semitism that powered and directed Nazi policies. However, this is not really the same as the arguments about biopolitics, advanced by Peukert in particular, which have little to do with Hitler individually but a lot to do with the process and structure of German modernity; see especially Detlev Peukert, 'The Genesis of the "Final Solution" from the Spirit of Science', in Thomas Childers and Jane Caplan (eds.), *Reevaluating the Third Reich* (New York 1993), pp. 234–52.

[72] P. 284 below.

work through the tangle, to produce some conclusions that are historically legitimate and politically meaningful. Mason's painstaking reconstruction of the timing and sequence of the Turin strikes in March 1943 was the groundwork, the precondition for explaining exactly what were the sources, the extent and the logic of the political resistance to fascism among the Italian industrial working class. Cautiously, the essay suggests that the origins and significance of the strikes have been misunderstood. Like the Italian new left historians among whom Mason was now working, he wanted to demonstrate that the Italian Communist Party had not had a monopoly on resistance activity and leadership. He wanted to extract the truth about the resistance from the official communist hagiography that had entangled it since the 1940s, while at the same time resisting the conservative consensus, represented most vigorously by the historian Renzo de Felice, that Italians had supported or at least passively accepted the fascist regime. If unprejudiced research revealed that the true story of working-class resistance was less heroic than the legend proposed, this did not, in Mason's eyes, mean that it was less admirable or meaningful. In this preliminary essay, Mason went no further than to probe and partially reconstruct the mix of political motives and human impulses that gave the events of March 1943 their character; however, behind this modest objective lay broader Italian debates about the class identity of the opposition to fascism which have now begun to be more openly addressed.[73]

The two remaining essays in this collection, 'The Origins of the Law on the Organization of National Labour' and 'Women in Germany 1925-1940', are at the same time exercises in detailed historical research and contributions to important debates that spring the boundaries of German history alone. Though both essays were early contributions to these debates, they were exceptionally subtle and insightful, and have remained standard reading on their subjects. The essay on the Labour Organization Law was written in the context of the debate about National Socialism and modernization in the early 1970s. It took issue with the view (originally proposed by Talcott Parsons and taken up again in the 1960s, most influentially by the West German sociologist Ralf Dahrendorf) that National Socialism represented an 'archaic' or anti-modernist response to the crisis of modernization in Germany. However, the essay was not an attempt simply to argue the other side of the case, but was a careful critique of the archaism/modernity dualism itself, and a more severe assault on the positive value attached by its theorists to the concept of modernization. Mason disputed the assumption that modernization equalled economic development, that it necessarily implied social rationalization and political democratization, and that what appeared

[73] See Claudio Pavone, *Una guerra civile. Saggio storico sulla moralità nella Resistenza* (Turin 1991).

contrary to this trend or was expressed in the language of tradition was therefore incompatible with or hostile to modernization. In Mason's contrary view (and here he correctly invoked Max Weber in his support), modernization was a dialectical, Janus-faced process, the complexity of which was belied by the simplistic teleological and ideological model adopted by modernization theorists. The concept of 'community' (*Gemeinschaft*) was his key example here. In the classic contrast proposed by Weber's contemporary Tönnies, 'community' was the traditional form of association that was superseded by the modern 'society' (*Gesellschaft*). Thus the preponderance of a language of 'community' and associated terms (notably *Volksgemeinschaft*) in the Nazi lexicon tended to be taken as *prima facie* evidence of Nazi anti-modernism. Mason argued that this conclusion was possible only if the word 'community' was given a single, fixed meaning, rather the polymorphous character he believed it had in the 1930s, which was compatible with a wide range of economic and social values.

The body of the essay demonstrated this claim through a close analysis of the origins and wording of the Nazis' new 1934 Labour Law, which designated each workplace as a 'factory community' (*Betriebsgemeinschaft*) composed of 'factory leader' (*Betriebsführer*) and 'retinue' (*Gefolgschaft*), regulated by a 'factory code of rules', and supervised by a state-appointed Trustee of Labour. The law might thus appear to have reconstructed the capitalist factory as a kind of neo-feudal community that would satisfy the most backward-looking petty bourgeois fantasies; but Mason argued that both the thinking from which the law emerged and the form which it took were profoundly in tune with unimpeachable capitalist values of maximized rationality, efficiency, labour discipline, and profits. The law, he concluded, 'appears as an inevitable consequence of industrial, economic and technical progress, of the appropriate representation of interests and the untamed pace of economic development peculiar to industrial capitalism'.[74] All that was needed to fulfil 'the dream of total managerial control of industry', already circulating in Weimar, was the physical destruction of the independent trade unions that in fact accompanied the drafting of the law in 1933. Mason returned to the problem of modernization in a later essay, in which he argued that this almost terminally confused term must ultimately be conceded a normative, positive content if it were to be of any value at all in the historian's interpretative armoury. This led him logically to deny that the Nazi or Italian Fascist regimes could have had genuinely 'modernizing' effects.[75] The scholarly debate about the 'modernity' of Weimar and Nazi Germany has continued and widened; it has been informed not only by new empirical research into the sources

---

[74] P. 102 below.
[75] 'Italy and Modernization: A Montage', *History Workshop Journal*, no. 25 (spring 1989), pp. 127–47.

and outcomes of modernizing processes, but also by some major reconceptualizations of the concept of modernity.[76]

As a counterpart to this discriminating reworking of a familiar concept, it is fitting to end this introduction with a pioneering piece of research, the long essay 'Women in Germany, 1925-1940', first published in 1976. It may be hard, now that women's history has secured itself a solid place as one of the most interesting and fertile areas of historical scholarship, to recall how little researched or understood it was among academics in the mid-1970s, especially in Britain. This is not to discount the pioneering work on German women's history that had already been published by a few scholars, to whom Mason gave full credit.[77] But Mason was unusual among his male peers in taking this new field seriously, and not just by taking note of its existence but by doing serious work on it himself. The postscript to the essay shows that this was a position Mason reached rather awkwardly and with some resistance; nevertheless, he made the journey earlier and in far more good faith than most. His comments about the problems of writing the history of 'people in the past who appear to have been largely passive in public affairs'[78] are also revealing of the time in which the essay was written. Mason's provisional resolution here was to concentrate on demographic 'facts' and on women as the object of social and familial policy. His conclusions were that the Nazis were largely unsuccessful in any of their policies that attempted to buck larger economic and demographic trends: for example, their procreationist policies did not succeed in removing married women from the labour market, and inadvertently led to more numerous, but smaller and more privatized families. It is clear that this foray into the new women's history did not entirely satisfy his growing interest in the detailed texture and experience of social history; he was unable, for example, to judge the extent to which Nazi eugenics and anti-feminism converged into a

---

[76] See Annemarie Tröger, 'The Creation of a Female Assembly-Line Proletariat', in Renate Bridenthal, Atina Grossmann and Marion Kaplan (eds.), *When Biology Became Destiny. Women in Weimar and Nazi Germany* (New York 1984), pp. 236–70; Zygmunt Baumann, *Modernity and the Holocaust* (Oxford 1989); Hans Mommsen, 'Nationalsozialismus als vorgetäuschte Modernisierung', in Walter H. Pehle (ed.), *Der historische Ort des Nationalsozialismus* (Frankfurt am Main 1990), pp. 31–46; Detlev Peukert, *The Weimar Republic. The Crisis of Classical Modernity* (London 1991); idem, 'The Genesis of the "Final Solution"'; Michael Prinz and Rainer Zitelmann (eds.), *Nationalsozialismus und Modernisierung* (Darmstadt 1991); Mary Nolan, *Visions of Modernity, American Business and the Modernization of Germany* (New York 1994). For the newer issue of post-modernism, see, in addition to the sources listed in note 59 above, Jean François Lyotard, *The Differend. Phrases in Dispute* (Minneapolis, MN 1988) and Dominick Lacapra, *Representing the Holocaust. History, Theory, Trauma* (Bloomington, IN 1994).

[77] Notably Renate Bridenthal, 'Beyond *Kinder, Küche, Kirche*. Weimar Women at Work', *Central European History*, vol. 6, no. 2 (1973), pp. 148–66 (reprinted in a revised and expanded form co-authored by Claudia Koonz in Bridenthal, Grossmann and Kaplan (eds.), *When Biology Became Destiny*, pp. 33–65); and Jill Stephenson, 'Women in German Society 1930–1940', Ph.D. thesis, Edinburgh 1974, later published as *Women in Nazi Society* (London 1975).   [78] P. 209 below.

punitive assault on so-called 'asocial' or feckless breeders, even if they were 'aryans'. Even so, he was able to broach numerous themes in the history of Nazi Germany that have since been more fully researched, among them the status of women in the labour market, women in the family, the welfare system, and the connection between anti-feminism and racism.[79] Mason's approach to these questions was heavily informed by his existing interpretative positions, especially in his emphasis on class and his use of the internal crisis of 1939 as the key to explaining apparent contradictions in Nazi policy towards women. Nevertheless, this essay was his closest approach to the writing of social history, as opposed to labour and political history. While it is true that debates about women and gender under National Socialism have expanded and ramified since the original publication of this essay, and an extensive new literature has accumulated to fill out the issues it raises, it remains one of the best short introductions to the position of women in Nazi Germany. Apart from summarizing a wealth of economic and demographic information, it is an example of open, undogmatic enquiry that, like the best of Mason's work, invites the reader to follow the author's thoughts not in order to agree with them but to criticize, amplify and refine.

Mason's ultimate but unrealized goal was to bring together the overarching themes in his published works and write a comprehensive 'political social history of Nazism':[80] one that would tell the history of the Nazi polity from the perspective of class experience, that would splice together the multiple strands spun out by the essays. The completion of this task ultimately eluded him, but the essays stand as so many gateways into this ambitious project of theoretically informed history. Throughout his life, Mason had remained sceptical of theory that was abstract, rigid or constraining. The motivating belief behind his work – that the National Socialist regime was 'unique in the history of modern bourgeois society'[81] – was necessarily rooted in a more generalizing political theory of the modern world, but although the elements of that theory were patently if eclectically marxist, his characteristic analytic approach could better be described as strategic rather than strictly theoretical. His political and historical temperament, though not particularist in any pedantic sense,

---

[79] On these themes, see especially Stephenson, *Women in Nazi Society*; idem, *The Nazi Organisation of Women* (London 1981); Frauengruppe Faschismusforschung (ed.), *Mutterkreuz und arbeitsbuch. Zur Geschichte der Frauen in der Weimarer Republik und im Nationalsozialismus* (Frankfurt am Main 1981); Marie-Luise Recker, *Nationalsozialistische Sozialpolitik im Zweiten Weltkrieg* (Munich 1985); Claudia Koonz, *Mothers in the Fatherland. Women, the Family and Nazi Politics* (London 1987); Gisela Bock, *Zwangssterilisation im Nationalsozialismus. Studien zur Rassenpolitik und Frauenpolitik* (Opladen 1988); also Michael Burleigh and Wolfgang Wippermann, *The Racial State. Germany 1933–1945* (Cambridge 1991), and Elizabeth Harvey, *Youth and the Welfare State in Weimar Germany* (Oxford 1993).
[80] See Mason, *Social Policy in the Third Reich*, pp. 275 f.
[81] 'The Primacy of Politics', p. 54 below.

was strongly committed to the documentary record, which for him provided the essential raw materials of the historian's craft. He was less interested in theorizing the general 'laws of motion' of capital than in exploring and explaining precisely how the relationship between the economic, the social, and the political worked in a particular instance, and what it meant to those who were its historical subjects. Mason had sound intellectual grounds for emphasizing class and class conflict in his accounts of National Socialism: historically, because the struggle between labour and capital, left and right, was arguably the definitive ground of European politics between the wars; and sociologically, given the evidence that the factory floor generates daily tensions between labour and capital that are the raw material of class consciousness. But Mason's concept of class was itself a profoundly dialectical and political one, far removed from the economism that ascribes fixed positions and rigid meanings to social collectives. For him, 'class' materialized, in specific historical contexts, the tensions between collective and individual, between experience and agency, between the social and the political, between domination and resistance that he understood as the heart of the human condition in the modern world.

In his one published contribution to the 'theory wars' that racked British marxist history in the 1970s, Mason demanded with some exasperation,

What . . . is a school of Marxist history worth, which does *not* place major crises of the political–economic order at *the centre* of its meditations? Nothing. And how can the word 'crisis' even be spoken, let alone conceptualised, without the bodies of dead revolutionaries, the historical presence of self-conscious political militants who died for their (our?) cause, bursting the seams of the files in which we order our notes on 'the mode of production'? No way.[82]

Mason's own work repeatedly sprang the conventions of the academy, and honoured not only 'the bodies of dead revolutionaries', but those of the anonymous millions slaughtered in the wake of Nazi dictatorship, imperialism and racism. At the same time, his unwavering respect for the evidence, intractable as it often was, was a professional duty, an academic warranty of his political respect for the ordinary working lives that ultimately underlay the real history he studied: lives crushed in struggle, brutally extinguished, forced into silence, shamefully acquiescent, fitfully heroic, but worthy of the dignity of being taken seriously.

[82] Tim Mason, 'The Making of the English Working Class', *History Workshop Journal*, no. 7 (spring 1979), p. 224. This was a letter criticizing Richard Johnson's controversial article, 'Thompson, Genovese, and Socialist–Humanist History', *History Workshop Journal*, no. 6 (autumn 1978), pp. 79–100, in which Mason also conceded, however, that Johnson had 'triggered off a historical debate of great significance for historians on the Left [and] forced a lot of un-theoretical historians to read a lot of "theory" in the past six months'. The issues raised in the article provoked Mason, as an editor of *History Workshop*, to a series of explosive internal memoranda, but these remained unpublished.

1

---- ❧ ----

SOME ORIGINS OF THE SECOND WORLD WAR

THE FIFTH impression of Mr A. J. P. Taylor's *The Origins of the Second World War* contains a new introductory essay entitled 'Second Thoughts', in which he makes explicit some of the important underlying propositions of the book, and deals in greater detail with a number of specific problems. The central issues are now clear beyond dispute.

'I wrote this book in order . . . to understand what happened and why it happened . . . when I speak of morality I refer to the moral feelings at the time I am writing about. I make no moral judgements of my own.'[1] One of the major themes of Mr Taylor's book is the inability of historians writing on the inter-war period to overcome their horror at the atrocities committed by the National Socialist regime; this horror has led them to mistake the general moral responsibility of the Third Reich for the greatest barbarities in the history of Western civilization for an assumed, concrete historical responsibility for the outbreak of the Second World War. There is certainly much truth in this contention,[2] and Mr Taylor has made a greater effort than any previous historian to achieve an emotional and moral detachment from the subject matter. The importance of making this effort is demonstrated by the brilliance and lucidity of many passages in *The Origins of the Second World War:* the account of the 1920s, the analysis of the international importance of the Italian conquest of Abyssinia, and the portrayal of relations between Britain, France and Russia in 1939 present most complex themes with outstanding clarity and objectivity.

[1] A. J. P. Taylor, *The Origins of the Second World War*, 5th impression (London 1963), with a new essay entitled 'Second Thoughts'; the essay is not paginated. The main text will be cited hereafter as Taylor, *Origins*; the essay as 'Second Thoughts'. The quotation above is from 'Second Thoughts'.

[2] See for example Chapter 1 of W. Hofer's book, *Die Entfesselung des zweiten Weltkrieges*, rev. edn (Frankfurt am Main 1960). Hofer's basic thesis that National Socialism was the major cause of the war (*Origins*, Introduction) *need not* lead to the moral determinism which Mr Taylor rightly criticizes.

It is no coincidence, however, that the best passages in Mr Taylor's book are those which deal with countries other than Germany, countries whose foreign policies were basically pragmatic, and whose statesmen were seeking more or less limited goals with more or less conventional means. It is the basic unspoken postulate of *The Origins of the Second World War* that the foreign policy of the Third Reich was also of this character. In attempting to lift the shadow cast by the Nuremburg Tribunals over the historiography of Nazi Germany, Mr Taylor reduces the international relations of the period to the obsolete formula of independent states pursuing intelligible national interests with varying degrees of diplomatic skill. 'What happened' is by this token the story of the complex interaction of these national policies, an interaction so complex and so swiftly changing that no statesman could come near to grasping it in its entirety; and the answer to the question 'why' lies largely in these inevitable shortcomings of the statesmen.

'The Second World War, too, has profound causes; but it also grew out of specific events, and these events are worth detailed examination.'[3] Yet Mr Taylor's formula largely excludes the profound causes from consideration;[4] it seems unable to accommodate political movements and ideologies. National Socialism was perhaps the profoundest cause of the Second World War, but Mr Taylor's book is not informed by any conception of the distinctive character and role of National Socialism in the history of twentieth-century Europe.[5]

Two main reasons are advanced for this partly deliberate omission: first, that foreign policies were determined rather by *raison d'état* and the need to respond to contingent international situations, than by internal political, ideological or economic pressures – international relations are portrayed as largely autonomous from other spheres of politics; and second, that in the period Britain and France dominated the international scene, their policies were decisive.

It will be argued below that these two theses are invalid, and then further reasons will be suggested as to why *The Origins of the Second World War* does not deal satisfactorily with the foreign policy of the Third Reich.

An experienced British observer who visited Germany in 1938 came away with the conviction that 'at that time, the great bulk of the German people (as distinct from the inner ring of leaders) were thinking of anything rather than war, and were inspired by the economic and social

---

[3] Taylor, *Origins*, p. 103.
[4] The brief discussion of profound causes (*Origins*, pp. 103–7) is such as to cast doubt on the very notion of a profound cause; see the review by F. H. Hinsley, *The Historical Journal*, no. 4 (1961), pp. 222–9.
[5] Neither National Socialism nor the National Socialist Party are mentioned in the very full index.

changes which they felt were taking place around them and which seemed to hold out such high hopes for the future. Their eyes were turned inwards, not outwards.'[6] This state of affairs was not congenial to a regime in whose very nature it lay to make continuous and total demands on the loyalty and activity of its subjects, to perpetuate an atmosphere of febrile political enthusiasm and tension. Hitler's remark to his military leaders in November 1937 reads almost as a direct response to the perceptive observation of Guillebaud just quoted:

If, territorially speaking, there existed no political result corresponding to this German racial core, that was a consequence of centuries of historical development, and *in the continuance of these political conditions lay the greatest danger to the preservation of the German race at its present peak.* To arrest the decline of Germanism (*Deutschtum*) in Austria and Czechoslovakia was as little possible as to maintain the present level in Germany itself. Instead of increase, sterility was setting in, and in its train disorders of a social character must arise in course of time, *since political and ideological ideas remain effective only as long as they furnish the basis for the realisation of the essential vital demands of a people.* Germany's future was therefore wholly conditional upon solving the need for space.[7]

Despite its turgid rhetoric, this passage contains a very clear and important judgement – the movement was becoming slack and sated, losing its demonic edge; the Third Reich had either to set itself new tasks by expanding, or to cease from being totalitarian.

Mr Taylor dismisses such considerations: 'The historian must try to push through the cloud of phrases to the realities beneath', and these realities were the attempts of Great Powers 'to maintain their interests and independence'.[8] This view leads to an overwhelming concentration on the sequence of diplomatic events, and a failure to see German foreign policy in the general context of National Socialist politics. The foreign policy of the Third Reich was dynamic in character, limitless in its aims to achieve domination and entirely lacking a conception of an 'ultimate status quo'.[9] This expansionist drive was the unique contribution of National Socialism, and the feature which most clearly distinguishes Hitler's foreign policy from that of his predecessors.[10] In concentrating the reader's attention on the detailed circumstances which enabled

[6] C. W. Guillebaud, *The Social Policy of Nazi Germany* (Cambridge 1941), p. 108.
[7] The Hossbach Protocoll, *Documents on German Foreign Policy*, ser. D., vol. I (Washington, DC 1949), pp. 29–30 (my italics). It is impossible to conceive of any other statesman of the period talking of foreign policy in these terms; for the language of the diplomatic documents see p. 39 below.   [8] Taylor, *Origins*, p. 107.
[9] See E. M. Robertson, *Hitler's Pre-War Policy and Military Plans 1933–1939* (London 1963), pp. 2–3.
[10] The view that National Socialist rule changed every aspect of German public life, but not foreign policy, is fundamentally implausible; why was it alone exempt? (See Taylor, *Origins*, p. 68.)

Germany to make territorial gains prior to the outbreak of war, Mr Taylor omits a satisfactory analysis of the mainsprings of German policy. Expansionism is sometimes taken for granted, sometimes represented merely as the restoration of German power in Europe or as the revision of Versailles,[11] and is sometimes dismissed adverbially;[12] it is never assigned any definite role among the causes of the Second World War.

This weakness is due in part to Mr Taylor's abrupt dismissal of 'the cloud of phrases' which enveloped German policy, his refusal to accept that policy was in any way determined by the ideology or by the internal political structure of the Third Reich. His choice of words is illuminating; in seeking a language to describe the phenomena of National Socialism, he is driven back on the vocabulary of nineteenth-century liberalism: the gas chambers were 'wicked', 'the rhetoric of the dictators was no worse than the "sabre-rattling" of the old monarchs', Hitler differed from other statesmen in that his appetite for success was greater, and his 'habits and nature' played their part in causing the war – 'it was easy for him to threaten and hard for him to conciliate'.[13] The vocabulary and the analogies are simply inadequate. The wickedness of the gas chambers is not at stake; of more importance for the historian is the light which they shed on the mentality of the regime and on the nature of its aims. Similarly, the terms 'rhetoric' and 'sabre-rattling' hardly do justice to a government which systematically militarized all social relations, turned employers and workers into 'leaders and followers',[14] had its youth do rifle-drill with spades,[15] elevated fanaticism to the supreme public virtue,[16] and saw all facets of life as *struggles* or *battles* for existence and domination.[17] This is the historical context in which Hitler's personal characteristics must be seen; the facility with which he resorted to force or the threat of force in international affairs, his need to achieve success after success in foreign policy were not minor contingent factors on the European scene, but basic traits of the political movement which he led.

The second thesis seems equally open to question: 'My book really has little to do with Hitler. The vital question, it seems to me, concerns Great Britain and France. They were the victors of the first World War. They

---

[11] It is questionable whether the latter 'aim' should be considered as more than a useful slogan for securing popular support.

[12] 'Hitler *undoubtedly* wished to "liberate" the Germans of Czechoslovakia' (my italics): Taylor, *Origins*, p. 152.

[13] Ibid., p. 71 and 'Second Thoughts', pp. 103, 106, 216.

[14] Law on the Organization of National Labour, 20 January 1934.

[15] See Erwin Leiser's film, *Mein Kampf*.

[16] V. Klemperer, *LTI. Notizbuch eines Philologen* (Berlin 1947), p. 65; this book is a brilliant portrayal of National Socialism by a German-Jewish professor of linguistics who stayed and survived.

[17] *Arbeitsschlacht*: the battle to create employment; *Kampf um Rohstoffe*: the fight for raw materials.

had the decision in their hands.'[18] Mr Taylor has clearly shown that in the individual crises which led up to the outbreak of war in 1939, many important initiatives came from Britain and France, but this is insufficient evidence that his general perspective is the right one. In the Europe of the 1930s the Third Reich was the most potent force for change – for change in boundaries no less than for change in political and economic techniques or social and cultural values. Mr Taylor insists that 'the crisis of March 1938 was provoked by Schuschnigg', and that the crisis which culminated in the Munich settlement was 'of British making', and he lays some emphasis on the fact that President Hacha of Czechoslovakia was not summoned to Berlin in March 1939 but asked to come of his own accord. In doing so he omits to ask why it was possible for these crises to arise at all – why Schuschnigg thought it necessary to call a plebiscite in Austria, why in the late spring of 1938, 'Everyone in Europe felt [that] . . . the Czechoslovak round was due to begin',[19] why Hacha saw no alternative but to turn to Hitler. It is a question of perspective; in a longer perspective the initiatives of other governments appear rather as responses to problems raised by Nazi Germany. Crucial decisions were certainly made in all the capitals of Europe, but the Third Reich determined what it was the victor powers had to decide about. The fact that the Sudetenland and Danzig arose at all as *acute, international* problems was due almost exclusively to the hegemony of the National Socialist party within Germany. In rightly insisting that the expansionist aims of the Reich were at no stage formulated into a comprehensive plan, Mr Taylor wrongly conveys the impression that they were of little importance.[20]

This impression is enhanced by the way in which the appeasers are saddled with the full historical responsibility for the results of their actions (whether these results were intended or not), whereas Hitler is deprived of this responsibility; his successes were largely unpremeditated. The results of the British agreement to guarantee the remains of Czechoslovakia on 18 September 1938, and of the German occupation of Bohemia in March 1939 are analysed at quite different levels. By the former Edouard Daladier unwittingly secured Britain's future opposition to German expansion in Eastern Europe; by the latter, 'Hitler . . . was . . . reverting in the most conservative way to the pattern of previous centuries', he was acting 'without design'.[21] The former analysis is rigorous, objective and forward-looking, the latter merely a subjective explanation – Hitler's prestige was threatened if either the Czechs or the

[18] Taylor, 'Second Thoughts'.
[19] Taylor, *Origins*, pp. 149, 155, 202 and 'Second Thoughts', and *Origins*, p. 151.
[20] This is one danger of relying largely upon the diplomatic documents; not every foreign service has its Sir Eyre Crowe; see also below, p. 39.
[21] Taylor, *Origins*, pp. 177, 202–3.

Hungarians attacked Slovakia. In order simply to understand what happened and why, more must be said about the regime which could make a basic foreign policy decision on such grounds, and more about the necessary logic in the development of German policy, which was no less marked than that of Anglo-French policy.

Similarly, the outbreak of a European war over Danzig was not just a matter of miscalculation on Hitler's part. Hitler took the very straightforward risk that Britain and France would declare war in the event of a German invasion of Poland. The decision to take this risk launched the Second World War. Clearly Hitler would have preferred Britain and France to remain inactive, but the risk was obvious enough for him to be presumed to have been ready to accept the consequences if they did not. Mr Taylor illuminates the reasons why Hitler may have thought the chance worth taking,[22] but this explanation is on a subjective level and the objective importance of the decision is missed.

The fundamental argument of Mr Taylor's book is that it takes two to make a war; more accurately, that it took Britain and France to make a European war. It does not really explain why the Third Reich was willing to risk a European war.

A number of further reasons may be suggested for the inadequate treatment of German foreign policy in *The Origins of the Second World War*;[23] two of these will be discussed below: the limited nature of the source material selected, and the way in which this material is used.

'"Le style c'est l'homme": a man may speak untruths, but his very being is laid bare in the style of his self-expression.'[24] Mr Taylor's judgements rest very largely upon the diplomatic documents. Some of the consequent disadvantages have already been mentioned above. In addition, these documents were primarily the work of conservative German diplomats, who, in dealing with their specific problems, were able to cover up or ignore the distinctive language and concepts of National Socialism. This helps to nurture the illusion that the foreign policy of the Third Reich was much the same as that of the Weimar Republic, and that it served the same functional purposes as the foreign policies of the other powers.

---

[22] Ibid., pp. 269 ff. There were also many good reasons why it was a bad risk: Neville Chamberlain regarded his written obligations a little more seriously than Hitler did, and the British public much more seriously.

[23] Anti-German prejudice perhaps plays a role; the insistence that there was nothing exceptional about the foreign policy of the Third Reich damns by implication that of the Weimar Republic and perhaps that of the Federal Republic – see the concluding notes by Professor M. Freund in the German edition of *The Origins of the Second World War*. Mr Taylor writes that 'most Germans vaguely believed' in racial doctrines, and that Hitler's *Lebensraum* aspirations 'echo the conversation of any Austrian café or German beer-house' (*Origins*, pp. 69, 71).

[24] Klemperer, *LTI*, p. 16.

Neither do the documents give an adequate picture of the role of the Nazi movements inside Austria and Czechoslovakia; their movements are portrayed as the objects of diplomacy, and Mr Taylor tends to reflect this emphasis.[25] Thus he adduces the existence of a militant pro-Nazi movement among the Sudeten Germans as further proof that Hitler did not initiate the crisis over Czechoslovakia. Though the point is illuminating in a sense, it encourages the making of too radical a distinction between Hitler the German statesman and Hitler the leader of the Nazi movement. The persistent and violent disruption of ordered life in Austria and Czechoslovakia was a crucial contribution of National Socialism to pre-war international relations. It severely weakened the internal structure of both states,[26] created an atmosphere of continual crisis, and in the latter case provided Hitler with the indispensable pretext of self-determination; in Austria it was Schuschnigg's discovery of plans for a Nazi insurrection which brought him to seek the fateful meeting with Hitler at Berchtesgaden on 12 February 1938. In short, the National Socialist movement created conditions in which the actual course of events in Central Europe was made very probable, if not fully predetermined. And the fact that the Austrian and the Sudeten parties often acted independently of the German leadership,[27] indicates in the first instance the central role of the movement in the history of the period; Hitler's opportunism is only meaningful within this context. The question 'why' cannot be asked of the diplomatic documents alone.

A further important reason for Mr Taylor's inadequate treatment of National Socialism is that his handling of the material which he does use is sometimes faulty.[28] Important conclusions are occasionally drawn from evidence of uncertain validity. On the question of factual accuracy this chapter will confine itself to two major problems: the Hossbach Protocoll, and Germany's economic preparations for war.

The so-called Hossbach conference has been investigated with some thoroughness by German historians,[29] and although Mr Taylor seems to

---

[25] Taylor, *Origins*, p. 152.

[26] The Czech defences in 1938 were manned in part by German-speaking troops. It must remain an open question how long either country could have withstood the economic and psychological pressures of a state of internal siege; for this dimension G. E. R. Gedye's *Fallen Bastions* (London 1939) is still necessary reading.

[27] See Robertson, *Hitler's Pre-War Policy*, pp. 123, 137; Taylor, *Origins*, p. 140.

[28] Contrast Mr Taylor's statement that the Saar plebiscite was 'unquestionably free' (*Origins*, p. 86) with the eyewitness account of Alexander Werth, *The Destiny of France* (London 1937), Chapter 7. Compare Taylor (*Origins*, p. 166) and Robertson (*Hitler's Pre-War Policy*, p. 135 n. 1) on German military planning against Czechoslovakia in the summer of 1938. See also the painstaking review article by P. A. Reynolds, 'Hitler's War?', *History*, no. 46 (1961), pp. 212–17.

[29] See especially G. Meinck, *Hitler und die deutsche Aufrüstung 1933–7* (Wiesbaden 1959), pp. 174–84, 236–7; and H. Gackenholz, 'Reichskanzlei den 5 November 1937', in *Forschungen zu Staat und Verfassung. Festgabe für Fritz Hartung* (Berlin 1958), pp. 460 ff.

have drawn on their research[30] his conclusions do not correspond with theirs. Mr Taylor advances the thesis that Hitler called together Neurath, Göring and his military leaders in November 1937 in order to gain their support in overcoming Hjalmar Schacht's resistance to increased armaments expenditure. No evidence is cited in support of this interpretation and a number of considerations weigh heavily against it. First of all, the conference was called by Blomberg who wished to press home a complaint against Göring: the latter was misusing his powers as Plenipotentiary for the Four Year Plan and Controller of raw materials and foreign exchange in order to favour the rearmament programme of the airforce (of which he was Marshal) at the expense of that of the army.[31] Hitler was thus faced wth the embarrassing situation of having to arbitrate an important dispute between two of his chief subordinates; it is plausible that he sought to escape from this dilemma by talking at length of the general aims of German strategy and impressing his listeners with the general political need for accelerating rearmament.[32] Thus the picture of Hitler calling and manipulating the conference for his own ends is, at the very least, overdrawn.[33] Given the immediate problem with which he was faced by the conference Schacht can hardly have played more than an incidental role in his calculations.

The evidence that the military leadership curtailed rearmament out of respect for Schacht's views of fiscal policy is very slight and fragmentary, and is not sufficient to bear out Mr Taylor's statement that 'Hitler's manoeuvre had succeeded: henceforward Fritsch, Blomberg and Raeder had no sympathy with Schacht's financial scruples'.[34] There is record of an agreement in March 1937 between Blomberg, Schacht and Krosigk that the military budget should not exceed RM 10 milliard per annum,[35] but it is not clear that the agreement was carried out;[36] Göring almost

[30] There are regrettably few references in *The Origins of the Second World War*. None are given to secondary works for the discussion of the Hossbach Protocoll in the main text; it is wrongly stated that the reasons why the conference was held have not been investigated (*Origins*, p. 133). Some references are given in the further discussion in 'Second Thoughts', where Mr Taylor casts grave doubts on the reliability of the extant text. Drawing upon the work of Meinck (*Hitler*, pp. 236–7), Mr Taylor notes that several days elapsed before Hossbach wrote up the minutes of the conference and that his manuscript was transcribed twice before being used as evidence at Nuremberg; only this last abbreviated version, which omits the discussion which followed Hitler's monologue, has survived. On the basis of considerable research, however, Meinck comes to the conclusion that Hossbach's original minutes were a reasonably accurate version of what Hitler said, and that the extant version is an accurate rendering of the original as far as it goes; it corresponds with the notes taken at the time by General Beck.

[31] Meinck, *Hitler*, p. 174; Gackenholz, 'Reichskanzlei', pp. 461–2.

[32] This does not necessarily detract from the importance of what Hitler said.

[33] Taylor, *Origins*, p. 133.   [34] Ibid., p. 134.   [35] Gackenholz, 'Reichskanzlei', p. 460.

[36] See below, note 81. There are other inconclusive hints that the military leadership did fear inflation: see Robertson, *Hitler's Pre-War Policy*, pp. 84–6; H. Schacht, *Account Settled* (London 1949), p. 90.

certainly did not feel himself bound by it, and fiscal control over the military establishment was anyway very weak. In April 1934 the Ministry for the Armed Forces was exempted from the requirement to submit detailed estimates to the Ministry of Finance, and the Ministry of Aviation was accorded the same privilege a year later; global estimates were submitted and bargained over; there was no 'Treasury control'.[37] It is also very doubtful whether Schacht's position in the autumn of 1937 was still strong enough to warrant Hitler's taking such drastic measures to undermine it.[38] His power and influence had already been appreciably reduced by the transfer to Göring of competence for raw materials and foreign exchange in April 1936,[39] and by the creation of the Four Year Plan Office in the autumn of the same year. Schacht could only secure the termination of the Mefo-bill issue by agreeing to an increase of one-third in its size, and the Mefo-bill was immediately replaced (1938–9) by the delivery note and the tax remission certificate; public expenditure was not reduced.[40] Hitler's reluctance to lose Schacht probably derived from the latter's reputation rather than from his power.

Thus the Hossbach Protocoll remains of vital interest to the student of German foreign policy, but the importance of the conference must first be demonstrated before valid conclusions can be drawn from the document. Of the practical effects of Hitler's monologue, Mr Taylor writes, 'There was here . . . no directive for German policy'; and, 'At the time, no one attached importance to the meeting.'[41] In the middle of December, seven weeks after the conference, the mobilization orders of the armed forces were changed; the orders of July 1937 envisaged a preventive German invasion of Czechoslovakia in the event of Franco-Russian aggression against the Reich. Those of December postulated (given favourable international circumstances) German aggression against Austria and Czechoslovakia.[42] This change mirrored the new temper and new aims of Hitler's policy as he had expounded it to his military leaders on 5 November. The conference marks the point at which the expansionism of the Third Reich ceased to be latent and became explicit. Hitler's prognostications at the conference were faulty, but the new temper of his

[37] H. Steubel, 'Die Finanzierung der Aufrüstung im Dritten Reich', *Europa Archiv* (June 1951), col. 4131.
[38] Mr Taylor even goes so far as to assert that the Reichswehr crisis of February 1938 was staged with the object of covering up Schacht's resignation (*Origins*, p. 141). No sources are quoted; it is very unlikely that any of the Nazi leaders thought that Schacht was a more influential opponent than the generals.
[39] Meinck, *Hitler*, pp. 159–64.
[40] Steubel, 'Die Finanzierung', cols. 4130–1.
[41] Taylor, *Origins*, p. 132 and 'Second Thoughts'.
[42] Gackenholz, 'Reichskanzlei', pp. 476–81. Göring changed the mobilization orders of the Luftwaffe in this sense immediately after the conference without waiting for orders from his superior Blomberg.

policy persisted, as Schuschnigg found to his cost on 12 February. The Protocoll is indeed a 'pledge to violence'.[43]

It is clear that political, strategic and geographical factors were of more importance in the history of Europe in the 1930s than the factor of sheer military strength. In comparison with British foreign policy, French military strategy and the fragmentation of Eastern Europe into a number of rival national states, the precise level of German rearmament was a matter of relative indifference in determining the development of international relations.[44] However, the extent and nature of German rearmament is not only an interesting question in its own right, but can (in principle) also throw light on the aims of German foreign policy. 'Far from wanting war, a general war was the last thing he [Hitler] wanted . . . This is not guesswork. It is demonstrated beyond peradventure by the record of German armament before the Second World War or even during it.'[45] The weakness of Mr Taylor's deduction is that it is based upon a very imperfect knowledge of the economic history of the Third Reich.[46] No authoritative study of this immensely complicated subject exists as yet;[47] the source material is enormous in bulk and of dubious quality. Some caution is thus called for, but Mr Taylor, citing the work of the American economist B. H. Klein,[48] makes a number of sweeping general assertions: the 'German recovery was caused by the return of private consumption and non-war types of investment to the prosperity levels of 1928 and 1929. Rearmament had little to do with it'; and, 'Hitler . . . was terrified of inflation.'[49]

The title of Mr Klein's book, *Germany's Economic Preparations for War*, is misleading, for the great bulk of it is in fact concerned with the performance of the German economy *in wartime*, a subject which it treats thoroughly and in some detail. The same cannot be said of the chapters on the pre-war period. Mr Klein's book appeared in 1959, but his bibliography indicates that he used only two works in this field published after 1948; he

---

[43] The title of Meinck's chapter on the conference.

[44] See Taylor, 'Second Thoughts'.

[45] Taylor, *Origins*, p. 218.

[46] Compare the judgements quoted at the end of the paragraph above with the following 'first thoughts': Full employment 'depended in larger part on the production of armaments' (p. 104); 'A dictatorship like Hitler's could escape the usual consequences of inflation' (p. 119); the judgements that the Third Reich was short of neither raw materials nor markets (pp. 105–6) are highly contentious.

[47] The work of Arthur Schweitzer, *Big Business in the Third Reich* (Bloomington, IN, 1964) appeared too late for consideration here.

[48] *Germany's Economic Preparations for War* (Cambridge MA 1959).

[49] Taylor, 'Second Thoughts'. Contrast the latter statement with Hitler's repeated insistence in his war economy memorandum of 1936, that the cost of putting industry on a war footing was a matter of absolute indifference. The memorandum has been published with a commentary by W. Treue: 'Hitlers Denkschrift zum Vierjahresplan 1936', *Vierteljahrshefte für Zeitgeschichte* vol. 3, no. 3 (1955).

shows no knowledge of the work done by British and German economic historians;[50] he makes firm judgements about Schacht's policies without having read either of the financier's autobiographies; he does not mention the Mefo-bill issue; his statistics (from which Mr Taylor has chosen a few 'at random') are often inscrutable and occasionally contradictory.[51] Mr Klein is no doubt right that contemporary observers exaggerated the predominance of the military sector in the German economy before 1939, but his own study cannot claim to be definitive; it cannot be described as 'the only book which has looked at what happened instead of repeating what Hitler and others said was happening', nor as a 'dispassionate analysis'.[52]

As the following table shows, categorical judgements are unwarranted; the study of the economy of the Third Reich is still in its infancy. One of the many elementary facts which has still to be established is the precise expenditure of the regime on rearmament; the problem is chiefly one of unsatisfactory source material.

The totals of Steubel, Klein I and Hillman are roughly reconcilable with one another, and that of Klein II could be brought within the same range by the addition of the Mefo-bill issue (RM 12 milliard), but their figures give rather different pictures of the development of armaments expenditure; this is of some importance in judging economic policy, especially in relation to the financial year 1937–8.[53] The most detailed and thorough investigation seems to be that of Steubel, though his final total may be a little high since not all of the Mefo-bill issue was used for projects of direct military importance.

This element of uncertainty together with the use of different economic concepts gives rise to a second set of statistics with an even wider range of divergence: Klein estimates German military expenditure at 15 per cent of the country's gross national product for the year 1938–9; the corresponding British figure for 1939, at almost 15 per cent.[54] Hillman's figures are percentages of the net national product for 1938 – Germany 16.6 per cent, Britain and France both 7.9 per cent.[55] Steubel's estimates of armaments expenditures as proportions of national incomes for the year 1938–9 provide a third series of figures – Germany 21 per cent, France 17 per cent and Britain 12 per cent.[56]

The picture of the strength of German military forces is not much

[50] See the references given below; they do not claim to be exhaustive.
[51] E.g. the figures for government deficits given in Tables 8, 45 and 60.
[52] Taylor, 'Second Thoughts'.   [53] See below, note 81.
[54] Klein, *Germany's Economic Preparations for War*, p. 19. Taylor quotes these figures in 'Second Thoughts' as though they *both* refer to 1938.
[55] Hillman, 'Great Powers', p. 456; quoted by Taylor (*Origins*, p. 116) who does not seem to notice the discrepancy between Klein's and Hillman's estimates.
[56] Steubel, 'Die Finanzierung', col. 4129; this does not exhaust the list of such estimates.

Estimates of German armaments expenditure, 1933–9*

	Stuebel	Klein I	Klein II	Hillman	Erbe
1932–3	(0.63)				(0.62)
1933–4	0.75⎱	5	1.9	1.9	0.72
1934–5	4.20⎰		1.9	2.8	3.30
1935–6	5.50	6	4.0	6.2	5.15
1936–7	10.27	10	5.8	10.0	9.00
1937–8	10.96	14	8.2	14.6	10.85
1938–9	17.25	16	18.4	16.0	15.50
Apr.-Sept. 1939	11.91	4	10.0	–	–
	60.84	55	50.2	(51.5)	(44.52)
	+ c. 3.00				
	c. 64.00				

*All figures in the table are in milliards RM; the figures for 1932–3 have been inserted in brackets for purposes of comparison and are not part of the totals; the totals in brackets refer to the period up to April 1939 only, no estimate having been made for the last five months of peace.

Sources: Steubel, col. 4129; his own total of RM 59.97 milliard seems to be an arithmetical mistake; about an extra RM 3 milliard are added to cover the rearmament expenditures of civilian ministries.

Klein I: Burton H. Klein, 'Germany's Preparation for War: A Re-examination', *American Historical Review*, vol. 38. (March, 1948), pp. 68–9; the figure for April–September 1939 is an estimate.

Klein II: *Germany's Economic Preparations for War* (Cambridge, MA 1959). In Table 60, p. 264, these figures are given as *budget* expenditure (as in *Die Deutsche Industrie im Kriege* (Berlin 1954), p. 17). No source is given for the figures, which appear in Table 6, p. 16 simply as 'Armament Expenditures'. He does not explain the difference between his estimates of 1948 and 1959.

H. Hillman, 'The Comparative Strength of the Great Powers', *Survey of International Affairs. The World in March 1939*, ed. A. Toynbee and F. T. Ashton-Gwatkin (London 1952), pp. 453–4.

R. Erbe, *Die nationalsozialistische Wirtschaftspolitik* (Zürich 1958), pp. 25 and 100. Erbe quotes Steubel's figures (p. 39) but uses his own set for calculations.

clearer. In 1938 Chilston estimated the front-line strength of the German airforce at the time of Munich as 'nearly 3,000 aircraft';[57] Mr Klein gives two different figures for its strength on the outbreak of war – 1,000 bombers and 1,500 fighters, and 800 bombers and 1,450 fighters; Hillman's estimate for September 1939 is 2,400 front-line planes, and the detailed figures of Kesselring give a total of 2,975 combat machines.[58]

These statistical uncertainties are a great impediment to any discussion of the German economy in the 1930s; they show very clearly the dangers

[57] 'The Rearmament of Britain, France and Germany down to the Munich Agreement of 30 September 1938', *Survey of International Affairs*, vol. 3 (1938), p. 529.

[58] Klein, *Germany's Economic Preparations for War*, pp. 19, 177 – the latter figures are quoted by Taylor in 'Second Thoughts'; Hillman, 'Great Powers', p. 395; Symposium, *Bilanz des zweiten Weltkrieges* (Oldenburg/Hamburg 1953), p. 159.

of making categorical judgements, and for this reason the following brief remarks must remain tentative and general.

The central historiographical question is once again that of perspective. In his concern to refute earlier works which exaggerated the war-orientation of the German economy before 1939, Mr Klein uses the performance of the economy in wartime as a yardstick for comparison; the pre-war effort is thus made to appear slight, and Part I of his book is an attempt to explain why it was not greater. This perspective harmonizes well with that of Mr Taylor and seems equally open to question. Comparisons should also be made with the performance of the German economy in 1928–9 and 1933, and with that of the British and French economies in the 1930s. If deductions about foreign policy are to be made from the realm of economics these are, in fact, the only legitimate comparisons.

The sole international comparative study of this question leaves no doubt as to Germany's overwhelming military–economic preponderance in Europe in 1939.[59] From March 1933 to March 1939 the Third Reich spent about half as much again on armaments as Britain and France put together. The steel production of Greater Germany in 1938 was one-quarter as much again as that of Britain and France put together, and by far the greater part of it was used domestically. As early as 1937 the capital goods sector[60] of the German economy accounted for an appreciably higher proportion of total manufacturing production than that of the British economy. Throughout the 1930s Germany exported more machine tools than Britain produced, and German machine tools were of a multi-purpose type permitting swift conversion from civilian to military production; British rearmament was hampered by a shortage of machine tools. Further, the British capital goods industries were heavily hit by the slump of early 1938; production of iron ore and pig-iron fell considerably, and in the latter case was slow to recover. Germany's autarkic economy remained unaffected by the slump. The briefest survey of the British economy in the 1930s yields many similar examples of events which are wholly inconceivable in the context of the Third Reich: in August 1937 the price of shares in the aircraft industry reached its lowest point since the start of rearmament; production was hemmed in by the reluctance of the government to give long-term and large-scale contracts; the structure of the British capital market was such that the announcement in February 1937 of a big increase in the military budget greatly handicapped private investment; and in April 1940 there were still one million unemployed in Britain.[61] War only replaced deterrence as the aim of British rearmament

[59] Hillman 'Great Powers'. This monograph is praised by Taylor (*Origins*, p. 284) but he makes no use of its admirably balanced conclusions.

[60] Hillman's definition of war-potential industries; for this and subsequent points above, see 'Great Powers', pp. 444 ff.

after Munich; military expenditure in 1939 was about twice as high as in 1938.[62] Thus the unadorned statement that in 1938–9 Britain and Germany spent the same proportions of their gross national products on armaments is not only incorrect; it is a highly misleading comparison.[63]

Of equal importance for purposes of comparison are the structural changes which occurred in the German economy between 1929 and 1939. The most striking of these was the steadily growing predominance of the heavy industrial sector. This sector suffered worst in the slump, enjoyed a swift rate of recovery and maintained this impetus throughout the 1930s. The figures for production are perhaps a better guide to this development than the investment statistics.[64] Thus the production of machine tools (measured in weight) doubled from 1928 to 1938; that of steel-rolling machinery trebled while that of textile machines fell by one-third over the same period. Steel production had already regained its 1929 level by 1936 and rose steadily thereafter, and the output of electricity increased by one-third 1928–36.[65] All branches of the engineering industry expanded,[66] and there was a marked increase in the labour force of the metal-working and chemical industries, while that of the consumer goods industries tended to remain stable or even to decline.[67] In 1929 the capital goods sector of the German economy accounted for 41 per cent of total manufacturing production; in 1937, 51 per cent.[68] This trend was present though less pronounced in the economies of all industrialized countries during the period; but the sharpness and peculiar form of the trend in Germany was due largely to the hegemony of National Socialism. The scale of the rearmament programme was sufficient all but to eliminate the element of entrepreneurial risk in the heavy industrial sector;[69] and secondly, a significant expansion of the consumer goods sector was impeded, partly by limiting demand through wage-controls and partly by an allocation of foreign exchange for the purchase of raw materials which

[61] Chilston, 'Rearmament', p. 492; ibid., p. 485; M. M. Postan, *British War Production*, History of the Second World War, UK Civil Series (London 1952), p. 43; Hillman, 'Great Powers', p. 466; A. J. Youngson, *The British Economy, 1920–57* (London 1960) p. 145.

[62] Hillmann, 'Great Powers', p. 453; *Statistical Digest of the War*, History of the Second World War, UK Civil Series (London 1951), p. 195.

[63] Taylor, 'Second Thoughts'; see note 54 above.

[64] The official investment statistics from the Third Reich are implausible; investment in armaments plants in 1935 (the year of conscription) is given as 25 per cent lower than that in 1928: Klein, *Germany's Economic Preparations for War*, p. 14. Most writers stress the extent of disinvestment caused by the slump, but the production indices tend to show that this had only slight effects on production levels during the 1930s: see *ibid.*, p. 35.

[65] G. Kroll, *Von der Weltwirtschaftskrise zur Staatskonjunktur* (Berlin 1958), pp. 611, 615; Klein, *Germany's Economic Preparations for War*, p. 41.

[66] Production of motor vehicles increased by 60 per cent 1928–36: Kroll, *Weltwirtschaftskrise*, p. 617.   [67] Klein, *Germany's Economic Preparations for War*, p. 74.

[68] Hillman, 'Great Powers', p. 444; the process was cumulative.

[69] In October 1938 Göring had to use the threat of nationalization to get industrialists to produce for the more risky export market: Steubel, 'Die Finanzierung', col. 4133.

was favourable to heavy industry.[70] Mr Klein and Mr Taylor give great weight to the fact that gross consumer expenditure in 1938 was at least as high as in 1929; the fact assumes a somewhat different significance from that which they attach to it,[71] when one considers that in this decade both the population and the employed labour force grew larger, the index of industrial production rose by some 20 per cent and the gross national product by almost 40 per cent.[72] This relative oppression of the consumer can be seen even more clearly from Mr Hillman's calculation that in 1938 63 per cent of the German net national product went on personal consumption; only in Japan and Russia was the proportion lower; in Britain and France it was c. 79 per cent and in the USA 84.6 per cent.[73] The consumer in the Third Reich was not getting butter instead of guns.

The second important structural change in the German economy was the trend towards autarky; international trade generally was very slow to recover after the slump, but in Germany the trend was deliberately fostered by the government for strategic reasons.[74] Domestic production of basic raw materials expanded significantly in the last three years of peace: the exploitation of metal ore deposits was intensified and refining capacities were increased;[75] production of synthetic rubber rose from almost nil in 1936 to 22,000 tons in 1939, and that of both synthetic and crude oil was roughly doubled in the same period.[76] The incompleteness of the programme on the outbreak of war[77] should not be allowed to detract from these very considerable changes. The autarky policy accentuated the predominance of the big production goods monopolies in the German economy;[78] it also illuminates the political intentions of the regime – a government not bent on war will not go to such very great lengths to secure its independence from international trade. The precise character of the war was not of course determined by the autarky policy, though this policy did make it easier for Hitler to risk conflict with Britain.

The third structural change, and that on which the other changes were in large measure dependent, was the very great increase in public

[70] Shortage of foreign exchange led to a reduction in the import of textile raw materials in 1934, and the introduction of a thirty-six hour week in many textile mills.
[71] Taylor 'Second Thoughts' goes so far as to say that butter was produced instead of guns.
[72] Guillebaud, *Social Policy*, p. 106; Klein, *Germany's Economic Preparations for War*, pp. 72, 10.   [73] Hillman, 'Great Powers', p. 456.   [74] See Treue, 'Hitlers Rede'.
[75] Klein, pp. 45–7. His Chapter 2 is the best discussion of this whole question, though he stresses the gap between programme and achievement rather than achievement itself.
[76] Ibid., pp. 45 and 40; Die Deutsche Industrie im Kriege, p. 18. Virtually no synthetic rubber was produced in Britain in 1939.
[77] On the outbreak of war Germany was dependent on imports for 80 per cent of her textile raw materials and 65 per cent of her iron ore and oil: see Klein, *Germany's Economic Preparations for War*, pp. 48–50.
[78] This judgement refers to economic structure; in matters of economic policy the big concerns did not form a monolithic bloc; the autarky policy rested on the support of the chemical industries.

spending. Reich expenditure increased roughly fourfold during the 1930s, and the government debt two-and-a-half-fold.[79] There was clearly a revolution in German public finance, and this fact should dominate discussion of the problem. Mr Klein thinks that fear of inflation seriously retarded German rearmament, but the evidence which he quotes proves only that the fears existed, not that they exercised a decisive influence on economic policy;[80] in the present state of research, this point can be neither proved nor disproved.[81]

However, as Mr Klein himself remarks, there were various other good reasons why Germany's preparations for war were not more extensive. Chief among these was the inability and/or unwillingness of the government to effect the necessary additional transfer of money and resources from the non-military sector of the economy. After 1936 such a transfer would have raised enormous administrative and political problems,[82] and it was not in fact achieved until the later stages of the war, under the stimulus of imminent defeat.

It was not achieved earlier because the party had to continue erecting its monumental buildings, and the size and cost of the administrative apparatus could not be held in check; more important, *le plebiscite de tous les jours* made a significant peacetime increase in taxation or reduction of consumer expenditure politically impossible.[83] Although the labour market in the key industries (construction, metals and mining) had been strained to breaking point since mid-1937, the government only began introducing maximum wage legislation and restricting the free choice of work in the shadow of the Sudetenland crisis.[84] And then, the inevitable

---

[79] For expenditure: Steubel, 'Die Finanzierung', col. 4132; this includes all rearmament expenditure, but not that of the Länder or local authorities; for debt: Erbe, *Wirtschaftspolitik*, p. 54.

[80] Klein, *Germany's Economic Preparations for War*, pp. 21–5. He does show, however, that financial considerations limited the scale of the autarky programmes for iron ore and synthetic oil: pp. 52–3, but see note 90 below.

[81] This is chiefly due to the unreliability of the statistics; if those of Steubel for armament expenditure are compared with those of Erbe for the growth of the debt, it seems that there was a reduction in the rate of growth of both in 1937; this could indicate fears of inflation affecting economic policy: Steubel, 'Die Finanzierung' col. 4129; Erbe, *Wirtschaftspolitik*, p. 54.

[82] Klein does not appreciate the scale of these problems, which he discusses at a mathematical level only: *Germany's Economic Preparations for War*, p. 21; contrast Kroll, *Weltwirtschaftskrise*, p. 560.

[83] The reports of the Gestapo (Secret State Police) on the mood of the population constantly make the mundane point that the popularity of the regime was largely dependent upon the standard of living: see B. Vollmer, *Volksopposition im Polizeistaat* (Stuttgart 1957), esp. p. 371; also the collections of police documents, R58 and 1010 EAP, in the Bundesarchiv Koblenz.

[84] 'Verordnung über die Lohngestaltung', 25 May 1938, *Reichsgesetzblatt*, 1, p. 691. Implementation was left to the Reich Trustees of Labour, and was a delicate and sometimes long-drawn-out task, frequently involving reductions in real wages. Attempts to restrict the free movement of labour began on a small scale at the end of 1936, and

consequences of this over-full employment: failure to meet delivery dates, a wage spiral, the enticement of scarce skilled workers from one firm to another, a very high and economically wasteful mobility of labour, and in many cases a drop in per capita productivity and a decline in 'work-morale'[85] – these consequences were combatted by the government with only very limited and delayed success; for instance, the abolition of paid holidays and of higher rates of pay for overtime on the outbreak of war produced so much bitter discontent and absenteeism in industry during the Polish campaign that the decrees had to be annulled in the winter of 1939–40.[86] The Labour Front, which depended for even the toleration of its 26 million compulsory members on the improvement of living standards, used the new balance of social forces brought about by full employment to make a bid for supreme power in the state in February 1938; the bid failed, but so did the counter-attack by the Reich Chamber of Economics, which aimed at reducing the influence of the Labour Front.[87]

Both crises, the economic and the institutional, were acute and insoluble. The Third Reich was the first modern state to face the many new problems raised by permanent full employment, and was totally unfitted to solve them: the Nazi Party had been brought to power to end unemployment, and in the later 1930s the government proved unable to make the great reappraisal and reorganization necessary to cope with its success;[88] second, the labour shortage could not be met by economic contraction since this would have slowed down rearmament; third, the built-in need of the totalitarian regime to obtain the constant loyalty and

became general in scope on 10 March 1939; they were not very effective before the outbreak of war.

[85] A lame rendering of *Arbeitsfreude*, literally, 'work-joy', which was the current term. The source materials on which these assertions are based are the documents of the Reich Ministries of Labour and Economics, now divided up among the Deutsches Zentralarchiv Potsdam, the Hauptarchiv West Berlin and the Bundesarchiv Koblenz; also the documents of the Reichskanzlei (now in the Bundesarchiv), which contain regular reports on these problems from the Reich Trustees of Labour (R43II, vol. 528). The material is vast; the writer is preparing a documentation on all the problems touched on in this paragraph.

[86] Deutsches Zentralarchiv Potsdam, Reich Ministry of Economics, file 10401.

[87] The Labour Front was technically responsible to the party (Rudolf Hess) rather than to the government; in fact, it was responsible to neither, since Robert Ley effectively insisted that his dual position as *Reichsorganisationsleiter* of the party and leader of the Labour Front gave him direct access to Hitler in *both* capacities – strictly speaking, he had direct access only in the former capacity. Material on this crisis can be found in the documents of most departments of the government; basic material in the Bundesarchiv, R43II, vols. 530, 530a, 548a, 548b.

[88] Not until 1 February 1939 was the Reich Ministry of Labour reorganized to permit the creation of a new Department 5 dealing solely with the direction and allocation of labour, subjects which had until then been handled by a subsection of the department dealing primarily with unemployment. I am grateful to Dr Dienwiebel of the Bundesarchiv for this point.

continuous adulation of those classes of society which had most reason to hate it, disabled it from effective intervention in the labour market until internal crisis had made such intervention essential and external crisis had provided the necessary justification.

Organizational problems also played their part in ruling out a further transfer of resources to the military sector in the immediate pre-war years. Behind the endlessly repeated official fiction of the 'organic, harmonious popular community', there existed a jungle of competing and overlapping economic organizations, interest groups and authorities, which was essential for preserving the political power of the Nazi leadership, but which precluded effective economic planning and administration. Göring could not secure the co-operation of the metal industry in exploiting low-grade domestic iron ores; the pre-war system of allocating the available supply of steel was quite unable to fulfil its function,[89] and the three branches of the armed forces competed ruthlessly with one another for priority status.

All these were necessary and immutable consequences of the style and structure of National Socialist government, and for these reasons, it must be doubted whether the Third Reich conceivably could have armed to a higher level before 1939.[90] With his acute sense of power politics Hitler saw that the strategic diplomatic position in Europe and recent developments in weaponry might exempt him from the need to face these structural problems; the *Blitzkrieg* strategy was perhaps as much a product of these problems, as *the* consideration which determined the level of rearmament: it cannot seriously be argued that real opportunities to rearm were neglected before 1939 as a result of the decision to adopt this strategy.

The economic, social and political tensions within the Reich became steadily more acute after the summer of 1937; while it seems safe to say that Hitler himself understood very little of their technical content, it can be proved that he was informed of their existence and was aware of their gravity.[91] If the existence in the winter of 1937–8 of a conscious connection in Hitler's mind between this general crisis and the need for a

---

[89] Klein, *Germany's Economic Preparations for War*, pp. 55, 76–82.

[90] Without a more drastic system of military priorities, increased government spending on armaments would have achieved very little; for this reason, too, it is hard to accept the overriding influence of fiscal policy, as put forward by Klein.

[91] The content of some of the reports of the Reich Trustees of Labour was brought to Hitler's attention by his Secretary of State, Lammers. The conflicts surrounding Schacht's resignation at the end of 1937 were repeatedly referred to Hitler (see A. E. Simpson, 'The Struggle for Control of the German Economy 1936–37', *Journal of Modern History*, vol. 31 (1959), pp. 37–45), as was the crisis brought about by the Labour Front, February–March 1938.

more dynamic foreign policy cannot yet be established,[92] functional relationships between these two aspects may nonetheless be suggested. The chain of international events unleashed by the browbeating of Schuschnigg on 12 February 1938 aggravated the shortages of labour, raw materials and money. *But* at the same time they provided the only conditions under which the government thought it safe to increase the coercion and exploitation of labour, to depart from conservative principles of sound finance, and to intensify government control over business – all measures which the survival of the system demanded anyway; and the seriousness of the crisis over the Labour Front was certainly lessened by the fact that it coincided with the Anschluss.[93] The only 'solution' open to this regime of the structural tensions and crises produced by dictatorship and rearmament was more dictatorship and more rearmament, then expansion, then war and terror, then plunder and enslavement. The stark, ever-present alternative was collapse and chaos, and so all solutions were temporary, hectic, hand-to-mouth affairs, increasingly barbaric improvizations around a brutal theme. Mr Taylor is perhaps nearer to the truth than he knows, in writing that, 'at best the argument was self-consuming. Germany needed the prizes of war solely in order to make war more successfully.'[94] A war for the plunder of manpower and materials lay square in the dreadful logic of German economic development under National Socialist rule. The sequence of international events was not thereby predetermined, but the range of possibilities was severely circumscribed.[95]

It has been wisely remarked that good works of history are informed by a sense of what could not have happened. The judgement, 'it seems from

[92] The only hint of such a conscious connection which the writer has found to date, is the passage from the Hossbach Protocoll, quoted above p. 35.
[93] The difficulties of writing about the Third Reich may be illustrated by the fact that it is also true to say that this crisis was caused by the intensity of the rearmament effort – cause, effect and response are almost inextricable.
[94] Taylor, *Origins*, p. 217. This is one of the few occasions when Mr Taylor hints that there may be a further dimension to historical reality, beyond the calculations and miscalculations of statesmen, but the point does not appear to be offered seriously and is not elaborated. Compare the judgement of General Thomas of the Armed Forces War Economy Staff, that Germany's 'economic collapse would have occurred much earlier except for the fact that Hitler's campaigns of conquest yielded the Wehrmacht tremendous booty in the way of raw materials and fuels' (quoted in L. P. Lochner, *Tycoons and Tyrants* (Chicago 1954), p. 210). Thomas might have added the materials and foodstuffs delivered to Germany under the terms of the Non-Aggression Pact with the Soviet Union.
[95] This cautious, negative formula is deliberate; there is no point in reviving obsolete slogans about the economic causes of war. Economics was not the only circumscribing factor; British public and backbench opinion greatly limited the freedom of action of the British government. Mr Taylor notes this (pp. 272, 276), but makes no attempt at all to establish a hierarchy of the causes of the war; rather he offers his readers a simplistic narrative, underlying which is the assumption that the debate about historical inevitability is a tiresome anachronism.

the record that Hitler became involved in war through launching on 29 August a diplomatic manoeuvre which he ought to have launched on 28 August',[96] is, even allowing for a degree of poetic licence, a flat denial of this dictum; neither factually nor logically is it a necessary consequence of the attempt to portray in moral detachment 'what happened and why it happened'; it is, on the contrary a judgement which destroys much of the point of studying history at all.

[96] Taylor, *Origins*, p. 278.

2

THE PRIMACY OF POLITICS. POLITICS AND ECONOMICS IN NATIONAL SOCIALIST GERMANY[1]

ONE OF the main concerns of marxist historiography is the question of the relationship between economics and politics in the capitalist epoch. Its central thesis can perhaps be outlined as follows: the sphere of politics represents, by and large, a super-structure of the specific economic and social system, and has the function of perpetuating that system. The existence of an autonomous political realm with its own self-determining laws is usually denied by marxist historians, and passing tendencies towards the development of such an autonomous political realm are ascribed to a temporary balance between the various social and economic forces. Politics as such are held to remain incomprehensible until those forces of economic and social development are elucidated, which determine the forms and substance of political life. All historical representations and analyses which do not attempt such an elucidation or which deny the point of such an attempt, are considered to be at best unscientific, at worst ideologically motivated justifications of the social status quo. The view that the economy gets the system of government which it needs is considered a better point of departure for historical enquiry than the saying that the people get the government which it deserves. It is not necessary to point out here that this marxist approach has proved its value in the practice of historical research and writing.[2] But the overwhelming majority of works on the history of National Socialism which have appeared in the West are characterized precisely by a rejection of this approach; they are all too quick to apostrophize the economy as just one more sphere of public life alongside many others, all of which are

---

[1] This is a revised version of an essay which first appeared in *Das Argument*, no. 41 (December 1966 pp. 165–95. I am grateful to Bernhard Blanke for his critical comments. Further debate on the subject appears in *Das Argument*, no. 47 July 1968).

[2] Franz Neumann, *Behemoth. The Structure and Practice of National Socialism* (London 1942), remains the best single work on the Third Reich.

supposed to have been subjected in like measure to the draconian coercion of an uninhibited political dictatorship.[3]

On the other hand, modern historical research in East Germany is still conducted in the light of Dmitrov's definition of fascism as 'the openly terroristic dictatorship of the most reactionary, most chauvinistic and most imperialistic elements of Finance-Capital'.[4] No doubt this definition had a function and a degree of plausibility in 1935, but today, in view of the later development of Nazi Germany, it can have only very limited use as a starting point for an investigation, and can certainly not be regarded as an answer to the problem of the relationship between politics and economics under National Socialism.

It is not that the truth lies somewhere in the middle, between these two interpretations (here almost caricatured). To anticipate the conclusion of this still very provisional study, it was apparently the case that both the domestic and the foreign policy of the National Socialist government became, from 1936 onwards, increasingly independent of the influence of the economic ruling classes, and even in some essential aspects ran contrary to their interests. *This relationship is, however, unique in the history of modern bourgeois society and its governments; it is precisely this that must be explained.*[5] According to marxist theory it cannot be explained *only* in terms of the establishment of an unlimited political despotism, that is, with reference only to the impact of state controls; the autonomy of the laws governing the workings of the capitalist economic system is too strong for this to have been the case, and the significance of the economy for the political sphere too great. It is rather that far-reaching structural changes *must* have taken place both in the economy and in society before it became possible for the National Socialist state to assume

---

[3] Thus Gerhard Schulz in Karl Dietrich Bracher, Wolfgang Sauer and Gerhard Schulz, *Die nationalsozialistische Machtergreifung. Studien zur Errichtung des totalitären Herrschaftssystems in Deutschand 1933–1934* (Cologne/Opladen 1960), Part II, Chapter 5; also Ingeborg Esenwein-Rothe, *Die Wirtschaftsverbände von 1933 bis 1945* (Berlin 1965) and David Schoenbaum, *Hitler's Social Revolution. Class and Status in Nazi Germany 1933–1939* (New York 1966). The controversy about totalitarianism rests on similar postulates. The only exceptions among the scholarly post-war works to have appeared in the West are Arthur Schweitzer, *Big Business in the Third Reich* (Bloomington, IN 1964) and Dietmar Petzina, 'Der nationalsozialistische Vierjahresplan' (diss., Mannheim 1965).

[4] Quoted after Dietrich Eichholtz, 'Probleme einer Wirtschaftsgeschichte des Faschismus in Deutschland', *Jahrbuch für Wirtschaftsgeschichte* (1963), Part III, p. 103. This essay brings some important refinements to the marxist–leninist concept of fascism and one awaits with interest the author's book on the German war economy 1939–45; but he still writes of 'the tasks allotted by finance-capital to its neo-fascism'. For a critical review of East German historiography see B. Blanke, R. Reiche and J. Werth, 'Die Faschismus-Theorie der DDR', *Das Argument*, no. 33 (May 1965), pp. 35–48.

[5] The New Deal in the USA, the Popular Front of 1936 in France and the Labour government of 1945 in Britain represented a different kind of variation from the norm – their limited reforms tended to strengthen the existing social order, the needs of which they understood better than the respective ruling classes.

a fully independent role, for the 'primacy of politics' to assert itself. The methodological starting point, the approach, must therefore owe much to the insights gained from marxist theory.

It is the aim of this essay to demonstrate the existence of a primacy of politics in Nazi Germany and to seek its roots in the economic history of the period. In order to avoid misunderstandings in advance, let it be emphasized that the question here is not what kind of an economic system existed at the time; whether it was a market economy, a centrally planned economy or a species of state-monopoly-capitalism.[6] Equally, it would exceed the bounds of this essay to portray in detail the actual structure of the governmental machine and to examine systematically the mainsprings of its policies and aims. The preliminary studies towards the clarification of this latter question do not yet permit more than suppositions to be made.[7] Even within these limits the present essay is highly speculative. The wide-ranging theoretical discussion of the 1930s about the nature and structure of National Socialist rule was not really taken up again after 1945;[8] the work of integrating the immense quantities of newly available documentary evidence into an interpretative framework will involve a high degree of co-operation among specialist historians and social scientists from a wide range of disciplines. The task has hardly begun to be faced and thus what is presented here is essentially a set of working hypotheses.

THE TRANSITION

National Socialist leaders constantly maintained that they had restored the primacy of politics. In the place of the weak governments of the Weimar Republic, which had acted largely under the influence of the interest groups with which they were connected, they had introduced, so the claim ran, a politically independent and energetic state leadership which was no longer forced to take into account the selfish, short-sighted wishes of special interests in the social or economic sphere when it had to make important decisions. As a slogan the primacy of politics was undoubtedly very effective, since it promised to put an end to the

---

[6] This question is of lesser importance; some light is thrown on it by J. S. Geer, *Der Markt der geschlossenen Nachfrage* (Berlin 1961).

[7] The recent works of Andreas Hillgruber, *Hitlers Strategie. Politik und Kriegführung 1940–41* (Frankfurt am Main, 1965); and Hans Mommsen, *Beamtentum im Dritten Reich* (Stuttgart 1966) are suggestive in this connection.

[8] Useful selections from the pre-war literature have been edited and published by Wolfgang Abendroth: O. Bauer, H. Marcuse, A. Rosenberg, *Faschismus und Kapitalismus. Theorien über die sozialen Ursprünge und die Funktion des Faschismus* (Frankfurt am Main/Vienna 1967); and Ernest Nolte, *Theorien über den Faschismus* (Cologne/Berlin 1967). See also R. Griepenburg and K. H. Tjaden, 'Faschismus und Bonapartismus', in *Das Argument*, no. 41 (December 1966), pp. 461–72.

apparently interminable economic and national distress of the years before 1933.

For the forces on which the Weimar Republic rested, this distress was rooted in the failure of the Republic to achieve any lasting compromises among its constituent social classes and interests and their political groupings. In the structure of the Republic a basic contradiction had been institutionalized: the working classes had the possibility of gaining political power but no social guarantees, and the propertied classes possessed social power but no political guarantees. Of greater, and directly political, significance was the fact that the propertied classes were not united among themselves: the political and social structure of bourgeois Germany, already shaken to its foundations by the First World War and the inflation, fell apart with a vengeance under the pressure of the world economic crisis. The causal relationship between the world economic crisis and the seizure of power by the National Socialists needs more detailed examination,[9] but the economic crisis can safely be said to have contributed in two decisive ways to the seizure of power: it deprived industry of the only political alternative left open to it by making economic co-operation with the USA impracticable. Thereupon the propertied classes disintegrated both economically and politically into their basically divergent groupings; the new rapprochement with the Western powers in July 1932 came too late to reverse this process. Second, mass unemployment meant that class conflict again came to be expressed immediately in political terms – which had been denied to it by the basic agreement which had obtained between the bourgeois parties, social democracy and the trade unions after 1924. The fundamental structural weakness of the Weimar Republic again became apparent in a politically intensified form; this time it entailed a marked growth in the power of the Communist Party (KPD) and a radicalization of the employers' organizations. The accumulated problems arising out of the unviable structure of German society were even less amenable to solution during the world economic crisis than at any other time. Faced with these problems, the bourgeoisie, the old and the new petty bourgeoisie and the rural population all sought their salvation in an unthinking flight into 'pure politics': politics-as-propaganda, national exaltation, the cult of the leader, anti-Semitism and anti-communism, a yearning for an idealized pre-industrial community all served as political pseudo-solutions to the structural problems of the social order of Weimar Germany. The

---

[9] Above all the social consequences of the crisis need detailed investigation. There was no simple correlation between mass unemployment and the rise of National Socialism; new, potentially fascist popular movements antedated the crisis by over a year: see Arthur Rosenberg, *A History of the German Republic* (London 1936), Chapter 9, and Rudolf Heberle, *From Democracy to Nazism* (Baton Rouge, LA 1945).

National Socialist movement was the vehicle of this flight from reality into the fancy-free world of affective racial–national harmony and unity, but the various social groups which joined it during the years 1930–3 saw no incompatibility between the new political style and the vigorous prosecution of their special (and incompatible) social and economic interests *within* the movement.

In the years between 1924 and 1929 the economic situation gave the various bourgeois coalition governments a certain freedom of action which permitted on the whole a conciliation of opposing class and group economic interests which did not seriously endanger the position of capital.[10] The growing economic crisis accentuated the struggles between classes and among interest groups and thus deprived the state of this latitude. For the same reason the freedom which the party leaders had had *vis-à-vis* their own supporters (especially that of the social democratic leadership) also disappeared, and with it the possibility of forming parliamentary coalition governments. In these circumstances the relative autonomy of the state, indeed its very existence, could only be preserved by the formation of presidential cabinets which promised to divorce government from the sphere of political interest-group conflicts. Although Brüning's cabinet brought about a significant reduction in the standard of living of the working population, it was incapable of solving the great problems of domestic, economic and foreign policy and of thereby giving bourgeois society a new structure and a new directon in which to develop. And during the 'unpolitical' rule of Brüning, public concern about the structure and aims of society had necessarily become more urgent and hysterical. In the year 1932 all political organizations, with the exception of the Social Democratic Party, were convinced that a completely new system of government was called for, whether a Catholic corporative state, a bonapartist autocracy (Schleicher), a National Socialist state based on the leader-principle, or a dictatorship of the proletariat. The machinery of state had admittedly increased its independence of social pressures during these years – Brüning's deflationary policy damaged the short-term material interests of every class of society and of every entrenched pressure group – but it had in fact ceased to function as a representation of the propertied classes as a whole, let alone of the whole people, and public opinion in Germany was very much aware of this.[11]

'Civil Society' was no longer able to reproduce itself. The basic precondition for overcoming this situation was the recovery of the

[10] For Stresemann's freedom of action *vis-à-vis* heavy industry, see Henry A. Turner, Jr, *Stresemann and the Politics of the Weimar Republic* (Princeton, NJ 1963).

[11] Bracher's concept of a 'political power-vacuum' in the years 1930–3 is useful, but needs to be underpinned by an analysis of the disintegration of social and economic power structures: see *Die Auflösung der Weimarer Republik*, 3rd edn (Villingen 1960), Part II, Section B.

economy. Capital could not bring this about by itself, principally because of the power of the heavy industrial cartels.[12] An economic recovery in the interests of the middle classes could only be implemented by a government that was strong enough to: (a) mediate between the contrary interests of the heavy and consumer goods sectors of industry, and protect the special interests of agriculture; (b) bring about general domestic 'peace and quiet' for industry;[13] (c) prevent the standard of living of the majority of the population from rising for some time above the crisis level – which meant effectively the elimination of the trade unions; (d) effect a strict control and management of foreign exchange resources which had become very scarce; (e) effectively combat the deeply rooted fear of inflation and so make possible a state-sponsored expansion of credit.

In short, the reproduction of society could only be guaranteed through radical political means.[14] Early in 1933 it was only National Socialism which fulfilled these minimal conditions. Its uncertainty and opportunism in many specific questions, the socially heterogeneous character of its following, the ruthlessness with which decisions, once taken, were implemented, and the proven success of its propaganda methods all contributed to make it appear the best suited vehicle for a renewal of civil society. At the latest when Chancellor Schleicher began to negotiate with the trade unions and the SA, heavy industry drew the necessary conclusions.

It is the main function of politics in a stable, liberal democracy to reconcile the interests of the ruling social groups with each other, to interpret their common needs and to cater for them by the most suitable means in their domestic and foreign policy aspects. This harmonious co-operation between the economy and the state demands in the long run the recognition, in a form which is acceptable to business, of the basic social and economic interests of the working class, and a consensus of the most powerful organs of opinion in matters of political principle. These are, generally speaking, rather functions of civil society than results of public policy. In Germany, on the other hand, it became the function of National Socialism to create a new social and economic compromise, a new public consensus, in fact a new general representation of the people, *by political means*; and in the context of 1933 that necessarily meant the open use of force. The primacy of politics, which was undeniably there in 1933 – the creation of a dictatorship, terrorism, political and cultural *Gleichschaltung* – was the result of a social disintegration which it was the

---

[12] The cartels kept up the price of coal, iron, steel, etc., thus ruling out the type of economic revival predicated by classical economic theory.

[13] *Ruhe und Ordnung* was the euphemism current among employers for the restoration of their managerial prerogatives, which were threatened by the working-class organizations.

[14] How exceptional this position was can be seen by comparison with the history of the Federal Republic since 1953: the sphere of high politics – though not that of administration – can be almost superfluous to the reproduction of society.

function of National Socialism to repair. Accordingly, Schacht, von Papen, groups in the Reichswehr and industry expected that it would be possible to push the National Socialists out again, at least to limit them to a decorative function in the state, as soon as the rebuilding of a viable civil society had made possible a new bid for political power on the part of its traditional ruling classes. These groups expected to be able to secure their own social supremacy, which was based on private property and threatened by the KPD, by *temporarily* giving up the *direct* execution of political power. This hope was, of course, not fulfilled. From a historical point of view, the incapacity of the political representatives of the propertied classes to formulate and implement their own policies, their abdication in favour of National Socialism, even if partly marked by unconcerned fellow-travelling, represented a great historical defeat. The political leadership of the Third Reich was able, through means unforeseen by anyone, to maintain the independence from the old ruling classes which it had gained in the crisis, 1930–3. It did not fulfil its function of becoming obsolete.

THE DISTRIBUTION OF POWER IN THE MACHINERY OF NATIONAL SOCIALIST GOVERNMENT

One fundamental condition of the primacy of politics was in any case a matter of course for National Socialism – a strong concentration of power in the hands of a leader who wholly dominated even his closest associates. For reasons of tactics as well as of disposition and character, Hitler largely kept out of routine governmental work; his function in the system of government of the Third Reich was, with the exception of foreign policy (later strategy) and of his personal hobbies (military weapons and architecture), chiefly that of a supreme arbiter. All important drafts of proposals by heads of departments and party leaders required his personal approval; there was never any collective responsibility within the government; after the event, Hitler's decisions could hardly ever be frustrated or changed by those responsible for their implementation. This should not, of course, be understood to imply that Hitler alone bears the historical responsiblity for all National socialist policies; it is rather that, in important questions, the various ruling groups within the Third Reich could only assert their interests through this one channel; and the approval of the Führer was no mere formality.[15] A supreme political arbiter was glorified whose understanding of politics was predominantly aesthetic, who tended to see politics in terms of will, spectacle, the

---

[15] Hitler several times withheld his approval from draft laws signed by all interested ministers; some of these concerned economic policy and did not come into force in the form of the drafts: examples in Bundesarchiv Koblenz, R43II vols. 417a, 810a.

enjoyment of power and tactical finesse, and who left all substantial problems in domestic policy to 'experts', but who either could not or would not take decisions about the contradictory solutions proposed to him by these experts. Thinking in economic terms was totally alien to the members of the old guard in the leadership of the National Socialist system, that is to those who had most ready access to Hitler.[16] By economics Hitler understood only *what was produced*. His memorandum on the second Four Year Plan demanded repeatedly and exclusively the simple accumulation of goods and armaments;[17] and his speech before the Reichstag on 20 February 1938 – probably his only one on this subject – consisted solely of a boastful list of the figures for the increases in production in Germany since the seizure of power. He had no grasp of the question of *how* things were done in economic policy, and there is hardly any indication that he ever worried about the economic consequences of his political goals or of the decisions he made in foreign policy.[18]

Until 1942 no economic expert worthy of mention was a member of the inner circle of Hitler's advisers. Of the first men who created links between the party and industry, Funk went to the Ministry of Propaganda, Kessler turned out to be incapable and Keppler's influence never matched his ambition.[19] As early as mid-1933 Fritz Thyssen's position as Hitler's favourite industrialist was undermined – his support of a guild system of social organization of the type advocated by Othmar Spann was irreconcilable with the claims of the NSDAP for a leading role in all spheres. In 1934 and 1935 Schacht, at once President of the Reichsbank and Minister of Economics, was allowed to make economic policy almost without hindrance. His contacts with banks, large firms and economic organizations were extremely close, but he never enjoyed the full confidence of the party or of the Führer. This system could only last as long as there were no signs of crisis in the domestic economic situation.

[16] Darré (Minister of Agriculture) and Gauleiter Wagner (Price Commissar) were both increasingly forced to think in economic categories by the steadily growing difficulties in their respective spheres of competence; neither of them had easy access to Hitler; both fell from power early in the war.

[17] Text of the memorandum in *Vierteljahrshefte für Zeitgeschichte* (1955), vol. 3, no. 3.

[18] Excerpts from the speech in Max Domarus (ed.), *Hitler. Reden und Proklamationen* (Würzburg 1962), vol. I, pp. 793 ff. A good example of Hitler's lack of concern for the economic consequences of his decisions is the hectic building of the Siegfried Line in the latter half of 1938, which brought the already over-strained building industry to the edge of chaos.

[19] Before 1933 Walther Funk was on the staff of the *Berliner Börsenzeitung*; he carried little weight as Minister of Economics from 1938 on. Kessler held the position of Leader of the Economy very briefly, 1933–4. Wilhelm Keppler was Hitler's personal economic adviser, held a post in the administration of the second Four Year Plan 1936–8 and then became Secretary of State in the Foreign Office; his political role remains unclear. The importance of Goerdeler as economic adviser to the Chancellery 1933–5 would bear further investigation.

By 1936 this was no longer the case. From the start of that year fundamental decisions had to be taken which constantly demanded reference to Hitler. For this reason, if for no other, it was necessary to appoint to the direction of economic policy a member of the old guard who enjoyed Hitler's confidence. This role suited Göring, the Prussian Minister President and Colonel-General of the Air Force, and suited him well in as much as his ideological prejudice was much less marked than that of most other top party functionaries; he seemed quite open to the factual arguments of the civil service. However, Göring was in no way up to the twofold task of forcing through necessary but unpopular measures of economic planning and of compelling some consideration of the interests of the economy in the formulation and execution of foreign policy. Whenever the civil service and representatives of industry thought they had him where they wanted him, he would tend to relapse and to sacrifice pragmatic arguments to his loyalty to the movement and to his fear of the Führer.[20] Not until February 1942, when Albert Speer was appointed Minister of Armaments and Munitions, did the effective scope of economic considerations extend to the ante-chamber of the political arbiter of the Third Reich.

Thus the political structure and the personality of the Führer provided a favourable basis for the maintenance of a 'primacy of politics', and it is in fact very difficult to demonstrate the participation of economic leaders or organizations, even in an indirect way, in the formation of overall policy in the Third Reich. One very important reason for this was the changed position of Germany in world trade and in the international capital market. During the Weimar Republic economic and foreign policy had been closely interwoven, but this relationship was largely dissolved by the termination of reparations. For this reason and also thanks to the extensive control of all foreign currency transactions which was a result of Schacht's 'New Plan', German foreign policy was no longer impeded by being forced to take into consideration possible economic sanctions on the part of the Western powers. So it is not surprising that pressure from economic interest groups played no significant role in the decisions to leave the League of Nations (November 1933), to reintroduce military service (March 1935) and to reoccupy the Rhineland in March 1936. It seems that they were not even consulted. From 1933 until 1936 economic policy, and in part also social policy, was left to the propertied classes, but they were not permitted to play any directly political role beyond these spheres. This division of labour and the approval given in economic

[20] Göring havered continually in the conflict between the Labour Front and industry (see below) and could reach no decisions on wage policy; he opposed Hitler's foreign policy, 1938–9, but dared not force the issue. He too had little understanding of economics, as he proudly proclaimed at the 1938 party rally.

circles to the aggressive moves in foreign policy in these years was based
on the belief that industry and the NSDAP shared a common imperialist
programme. This apparent consensus of opinion is not only evident in the
co-operation between heavy industry, the military, the party and the civil
service in the question of rearmament;[21] as far as resistance to Hitler is
concerned, there were no doubt many managers and industrialists who
regarded the new foreign policy as 'a bit risky', and the persecution of
communists and Jews as 'unnecessary' or even wrong; but the fact
remains that no effective resistance whatsoever was offered by these
circles during the years in question, and that they were the very groups
whose social position gave them the greatest scope for such action. This
apparent harmony in the aims of the ruling groups had one by-product
which at first sight looks paradoxical: the *direct* links between the
economic and political elites became weaker than they had been in the
Weimar Republic. During the years of relatively unproblematic economic
and military reconstruction, industry had neglected to maintain and
safeguard its power at the political level. Alfred Hugenberg had resigned
as Minister of Economics, all parties except the NSDAP had been
prohibited; Franz Seldte, the Minister of Labour, had simply looked on
and done nothing as the Stahlhelm, which he had controlled, was taken
out of his charge and handed over to the SA, and von Papen had been
relegated in autumn 1934 from Vice-Chancellor to Special Ambassador
in Vienna – after these changes, the only representative of the old
bourgeoisie left in the government was Schacht.[22] Much was made to
depend on his influence. In 1936 Schacht reconstructed the former
employers' organizations, chambers of trade and industrial groups into a
comprehensive 'Organization of Industry' and, in the shape of the
Reichswirtschaftskammer, created a new summit organization for it. His
aim was, on the one hand, to enable the state to manipulate the economy
more easily in technical matters (rationing of foreign exchange, etc.), on
the other, to consolidate the position and power of industry within the
overall system.[23] In a liberal or in an authoritarian state, profitable and
lasting co-operation between the state and the economy might perhaps
have been possible on the basis of this modern corporativism, to the end
of achieving a gradual imperialist expansion, *without* further extending

---

[21] Apart from the working-class organizations, the other victims of this alliance were
sections of the Nazi movement itself – the handicraft and factory cell organizations and
the SA, whose populistic and anti-industrial tendencies caused the business world a great
deal of concern in 1933.
[22] Constantin Freiherr von Neurath's position as Foreign Minister till early 1938 may have
acted as a reassurance to some, and the army was not purged until this date either. There
seem to have been no contacts between industry and the first oppositional groups within
the army in 1938; it is noteworthy that industry has hardly claimed any role at all in the
conservative resistance.   [23] Esenwein-Rothe, *Die Wirtschaftsverbände*, p. 72.

the political power of industry. But the consequences of the forced rearmament drive eliminated this possibility.

THE DISINTEGRATION OF THE INDUSTRIAL POWER BLOCK

Since 1879 heavy industry had been the determining factor in the political economy of Germany. It had been – in contrast with British experience – the vehicle of the industrial revolution, and in the many confrontations with the consumer goods sector, handicraft organizations and trading interests about protective tariffs, price agreements and most recently over civilian work-creation measures (1932–3), heavy industry had always got its own way. The seizure of power by the National Socialists would hardly have been possible without the support of considerable circles in heavy industry during the years of crisis. But in 1936 a great change in the structure of the German economy became apparent, which, although inherent in the system, was not apparently foreseen by any of the ruling groups. Whereas under the Weimar Republic industrial production had been inhibited by a lack of liquid capital, now, as a result of the rearmament boom, more tangible limits on production became apparent – shortages of raw materials from abroad, and of labour. These became the two decisive factors in the German arms and war economy and resulted in a far-reaching transformation of the economic power structure; and hence in a change in the relationship between economics and politics, industry and the state.

First, the lack of foreign exchange: rearmament demanded increasingly large imports of raw materials but did not contribute to a corresponding increase in exports;[24] added to this was the necessity of importing increased quantities of foodstuffs for a population whose overall purchasing power slowly rose with the disappearance of unemployment. If rearmament was not to be scaled down, the only way to avoid a repetition of the foreign trade crisis of 1936 was to bring about an immense increase in the domestic production of raw materials.[25] But to curtail rearmament was a *political* impossibility for National Socialism. Schacht vainly urged this course of action and the leaders of the iron and steel industries gave him objective, if not deliberate, support by opposing the exploitation of low-grade German iron ores. The chemical industry (i.e. IG-Farben) became the new economic pillar of the Third Reich; it urged the large-scale synthetic production of vital raw materials such as rubber and

[24] So great was the shortage of foreign exchange that considerable quantities of weapons and machine tools for their production were exported.
[25] For the crisis see Arthur Schweitzer, 'The Foreign Exchange Crisis of 1936', *Zeitschrift für die gesamte Staatswissenschaft*, vol. 118, no. 2 (April 1962), pp. 243–77. The autarky programme needed time and the continued acceleration of rearmament was in fact only made possible by the unforeseeable revival of international trade during 1937.

petrol. The decision in its favour by the state leadership and the announcement of the second Four Year Plan in September 1936 – in its final phase a personal decision by Hitler – finally broke the economic and political supremacy of heavy industry. At the same time this meant an end to the formation of any general and unified political will or representation of interests on the part of German capital, such as the employers' association (Reichsverband) had achieved under the Weimar Republic. In the forced rearmament of the last years before the war, the top industrial organizations lost their overall vision and control of the general economic development – all that was left were the special interests of individual firms, at most of certain branches of the economy. Heavy industry could no longer maintain that its interests were identical with those of German imperialism in general, let alone make this claim good. As a result of technological developments, rearmament, for which heavy industry had fought so bitterly and doggedly since 1919, marked the start of its own downfall. Heavy industry became the victim of its own expansionism. The direction and the dynamic of National Socialist economic and foreign policy after 1936 were predicated on the domestic production of raw materials. Without the accelerated expansion of the chemical industry a European war could never have been risked in 1939.[26]

These structural changes were strengthened and speeded up by developments in the labour market. In this period of rapidly advancing rearmament, the public purse became the decisive factor in the shaping of the German economy. In 1939 the share of Reich expenditure in the gross social product was 34 to 35 per cent, of which two-thirds went towards preparation for war. Armaments expenditure had increased fifteenfold in seven years.[27] Up to January 1939, public contracts were not subject to the price-freeze – on the contrary, most were calculated on a 'cost plus' basis. To increase his own profits, every contractor tried to obtain these orders and to fulfil them as punctually as possible, so that he would be taken into consideration when contracts were next distributed. This, in conjunction with the shortage of labour and raw materials brought about by the rearmament drive, led to ruthless competition between firms, not for markets, which were well-nigh unlimited for the industries concerned, but for the basic factors of production. The firms which produced goods needed in the armaments drive had an advantageous position in the struggle for raw materials, and were, by virtue of the generously calculated estimates, able to attract workers by increased wages, to lure

[26] Hardly any of the production goals of the Four Year Plan were in fact reached, but the achievement was considerable in relation to the narrow margin of German reserves in September 1939: full figure in Petzina, *Der Vierjahresplan*, pp. 249 f.

[27] See T. W. Mason, 'Some Origins of the Second World War', *Past and Present*, no. 29 (December 1964), pp. 67–87.

them away from other firms. So a second rift was added to the division in the economy caused by the rise of the chemical industry: that between firms primarily engaged in the armaments drive and those which produced primarily consumer goods or exports. Although the coal mines, for example, were indispensable to the war economy, this industry exported about one-sixth of its production and did not deliver direct to the armed forces; consequently, wages remained low and miners left in increasing numbers for other branches of industry; the per capita productivity of the miners decreased and, at the outbreak of war, there was a shortage of coal which looked like presenting a severe threat to the army's rail transport programme. The same factors threatened agricultural production too, whereas the building, chemical and engineering industries enjoyed an unprecedented prosperity.[28]

This intensification and change in the character of capitalist competition contributed further to the disintegration of the political power of industry in general. Once freed by the terrorist methods of the Gestapo from the necessity of defending themselves against an organized working class, and relieved by the armaments boom from the necessity of planning and limiting production on a cartel basis, the propertied classes lost their sense of common interest. The collective interest of the capitalistic economic system dissolved progressively from 1936 to 1939 into a mere agglomeration of the short-term interests of individual firms, which, to reverse a dictum of Lenin, marched separately and fell together. It is not a gross oversimplification to say that they were bought by the government.[29] The public purse, that is, a part of the same institution which determined foreign policy, became the interpreter of the interests of the economy, by sole virtue of its financial resources. The Reichswirtschaftskammer, which had been called into being in 1936 to head the new and strengthened Organization of Industry, in fact carried out only technical and administrative tasks for the Reich government and was incapable of making itself felt in the realm of high politics.

As far as the distribution of raw materials was concerned, the state did not succeed in curbing the competition among the firms and the growing number of public agencies issuing contracts until 1941–2. On the other hand, the state had, for political reasons, only a limited interest in regulating the labour market in favour of industry. By the autumn of 1936 the shortage of labour in the building and metal industries had led to considerable pay increases, partly forced by strikes, and to the widespread

---

[28] Bundesarchiv Koblenz, R43II, vol. 528; R41I, vol. 174; WiIF5, vols. 560/1 and 2; R22Gr. 5, vol. 1206.
[29] The quarterly reports on the economy of Berlin 1938–9 give a good picture of this process: Bundesarchiv Koblenz, R41, vols. 155–6. The role of the cartels in the 1930s has not yet been properly studied.

practice of luring skilled workers from one firm to another by the offer of improved working conditions. It ought to have been clear at this juncture that these were not merely temporary phenomena, but in fact represented the necessary consequences of a rearmament programme which was itself only in its initial stages. Three measures were necessary to forestall the spread of these conditions to the entire labour market and to prevent them from having a harmful effect on the course of rearmament through lowering productivity and increasing the purchasing power of the population: a general limitation of the freedom of movement of labour, the fixing of maximum wages and a more stringent allocation of economic resources to priority tasks. The National Socialist leadership deliberately omitted to take these steps, which were advocated by several ministries, until the international crisis over the Sudetenland came to a head in the summer of 1938 and not only provided the pretext (which domestic propaganda considerations demanded), but also made such state controls quite unavoidable.[30] By that time the shortage of labour had long become general – shop assistants and hairdressers were in as short supply as lathe hands. The reasons for this inaction by the government were quite obvious and at the same time throw a clear light on the problem of the primacy of politics: all the above-mentioned measures were rejected for two years by the political leadership because such radical steps against the material interests of workers and consumers were not reconcilable with the *political* task of 'educating' them in National Socialism. It was absolutely necessary for the National Socialist system, at least until well into the war years, to be quite sure of the active sympathy and agreement of the mass of the population with its ideology, goals and policies. The attempt to achieve this through pseudo-egalitarian demagogy, by improving social amenities in the factories and through 'Strength through Joy', etc., had clearly failed – so the workers' approval of the system had to be bought by high wages, paid holidays and the like,[31] although such measures were in direct contradiction to the demands of the rearmament drive, which the government was, at the same time, determined to speed up. For the same reason the political leaders obstructed the efforts of industry (led by the Reichswirtschaftskammer) to limit the growing power of the Labour Front. This organization had been given the task of winning over the workers to National Socialism and nothing, not even the smooth running of the arms economy, was allowed to impede its efforts, even though the Labour Front acted in a disguised form, but after 1936 in

---

[30] The measures were first considered in September 1936; the building of the Siegfried Line was the immediate cause of their introduction.

[31] Memories of the November revolution of 1918 were in some measure responsible for the stress which the Nazi leadership placed on this problem.

increasing measure, as bearer of the economic interests of the working classes.[32]

The old contradiction between the potential political power and the economic impotence of the working class had apparently been 'solved' when the National Socialists destroyed the workers' organizations in 1933, but the plebiscitary elements of the system, which necessarily came more to the forefront after full employment had been reached, made the political and economic repression of the working class more difficult and necessitated the sanctioning of material improvements to mobilize its support. The contradiction between demagogy (Strength through Joy) and political practice (forced rearmament) reproduced the contradiction between the mass basis necessary to National Socialism and the unchanged structure of property relationships. Labour exploited its own growing scarcity and the government had to acquiesce in this.

While the suggestion that the freedom of the workers to change their jobs should be curtailed met with hardly any resistance among employers,[33] their reaction to the proposal that an upper limit to wages should be fixed was different. Those firms which were directly or indirectly involved with rearmament needed more and more labour. A reserve army of unemployed workers 'capable of being used anywhere'[34] had ceased effectively to exist since early 1937. Additional workers thus had to be lured away from other firms and the decisive means of achieving this was the offer of higher pay. Until an efficient form of state-controlled labour deployment had been developed late in 1939, which was able to direct workers into the armaments sector and force them to stay there, a wage-freeze was by no means in the interests of all employers. The maximum-wage-scales which were introduced in the last twelve months before the outbreak of war were in practice circumvented by many employers by means of gifts and concealed bonuses to their workers.[35] There was also the further problem of the generally declining productivity of labour; this was a consequence in part of the physical over-taxation of the workers (too much overtime), in part of inadequate food (shortage of fats), but also of the new job-security resulting from full employment, and of the sullen indifference of most industrial workers towards the whole social and political system of National Socialism. The only counter-measure and inducement to higher output which many employers

---

[32] See T. W. Mason, 'Labour in the Third Reich 1933–39', *Past and Present*, no. 33 (April 1966), pp. 112–41.

[33] The controls were introduced gradually in 1936–9 and proved very difficult to enforce.

[34] The unemployed were divided into categories; only those who were physically fit and in a position to take up work away from their homes qualified as *volleinsatzfähig* after 1936.

[35] Reports of the Reich Trustees of Labour for June 1938–March 1939: Bundesarchiv Koblenz, R43II, vol. 528. Average hourly wage rates in industry rose by 25 per cent from January 1933 to mid-1943 (ibid., R41, vol. 60, p. 200).

could think of was an increase in wages. This line of argument, which was still implemented in a more modest way during the war, rested as far as the employers were concerned on an extraordinary indifference to the wider economic consequences of such a policy (inflation) and on a neglect, which was determined by the generosity of the public purse, of normal procedures of economic calculation within the firm. The historically typical behaviour-patterns of capitalist economic policy and management had, thanks to the forced rearmament drive, become largely irrelevant; all that was left were the primitive and short-term interests of each and every firm.

In these conditions the large firms became larger still. For various reasons rearmament necessarily accelerated the process of concentration in the German economy. This tendency was particularly obvious in the electrical industry (Siemens), in the chemical industry (IG-Farben), and in the iron and metal industries (Reichswerke Hermann Göring). By virtue of their position as monopolies and of the importance of their products for the war economy, these firms maintained close and direct contacts with the machinery of state and with the military; sometimes they even achieved through their personnel the equation of the interests of the state with those of their firms – leading managers were seconded to public economic agencies.[36] But rearmament also meant that the *direct* relationships with the agencies distributing contracts became more important for most big firms than *collective* dealings with the state through the channels of the economic and industrial organizations. Once the problem of the allocation of raw materials and labour had become crucial, this traditional form of collaboration between industry and the state had become secondary. For all these reasons, which were inherent in the political and economic system, the capitalist economic structure largely disintegrated into its constituent components. It was easy for the huge armaments firms to prosecute their immediate material interests, but in the process, the responsibility for the overall economic system was left to a political leadership whose final arbiter, Hitler, saw in the economy merely a means for attaining certain vaguely outlined yet, in principle, quite unattainable political goals – goals which, though certainly of great incidental benefit to German industry, were not determined by economic considerations. Even the fact that Speer called in 'Leaders of the Economy' in 1942–4, to help with the distribution of public contracts and raw materials, did little to alter this situation. The 'rings' and committees in his system of the 'self-government of German

---

[36] On the trend towards concentration in industry, see the reports on the economy of Berlin: Bundesarchiv Koblenz, R41, vols. 155–6. Dr Karl Krauch of IG-Farben was in charge of chemical production under the Four Year Plan; 30 per cent of his staff in this office came from IG-Farben (Petzina, *Der Vierjahresplan*, p. 147).

industry' were indeed run by industrialists, but they were responsible, in accordance with the *Führerprinzip*, only for ensuring that the rulings and plans made by Speer's ministry were carried out. They were given considerable freedom of action in this sphere, but on decisive questions of strategy, foreign policy and war aims their opinion was not sought. Their competence was limited entirely to the question of *how* things were done.[37]

INDUSTRY AND THE WORLD WAR

All the important foreign policy decisions in 1938 and 1939 were taken by Hitler personally. It is not yet possible to state with any degree of certainty how far he may have taken economic factors into consideration in these decisions. As yet there are hardly any positive proofs that he did.[38] Göring and General Thomas, who were both in close contact with industrial leaders and may well have been influenced by them, concluded from Germany's shortage of almost all strategic economic reserves that Hitler's foreign policy was rash and that the great war would have to be postponed. Their doubts were dismissed by Hitler. The fact that their pessimistic economic prognoses were not fulfilled until later was largely due to the military inactivity, or rather weakness, of the Western powers in 1939–40 (a factor which Hitler had at least in part reckoned with in his plans for a *Blitzkrieg*), to deliveries of goods from the Soviet Union under the Non-Aggression Pact in 1939–41 and to the plundering of occupied territories. 'Rearmament in depth' as demanded by Thomas remained, for the plebiscitary reasons noted above, a political impossibility for National Socialism until the defeat at Stalingrad; it would have demanded a drastic lowering of the standard of living. The domestic– political function of the *Blitzkrieg* plans resided in their promise of bringing the war to a swift and successful conclusion *without* demanding any undue sacrifices of the German people; and thereby providing a basis of tangible social and economic privilege for the alleged racial superiority of the German people in Europe.

Although the lack of raw materials and of labour therefore can still not be cited as a direct or immediate cause of the war of 1939, the war, once started, was of necessity transformed into an even more intensive economic exploitation of the whole of Europe.[39] The war made plunder possible – and also essential. In this connection the Second World War

---

[37] See Alan Milward, *The German Economy at War* (London 1965), Chapter 4.
[38] Hitler mentioned Germany's need to annex agricultural land at the so-called Hossbach conference of 5 November 1937 and there are many *post factum* utterances by political leaders on the economic functions of territorial expansion. The subject may not have been discussed before the war because such a justification for expansion implied a certain weakness on Germany's part, of a kind which Hitler always refused to acknowledge.
[39] This subject has hardly been investigated by historians yet.

differed in two essential respects from earlier imperialist wars: the economic need which was to be satisfied by military expansion was by no means of an autonomous economic nature (lack of markets or openings for investment), but was heavily determined by political factors. It was only the forced rearmament drive of 1936–9 which brought about the shortages of the basic factors of production; these were in turn intensified by the war, but could at the same time through war be alleviated in the most brutal way. Wartime plunder thus had its roots in political considerations: rearmament, the rapid extension by force of the German sphere of influence. These considerations had appeared to be based on a consensus of opinion between the Nazi leadership and industry, but the course of their translation into practice changed the terms of the partnership; control had largely slipped from the hands of industry from 1936 onwards, partly as a result of the political structure of the Third Reich, but also partly because of the inevitable changes in the structure of the economy. The high taxation rates and the control exercised by the state over the capital market did not trouble industry because it got the money back again in the form of public contracts. Thus the pursuit of war and the pursuit of profit became under National Socialism a closed system, a vicious circle of almost complete mutual dependence. What this closed system was for remained unclear.

This was the second peculiarity of German policy in 1939–45. National Socialism lacked concrete war aims; accordingly there was no conception of a new imperial order in Europe which was based on the needs of the economy – extensive plundering simply permitted the war to be continued. German industrialists certainly took advantage of the victories of the Wehrmacht to eliminate or take over foreign competitors and to extend the interests of their firms into France and Eastern Europe; they sometimes took the initiative in submitting takeover plans to the government.[40] Yet it cannot be said that this was what the war was really about; no compelling economic necessity lay behind such private industrial annexations. Final victory would have brought German industry dominance over the whole European economy – which would obviously have been welcome (though it must be doubted whether the NSDAP and the SS would have left the pickings to industry alone). It is, however, very hard to underpin such a statement with examples of pre-conquest expansionist designs either from within industry or at the level of government economic policy, and it is even harder to build bridges from 'economic

---

[40] E.g. D. Eichholtz, 'Die IG-Farben – "Friedensplanung"', *Jahrbuch für Wirtschaftsgeschichte*, Part III, 1966, pp. 271–332. Further examples cited by E. Czichon, 'Das Primat der Industrie im Kartell der nationalsozialistischen Macht', *Das Argument*, no. 47 (July 1968), pp. 168–92; but the discovery of such evidence alone does not prove the significance of industrial expansionism.

imperialism' in this sense to the crucial decisions of high policy which were taken in 1939–41. It may be misplaced to look for such designs and interconnections; perhaps the various elites of Nazi Germany all had their own different views of what the war was about, views which remained roughly compatible with each other as long as the war continued. The question requires more systematic investigation, but it is difficult to detect any coherent economic vision of empire behind the conquests and occupations of the period 1938–42. Neither in a political nor in an economic sense did the Nazi system produce a realistic conception of an ultimate status quo. For this reason, if for no other, a *victory* of National Socialism in the usual sense, which presupposes the goal of a post-war order, is unthinkable. Further, by 1942 the armaments drive had brought about such a great change in the industrial structure in favour of the production of basic materials and capital goods, that a peacetime market economy could scarcely be visualized. Even the gradual termination of the state's demand for military goods would have entailed a radical change in the economic and political system.[41] In all respects war had become an end in itself; the boundless expansionism of National Socialism gave rise to an international alliance which was bound to bring about its destruction.

SUMMARY

From 1936 onwards the framework of economic action in Germany was increasingly defined by the political leadership. The needs of the economy were determined by political decisions, principally by decisions in foreign policy, and the satisfaction of these needs was provided for by military victories. The fact that numerous industrialists not only passively co-operated in the 'Aryanization' of the economy, in the confiscation of firms in occupied territory, in the enslavement of many million people from Eastern Europe and in the employment of concentration camp prisoners, but indeed often took the initiative in these actions, constitutes a damning judgement on the economic system whose essential organizing principle (competition) gave rise to such conduct. But it cannot be maintained that even these actions had an important formative influence on the history of the Third Reich; they rather filled out in a barbaric manner a framework which was already given. The large firms identified themselves with National Socialism for the sake of their own further

---

[41] During 1941 and 1942, when final victory seemed near, the government gave some thought to this question; it was decided to solve it through a large-scale housing programme – there was a shortage of some 3 million dwellings at the outbreak of war. But this solution would have been of no benefit to the chemical and engineering industries. The post-war plans of the Nazi leadership would repay detailed investigation.

economic development. Their desire for profit and expansion, which was fully met by the political system, together with the stubborn nationalism of their leaders did, however, bind them to a government on whose aims, in as much as they were subject to control at all, they had virtually no influence.

Only between 1934 and 1936 was there a degree of elastic co-operation between the economy and the state to the advantage of the economic system, and that only in a simulated form, for it was not based on a stable balance between the various class interests but on the terroristic suppression of the workers' organizations and on totalitarian propaganda. The political leadership constructed for itself a position of supremacy which in institutional terms was autonomous and unshakeable and which, through its control of foreign policy, determined the direction of the system as a whole.

The seizure of power by the National Socialists can be traced back to a fundamental disintegration of bourgeois society in Germany, and the primacy of politics in its mature form was based on a renewed disintegration in the years 1936–8. This lack of unity and of co-ordination was by no means limited to the economy; on the contrary, it became the basic organizing principle of the National Socialist system of rule. A new stable and general representation of the people could not be achieved only by terror, propaganda and successes in foreign policy (i.e. through politics). This would have required a rational restructuring of society and neither in industry nor in the NSDAP was there the slightest inclination to attempt this. The old conflicts between agriculture and industry, capital and the working classes continued with the old intensity, though in new institutional forms. To these, new structural conflicts were added: *Gauleiter* against the central government, the party against the Wehrmacht and the civil service, the SS and the SD against everybody else. In 1938 General Keitel characterized the social and economic system as 'a war of all against all'.[42] It was no less warlike for being fought in silence. Debates in Germany as elsewhere about the social distribution of the national wealth had always been public and ideological. The monolithic front which National Socialism wished to present to the outside world forbade such debate, and the ideology did not furnish a language in which it could be conducted. The differences between the various ruling groups were thus fought out behind closed doors and in the form of straightforward, unideological battles for power and economic resources. The constantly invoked 'national community' (*Volksgemeinschaft*) of the propaganda concealed a reality in which the only acknowledged conformism was the

---

[42] 'Kampf aller Bedarfsträger um menschliche Arbeitskräfte, Rohstoffe und Geld'; minutes of meeting of Reich Defence Committee, 15 December 1938. Bundesarchiv Koblenz, WiIF5, vol. 560, no. 2, pp. 5 f.

cynical prosecution of one's own material interests; there developed as a result a broad, complex and 'modern' pluralism of political and economic interests which, until the military recovery of the Soviet Union in 1942, defeated most of the government's efforts to simplify and unify the power structure. Until 1942 the system was held together by two things: the frenetic, aimless dynamism of expansion, in which the constant setting of new tasks compelled the various organizations and interests to co-operate with each other – standstill would have meant decay; and second, by the function of the *Führerprinzip*. Hitler's alleged technique of extending his own sphere of influence by tactics of *divide et impera* was in reality a necessity dictated by the system, since the plurality of interests and organizations was already in existence.[43] Attempts to secure unitary structures of command foundered not so much on Hitler's desire to play the arbiter wherever he could, but on the power of those interest groups whose influence would have had to be curtailed if the various decisions on matters of principle were made. To decide between the rival claims of the Labour Front and industry, the contradictory interests of the farmers and the consumers or the different views of Göring and the *Gauleiter* on the need for stringent war economy measures was a very delicate and thankless task, which Hitler usually preferred simply to avoid. Speer was one of the few who could force him to take such decisions. Loyalty to the Führer and the willingness of the leaders of state and party organs to accept Hitler's decisions often seemed to be the barrier standing between the 'Thousand Year Reich' and anarchy.[44]

The self-destructive measures of the National Socialist system can only be understood in the context of the primacy of politics and of the material plurality of the power structure from which the state derived its autonomy. Among the first Polish Jews who were gassed in the extermination camps were thousands of skilled metal workers from Polish armament factories. This was in the autumn of 1942, at the turning point in the campaign against the Soviet Union, which was to increase still further the demands made by the Wehrmacht on the German war economy. The army emphasized the irrational nature of this action in view of the great shortage of skilled labour, but was unable to save the Jewish armament workers for industry. The general who made the formal complaint was relieved of his post.[45] The same internal power relationship lay behind the use of scarce railway installations for the deportation of

[43] For the war period, there is evidence that Hitler *deliberately* created agencies with overlapping competences.

[44] Not least important was his considerable personal popularity among the people at large, which went a long way towards countering the unpopularity of the 'little Hitlers', the war, etc. See Heinz Boberach, *Meldungen aus dem Reich* (Neuwied/Berlin 1965).

[45] Testimony of Dr H. von Krannhals in the trial of SS-Obergruppenführer Karl Wolff, Munich, September 1964.

persecuted Jews towards the end of the war, instead of for the provisioning of the forces on the Eastern Front. The SS was able, by virtue of its monopoly over the information services and the machinery of terror, of its position outside the legal framework and lastly by virtue of Himmler's special relationship with Hitler, to execute its ideologically determined task of the destruction of the Jews to the material detriment of the whole system. The way in which the political sphere emancipated itself from all reference to the needs of society is nowhere clearer than in the example of the SS, where the translation of ideology into practice was in flat contradiction to the interests of the war economy and yet was allowed to continue.

Another slightly less crass example was the decision of March 1942 to enslave the populations of Eastern Europe systematically and put them at the disposal of the German war economy. Gauleiter Sauckel, who was given control over all labour deployment at that time, suggested that the problem of labour shortage could be solved by rationalization of the methods of production and by conscripting German women to work in industry. Slave labour, he maintained, was politically and technically unreliable, unproductive, and represented a 'racial danger' to the German people. His programme was rejected by Hitler on the grounds that there was no time to rationalize the economy and that the German woman's place was in the home. After this a further 5 million 'foreign and Russian workers' were brought forcibly into Germany, and Sauckel's doubts were confirmed.[46] Again an ideologically determined policy triumphed over economic calculation.

Any attempt to find a common denominator in this ideology, to interpret it as if it were systematic, is doomed to failure. Goebbels and his team tended to understand and use the ideology as an instrument of domination, the contents of which could be manipulated almost at will. But in the end, the racial–ethical utopia at its core was taken so seriously by the political leadership, in particular by Hitler and by the SS, that in decisive questions even the urgent material needs of the system were sacrificed to it. Precisely in the case of the destruction of the Jews and in the question of conscripting women into industry, the ideology was *not* any longer a necessary pillar of the system – as it perhaps had been in the early years of the Third Reich. For the destruction of the Jews was carried out *in secret* in Poland; and according to the reports of the security services on public opinion within Germany, the majority of the population would have approved of measures to compel women to work. What held

---

[46] See trial of Fritz Sauckel before the International Military Tribunal at Nuremberg: *Trial of the Major War Criminals*, esp. vol. XV. Russian workers (*Ostarbeiter*) were treated even worse than other foreign workers. The mobilization of female labour was more complete in Britain than in Germany.

the system together as late as 1944 was neither common interest nor a consensus, but fear – fear of the 'Russian hordes', and of the now indiscriminate terror of the Gestapo.

Under the conditions of capitalist production there is always something irrational about the assertion of a primacy of politics, since that which alone can legitimate this primacy, a commonweal, can only be simulated. It is only possible to talk of a rational primacy of politics when the state can act as trustee of a homogeneous society and base its policies on the needs and resources of the society. The radical nature of the primacy of politics under National Socialism, however, was rooted in the specific historical disintegration of bourgeois German society (1929–33), of German capitalism (1936–8), and of international politics in the 1930s. The immense political scope of the National Socialist government was not based on the confidence of a politically and economically homogeneous society; on the contrary, it was a result precisely of the disintegration of society. The coincidence of this with the collapse of the international order in the 1930s enabled the National Socialist state to achieve a degree of independence of society which is unparalleled in history. The development of the National Socialist system of rule tended inevitably towards *self-destruction*, for a political system which is not based on the requirements of social reproduction is no longer in a position to set itself limited and rational aims. This autonomy of the political sphere led to a blind, goalless activism in all spheres of public life – a tendency to which the capitalist economy, based as it was on competition and the maximization of profit, was particularly susceptible. The separation of the economic principle of competition from all institutional limitations designed to ensure the continued reproduction of society was part of the dialectic of National Socialism. The economic power of the state as an unlimited source of demand for armaments gave free rein to destructive tendencies in the economic system.

The fundamental irrationality of the system had in part its origin and found its concrete expression in the specific irrationality of the National Socialist ideology. This ideology was the product of a declining social class and came increasingly into conflict with the social realities created by National Socialist rule itself: the movement whose ideology had been directed towards the construction of a society of small traders, craftsmen and smallholders brought about a tremendous acceleration in the process of concentration in industry and trade, and intensified the drift of population from the countryside into the towns; industry was concentrated in central and western Germany and drew increasingly on the population of the poorer eastern regions as a source of labour, thus making nonsense of the policy of colonizing and settling Eastern Europe with German farmers – the one attempt at this in western Poland was a signal failure.

Likewise the attempt to educate the working classes to idealism – the workers had to be bought at a cost to military strength, and yet even this method did not suffice. In the end the ideology could only find a secure place in the 'reality' of everyday life in and through the SS – and that only through terror and bureaucratic norms.

Fighting spirit and the willingness to make sacrifices, on the one hand, and comprehensive military–economic planning, on the other, were only realized under pressure of imminent defeat. Self-destruction was the preordained end of a system in which politics was synonymous with the boundless pursuit of political power; destruction its only achievement.[47]

---

[47] See Norman Cohn's illuminating discussion of the self-destructive elements in the psychology of the anti-Semite in *Warrant for Genocide* (London 1967), Conclusion, esp. pp. 265 f. 'Self-destruction' appears to be the only universal theme in the history of National Socialist Germany, but the universality may only be verbal: it is difficult to relate the various manifestations – political, economic, psychological – with one another.

3

❦

THE ORIGINS OF THE LAW ON THE ORGANIZATION OF NATIONAL LABOUR OF 20 JANUARY 1934. AN INVESTIGATION INTO THE RELATIONSHIP BETWEEN 'ARCHAIC' AND 'MODERN' ELEMENTS IN RECENT GERMAN HISTORY[1]

INTRODUCTION

SCHOLARLY DEBATE and research into National Socialism has made use of various more or less clearly defined models, such as totalitarianism theory, marxist interpretations, or the application of social and psychological concepts. More recently another approach has emerged which, while by no means new, has been attracting renewed attention. It starts from the assumption that the rise and dominance of National Socialism was a *specifically German crisis within a general process of modernization,* and it emphasizes those aspects of the movement and of the policies of its leaders which originated in 'pre-modern' structures, or which give an impression of hostility to modernization, or else were simply archaic. Certain economic interests and class-specific (particularly middle-class) values and behaviour; certain ideological slogans (*Gemeinschaft* or community), together with some important aspects of the practical politics of the Nazi regime (such as the persecution of the Jews) all fall easily in with this line. Thus the twin polarities of 'modernity' and 'archaism' seem to offer a useful tool for the analysis of recent German history.

One aim of this study is to challenge that assumption, though it is an aim that can be only partially accomplished here. A thorough examination of the question would require a more detailed theoretical discussion and a more precise definition of the diverse sensitive and complex concepts

---

This chapter was translated by Rosemary Morris.

[1] This study emerged largely in the course of many years of dialogue with David Schoenbaum, one of the few colleagues with whom disagreement is both pleasant and profitable.

77

involved than I can undertake here. What I offer here is therefore more like an interim report, which points to some still open questions of theory and research. My objection to the application of 'modernization' theory to German history in the last century is broad and simple, and can be best explained with reference to a notable example of National Socialist policy. To highlight this example I have kept my initial theoretical claims to a minimum, and my conceptual definitions fairly broad.

Modernization theory almost always lays stress on the progressive, positive side of modernization itself – in which it diverges notably from the ideas of Max Weber, often considered the father of this particular sociological approach. In modernization theory, economic growth, the pursuit of ever more clearly defined aims, and an ever clearer differentiation of economic and social roles, are paradigmatically opposed to attitudes and structures which are seen as obstructive and restrictive, and can be described as irrational, traditional, backward-looking or – in their more aggressive form – archaic. The appropriateness of these categories (borrowed from the sociological school of structural functionalism) to the analysis of today's so-called developing countries is not the question here; but with regard to European history they are a source of confusion. Our present example, which in 1934 laid the legislative basis for labour policy in Nazi Germany, shows that the apparently retrograde intention of this measure was indeed only apparent. It is simply not true that the roots of Nazi policy in this area are to be found in a revolt against modernization; on the contrary, they sprang from essential, if latent, directions being taken within 'modernity' itself. And it is still an open question whether other sectors of public life, such as the civil service and the military, which have been classified as equally antiquated, did not also in the 1920s contain some positively forward-looking and direction-setting structural elements.

Such confusions spring initially from the fact that the evidence for modernization theory is usually sought in phenomenological descriptions and the history and critique of ideas: behavioural patterns and social structures are derived principally, if not exclusively, from ideology. This approach is unsatisfactory for three reasons. First, we must always ask who is speaking, for whom and about whom: to take an example from Parsons and Dahrendorf, it is not possible to derive the fundamental attitudes of the imperial political leadership towards private property from Bismarck's speech on the nationalization of the railways (see note 8 below). In dealing with National Socialism we cannot assume that remarks by political leaders always reflected the current ideology, nor that they always derived closely from Nazi ideology itself. The ideological components of labour law after 1934 certainly agreed with basic Nazi thinking, but (as will be shown later) their roots lay in a quite different context. Second, and consequently, we must always ask about the purpose and function of ideological principles; an interpretation of ideology drawn from the texts alone, which infers their meaning *directly* from an implied social totality, leaves no room at all for Horkheimer's *'cui bono?'* Third, we must be aware of possible shifts in the content of key ideological concepts: the mere fact that some special interest group sings the praises of community values as an ordering principle of society does not mean that it must immediately be identified as 'anti-modern'. For notions of community (*Gemeinschaft*) in the Germany of the 1920s and 1930s differed widely from one another, and the verbal homogeneity disguised fundamentally incompatible socio-political and politico-economic tendencies. The example of labour law again indicates that the community slogan was manipulated by interests whose real ideas of the social order were radically and consciously pro-modern. Nonetheless, it was much more than a verbal ruse aiming to imply some sort of fundamental common ground between industry and the middle classes where none existed: it implied a redefinition, grounded in some sort of reality, of the concept of community itself. It is irrelevant to observe that both the modern and the retrogressive ideas of community were authoritarian, because it is wrong to postulate a pluralistic and democratic welfare state as the inevitable outcome of the process of modernization in Germany. For modernization itself has the face of Janus. A complacently teleological view, angled on the present, can only be harmful to historical research.

In the discussion that follows I shall continue to make use of this sociological vocabulary, in order to highlight how the evidence might affect a historiography derived from modernization theory. This is a deliberately critical strategy, and is intended to expose the limits of this theory as an analytical tool. I am sceptical about it, first, because it leads to over-hasty generalizations; second (and these two points are closely related), because there seems to me to be a circular relationship between theory and proof, so that descriptive elements are immediately pressed into service as analyses.

However, the term 'archaism' does seem to be an irreplaceable heuristic concept, always provided that it is accurately defined. If we meet with a spontaneous recrudescence of specific and clearly identifiable patterns of behaviour typical of a past social order, then its manifestations can scarcely be described otherwise than as 'archaic'. The political and racist pogroms which sprang out of the National Socialist movement in early 1933 are a typical example, and also had great political significance: a collective lapse into a type of behaviour which was fundamentally anachronistic. (Even the party leadership found it to be so, and this was one of the reasons for the mass killings of 30 June 1934.) At times it may also be appropriate to describe as archaic certain schools of social theory that deliberately turn their backs on modern methods and approaches. In other respects, however, the term should be treated with caution.

I

We must attempt to awaken the power of the worker's inner commitment to his firm, which has hitherto been absent, extinct or destroyed. He must stop thinking that it does not matter to him how his plant is doing so long as he can do his work and get his pay; he should have a strong feeling that he is bound to his plant for better and for worse, that he is, as it were, working in his own undertaking. This goal can be reached only through participation and shared responsibility. (Ernst Francke, 1921)[2]

We must all share in the workplace where we are employed. Share in every stone, every machine, everything. Yes, my friend: if you work there, it belongs to you! In law it may be the property of another, but that means nothing. The workplace is yours, and you must learn to love the machine like a bride. (Robert Ley, at the Siemens Jubilee in Berlin, October 1933)[3]

The Law on the Organization of National Labour (Arbeitsordnungsgesetz, or AOG) was one of the most all-embracing and rigorous legislative products of National Socialism, and few enactments bore a clearer stamp of Nazi ideology. In terms of both labour law and ideology, it was the 'factory community' (*Betriebsgemeinschaft*) that was the crux of the new order. It replaced all previous institutions of industrial labour relations: associations, state arbitration authorities and mass organizations.[4]

At the head of the workforce was the employer, the *Betriebsführer* (factory leader). His workers, now called his *Gefolgschaft* (followers or 'retinue'), had to swear 'fealty and obedience' (*Treue und Gehorsam*) to him: 'The factory leader makes decisions on the followers' behalf in all factory affairs... He shall look after the well-being of the followers.' The factory leader was backed by a 'council of trust' (*Vertrauensrat*) whose duty was to 'deepen the mutual trust within the factory community'. It was to discuss all measures 'pertaining to the improvement of efficiency, the establishment and supervision of working conditions in general...the strengthening of the bonds of factory members with one another and with

[2] Quoted in Ludwig Preller, *Sozialpolitik in der Weimarer Republik* (Stuttgart 1949), p. 206.
[3] *Siemens-Mitteilungen*, 12 October 1933.
[4] *Reichsgesetzblatt (RGBl)* (1934), I, p. 45. All quotations in the next three paragraphs are from the text of the law. The first commentary was written by the draftsmen themselves, Werner Mansfield, Wolfgang Pohl, G. Steinmann and A. B. Krause: *Die Ordnung der nationalen Arbeit* (Berlin/Leipzig/Mannheim/Munich 1934). This work represents the intentions of the legislators. The most comprehensive commentary is by Alfred Hueck, Hans Carl Nipperdey and Rolf Dietz, *Gesetz zur Ordnung der Nationalen Arbeit*, 3rd edn (Munich/Berlin 1939). A brief analysis of the problems is in the article by Thilo Ramm, 'Nationalsozialismus und Arbeitsrecht', *Kritische Justiz*, no. 2 (1969), pp. 108–20.

the factory, and the welfare of all members of the community'. This council was 'elected' by the workforce from a slate previously drawn up by the factory leader together with the representative of the German Labour Front. The council had no authority in the absence of the plant leader, so that it was prevented by law from acting as an independent representative of workers' interests. All aspects of labour relations which had not already been regulated by law (as had maximum working hours, minimum wage-rates, health and safety, etc.) had to be regulated by a 'factory code of rules' (*Betriebsordnung*): this was discussed by the council of trust and by the Trustee of Labour, but its content was decided substantially by the factory leader himself; similarly, pay scales above the legal minimum were now the affair of this new disciplinary authority in private industry.

The state's provisional oversight over industrial class conflict, which had been instituted in May 1933 with the appointment of the Trustees of Labour,[5] was confirmed and given more precise expression in January 1934. The Trustees were state employees subject to the Reich Minister of Labour, who fixed their general responsibilities in collaboration with the Minister of Economics. Their task was to 'maintain industrial peace' in individual industries, and later in entire branches of economic activity. In accordance with the spirit of the AOG this task required a certain deliberate restraint on the part of the Trustees, rather than a broad involvement in organizational and supervisory activity. A genuine, lasting solution to class conflict – which for the Nazis meant an ideological solution – could be achieved only if responsibility for day-to-day problems was assigned to cells of the social organism itself. The Trustees' function was to protect the interests of the state by a cautious application of its wide-ranging authority in labour relations, so that class conflict would not be reignited by brutal economic repression (and if such conflict did break out among the workers there were other means of control to hand – the Gestapo and the concentration camp). The Trustees were thus supposed to interfere as little as possible in the internal affairs of the industrial community; and the Labour Front could not interfere at all. The office of Trustee was thought of as a sort of last instance in social and labour policy, and its legally constituted duties were confined to checking the need for any proposed mass redundancies; ensuring that minimum working conditions conformed to the existing agreements, which had been taken over by the regime and imposed on the employers, and gradually transforming these into a new type of 'wage code'; monitoring the constitution and activities of the councils of trust; and keeping the Reich government informed of developments on the social policy front.

[5] Law on the Trustees of Labour (Gesetz über die Treuhänder der Arbeit), 29 May 1933, *RGBl* (1933), I, p. 285.

The drafters of the new law knew that it would take a long time before class conflict could be eliminated by the closer relations that were being established between management and workforce through indoctrination, increased trust, and so on. They did not, however, take the obvious route of giving the Labour Front the necessary powers to force this process through. Instead, they decided to deal with incorrigibles through a new system of 'social honour courts': 'Gross violations of the social duties laid down by the factory community will be penalized by the courts as offences against social honour.' Thus it was an 'offence' for the factory leader to maliciously exploit his labour force, and, similarly, for individual members of the workforce to endanger industrial peace by maliciously sowing sedition among them. Only the Trustees could institute legal proceedings. The social honour courts were initially conceived as a means of education, and their sanctions were correspondingly mild and more or less symbolic in character. The new law omitted virtually any reference to the Labour Front.

There seems little disagreement among historians about how this law worked in practice, or about its role in the political and economic preparations for the Second World War. The lengthy educational stipulations remained a dead letter: councils of trust and social honour courts led a miserable existence on the fringes of the most important developments in social and labour policy, which were determined on the one hand by the instability of the labour market, and on the other by the institutional imperialism of the Labour Front. The chief beneficiaries of this new regulation of socio-political institutions were the big enterprises which, for the first time since the world war, were entering on a phase of vast and solidly based expansion with increased profit margins.[6]

The origins of this legislation are, however, another story, and here there is neither clarity nor agreement. The mere fact that the declared intentions of the legislator largely remained unrealized should serve to warn us against assuming that the chief beneficiaries of the law were also responsible for its genesis. Here it is worth remembering Ernst Fraenkel's observation that the history of a statute 'does not conclude with its legislative enactment: that is merely the first decisive step'.[7] At first glance its wording looks much like a typical product of the petty bourgeois (mittelständisch) attitudes which the NSDAP succeeded in

---

[6] See Franz Neumann, *Behemoth. The Structure and Practice of National Socialism* (New York 1972); Hans-Gerd Schumann, *Nationalsozialismus und Gewerkschaftsbewegung* (Hanover/Frankfurt am Main 1958). The social policy of the National Socialist state and the role of the Labour Front can also be studied in my collection of documents, *Arbeiterklasse und Volksgemeinschaft. Dokumente und Materialien zur deutschen Arbeiterpolitik 1936–39* (Opladen 1975).

[7] See Thilo Ramm (ed.), *Arbeitsrecht und Politik. Quellentexte 1918–1933* (Neuwied 1966), p. 948 note.

mobilizing between 1930 and 1933. In this sense David Schoenbaum categorizes the AOG as 'a kind of countermanagerial revolution': an attempt to shape the whole economy on the model of the independently responsible owner and factory leader.[8] At the 1934 Berlin exhibition 'German People – German Labour', the AOG was represented in the following way: a vast mural depicting a handful of craftsmen and labourers who were putting together a small housing estate in a harmony undisturbed by either class conflict or noisy machinery.[9] It would be easy to find similar examples from the propaganda of the time; but an interpretation of the AOG which stresses only the archaic traits in its provisions and language cannot hope to give adequate answers to all the questions about its origins.

First, it is notable that the overwhelming majority of handicraft workshops were exempted from the legislation: only employers of over twenty workers were obliged to issue a factory code of rules and establish a council of trust. Doubtless this must be seen as a concession to what was then still a powerful interest group; in itself, however, it tells us nothing about the origins of these provisions. By contrast, the law pays detailed attention to the particular situation of large concerns comprising several plants. Second, it must be emphasized that the AOG established a 'duty of care' on the part of the employer, but without giving any further details. The earliest statements of the new rulers after 2 May 1933 already make it clear that the regime was going to take this point seriously, for obvious reasons of its own. And yet it was precisely the handicraft firms and small enterprises that were ruthlessly exploiting their workers. It was they, and not the big industrialists, who saw the Nazi seizure of power as a welcome opportunity to depress the condition of wage-earners directly and decisively – and this brought them up against the implacable opposition of the factory inspectorate, the Labour Front, the Reich

---

[8] David Schoenbaum, *Hitler's Social Revolution. Class and Status in Nazi Germany 1933–1939* (New York 1966), p. 91. Basically similar, but undialectic, are the interpretations of National Socialism by Ralf Dahrendorf, *Gesellschaft und Demokratie in Deutschland* (Munich 1965) and Henry Ashby Turner Jr, *Faschismus und Kapitalismus in Deutschland* (Göttingen, 1973), Chapter 6. This direction in recent research largely goes back to two 1942 articles by Talcott Parsons, republished in his collected *Essays in Social Theory* (Glencoe 1964), pp. 104–41. For a critique of Parsons' method see especially Alvin W. Gouldner, *The Coming Crisis of Western Sociology* (London 1971). The most effective attempt to link Parsons' theory to empirical historical research is Neil J. Smelser, *Social Change in the Industrial Revolution. An Application of Theory to the Lancashire Cotton Industry, 1770–1840* (London 1959). Recently, however, Smelser's results have been fundamentally challenged on both the theoretical and empirical levels: I owe ideas on this subject to unpublished critical material by Michael Anderson (Edinburgh) and Michael Pickering (Cambridge).

[9] Abundant documentary evidence on this notable exhibition is to be found in Deutsches Zentralarchiv (DZA) Potsdam, Reichsarbeitsministerium (RAM) vol. 7247.

Ministry of Labour and occasionally even the Gestapo.[10] In these circumstances we can scarcely talk about a successful attempt by the *Mittelstand* to influence government policies. On the contrary, small employers soon made up the majority of those condemned by the social honour courts.[11]

Third, it has yet to be proved that the specific ideology exhibited in the AOG had already been fully developed in the National Socialist Party by the end of 1933. The question needs further investigation; but to all appearances the party leadership had hardly even considered the form that any new socio-political institutions ought to take; in fact it was still in thrall to various concepts of corporatism which were quite alien to the text of the law. Certainly the AOG stood out among Nazi legislative measures for its exceptional ideological stringency; but there is no proof that the ideology that it expressed was, in any precise sense, of National Socialist origin.

This criticism of the petty bourgeois interpretation is highly speculative, for the very good reason that all the Reich Ministry of Labour's documentation on the AOG was destroyed during a bombing raid on Berlin towards the end of the war. Scholarly discussion thus remains on an uncertain footing of circumstantial evidence. One of the most important pieces of evidence is the author of the AOG himself. Other records show that it was Dr Werner Mansfeld, ministerial director and head of a division in the Ministry of Labour from 1933 to 1942, who drafted the essential proposals. Mansfeld (b. 1893), a lawyer who had been an officer on the Western Front, a member of the Freikorps and probably of the Stahlhelm, was counsel to the Association of Mining Interests in Essen from 1924 to 1933. He specialized in labour law, and represented the Association in wage negotiations with the unions. He did not join the Nazi Party until early 1933. Mansfeld's closest colleague in the autumn of 1933 was Dr Wolfgang Pohl, an official in the Ministry of Economics since 1927 who had been seconded to the Ministry of Labour in July 1933; Pohl had previously worked in the social policy department of the Allgemeine Elektrizitätsgemeinschaft (AEG), and later as an editor of the *Deutsche Allgemeine Zeitung*.[12] It was, however, Mansfeld who was the decisive influence in the Reich government.

From the viewpoint of social policy the Ruhr mining industry, in which Mansfeld had gained his experience, was by no means typical of

[10] The annual reports of the factory inspectorate (*Jahresberichte der Gewerbeaufsichtsbehörden*) 1933–4, contain much material on this theme. See von der Goltz's memorandum on the Labour Front of October 1934, Bundesarchiv Koblenz, R43II, vol. 530.

[11] See Nathan A. Pelcovits, 'The Social Honor Courts of Nazi Germany', *Political Science Quarterly*, vol. 53 (1938), pp. 350–71.

[12] Mansfeld's personal papers: Geheimes Preussisches Staatsarchiv (GPSA) Berlin, Rep. 318 PA, vol. 213.

German industry as a whole. The mines, as a Siemens manager once remarked, had to make do with 'very inferior human material'.[13] Even in the 1920s most mine managers were still looking back to the rigid patriarchal authoritarianism of their founding fathers as a model for their relations with factory councils and unions – and even today they are still commonly referred to as 'factory leaders' by their workforce. The wording of the AOG expressed this nostalgic desire to be masters in their own house again: even the biggest industries were not free of ideological archaism. H.-A. Winkler has rightly drawn attention to the fundamental similarity in the social policy views of both heavy industry and handicrafts in the last years of the Weimar Republic. But even here certain reservations seem in order.[14] As will be explained later, this attitude represented above all a compelling, comprehensive aim of economic 'rationalization' which was not restricted to one industry alone. It would also be quite wrong to dismiss Mansfeld as simply the stereotypical agent and mouthpiece of west German heavy industry. He evidently had broader interests: he was academically qualified, and was a part-time university lecturer in Münster after 1930.[15]

It should also be noted that the basic principles of the AOG were by no means peculiar to heavy industry. In the surviving archives of the Ministry of Economics there is a no-nonsense memorandum by Goerdeler, dated 7 September 1933, in which he unreservedly approves the destruction of the trade unions and describes both the eight-hour day and wage settlements through negotiation and strikes as 'unnatural'. This advice was obviously unsolicited and may well have had no influence on the decisions which were shortly to follow. However, it is probably not insignificant that his positive suggestions agree on every essential point with the institutional regulations of the AOG: the aim was to reduce the working classes to total impotence and give the factory leadership the greatest possible autonomy in setting working conditions. The industrialist Fritz Thyssen's much less down-to-earth suggestions boiled down to exactly the same conclusions.[16]

An exhaustive study of the printed sources would surely help to fill the gaps in our evidence and clarify our picture of how the AOG emerged during the autumn of 1933. It is, however, unlikely that we would come across any single personality or special interest that could be said to have played a key part in the process. At most, Goerdeler, Thyssen and Mansfeld shared a deep hostility to the labour movement and all its

[13] In conversation with the author.
[14] Heinrich-August Winkler, *Mittelstand, Demokratie und Nationalsozialismus. Die politische Entwicklung von Handwerk und Kleinhandel in der Weimarer Republik* (Cologne 1972), p. 130.
[15] See note 12, above, and Section III below.
[16] DZA Potsdam, Reichswirtschaftsministerium (RWM), vol. 9931, pp. 119–34; cf. also Arthur Schweitzer, *Big Business in the Third Reich* (Bloomington, IN 1964), p. 361.

works, and a resolve to re-establish Germany as a great power. But in 1933 even this somewhat narrow basis of agreement proved quite adequate for drafting a new social contract. For the AOG was concerned not with the success of any particular industry or segment of the German ruling class, but with providing statutory anchorage for domestic political aims which had become the common property of almost all conservative elements.

Significant, from this viewpoint, are the cabinet meetings in which the draft law was adopted. Not a single word was wasted on the fundamental principles of this radical reconstruction of industrial labour relations; the file did not even include the usual explanatory memorandum to the law (*Begründung*). The only debate was over the public services, with the largest administrative ministries stubbornly insisting that they should retain completely unrestricted authority and sole responsibility in their own administrations and quasi-industrial enterprises.[17] Given this broad and secure consensus among all leading groups, it seems appropriate to expand our search for the origins of the AOG considerably, and turn to the general historical background and the relevant long-term trends in the German economy which contributed to the formulation of this 'solution' to industrial class conflict. In so doing I shall confine my remarks to four themes which seem likely to prove fertile ground for further research into the question, though here they can be treated only briefly and theoretically: the effects of the world economic crisis on class relationships in industry (Section II of this essay); the consequences of rationalization for the leadership structure of the plant (Section III); the role of the Reich labour court from 1927 to 1932 (Section IV); and the activity of the National Socialist Workers' Cell Organization (NSBO) and the German Labour Front (DAF) in summer and autumn 1933 (Section V).

II

The world economic crisis contributed decisively to the exacerbation of political class conflict and the rise of the German Communist Party (KPD) between 1928 and 1932: so much is undeniable. Less well known, but not less interesting, is a counter-tendency which made itself particularly felt on the shop-floor, but to some extent affected the stance of the trade unions too. Mass unemployment destroyed the power of the working class on the labour market. Workers, whether as individuals or as union members, were at the mercy of the laws of economic contraction, subject to the inexorable decisions of employers regarding both job opportunities

---

[17] Bundesarchiv Koblenz, R43II, vol. 531.

and wages. Fear of unemployment, combined with extraordinarily strong disciplinary pressures, gave a sharp edge to their collective and personal subordination within the plant. Whole paragraphs from the reports of the health and safety inspectorate at this time already read like an anticipation of the conditions that the authors of the AOG planned to enshrine in law. One example among many must suffice:

Generally it can be said that for the most part the representatives of the workforce and the workers' organizations showed full understanding of the difficult situation of the plants and had put off many justified claims until better times...In the Rhineland it was observed in many plants that the workers were doing their best to work harder and better to improve the business standing of the company and so safeguard their own jobs. But the diligence of the workers could not prevent a general decline in wages . . . especially as many workers were prepared to work for less than the minimum wage.[18]

Needless to say, it was the less 'understanding' workers who were the first to face redundancy. So strong was the compulsion of the labour market that output per head and per shift in the coal industry during the crisis years was higher than at any other time between the two world wars.[19]

To be sure, such conditions were at best a frail basis for the class harmony and plant unity that the AOG prescribed: gratitude for simply being in work was tempered with a considerable resentment at the constant wage cuts and fear of ever greater demands. Insofar as industry could spread the impression that the crisis was a sort of natural catastrophe whose consequences bore equally on workers, employers and the nation as a whole, mass unemployment may have been of even wider socio-political significance. The Communist Party did take up a critical attitude towards such propaganda; but the Social Democrats (SPD) and the free trade unions did not. And those who were prepared to blame the crisis on the capitalist economic order rather than on blind fate often found it cost them their jobs. To paraphrase Brecht, it was food first, theory second. Moreover, the propaganda from the ruling classes did not stop at slogans. Despite their undeniably difficult circumstances, employers were far from being uniformly merciless and inhuman: the bitter disputes at the level of the national organizations about issues such as the distribution of work should not blind us to the fact that many firms were troubled by the desperate straits of their workers, or at any rate acted as if they were – this was the basis for a number of purely charitable initiatives. More interesting, and more promising (because they were prompted by the aim of economic rationalization), were the equally frequent attempts

[18] *Jahresberichte der Gewerbeaufsichtsbeamten* (Prussia), 1931–2, pp. 11, 24
[19] See my *Arbeiterklasse und Volksgemeinschaft*, Document Section, Chapter xi.

by big firms to retain their skilled workers through planned reductions in working hours. Not infrequently this kind of redistribution of work was used as an alternative to a total loss of wages,[20] and it was thus a way to reconcile the workers' needs with the interests of the plant. Workers could have rejected such arrangements only on blatantly partisan political grounds.

This should not give the impression that German industry behaved through the crisis like some kind of conscientious welfare system. Firms that protected at least some of their workers from the worst consequences of the crisis, either out of charity or in their own interests, must have been in the minority. In some industries, such as the building trade, they simply did not exist. But, as regards the phenomenology of class relations, it seems possible that the crisis created two short-term trends which did something to pave the way for the National Socialist legislation. First, it further aroused and sharpened the employers' appetite for unlimited power over their workers: it opened vistas which in the 1920s had been blocked by the strong position of the unions. Second, there are indications that as the crisis dragged on, many workers began to lose confidence in a class identity that was opposed to the economic system, since their organizations could no longer effectively represent them. This hypothesis is supported by the fact that the working class put up no determined resistance after March 1933. There was a wave of opportunism among those who hoped that political conformism would get them or keep them in work.[21] The first point must remain tentative for two reasons: first, because our knowledge of the sources is still insufficient for further proof, and second because the very grounds for the argument, i.e. the contradictory experiences and shifting and indirect reactions of those concerned, allow no more precise pronouncement.[22] However, the ambitions of the ruling class, as they unfolded through the crisis, were much more than a momentary reaction to the extreme conditions of mass unemployment. The intensification and extension of the system of internal factory authority was integral to the 1920s rationalization movement.

---

[20] See inter alia Friedrich Syrup, *Hundert Jahre staatlicher Sozialpolitik*, ed. Julius Scheuble; rev. Otto Neuloh (Stuttgart 1957), p. 283.

[21] See my *Arbeiterklasse und Volksgemeinschaft*. The introduction deals briefly with this question.

[22] See Rudolf Vierhaus, 'Auswirkungen der Krise um 1930 in Deutschland. Beiträge zu einer historisch-psychologischen Analyse', in W. Conze and H. Raupach (eds.), *Die Staats- und Wirtschaftskrise des Deutschen Reiches* (Stuttgart 1967). The fact that the German sociologists of the 1920s never did any empirical or descriptive research whatsoever into the mass unemployment of those years speaks volumes for the way they saw themselves at the time; compare the contemporary research in the USA, England and Austria.

III

Labour relations before the war were...still strongly influenced by the more easy-going and 'cosy' way of working that had come down from the old handicraft days. This changed fundamentally with the rationalization process after the war...Work became subject to the calculations of factory management. And this attitude was no longer confined to the larger firms.[23]

This abrupt and radical transformation of the character of work in industry – minute division of labour, all-embracing surveillance of behaviour in the workplace, psychological and technical aptitude testing, prescriptions for improved productivity which affected even the smallest procedures, etc. – has already been described in detail by a number of authors.[24] The following grotesquely exaggerated examples of this pressure for increased productivity may not be entirely typical, but they show very clearly the fundamental tendency for the worker to become ever more subordinate to management. Thus, a large Berlin office instituted an optimal procedure for the opening of envelopes, and also attempted to pay its shorthand typists by the syllable. Because order in the workplace was not only aesthetically satisfying (one wonders for whom), but was also conducive to efficiency, the Siemens-Schuckert switch-gear factory introduced a tool box whose drawers would close only if the workers had put every tool back in its correct place. The psychological and technical aptitude test for prospective post-bus drivers was so tough that it soon became notorious as the 'torture chamber' and eventually had to be toned down. Many new production processes demanded (for safety reasons) interference in workers' clothing and even their hair-styles; it was even thought that productivity improved if people assigned to particularly mindless tasks were subjected to incessant light music.[25]

In terms of political economy, this wave of rationalization broke on two opposing shores. On one side it promised to mitigate the struggle for fairer distribution of the social product by improving productivity throughout the economy as a whole: this would be of material advantage

---

[23] See Preller, *Sozialpolitik*, p. 130.
[24] Ibid.; also, and especially, Robert A. Brady, *The Rationalization Movement in German Industry* (Berkeley, CA 1933). In my opinion these two contemporary studies are still superior to all the more recent work on the political economy of the Weimar Republic. However, there is also a very rewarding comparative perspective in Charles Maier, 'Between Taylorism and Technocracy', *Journal of Contemporary History*, vol. 5, no. 2 (1970), pp. 27–61. It is perhaps not quite out of place here to draw attention to Hitler's repeated declarations that under National Socialism everyone would have 'his own' work to go to – a primitive version of this same notion of productivity.
[25] Preller, *Sozialpolitik*, p. 136; Brady, *Rationalization Movement*, pp. 255, 261–2; see also Hans Dominik, *Das Schaltwerk der Siemens-Schuckertwerke AG Berlin* (Berlin 1929), pp. 21–2.

both to capital and to labour and would make them into partners in technical progress. On the other, it gave some impetus to trade union militancy, which drew some of its strength from the demand for monetary compensation for increased pressure of work. As human workers were treated more and more like machines, this created new impulses and expressions of class struggle in industry. Preller has made this twofold development quite clear:

> Throughout the labour process . . . a tendency to objectify and depersonalize labour relations . . . was discernible. The regulation of production techniques brought the human side of labour more directly into managerial calculations: to the advantage of labour insofar as both performance at work and its effect on people were considered and investigated, but to its disadvantage insofar as the purely arithmetical standards of business were extensively applied to the activities of both blue- and white-collar workers. This development was of only limited help in labour relations. As labour relations in private industry came under closer scrutiny, and as they became ever more regulated by [labour] law, it became less easy to represent all physical and mental work as a collaborative effort for the good of the company and thus of the economy as a whole: instead, the dependency of the workers and the divide between workers and employers became ever more prominent.[26]

It was axiomatic in industrial circles that if the capitalist economic order was to be preserved, it had to be shown in practice that 'all physical and mental work was a collaborative effort'. Albert Vögler put it with characteristic directness at an association meeting:

> What good is it if you [employers] put your newly acquired knowledge into practice straight away, if a factor as powerful as the workforce isn't fully involved in your work?...and acts like a stranger, or even an enemy, to the works and what goes on there?[27]

It was Vögler again who made one of the most significant attempts to bind the workers closely to the firm in these radically changed circumstances. In Carl Arnhold's German Institute for Technical Training (DINTA), which soon earned itself an extraordinarily high reputation, not just in heavy industry, apprentices were given training in a skilled trade that not only imparted technical proficiency but also nurtured submissiveness and nationalism. The schools were organized on quasi-military principles. In February 1934 Hess took over the Institute as a National Socialist organization, rechristened it as the 'Office for Technical Education and Plant Leadership (Amt für Berufserziehung und Betriebsführung), and incorporated it into the Labour Front. During the war Arnhold was

---

[26] Preller, *Sozialpolitik*, pp. 137–8.   [27] Quoted in ibid., p. 202.

appointed to a high position in the Ministry of Economics.[28] The Institute and the 'yellow' (pro-employer) unions constituted only the most striking and extreme manifestation of a new class conflict waged from above. In virtually every industry a whole series of attempts was made to confirm and increase the power of employers through an ostensibly scientific industrial social policy. The aim was 'to grasp the worker as a whole person and reincorporate him as such in the organism of the plant'.[29]

The big capital-intensive companies in the chemical and electrical industries went to considerable expense to implement this strategy of social gratification and improved productivity, not least because the increased costs scarcely affected their overall balance sheet. Thus by the end of the 1920s IG-Farben was spending over 8 per cent of its salary budget on its social policy, but this represented only a vanishingly small proportion of its total production costs, and the outlay was tax-free.[30] (We may note in passing that the frequent complaints from employers about the supposedly intolerable financial burden of the state's new social policies at this time went hand in hand with a growing readiness to devote considerable resources of their own to specific social welfare policies that served their own interests.) Almost everything that the Labour Front trumpeted in the 1930s as the proud achievements of the Third Reich – 'Beauty of Labour', 'Strength through Joy' and so on – had already been tried and tested in the late 1920s. Rest homes for workers, relaxation rooms in the plant, subsidized hot meals in the works canteen, green spaces round factories, industrial nurses, supplementary insurance, edifying factory news-sheets, propaganda for caring and sympathetic treatment of the workforce, evening events for employees and their families – all these were part of an industrial social policy which in the 1930s became the highly stylized cornerstone of an allegedly unprecedented and unshakable class harmony within the factory community, yet all had already been spreading rapidly before 1930. All that was new after 1933 was the attempt to replace clocking-in with a roll-call, and the organized mass tourism of the Strength through Joy movement. Even the characteristic vocabulary of Nazi rhetoric, with its 'human factor', 'work in its totality as a social institution', 'community thinking', 'leadership quality', the 'joy of work' and the 'factory leader's sense of responsibility' to his workforce, can be found throughout the writings of those who

---

[28] See Robert A. Brady, *The Spirit and Structure of German Fascism* (London 1937); Wolfgang Schlicker, 'Arbeitsdienstbestrebungen des deutschen Monopolkapitals in der Weimarer Republik unter besonderer Berücksichtigung des Deutschen Instituts für technische Arbeitsschulung', *Jahrbuch für Wirtschaftsgeschichte*, 1971, Part III, esp. pp. 102–4; DZA Potsdam, RWM, vol. 10249.

[29] Preller, *Sozialpolitik*, p. 131.   [30] Brady, *Rationalization Movement*, pp. 239–40.

originally advocated this new course in social policy: Goetz Briefs and his school, for example. The really original traits of the system established by the AOG sprang mainly from the dictatorial monopoly which the new philosophy and its attendant institutions could now claim, which also explains in part (though only in part) its astonishingly rapid spread from 1935 onwards.

It seems important to emphasize that the evolution of this industrial social policy into a quasi-scientific and comprehensive method of social control went hand in hand with rationalization. The various forms of this process represented industry's response to the self-inflicted perils of persistent economic class conflict. To its supporters it was the only effective way to endow industry with the peaceful, submissive workforce which the new methods of production required. A powerful impulse in this direction was given by the greatly increased participation of women in industry during the war. Partly owing to the wave of rationalization, this development was not reversed in Germany in the 1920s to the same extent as in England. The prevailing anti-feminist opinion was that women were constitutionally easier to influence than men, and better adapted to boring working procedures; moreover, they were paid less. If women were believed to need special help and protection, this was an even more important argument in this context for it made them into both an appropriate object and a rewarding challenge for a modern approach to management.[31]

As Briefs, Schwenger and others clearly recognized, this approach had very little in common with the archaic paternalism of heavy industry before 1914. The latter had chiefly been concerned with welfare, principally in order to control fluctuations in the workforce. Both the aims and the means of the new industrial social policy were far more extensive: taken together, they constituted a potential programme for stabilizing the social order, and their attention to productivity seemed dynamic and future-oriented. The indispensable prerequisite for this, as both theorists and practitioners were well aware, was a decisive increase in the power of the factory leadership. This was not the defensive make-and-mend of Bismarck's social policy: it was a vision of a new technocratic capitalism, legitimized by its own efficiency, in which the capacity to satisfy the workers by scientifically tested welfare measures and a steady, performance-related improvement in their income played the decisive role.

This vision remained on the far horizon until the world economic

---

[31] See Judith Grünfeld, 'Rationalization and the Employment and Wages of Women in Germany', *International Labour Review*, vol. 29, no. 5 (May 1934), pp. 605–32. The textile industry, which employed many women, was in fact hardly rationalized at all, with the notable exception of Nordwolle AG. See Brady, *Rationalization Movement*, pp. 263 ff.

crisis, but it was also this consciously progressive tendency that found expression in the AOG. And after 1935/6 it became the prime impulse behind National Socialist labour policy. It all came together in a formula whose etymology encapsulates the main argument of this essay: the *Leistungsgemeinschaft* or 'performance-oriented community', which was the ideal of the later 1930s. This community had little room for small farmers, tradesmen or artisans. And it was not Krupp or the Steel Association, and certainly not the artisan trades, that designed and tested the Strength through Joy programme, but Siemens in Berlin. Early in 1934 Siemens asked all its workers to complete a questionnaire on how they spent their free time. The results showed a large unfulfilled demand for holidays away.[32] Vacation programmes were then based on the notion that relaxation would increase production.

We must end this section by raising another difficult set of questions. Practitioners and theorists of industrial social policy both took the view that the problem of immanent social conflict could best be grasped and solved at the point of its sharpest expression, i.e. in the factory. After 1933 this led to the revealing and typically Nazi way of referring to the factory community (*Betriebsgemeinschaft*) as the 'cell' of the national community (*Volksgemeinschaft*), and thus to turns of phrase which, insofar as they were not merely cynical, undeniably had a certain archaic flavour. This could not be said of developments in the 1920s. These later efforts derived from a social vision that was more or less deliberately narrowed to the industrial production process alone, a limited perspective that made it possible to imply that everyone involved belonged to the same community of interests. To promote this, industry's sphere of influence was expanded to take in every aspect of social life that seemed relevant to the production process, and the former was subordinated to the latter. In principle, then, the new industrial social policy claimed a total ascendancy over the worker; his own autonomous impulses, and indeed any undirected or unplanned behaviour, were considered a disruptive factor.

At the same time, it is important to note a radical dichotomy between theory and practice in 1920s social policy, which is being analysed here as an ideal type. In view of the identical development of industrial social policies in the larger American and British industries both before and after the Second World War, it is scarcely appropriate to label the new management techniques of German industrialists before 1933 as a specifically German archaism, as if they were a modern means of manipulation serving a romantic nostalgia for a healthily hierarchical national community. Even if such irrational motives were a personal inspiration to the Thyssens or Kirdorfs, the adoption of these forms of

---

[32] *Siemens-Mitteilungen*, February and July 1934.

industrial social policy was nonetheless a sober, rational and hence compelling way, given the rationalization imposed by economic crisis, to increase the profitability of industry and to tame the militancy of the labour movement. Similarly, the related social ideology, which represents the capitalist enterprise as the heart of the social order, is necessarily shared by any industrialist in an economic system geared to the accumulation of private wealth, whatever his own ideas on the extent to which the social system is relevant to the production process. But even from this viewpoint we can scarcely say that German industry in the 1920s was more narrow-minded, old-fashioned or ruthless in the promotion of its own interests than that of Britain the USA.[33] Things look rather different if we turn from industry to the social sciences or propaganda – areas which cannot clearly be separated from each other in this context. Here the narrow emphasis on shop-floor working conditions as the arena in which class conflict arose and had to be dealt with bears witness to an academic outlook which even then was making a mockery of every tendency in modern social science. The intellectual horizon of most authors can be defined without further qualification as reactionary, and even as specifically German, for it scarcely reached beyond the world imagined by the German romantics, even if this inheritance was enriched by occasional slogans from Catholic social teaching or (more seldom) solid empirical research. As an example we may take Goetz Briefs' great work *The Proletariat. A Challenge to Western Civilization*, published after he went into exile: it is a systematic study of class relations in which he manages to neglect every question of real economic importance (notably growth) and leaves such vital issues as educational opportunity and social mobility entirely out of account.[34] This extremely narrow and static perspective, which is perhaps particularly characteristic of Briefs' work, reduced the whole problematic of class conflict to a question of attitudes, and this left the door wide open for every kind of manipulation. The missionary element in his work wholly outweighed the analysis. His concepts of the joy of work, faithfulness, community and plant unity are admittedly somewhat different from the National Socialists', though it is not easy to show exactly how and why; certainly they were less realistic, because they failed to acknowledge any need for compulsion.[35] But here

---

[33] For a brilliant introduction to the American question see Loren Baritz, *The Servants of Power. A History of the Use of Social Science in American Industry*, 2nd edn (New York 1965). See also Sheldon Wolin, *Politics and Vision* (New York 1960), Chapter 10. On Britain see B. Seebohm Rowntree, *The Human Factor in Business*, 3rd edn (London 1938).

[34] Goetz Briefs, *The Proletariat. A Challenge to Western Civilization* (New York/London 1937).

[35] On this see the remarks by Rene König, *Die Zeit ohne Eigenschaften*, ed. L. Reinisch (Stuttgart 1961) and the devastating methodological criticism by L. von Friedeburg in *Betriebsklima. Eine industriesoziologische Untersuchung aus dem Ruhrgebiet*, ed. T. W. Adorno and W. Dirks, Frankfurter Beiträge zur Soziologie (Frankfurt am Main, 1955), vol. III, p. 14.

again some reservations seem necessary. Although this did not become entirely clear until the years of the Nazi hegemony, a superficially archaic vocabulary could actually disguise thoroughly modern concepts; even if these were only limited in scope, they were solidly built on new techniques of manipulation that were heavy with significance for the future. The language of social ideology alone is not a wholly reliable index of the character of the corresponding social processes; indeed, it is often not even a clue to the intentions of the writers concerned.[36] The complacent and fatal aim of contributing through applied social science to the reconciliation of the German people produced a theory of industrial social policy which inevitably contained a doctrine of political salvation. This outcome could have been prevented only if social scientists had taken the whole phenomenon of class antagonism as their field and investigated the real status of fringe benefits and the 'psychology of labour'. Even reputable social scientists were unable to resist the temptation of trying to resolve class conflict in a solo flight of literary fancy: and a perspective that confined itself to the factory alone was unlikely to question the dubious methodology of the enterprise. Thus, for example, in 1932 Rudolf Schwenger was still writing relatively sensibly about the limits of industrial social policy, but one can already hear the cadences of the technocratic salvationist and his overweening political agenda:

These assumptions suggest a number of positive tasks which arise from the social and human needs of the workplace in the twofold sense we have already mentioned: namely, the careful treatment of the individual in the factory – his effective incorporation into its social order – and the methodical supervision of all interpersonal relations.

Alongside these positive tasks and demands that face each industrial plant, we must also draw attention to the need for defence against any disturbing influences that might put at risk the survival of social order within it. These social disruptions are the main cause of the phenomenon of social unrest. On the one hand, they arise within the plant, from e.g. the deficiencies of labour regulations or factory organization, the inadequate adaption of individuals to the demands of the plant, and interpersonal frictions. Besides these internal disruptions there are

---

[36] To further discussion on the meaning of pre-industrial or archaic elements in recent German history, we urgently need an analysis of political language which would include both a historical and a comparative dimension. Why do people in Britain and the USA not start nervously when they hear the words 'community' or 'leadership'? These and similar terms were frequently bandied about among English and American industrial sociologists at the time. In spite of its fragmentary character and occasionally awkward methodology, I consider that the book by Victor Klemperer, *LTI. Notzibuch eines Philogen* (Berlin 1947), is still the best work in this field. See also Lutz Winkler, *Studie zur gesellschaftliche Funktion faschistischer Sprache* (Frankfurt am Main 1970), and the literature survey by G. Voigt, 'Zur sprache des Faschismus', in *Das Argument*, no. 43 (July 1967), pp. 154–65.

also elements of social disturbance that enter the factory from the outside. These additional entanglements can be understood if we bear in mind that the people in the plant also belong to groups and institutions of other kinds: the worker may be a member of a union, a party or a church. Thus people meet as representatives of organizations and powers alien to the plant and in this way also bring their external social interests and motives with them into the workplace. This gives rise to every conceivable kind of tension, since it means that the struggle between competing spheres of interest is also being fought out within the plant. Today, more than ever, we can speak of a front hostile to the factory that is trying to restrict the latter's autonomy and bring it under the influence of the state or of collective labour law. These influences, internal and external, all tend to alienate the worker further from his workplace. In the interests of self-preservation, therefore, every effort must be made to reduce social disorder in the plant. Alongside its positive tasks, then, the plant is also faced with the defensive task of resisting influences which are alien or hostile to it.[37]

The author's frustration at the disruptive influence of hostile factors and organizations is clearly audible here: without them, he seems to be saying, the plant would become a paradise of peaceful and mutually beneficial co-operation. In 1933 these hostile influences were in fact destroyed, and the worthy Schwenger went on to his next study, industrial social policy in the large industries of western Germany. The results were published in 1934. Schwenger again warned that the limited scope of industrial social policy must be borne in mind, but the words sound like an empty, half-remembered formula, a foreign body in an account which had gained a good deal in frankness and confidence and lost much of its frustration:

Until recently, industrial social policy was not an officially recognized policy with a clearly defined position within social policy as a whole; it was merely tolerated. It was marginal, unobtrusive; sometimes it was even expressly rejected. The marxist parties denied it altogether on principle. The aims of industrial social policy – to pacify the workforce, eliminate disputes, remove the objective grounds for social tension, encourage the worker towards self-help; to stress leadership and productivity, safeguard the existence of the plant, try to turn the worker into a property owner, through industrial housing estates and the allotments movement; to foster national ideas and reject class conflict – all these practical aims of industrial social policy, which are now in the course of being widely realized by the national state, met with determined resistance from that side and also from a section of the trade unions. The living multiplicity of industrial social policies, which arose from specific local and plant conditions, contradicted the ideology and the socio-political concepts of this circle.[38]

[37] 'Die betriebliche Sozialpolitik im Ruhrkohlenbergbau', *Schriften des Vereins für Sozialpolitik*, vol. 186, no. 1 (1932), p. 4.
[38] 'Die betriebliche Sozialpolitik in der westdeutsche Grosseisenindustrie', *Schriften des Vereins für Sozialpolitik*, vol. 186, no. 2 (1934), p. 1. The openness of Briefs and his school to the aggressive radicalism of the right in industrial social policy was clearly revealed by Peter C. Bäumer as early as 1933, in his study 'Das Deutsche Institut für

Schwenger was certainly no Nazi, and his comments on political economy in his second book witness to a conservative reserve *vis-à-vis* those now in power (he himself was more interested in corporatist ideas). But he could feel quite at home in the world of the AOG.

IV

It is probably safe to assume that the pseudo-scientific archaisms of industrial sociology had a good deal less political influence than the tried and tested measures taken by the managers who became factory leaders in January 1934 – men with a sound technical training who were well aware of their duty to look after their employees. A second group of intellectuals demands more attention in this respect, however. The judges in the Reich Labour Court (Reichsarbeitsgericht) probably had far greater influence on the directors of the employers' associations and on the civil service. Their contribution to the AOG needs no very detailed attention here, since Thilo Ramm has recently published a new edition of the outstanding contemporary analysis of their juridical activities by Otto Kahn-Freund.[39] The parallelism between the guiding principles of the Reich Labour Court and the overt aims of the technical innovators in industrial social policy is astonishing. The judges had obviously taken it upon themselves to abolish all the positive rights of individual workers, works councils and unions in every area in which they clashed with the economic interests of the plant. In 1931 Kahn-Freund summed up this tendency as follows:

The Reich Labour Court has licensed an enormous extension of the dictatorial power of the employer: as the court itself has repeatedly emphasized, its object here was to establish the discipline necessary for productivity, which is closely associated with the idea of unity within the plant. This idea is linked to that of the plant as an organism, of the productive community as a collectivity organized on almost romantic, military lines. Employers and employees [are] united in a single organism, as a working community, in which the voluntary subjugation of the one to the command of the other arises in the interests of the common goal of productivity.[40]

One would like to put a question mark, however, after the words 'romantic' and 'military'. We do not yet have adequate research into what aspects of German thought were in fact the source for the social policy

technische Arbeitsschulung (DINTA)', *Schriften des Vereins für Sozialpolitik*, vol. 181 (Munich/Leipzig 1930). Bäumer saw the aims of Arnhold's institute as a form of Taylorism suited to the German character.

[39] Otto Kahn-Freund, 'Das soziale Ideal des Reichsarbeitsgerichts', in T. Ramm (ed.), *Arbeitsrecht und Politik. Quellentexte 1918–1933* (Neuwied 1966).

[40] Ibid., p. 187.

norms of the Labour Court judges.[41] It is at least questionable whether we can isolate their decisions and reasons from the fundamental transformation of industrial relations which was then taking place, and attribute them simply to nostalgia for a healthy *Volksgemeinschaft*. In fact the judges, as Kahn-Freund himself pointed out, showed a very precise understanding of modern factory relations, and were in tune with the times in their readiness to acknowledge, and even reinforce, the formal juridical bases of union organization. But, while the pronouncements of the Labour Court did not challenge the actual existence of the unions, it nonetheless presumed to subject their activities to a rigorous juristic examination: only if they confined themselves to keeping order and supporting the employer could they escape the restrictive and repressive judgements of the court. This massive emphasis on the criteria of economic performance in the pronouncements of the Labour Court casts some doubt on its description as 'romantic' and 'military'.

The economic profitability of the plant was also the chief criterion when the court deliberated on the rights of individual workers, and it was the former that took priority. What was in question was no longer personal freedom, but the economic imperative of modern production methods, the efficiency of which might be seriously damaged by a single unruly worker stubbornly insisting on his rights – not to be required to do overtime, for example. As Kahn-Freund concluded, the Reich Labour Court had

gone a long way towards assuming that the employer has disciplinary powers over the employee; it saw the employee *vis-à-vis* the employer no longer as a party to a contract on equal terms, but as a subordinate under his power. It has replaced the specific obligation to perform labour, which is an essential part of the contractual relationship, by a general subordination.[42]

This finds an echo in Mansfeld's 1941 commentary on the AOG:

Individual labour contracts had hitherto been understood in materialist terms and established only a contractual relation between 'employer' and 'workforce'. This has been replaced by the 'loyalty relationship' [*Treueverhältnis*] between leader and followers which is the foundation of their common activity, and has (along with the employer's welfare responsibilities) to a large extent become the

---

[41] An essential influence was civil service law, with which the judges were surely familiar. At several points in the judgements cited by Kahn-Freund we get the impression of an attempt to apply current aspects of civil service law to industrial relations: see Jane Caplan, 'The Civil Servant in the Third Reich' (D. Phil. thesis, Oxford, 1974). This tradition was not particularly 'romantic' or 'military', and how far it was 'pre-modern' or 'archaic' in the sense I am using here has still to be investigated in detail. The special position of the civil service is often cited as an important example of the specifically German survival of pre-industrial structures, but in fact any modern industrial concern demands a similarly comprehensive, and privileged, subjection of its managers.

[42] Kahn-Freund, 'Das soziale Ideal', pp. 188–9.

juridical foundation of the rights and duties that derive from labour relations. Of course, the contract remains indispensable as the basis for labour relations, and certain material details must be regulated by it. But the contractual relationship with mutual and interdependent rights and duties has been eliminated from the relationship between the entrepreneur and his followers. Their relationship is governed and stipulated by mutual loyalty, loyalty which is, moreover, protected by the precepts of social honour, which for the first time has become the subject of statutory regulation.[43]

Eight years after the Nazi seizure of power, this account was pure wishful thinking, for the state had assumed comprehensive powers over the allocation of labour. However, it faithfully reflected the *intentions* of the legislators, intentions which the Academy of German Law undertook to specify further in 1938, when it proposed a statute intended to remove the contractual element altogether and put the whole of labour law on the basis of a 'community relationship in personal law' (*personenrechtliches Gemeinschaftsverhältnis*).[44] The draft subjected workers to the absolute power of the employer, a power backed up by police terror; and, as became unmistakably clear during the Second World War, this represented one (though certainly not the only one) of the latent tendencies of *modern* capitalism. The economic system, backed up by law, was moving closer to this aim, and there was no opposing power to prevent it.

V

This brings us to the fourth theme of this study. Why did the AOG allow no workers' representation, even a system under strict National Socialist control? A brief answer will suffice here, since Broszat and Sauer have already analysed some of the relevant documentary material.[45] After the destruction of the trade unions the NSBO and the Labour Front quickly grew into a rabidly populist movement which threatened to escape all control, unleashed strikes, tried to enforce wage demands by main force, and insulted respectable industrialists or threatened them with political persecution. For months it remained quite unclear what functions the Labour Front (founded in May 1933) was to have in this field. To prevent the threatened general strike, the Labour Front leader Ley was forced to acknowledge the organization publicly as the unified trade union and to

---

[43] *Die Ordnung der nationalen Arbeit. Handausgabe mit Erläuterungen* (Berlin 1941), p. 3.
[44] The draft can be found for example in W. Siebert, *Das Recht der Arbeit* (Berlin/Leipzig/Vienna 1941).
[45] Martin Broszat, *Der Staat Hitlers. Grundlegung und Entwicklung seiner innerer Verfassung* (Stuttgart 1969), Chapter 5; Wolfgang Sauer, Gerhard Schulz and Karl Dietrich Bracher, *Die nationalsozialistische Machtergreifung* (Cologne/Opladen 1960), Chapter 3, Sections 2 and 3 (Sauer) and Chapter 5, Section 3 (Schulz). My dissertation goes into the following problems in detail.

distance himself sharply from the 'yellow' unions. He cannot have been greatly surprised if his (perfectly sincere) disclaimers to the General German Economic Council (Generalat der deutschen Wirtschaft) on 20 September 1933 met with complete scepticism.[46] For the chief anxiety of the council in summer and autumn of that year was precisely the future of this peculiar and chaotic mass organization, including its immensely swollen and unpredictable wing on the shop-floor, the NSBO. The documentation is extremely patchy and leaves important aspects of industry's defensive fightback unexplained. However, the latter's success was apparent by 27 November when Ley, completely isolated between the NSBO and the industrial associations, was forced to subscribe to an agreement whereby the Labour Front renounced anything resembling union activity and confined itself to education and training. In compensation, and to distract public attention, the agreement was made known at the same rally at which Ley was to announce the foundation of Strength through Joy. Only after that was the minister in a position to open discussions on the final text of the AOG. Amidst the political manoeuvrings of those months the strong emphasis on the factory community represented, above all, a rejection of the indistinct, but radically formulated ambitions of the Nazi mass organizations.[47] Together, the agreement and the Act constituted an important stage in the taming process which turned the Nazi labour movement into a servant of the political and economic elites; and this was an important precursor of the events of 30 June 1934.

If the foregoing remarks have conveyed the impression that the AOG, and the solution it prescribed to social conflict, were a necessary stage in the development of German capitalism, let us end by testing this thesis against a wider background of political and economic history. Without the economic slump and the Nazi seizure of power, the principles of the AOG would surely have remained wishful thinking on the part of the big industrialists and technocrats. The crisis forced German industry to aspire to a solution of this kind, but only the seizure of power made it possible.

If the economic boom had continued, surely no rationalization or innovations in industrial social policy would ever have brought about a fundamental revolution in labour and social policy. If sales had continued to increase, the high investment costs would have been largely covered, and this would have given the industrialists enough room to rein in the unions via concessions on wage policy and legal pressures. This was indeed how German industry – especially the electrical and chemical industries – envisaged the future up to 1929. But the crisis – which is attributable in no small measure to those same large investments – created

[46] A verbal report of this important speech is in Bundesarchiv Koblenz, R43II, vol. 321, no. 1.
[47] There is fresh material on the radicalism of the NSBO in Max Kele, *Nazis and Workers. National Socialist Appeals to German Labor 1919–1945* (Chapel Hill, NC 1972).

a completely new situation in which it became a life-and-death matter for German industry to break the power of the labour movement and pass the costs of the previous increase in capacity on to the working class. As the crisis deepened and widened, this aim extended to the creation of a completely new basis for any future economic upswing: never again should the competitiveness of German industry, and the profitability of individual firms, be endangered by union wage demands backed up by the state. The titanic struggle waged in 1930/2 by the industrial associations against the existing collective wage legislation needs no further description here. In general it was aimed not at the complete destruction of the unions, but at cutting back their functions so drastically that – if industry had had its way – they would scarcely have had the right to call themselves unions at all. This, like the undermining of trade union power by mass unemployment, mentioned above, inevitably set up some of the important preconditions for the events of 2 May 1933.

One aspect of the anti-union struggle deserves special emphasis here: the question of industry-wide settlements. The demand for a return to the 'organic', 'natural', or 'flexible' and 'elastic' system of wage-structuring within each plant was perhaps the spearpoint of the attack on the unions. It united almost all branches of the German economy – handicrafts, heavy industry and farming – in their attack on the labour movement: it was the bond of common political interest which held together their otherwise divergent, and often flatly opposing, political and economic demands. In the economic crisis, the binding nature of wage agreements and the declaration of generally binding agreements by the Ministry of Labour seemed even more totally incompatible with the capitalist economic order. No matter whether this demand was expressed in quaintly old-fashioned or in technocratic terms – it sprang from the laws of urgent economic necessity. The remorseless rise in prices made the question of production costs one of life and death for every single plant; and except for the few industries which were thoroughly cartellized or monopolistic, production costs in the German economy were in fact still very variable.

Preller's argument, that this campaign against standardized wage costs shows some archaic traits, and that the modern sectors of German industry actually found, in the course of von Papen's experiment, that it was in their own interests to maintain the binding nature of wage agreements, has not yet been thoroughly verified. His justification, which is borrowed from the modern theory of market regulation by private industry, is logically convincing, and the argument seems to be supported by the wage policy of the Ministry of Labour after 1934.[48] But we must then ask why the AOG laid so much stress on the individual plant, why

[48] Preller, *Sozialpolitik*, pp. 399 ff.

Reich Minister of Economics Schmitt emphasized just this aspect of the new regulation when he presented the draft to the cabinet.[49] One explanation might invoke the political danger of labour unrest, to which the regime was still exposed in the second half of 1933. In May, to avert the universally feared general strike, the government had decided that the wage levels obtaining at the time of the destruction of the unions could be undercut only in extreme and exceptional circumstances; in general they remained in force, under the supervision of the newly appointed Trustees of Labour. To rescind this concession immediately, at the end of 1933, would have been an act of political suicide. Moreover, the employers discovered that state supervision of wage policy and working conditions, which they had generally regarded with such suspicion, offered in summer and autumn of 1933 a very welcome protection against the incursions of the NSBO. Finally, we must point out that the imposition of obligatory minimum wage levels seemed less intolerable to industry as a whole as the levels themselves were reduced: by May 1933 the cutback in standard wage-rates had already been very considerable. The AOG then empowered employers to structure wages as they saw fit on the basis of the current minimums; to this was added in October 1935 an executive order by which the Trustees could authorize the minimum wage to be undercut in exceptional circumstances.[50] In this admittedly somewhat milder form, the principle of plant autonomy seems to have been most beneficial to all of German industry, at least until the time when labour shortages began to demand an altogether different approach.

These observations tend to confirm the idea that the origins of the AOG are to be sought in historical necessity: the law appears as an inevitable consequence of industrial, economic and technical progress, of the appropriate representation of interests and the unbridled pace of economic development peculiar to industrial capitalism. One important question still remains untouched, however. Without the ruthless destruction of the unions and the works councils, the dream of total managerial control of industry would have remained just a dream; the rationalization and refinement of labour and social policy would have remained without any real direct influence on political and economic class relationships. So long as the mass basis and independence of the trade unions had been assured, the plant leadership's aspiration to total power could never develop beyond a latent potential. The unions were an opposing power capable of limiting and controlling it. The one fundamental political prerequisite for the AOG was not realized until early in 1933.

While during March and April the functionaries in the Ministry of Labour chiselled away at draft regulations to give wage-bargaining

---

[49] See note 17 above.
[50] Fourteenth executive order to the AOG, 15 October 1935 *RGBl* (1935), I, p. 1240.

powers to the 'yellow' unions and suppress the communist works councils, the labour movement was being destroyed root and branch. Although the Reich government itself had obviously decided on a war of attrition against the unions and works councils, bands of fanatical SA men were already ranging through industrial areas of Germany, smashing up trade union offices, killing and torturing innumerable officials, destroying all documents and ransacking safes. At the same time works councils of every union persuasion were being thrown out. When on 16 April 1933 the Nazi leaders resolved to bring the unions to heel and then liquidate them, the German Trade Union Federation (ADGB) had long been reduced to a set of generals without footsoldiers. These leaders had difficulty keeping in step with their own followers. A good many of the trade union offices that were dramatically occupied on 2 May had been under the supervision of NSBO officials for weeks past. The Reich government and the party leadership had certainly taken no effective steps to stem the terror, but there is no convincing evidence that they deliberately planned and unleashed it. The 'brown terror' was the last decisive manifestation of a truly archaic political culture. As soon as it had done its first political service, it immediately became a danger to both the old and the new power elites.

Meanwhile, however, not a single voice was raised among the employers to protest against the destruction of the unions. This turn of events could scarcely have been foreseen in entrepreneurial circles, but nor did it seem particularly ominous to them. As early as 10 March the representatives of German nationalist industrialists had asked the Ministry of Labour whether there was any point in starting wage negotiations in the building industry, since the new agreement might well outlive the partner with which it was made. And on 22 March the employers' association of the German chemical industry was encouraging its members to dismiss any workers who were kept away from work because they had been arrested. The way to the far from archaic utopia of 20 January 1934 was recognizable even in its beginnings.[51]

The basic principle of the new regulation was surely most accurately formulated by Speer: 'Idealism is the best economics [*Wirtschaftlichkeit*].' At that time he was still head of the office for the 'Beauty of Labour'.[52]

[51] DZA Potsdam, RAM, vol. 2185, pp. 90–3; Orwo-Wolfen film factory, company archive, vol. A 3713, fol. 410.
[52] *Die Gemeinschaft*, ed. Gauverwaltung of the Labour Front in Düsseldorf, April 1937.

4

ॐ

INTERNAL CRISIS AND WAR OF AGGRESSION, 1938–1939[1]

I

ACCORDING TO the present state of scholarly knowledge and opinion, Hitler's *Blitzkrieg* strategy was a concept which transformed itself almost directly into an initially successful process of conquest. That is to say, the course of the war until the middle or end of 1941 corresponded to, and at the same time justified, an original, well thought out and long-premeditated strategic concept. Reduced to its essentials, the argument runs approximately as follows. Hitler very soon realized that Germany's economic resources were insufficient for a European war. What the Four Year Plan dubbed a 'policy of autarky' was so called for purely propagandist reasons, while the real aim was simply forced rearmament – not economic independence from possibly unfriendly powers, which was generally acknowledged to be impossible within Germany's existing frontiers. The conditions for a policy of autarky could be produced only by a step-by-step expansion of the area of Central Europe under German control. Only the economic potential of a Greater German Reich, enlarged by annexations and by the creation of satellite states, could support the decisive struggle, a war against France and the USSR. And only the conquest of the Ukraine could create the basis for a world war against Britain, which would then no longer be in a position to reduce Germany to submission by blockade.

This chapter was translated by Rosemary Morris.
[1] This contribution has also been published in a slightly altered form, in Gilbert Ziebura (ed.), *Grundfragen deutscher Aussenpolitik seit 1871* (Darmstadt 1975). I am grateful to the Wissenschaftliche Buchgesellschaft for their permission to republish. I have published and discussed the source material on the economic and social history of Nazi Germany on which I have drawn for this study in my document edition, *Arbeiterklasse und Volksgemeinschaft. Dokumente und Materialien zur deutschen Arbeiterpolitik 1936–1939* (Opladen 1975). For this reason I have dispensed here with a full critical apparatus of sources, and have restricted myself to brief references.

In the light of this hypothesis, the phase of annexations and *Blitzkrieg* appears as the means to an end, the end being to create the preconditions for waging a war for world conquest. Timing was of the essence for this strategic concept. The initiative had always to remain with the German leadership, so that the European war would not break out prematurely, before Germany's economic potential for war was equal to the task. One step must follow another, with the task of German diplomacy being to maintain the isolation of each targeted state in turn.

Scholarly research into the origins of the Second World War has concentrated overwhelmingly on just this aspect. It has attributed a breathtakingly brutal realism to Hitler's underlying strategy, which so nearly led to the subjugation of Europe. The vital mistake, in fact, is said to have been Germany's inadequate diplomatic preparation for the attack on Poland, which led to the fatally premature declaration of war by England. This entailed tactical and political misjudgements that doomed the Nazi bid for world power, because the conflict with England got in the way of the attack on Russia. Long before Germany had had a chance to complete the economic reordering and absorption of the European territories it had annexed, occupied and reduced to dependency, the Nazi regime was embroiled in a world war, against powers that were its economic superiors in every way. It was not the *Blitzkrieg* concept itself that entailed defeat and collapse, but the mistaken way its inventor put it into practice: such, in sum, seems to be the generally accepted Western view of this question.[2]

The last five years have seen more intensive research into the economic and social history of the Third Reich, and it now seems time to subject the above version of the outbreak of war in 1939 to a critical examination. If we approach the question from this point of view, two big questions arise. The first is somewhat hypothetical. Up to November 1937, Hitler still thought that the best strategy would be to unleash the European war sometime between 1943 and 1945. But was this economically and socially feasible? Could Germany have waited so long? Second, we need to take a closer look at the domestic significance of the occupation of Prague and the invasion of Poland, which means above all their significance in terms of economic policy. Here we need to ask whether the room for diplomatic calculation was not greatly circumscribed by the symptoms of domestic crisis. The answers that I will propose to this second question go far to reduce the purely hypothetical character of the first. The Nazi leaders' intense antipathy to the written word and the consequent paucity of

---

[2] A. J. P. Taylor, *The Origins of the Second World War*, 5th impression (London 1963), takes this argument to absurd lengths. The fundamental principles of Hitler's *Blitzkrieg* concept are given detailed and discriminating treatment in Berenice A. Carroll, *Design for Total War. Arms and Economics in the Third Reich* (The Hague 1968), Chapter 5.

sources, especially of verbatim reports of Hitler's discussions of the strategic situation, prevent us from making any unambiguous connections between the two questions. What follows is therefore – to borrow an entirely appropriate phrase from the criminal law – circumstantial evidence.

To decide how far Hitler's freedom of manoeuvre in foreign policy was circumscribed by domestic and economic circumstances in Germany, we must first establish the essential features of the situation. The following, very abbreviated, analysis therefore concentrates exclusively on the most important crises of that crisis-ridden time. This is not just because these crisis-related phenomena are especially relevant to my argument about the function of the war of aggression. My emphasis is consistent with the tenor of all the surviving documents from the relevant ministries: from their point of view, there seem to have been no problems of economic or social policy in 1938/9 for which unambiguous solutions were ready to hand. The forced preparation for war from early 1938 had overstrained capacity and reserves on every side. The situation was especially critical with regard to financial policy, foreign trade, agriculture and the labour market. Difficulties in these areas then merged into an all-embracing crisis of the entire economic and governmental system; at the heart of it lay the question of how the social product should be divided between military and civil needs. To put it another way, the government was faced with the acute political problem of how much sacrifice they could demand of the people for the sake of rearmament and war. However, before we can understand and evaluate this all-embracing crisis in domestic policy, and its influence on foreign policy, we must first say a little about its individual components.

Schacht's resignation as president of the Reichsbank in January 1939 was only the most striking sign that public finances had got out of hand. The enormous increases in expenditure on armaments between 1936 and 1938 had produced two separate financial problems, which became even more acute before the beginning of the war. On the one hand, to ensure the availability of funds for armaments the government was forced to use methods which – as Schacht and his colleagues rightly warned – entailed great dangers for the domestic economy.[3] The national debt had tripled since 1933, burdening the budget with ever-increasing interest payments and leaving the capital market in a state which made private investment increasingly difficult. Following the New Financial Plan of March 1939, tax vouchers were issued as payment for the delivery of armaments: this was at most a very short-term solution, and it meant that the state had to sacrifice a considerable part of its future income.[4] The government's

[3] Edward N. Peterson, *Hjalmar Schacht. For and Against Hitler* (Boston MA 1954), p. 304.
[4] Note by the Reich Chancellery, 16 January 1939. Bundesarchiv Koblenz R43II, vol. 417b. Fritz Federau, *Der Zweite Weltkrieg. Seine Finanzierung in Deutschland* (Tübingen 1962), pp. 22 ff.

framework for future financial planning was quite unclear and confused, including in technical details. In May 1939, for example, Hans Posse, Secretary of State in the Ministry of Economics, could see no way to finance the war and wrote a detailed memorandum to that effect, concluding that at best part of the national debt would simply have to be written off after the war.[5] The same anxieties were expressed even more clearly in Hitler's order to the Wehrmacht to cut back sharply in expenditure in the first quarter of 1939 (the fact that the order was evidently ignored is of secondary importance for our present purposes).[6] This, like the fact that new investments in the production of synthetic fuels were postponed, allegedly for lack of capital, may point to a lingering influence of Schacht's ideas. All in all, the political, military and economic leaderships were building up uncontrollable inflationary pressures as a consequence of the rearmament programme; but until summer 1939 they remained unreconciled to the fact, or could not see the fiscal way to this goal in the face of Schacht's criticisms. Thus there were certain financial and political bottlenecks which partially and temporarily slowed down rearmament and the preparations for war.

Especially noteworthy is the fact that the Reich government felt unable to implement a decisive tax increase before the beginning of the war. The only exception was the gradual rise in corporation tax from 15 per cent to 40 per cent, whereas the vast majority of the population was unaffected by the supertax introduced in the New Financial Plan. In spite of the inescapable worsening of the financial crisis, the regular levels of sales and income tax remained unaltered until September 1939. The policy which was to be both consequence and solution was sketched out by Göring as early as December 1936: compensation through victory, and no delay in order to calculate costs.[7] During the war Hitler gave somewhat clearer expression to the same idea:

Since we brought back compulsory military service our armaments have swallowed huge deficit expenditures. Now there are just two ways: either this debt will be passed on in the course of time to the German people in the Reich, or it will be paid out of the potential profits from the conquered eastern regions. The last solution is obviously the right one.[8]

However, finding the resources was only one side of the financial and

---

[5] Bundesarchiv/Militärarchiv Freiburg im Breisgau (Military Department of the West German Federal Archives, files of the War Economy Staff of the High Command of the Armed Forces; henceforth BA/MA Freiburg), WiIF5, vol. 420/3.

[6] Decree of 7 December 1938; ibid., vol. 203; see Burton H. Klein, *Germany's Economic Preparations for War* (Cambridge, MA 1959), Chapter 1.

[7] Peterson, *Hjalmar Schacht*, pp. 280–2. We still lack a detailed examination of this whole question.

[8] Henry Picker and Percy Ernst Schramm (eds.), *Hitlers Tischgespräche im Führerhauptquartier 1941/42*, 2nd edn (Stuttgart, 1965), p. 208 (25 March 1942). Federau gives a brief but sound survey of this very important aspect of Hitler's war of plunder.

political problem: the effects of state expenditure on the domestic economy must also be examined. There can no longer be much doubt that a colossal inflation was in progress, although the inadequate price statistics of the time make it impossible to illustrate this development with reliable figures.[9] The basic problem was that the effective domestic demand stimulated by the armaments boom had outstripped the productive capacity of the German economy. This development can be seen (inter alia) in the fact that the national income (in relation to actual prices) rose faster after 1937 than industrial production.[10] Scholars have credited the Reich Commissariat for Price Control, set up in autumn 1936, with considerable efficiency, but the impression given by the flood of ordinances and regulations proceeding from that quarter is deceptive. From ministry to ministry, the complaints about ever-rising prices refused to go away; one Trustee of Labour recorded more than a thousand price increases in his district in a single day. Reich Price Commissar Josef Wagner himself soon came to the conclusion that the plenary powers he had been given to stabilize prices would remain meaningless unless these purely formal, toothless means of administrative control were extended by giving his officials real powers in wage-setting and in the entire system of government contracts: prices were the end product of economic processes, and could be influenced only by a planned intervention in those same processes.[11] Even more critical for the development of the price situation over the years was the fact that it was not until the beginning of 1939 that government contracting was subjected, gradually, to unified price controls. Until then, in the absence of comprehensive economic planning, government purchasing agents had basically to depend on financial power in order to satisfy the increasing demands: the dominant position of the military sector of the economy was achieved by credit expansion rather than by rational planning and distribution of resources. Because of the accelerated pace of rearmament the armed forces, the Autobahn Commission, the Labour Front and others were very generous in their patronage of industry. This situation gave a hefty impulse to inflation, which by 1939 was proving extremely difficult to control. If we consider that in 1938 public expenditure as a whole took up some 50 per cent of the national income, it becomes easy to trace the vicious circle in which the economy was trapped. Long before the outbreak of war the government's inflationary spending policy had meant that the purchasing power of the

[9] Thus, for example, the official building price index was based on the by now largely irrelevant standard wage levels, not on what workers actually earned.

[10] Figures in Carroll, *Design for Total War*, pp. 184 ff., and Walter Hoffman, *Das Wachstum der deutschen Wirtschaft seit der Mitte des 19. Jahrhunderts* (Berlin/Heidelberg, 1965), justify this – necessarily very broad – calculation.

[11] Detailed petition to Göring from Wagner, 12 December 1937; Bundesarchiv Koblenz R43II, vol. 355.

government's contract agents was itself being eroded. At the same time, and for the same reason, the bigger the deficit in the domestic economy, the more expensive became the very goods and services which the state most urgently needed. Göring's remark at the first session of the Reich Defence Council (Reichsverteidigungsrat) in November 1938 was perfectly justified: 'Gentlemen, the financial situation looks very critical.' But he could not yet bring himself to accept a solution in the form of a planned redistribution of economic capacity to the advantage of the armaments sector.[12]

As early as September 1936, the adoption of the Four Year Plan represented a more or less deliberate decision to let inflation destroy the German money and credit economy and throw the real costs of rearmament on to other peoples and economies which would be conquered in the future. The fiscal consequences of this policy were only thinly veiled up to the outbreak of war. Allowing this crisis to develop, however, was supposed to help contain another source of crisis: the permanent shortage of foreign exchange, a consequence of the First World War and the slump, had been made many times more acute by rearmament. The demand for strategically important raw materials from abroad was rising inexorably; the capacity of important export industries was being increasingly concentrated on economically attractive military projects, so that in 1938 there was a clear 'export fatigue'; the export market's lack of raw materials and personnel became more and more serious as the demand from the armaments sector went on growing, so that inflation made German exports yet more difficult; and, finally, the international armaments boom Germany had unleashed had caused a general increase in the price of imported raw materials. The increased domestic production of synthetics following the Four Year Plan had some modest success up to the outbreak of war, but the anticipated improvement in the balance of payments never took place, since demand in all sectors was rising faster than supply.

It was only a significant and completely unexpected improvement in world trade in 1937, which increased German imports by 30 per cent and exports by 25 per cent, that created the basis for accelerated rearmament foreseen by the Four Year Plan. This respite came to an abrupt end with the American recession late in 1937, after which the difficulties of German exporters became more acute just as the preparations for war were increasing the demand for imports. Repeated orders from Göring to give absolute priority to export orders had little effect. So serious was the position that Germany began systematically to export the very weapons that were so urgently needed by the armed forces. From mid-1938

---

[12] Minutes and memorandum on the meeting, 18 November 1938; BA/MA Freiburg, WiIF5, vol. 560/1.

Germany's trade position was marked by considerable fluctuations.[13] The annexations between March 1938 and March 1939 initially brought a temporary respite in the form of plundered weapons, cash and stocks of raw materials. When considering how the future then looked it is important to remember that the newly incorporated areas were themselves heavily dependent on foreign trade. The takeover of Vienna and Prague certainly strengthened Germany's trade position in south-eastern Europe, but a study by the War Economy Staff (Wehrwirtschaftsstab) showed that all these regions together could meet, at most, one-third of Germany's import requirements.[14] The accumulation of clearing debts and devaluation of the 'Aski-mark' in the last eighteen months before the war offered further evidence of the imminent collapse of the whole exchange system.

Considering this situation, the management of the available foreign exchange was remarkably lax. Although the distribution of reserves could have been rationally administered by the supervisory offices, the armaments sector gained only limited benefits from the controls. Thus, food imports never again reached either the value or the volume of the 1928/9 level, but the upward trend after the turnabout of 1935/6 (the Darré-Schacht controversy) was unmistakable. The actual value of these exports was RM 1.44 billion in 1935, RM 2.39 billion by 1938; during the same period the proportion of food imports to total imports rose from 34.5 per cent to 39.5 per cent. Among these imported goods were quasi-luxuries like leaf tobacco, coffee, cocoa, etc., imports of which in 1938/9 were both absolutely and proportionately considerably above the 1929 level. The steering of industrial imports towards the rearmament programme was more successful, but in 1938 the clothing needs of the German people still accounted for a good 30 per cent of industrial imports; the rise in living standards from 1936 to 1938 further increased imports of wool, yarn and woollen goods.[15]

But only if we contrast these facts with the gaping holes in supplies of imported raw materials to the armed forces can we see their relevance to the regime's policy of expansion. For these exchange concessions to the consumer coincided with an acute shortage of steel, various light metals, rubber, petrol and oil, to mention only a few of the most serious gaps in the drive for rearmament which cast doubt on the preparedness of the armed forces. Even in the summer of 1939 a war of plunder was certainly

---

[13] This is another problem that requires further research. There is an outline in Dietmar Petzina, *Autarkiepolitik im Dritten Reich. Der nationalsozialistische Vierjahresplan* (Stuttgart 1968). See also the excellent treatment by Hans-Erich Volkmann, 'Aussenhandel und Aufrüstung in Deutschland 1933 bis 1939', in F. Forstmeier and H.-E. Volkmann (eds.), *Wirtschaft und Rüstung am Vorabend des zweiten Weltkrieges* (Düsseldorf 1975), pp. 81–131.

[14] 'Stand der wirtschaftlichen Lage', February 1939; BA/MA Freiburg, Wi I5, vol. 176.

[15] *Statistisches Handbuch von Deutschland 1928–1944* (Munich 1949), pp. 396–408.

not the only way out of the impasse, but anyone proposing such a strategy did not have to look too hard for justifications, especially if he were unwilling to limit the use of private cars so that the armed forces could have their desperately needed petrol.

In the two areas of domestic policy so far examined, the political leadership retained a certain room for manoeuvre up to, and even after, the outbreak of war. But there was really no way to stem the crisis in agriculture – at least, not without facing up to quite radical changes of course in both the economic and the political spheres. Owing to its subordination to rearmament, by 1938 the 'battle for production' had gone as far as it could reasonably go. In that year there was an exceptionally good grain harvest, but if the weather was friendly it only contrasted with the far from friendly outlook in social relations in every other aspect of agriculture. Production for that year in almost all the labour-intensive areas fell back sharply, reaching at best the previous year's levels; and if this was less often mentioned in public than the record harvest, it occupied all the more space in internal government memoranda. However welcome the build-up of grain stocks for the army in the forthcoming war, it was no less worrying to consider the shortage of foods such as dairy products, fruit and vegetables, i.e. the very foods that had to be imported and paid for with foreign exchange. Although a foot-and-mouth epidemic had something to do with it, the falling production and rising imports of 1938 were due above all to a shortage of labour. For various reasons it is not easy to give a precise statistical account of the flight from the land in the 1930s. The Ministry of Labour estimated that the number of those employed on the land fell by about half a million between June 1933 and June 1938. That meant a total drop of only some 6 per cent. But those who left were almost all agricultural wage-workers, a group agriculture was least able to do without; their numbers fell from 2.5 million to 2.1 million, i.e. by 16 per cent.[16]

These workers were forbidden to leave the land and bombarded with propaganda, but to no effect: the attraction of industry for the rural population strengthened as wages increased and the agricultural and industrial price scissors began to widen once more. All interested parties were agreed that the flight from the land was attributable in the first place to the difference in living standards between town and country. Here again statistics are lacking, but there is no doubt that the difference had increased between 1936 and 1939. After the controversies of 1935, it became almost impossible to increase the price of any agricultural product: in January 1939 Reichsminister Darré tried in vain to convince Hitler of the need for a modest increase in the price of milk and fats and a

[16] Ibid., pp. 31–2, 124–5, 190–3, 215.

big (25 per cent) rise in the price of butter. On the other side, with few exceptions (the most important being artificial fertilizers), the prices of industrial products required for agriculture rose sharply – that of artificial fertilizers comparatively least. This threatened to plunge farmers back into debt; and for all these reasons they were in no position to offer wages and conditions that could compete with those in industry. Darré spared no effort to convince the government of the seriousness of the problem. In the Reich Chancellery the detailed descriptions piled up: villages where the farmers were selling their milk cows to the knacker, farmers' wives collapsing under the weight of overwork, and sons and labourers who would do anything to get a job in industry.[17] Information from other authorities told the same story. In April 1938 the Minister of Labour himself reckoned that agriculture was short of 250,000 labourers, but he could suggest no solution other than to reintroduce and stiffen the licence requirement for agricultural labourers seeking to change their jobs (10 March 1939). But in 1936 such compulsion had already proved a complete failure.[18]

Darré's own diagnosis was as unanswerable as the demands he derived from it were unachievable: the number of government contracts (by which he meant armaments orders, though he dared not say so) must be drastically cut so as to free industry from inflationary pressures and relieve the labour market to the point where the number of jobs would be equal to that of the available workers. If there was no chance of raising prices for agricultural products, then at least all industrial prices and wages should be reduced by at least one-quarter. Typically, Hitler found no time to discuss this programme with Darré.[19] Industry could not do without the flight from the land; agriculture would have to wait for the war to resolve its labour problem, with the transfer of hundreds of thousands of forced labourers and prisoners of war. Just as the attack on Poland was ending, the government was in process of detailing German schoolchildren for compulsory labour to bring in the harvest. Luckily, it then proved possible to use not only prisoners, but also several army divisions which were not needed on any front during the succeeding weeks.

However, the flight from the land was by no means sufficient to meet industry's growing need for labour. What in summer 1936 could be described as bottlenecks in one particular region, skill or industry grew,

---

[17] Numerous reports from Darré and his colleagues: Bundesarchiv Koblenz R43II, vol. 213b, p. 611.

[18] Second Executive Order to the Decree on the Supply of Adequate Labour for Projects of Exceptional National Political Importance (*VO zur Sicherstellung des Kräftebedarfs für Aufgaben von besonderer staatspolitischer Bedeutung*), *Reichsgesetzblatt (RGBl)* (1939), I, p. 444. Similar restrictions had been in force between 1934 and 1936.

[19] Darré's comprehensive memorandum of 21 January 1939; Bundesarchiv Koblenz R43II, vol. 213b.

in the course of the Four Year Plan, into a generalized discrepancy between the productive capacity of the German economy and the size of the working population. The multiple consequences of this development, whose importance can scarcely be over-estimated, will be indicated in due course. First, however, we must sketch the general extent of the problem. After May 1938 there were no more reserves to be found among the registered unemployed: on the day of registration they were either in process of changing their jobs, or had only a limited capacity for work. The most important industries – agriculture, building, metals – had already reached this stage nine months earlier. In December 1938 the Minister of Labour estimated that the economy was short of about one million workers. The shortage had increased further by the time war broke out.[20]

The surviving sources leave no doubt that this was the most significant constraint in the economics of rearmament. After May 1938 the various responsible (but impotent) departments were beset by a sea of ever-increasing troubles both in state concerns and in big private companies: late deliveries, unfilled export orders, major building projects left uncompleted, etc., were all to be blamed chiefly on the shortage of labour. Even Carl Krauch, with plenary powers over special problems of chemical production, an area which enjoyed a high priority, saw his plans endangered from the same cause. Thus, in summer 1939 one group of munitions factories in central Germany was short of 3,000 workers; only with the greatest difficulty, and after a considerable time, were they able to reduce this figure by two-thirds. Krauch was in charge of sites for new factories destined to produce fuel and artificial rubber (*Buna*) for the Wehrmacht: in August 1939 they were short of 13,000 building workers. The Luftwaffe estimated that the aircraft industry was in need of 2,600 additional engineers. The Ministry of Labour screwed this demand down to 1,500, but in the end only 153 engineers could be supplied. In the Ruhr there was a shortfall of 30,000 miners, so that in early 1939 the government had no choice but to stop coal exports and cut back on the already inadequate deliveries to the railways. At about the same time the president of the Hanover labour exchange announced that there were 100,000 jobs vacant in his district. In August 1939 the Postal Minister opined that the telephone service, which was of critical wartime importance, was no longer fully functional owing to the shortage of personnel. In the same month, the harbour at Königsberg was blocked for over a week because the available dockers were quite unable to cope with the volume of work. At this juncture Hitler made the rather surprising suggestion

[20] Seldte to Lammers, 17 December 1938; Bundesarchiv Koblenz R43II, vol. 533. Essential sources for this whole problem are the extracts from the reports by the Trustees of Labour; ibid., vol. 528.

that 70,000 policemen should be made available; but attempts to relieve the labour market through a general squeeze on the administration failed because no civil servants could be freed for these heavy tasks: the state apparatus was itself swamped by the flood of new duties. Government and industry devised a whole series of possible measures for dealing with this key problem, but they were all either long term (rationalization) or politically unacceptable (conscription of women's labour). Plundering workers from other countries was not only quicker, but also posed fewer political problems.

As pointed out at the beginning of this essay, these four emerging crises in economic and social policy came together as a comprehensive politico-economic crisis of the whole system of government. From the economic viewpoint the issues were the relationship between military and non-military needs, and the distribution of resources and of the social product. The labour shortage itself had a critical effect on the economic aspects of this crisis: in the last years before the war it caused a great surge in wage levels. On the one side, industrial workers were trying to make up for the long years of deprivation and oppression by a determined use of their newly acquired market value; on the other, employers in the expanding armaments sector had no choice but to attract the ever-increasing number of workers they needed by offering higher wages. The position of white-collar workers was much the same. The result was an increase in the buying power of working people which led to a full exploitation of capacity in the consumer goods sector, where wage levels also rose sharply after 1936. Between December 1935 and June 1939 the average hourly wage in industry rose by 10 per cent. Because of the sometimes considerable lengthening of working hours, the weekly wage rose by 17.4 per cent, with the rate of increase growing higher all the time.[21] It was armaments workers who received the greatest increases. In 1939 the average German male worker's pay-packet contained RM 5.80 more than it had in 1936, a female worker's RM 2.50 more. If we also take into account the increase in jobs, the buying power of wage-earners alone rose by about RM 200 million per week between 1936 and 1939. Private expenditure for the year 1939 amounted to about RM 66 billion – RM 2 billion more than in 1929, to which one must add the fact that living costs had decreased by a good 10 per cent over the previous ten years. Thus on the eve of war, the consumer power of the German people was quite markedly higher than it had been before the slump. The only contrary trend was the 5.5 million increase in the population during the same period, which meant that the total purchasing power was somewhat more thinly spread. Let us conclude by saying that not only were all classes

[21] Gerhard Bry, *Wages in Germany, 1871–1945* (Princeton, NJ 1960), pp. 242–3.

doing much better economically in 1939 than in 1929, but also – contrary to a widespread assumption – the average real weekly wage of workers had regained the 1929 level, and in most cases significantly overtaken it. This impression is fully confirmed by the development of official figures for consumption and turnover.[22]

It is by no means easy to evaluate this state of affairs. Insofar as it has been noticed at all in the literature, it has been evaluated in a different context of interpretation from the one that seems appropriate here. Thus it has been rightly emphasized that civilian consumption as a proportion of the social product, and wages as a proportion of the national income, both fell steadily after 1935/6: in other words, that the National Socialist system was successful in intensifying economic exploitation in the interests of rearmament and capital accumulation. It is, however, indisputable – and this is decisive for our present purposes – that the sharp cutback in consumption in 1937-9 was quite inadequate for the urgent rearmament programme. On the contrary, it was in those years that the reins began to slip from the government's grasp. Thus up to 1939 investment in new plant for the consumer industry far exceeded the highest levels since 1918[23] – but this utilized capacity and reserves that could have been put at the disposal of the armaments industry. In November 1939 General Thomas made the bitter, but hardly unjustified remark that 'we are never going to conquer England with radios, vacuum cleaners and kitchen equipment'.[24]

Ignoring for the moment the expansionist policies of the regime, we can see two additional elements that determined the politicization of this latent crisis and so turned it into a crisis of the whole system of rule. Even in 1938 the government's policy of unplanned expansion of credit and production had led it up a blind alley. It had put the economy as a whole under an intolerable strain, and the word 'overburdened' (*überbelastet*) features in almost every report on the economy from 1938 and 1939. Then the blinkered insistence on the end product that marked this policy began to produce grotesque consequences: output of munitions was limited by a shortage of machine tools, because the tool factories were short of workers and raw materials; the building industry had succeeded in attracting many additional workers from the building materials industry, and consequently ran into a serious shortage of such materials. The railways had failed to build up their rolling stock, so that the transport system was quite unequal to the increased demands made on it.

[22] This complex nexus of problems is analysed in detail in the Introduction to my *Arbeiterklasse und Volksgemeinschaft* (see note 1 above). As the cost-of-living index was being deliberately falsified at that time, all figures must be treated with caution.

[23] Petzina, *Autarkiepolitik*, p. 185.

[24] Georg Thomas, *Geschichte der deutschen Wehr- und Rüstungswirtschaft (1918–1943/45)*, ed. W. Birkenfeld (Boppard am Rhein 1966), p. 501.

The whole economic system was so strained that any one hold-up immediately caused another. These multiple shortages, which constituted a kind of negative multiplier effect, were the chief distinguishing mark of the situation just before the outbreak of war. It was not, as has often been maintained, a case of a few bottlenecks here and there: it was a general economic crisis. The ensuing frictions and delays in production, together with the increased wear and tear on men and machines, drew complaints from industry that the viability of their plants was threatened. By summer 1939 all departments concerned were up to their necks in the crisis and could see no way out of it, as several big armaments firms refused to accept any more orders from the armed forces because they could no longer guarantee delivery.[25] The strain on the economy had got to the point where the long-overdue redistribution of capacities and resources could not be further postponed. It was simply no longer possible to finance further expansion of the armaments sector by inflationary credit expansion.

Set alongside this was the second element in the overall crisis. As we can deduce from Hitler's ever-rarer public appearances, the regime was beginning to admit to itself that its hopes of maintaining mass enthusiasm for its project of racist imperialism had not been entirely fulfilled. After the summer of 1938 it was more a case of holding the population down and stemming the rising wave of discontent, opposition and demoralization. State-backed police terror, so effective against political opposition, proved quite inadequate to the changed circumstances. Exemplary punishment of randomly selected 'layabouts', contract-breakers or 'saboteurs' had little success. The government was reduced to bribing the population as a whole: they had to buy back the goodwill of the governed. Hitler had long ago recognized that the living standards of the German people could only be kept down for a short time while war was being prepared.[26] This was also the background for a series of decisions which were either made or neglected between 1936 and 1942. Thus in 1936 the Labour Front increased pressure on companies to improve their welfare provision, despite opposition from industry and the ministerial bureaucracy.[27] From 1937 wage-earners were once again paid for national holidays.[28] In 1938 Hitler categorically refused to agree to a plan for priorities in the national economy; a year later he refused even to discuss the acute crisis in agriculture with Darré, let alone accept food-price increases. Evidently it was Hitler's and Göring's attitude that lay behind

---

[25] The most important sources on the crisis in the armaments industry in 1939 are the comprehensive analyses by the War Economy Staff (Wehrwirtschaftsstab) based on reports of the individual defence inspectors; BA/MA Freiburg, WiIF5, vol. 176.

[26] *Hitlers Zweites Buch*, ed. Gerhard Weinberg, (Stuttgart 1961), pp. 53, 121.

[27] Hitler was patron of the Campaign for Productivity in German Industry.

[28] Order of 3 December 1937: *Deutscher Reichsanzeiger (DRA)* 1937, no. 280.

the refusal to increase taxes. When in 1939 a coupon system for food rationing was introduced, Hitler was angry and disturbed to think of the probable effects on popular opinion.[29] This anxiously concessionary and cautious approach did not simply coincide with the achievement of full employment, although that massively increased the pressure on government. The relaxation in attitudes, in areas so vital to the armaments economy, went back much further, perhaps to May 1935 when the attempt to hold down wage increases was deliberately abandoned, or to September 1936, when ministerial proposals for labour conscription were significantly toned down by Hitler and Göring. Afterwards it was almost too late, as Göring himself admitted. In November 1938 he told the assembled Reich ministers, commanders of the armed forces and secretaries of state that shutting down part of the consumer sector for the benefit of the armaments industry was simply impracticable: buying power being what it was, any such step would only lead to inflation.[30] Even in cases where the political leadership had attempted to promote rearmament by introducing an element of overt compulsion, the results, owing to a less than rigorous enforcement, fell far short of what was required. The clearest example of this is the effect of the state wages policy introduced in June 1938. The first year of would-be stabilization and cutbacks saw the average hourly and weekly wage in industry rise significantly faster than in the previous twelve months.[31] The introduction of civilian labour conscription produced similar results. This brutal attack on the few surviving rights of the working class did have some success in short-term crisis situations (the building of the West Wall, redeployment at the beginning of the war); but before then the government obviously shrank from the systematic use of its plenary powers in order to cover the 'normal', urgent manpower shortage in the armaments industry.[32] One of the main reasons for this irresolution was briefly referred to by Göring in a meeting with representatives of the War Economy Staff; the stenographer noted succinctly: 'Führer wants to take as few decisions as possible.'[33]

Such an accommodating economic attitude may have had its uses as a political bribe, but the economic overstrain already briefly described is enough to explain why it was bound to lead to trouble. Moreover, the

[29] Elisabeth Wagner (ed.), *Der Generalquartiermeister. Briefe und Tagebuchaufzeichnungen des Generalquartiermeisters des Heeres General der Artillerie Eduard Wagner* (Munich/Vienna 1963), p. 106.
[30] Speech before the National Defence Council, 18 November 1938. See note 12 above.
[31] Wage regulation of 25 June 1938; *RGBl* I, p. 91; Bry, *Wages in Germany*, pp. 242–3.
[32] Decree on the Supply of Adequate Labour for Projects of Exceptional National Importance, 22 June 1938, *RGBl* I, p. 652; executive order, 11 July 1939, *Reichsarbeitsblatt* (*RArbBl*) I, p. 345.
[33] Note on a conference of 18 July 1938; BA/MA Freiburg, WiIF5, vol. 412.

working population did not respond to the concessions with the hoped-for political loyalty or harder work. When Göring, at the Nazi Party rally of 1938, announced that the cultivation of hops was to be increased in the coming year, he was warmly applauded, it is true, and the numbers of those holidaying with the Strength through Joy organization grew every year, but neither rewards of this kind nor the bait of higher wages could turn the working class into a willing tool of fascist expansionism. The economic and political causes of this growing resistance, already perceptible at the end of 1937, were hard to disentangle. Job security and narrow defence of personal interests were accompanied by an unbroken consciousness and a rejection of the entire regime. State, Labour Front and employers worked unremittingly to politicize workers' attitudes through their ordinances, punishments, exhortations and appeals, all of which unmistakably showed the consequences for rearmament of sinking morale. And yet discipline at work declined sharply. The chorus of complaints about open rebelliousness, skiving off, unpunctuality, absenteeism, poor performance etc., grew even louder through 1938 and 1939. Productivity in the two industries where it was easiest to measure – mining and building – fell sharply during this time. Similar, though less precise, reports issued from other industries. Moreover, the figures for 'genuine' illness rose; this was generally attributed to exhaustion, but behind it both employers and leading civil servants scented gross negligence on the part of equally overworked doctors. Passive or active opposition was particularly stimulated by occasional state interventions like the fixing of maximum wage rates or the compulsory relocation of workers. Such measures repeatedly met with decisive rejection by the workers, making the authorities even more doubtful that an adequate economic and social policy for rearmament could ever be implemented. They were not helped by the National Socialist press, which had long sought superficial popularity by empty claims of success. Goebbels and his colleagues evidently thought that the task of persuading the workers of the need for personal sacrifice and renunciation to promote the regime's main aims was simply too difficult. The Labour Front, too, failed completely in its allotted task of turning the working class into the mindless instrument of the ruling power. Leading functionaries in this mammoth organization were not backward with their criticisms of interference by state authorities, and stuck to their demands for increased welfare provision – otherwise they would scarcely have dared to show their faces before their clientele. They even tried to monopolize responsibility for the whole of social policy.

In view of the uncertainty and disputes over these questions within the political leadership, it was left to understaffed and uninfluential organizations like the Trustees of Labour and the labour exchanges to respond to the insatiable demands of the armed forces and the armaments industry, by concentrating all their forces on meeting the latter's requirements. Co-operation from the Gestapo was only intermittent and seldom effective; and many employers still took the view that higher material inducements were the only way to deal with the demoralization in industry, which was now threatening to get out of control. In such a situation it is not at all surprising that all the official efforts to restrict freedom and consumption were in vain. The owner of a tannery in Dresden spoke for many businessmen when he described the attitude of his workers as a 'strike in disguise'.[34]

II

The value of an analytical approach to the issue will emerge if we now relate the facts discussed above to the foreign policy of the regime. This brings the argument back to our opening question: how much room for manoeuvre in foreign policy did the Reich government have in 1938/9? Given the domestic situation, was it in any position to make effective use of *Blitzkrieg* as a concept? Could it have waited any longer before embarking on war and the annexation of foreign territory? To give even a partial answer to these questions we must consider two sorts of evidence: first, we must clarify the relationship of economic and social policy to the strategy of expansion; thereafter, we may profitably examine decisions and pronouncements on the subject made by Hitler.

Crucial to the strategy of expansion was the assumption that internal politics would be wholly subordinated to the demands of foreign policy: what Hitler, in an early discussion of the subject, called the 'internal victory'.[35] This did not mean that the whole country had been turned into one vast military encampment even before the war, but that the military attacks which had already been decided on were to be prepared and carried out without the slightest regard to domestic pressures and dangers. The Wehrmacht was to be deployed in accordance with precise objectives, limited only by the international balance of forces. To create the preconditions for expansion, certain precautions were necessary, yet the regime's capacity to undertake them was limited. The only part of its programme that was ruthlessly enforced was the destruction and terrorist persecution of left-wing resistance in Germany. By contrast, the attempt to make the masses enthusiastic about the political aims of National Socialism, and enlist their spontaneous and obedient co-operation, was

---

[34] Report of the defence inspectorate of Dresden to the War Economy Staff, 17 August 1939; BA/MA Freiburg, WO 1–8, vol. 283.
[35] Adolf Hitler, 'Warum musste ein 8. November kommen?', *Deutschlands Erneuerung*, vol. 4 (1924), pp. 199–207.

completely unsuccessful. On this point all German and foreign observers, including the Gestapo, were in agreement. In political terms the consciousness of this failure was the reason for that anxious attention to the material interests of the governed that made it more or less impossible to apply strategically necessary prophylactic measures in the socio-economic sphere.

'Prophylactic' indeed were the exceedingly feeble labour ordinances and attempts to control consumption which were put into force at the end of 1936 as part of the Four Year Plan. All subsequent attempts worth mentioning to reduce living standards and mobility of labour bore the unmistakable stamp of internal reactions to already acute international crises. This applies to the wage intervention and labour conscription measures adopted in 1938, and especially to the radical social policy decrees of September 1939.[36] The former decision followed a good eighteen months of ever more drastic demands from the Wehrmacht, the ministerial bureaucracy and industry for the concentration of all economic forces on their most urgent needs.[37] These demands focused on the disruptions in agriculture, the labour market, and pricing policy for government contracts, all of which posed a threat to rearmament and to economic stability. It was repeatedly emphasized that if the system was to be protected against economic upheaval, then the government must identify its priorities and stick to them. In view of Germany's limited economic potential it was impossible to meet all requirements at once: this would only lead to frictions and hold-ups that were in principle avoidable. Among those who took this line, Major-General Thomas and Darré were the only ones who dared to state the obvious out loud: the required policy could not be carried out unless the whole population made greater personal and material sacrifices. This disagreeable fact was actually common knowledge in government circles. But until summer 1938 almost all ideas, suggestions and proposals on the subject went straight down the drain. On this most important question the willpower of the regime was blocked by fear. It was only the partial mobilization of the Czech armed forces in May 1938, and the subsequent decision to attack Czechoslovakia and finish building the West Wall in record time, that finally forced through some long-overdue interventions. How the government dragged its feet over the use of these new compulsions has already been told.

The government's last and decisive attempt to subordinate all non-military aspects of social and economic life to the demands of the armaments industry did not come until the war had started. Then there

---

[36] In the meantime there was only a timid effort to close down unprofitable handicrafts firms and individual businesses and to shorten the training period for apprentices.

[37] Schacht was the only one not to take this line.

was not even any propaganda to prepare for it; indeed, there was *no* internal preparation for this decisive turning point. Until the last possible moment even the directly responsible departments were irresolute and divided over the policy to be followed. The ministers' original plans stipulated that in case of war, wages should return to the official minimum, which would mean a reduction of between 10 per cent and 25 per cent, depending on occupation. But the Minister of Labour, who already had experience of state wage-controls, was by now convinced that such cuts would lead to great unrest and reduced productivity in industry. The same experiences lay behind the completely altered attitude of the War Economy Staff towards the usual wage supplements for night work and overtime: they pleaded at the last minute for their retention.[38] Was the increased buying power thus produced to be spent on consumer goods or siphoned off by some other means? Nobody had any idea. A series of hectic discussions led to a weasel compromise which was imposed on 4 September as a 'War Economy Decree'.[39] It must be strongly emphasized that the fatal contradictions in this regulation were in no way due to incompetence on the part of the politicians and civil servants concerned. A war of aggression, increased productivity alongside drastically reduced living standards *and* the political loyalty of the population together formed a circle which it was quite impossible to square.

Even more significant for our purposes than this confusion in high places was the fact that four of the measures taken in September 1939 had already been deemed impracticable by the specialist ministries, irrespective of whether or not it came to war. Thus the summer of 1939 saw the same constellation of forces forming as had been typical for the period since 1938. The progress of rearmament alone had called for harsh measures against the civilian population, but these were actually adopted only in direct response to a crisis in foreign policy. In 1939 this meant tighter controls over prices and wages, a drive to further limit labour mobility in all branches of industry, and the introduction of penal powers for the Trustees of Labour, which enabled them to deal with indiscipline and wage demands in industry without taking the long and weary path through the courts. These repressions, necessary in any case, constituted an important part of the war regulations.[40]

Whether the government could still have imposed these measures even

---

[38] Lecture notes for General Thomas, 24 June 1939; BA/MA Freiburg, WiIF5, vol. 319. Decree of the Minister of Labour, 9 August 1939 (ibid.)

[39] *RGBl* (1939), I, p. 1609.

[40] Prices: Lammers to Wagner, 1 July 1939; circular by Wagner, 9 September 1939; Bundesarchiv Koblenz R332II, vol. 611. Wages: Werner Mansfeld, 'Lohnpolitik im Kriege', in *Monatshefte für NS-Sozialpolitik*, vol. 6 (1939), pp. 383–6. Change of workplace: note from the Ministry of Economics, 25 August 1939; Deutsches Zentralarchiv (DZA), Potsdam, Ministry of Economics, vol. 10401, p. 2. Penal powers: ibid. vol. 55.

without the pretext of war cannot, of course, be known with certainty. Nor can we seriously expect to find evidence in writing to the effect that the outbreak of war had finally created the opportunity to clean things up at home. But the conclusion is inescapable that one of the functions of the war of aggression was indeed to clear the way to a 'solution' of this backlog of economic and social problems. The international crises of May–September 1938 and August–September 1939 made severe measures at home indispensable; but they also enabled the government to make decisions which it had been putting off up to that time.

Until the political leadership was in a position to fall back on that deceptive slogan 'Reich in danger', it did not have the courage to present its people with the bill for its rearmament policy. This put it in a quandary which contradicted the original concept of *Blitzkrieg*. The political leadership had no freedom of manoeuvre to deploy its sovereign powers to achieve what seemed to be the strategically necessary preliminaries for the war of aggression. It was only in a position to take the big political risk of imposing really heavy sacrifices on the people when it could use the war as immediate justification. Glittering but distant goals, ideological fanaticism and stirring oaths of national solidarity never failed to have their effect at a Nuremberg rally, but when it came down to wages, working hours and standards of living they were an unsafe basis for a long-term policy.

Thus, in September 1939 the government embarked on the twofold task of catching up on neglected business and subjecting the German economy to wartime conditions. On top of the measures already described, they resolved on a wartime income tax, which put 40 per cent of industrial workers above the threshold; all wage supplements were abolished and protective legislation largely suspended; on wage settlements they compromised on a universal wage cut of (on average) 10 per cent, which was to produce a drop in price levels over the whole economy, except in agriculture. All holiday entitlements lapsed, and companies' social obligations towards their workers were to be restricted.[41] If this programme had been implemented it would undoubtedly have speeded the expansion of the armaments sector very considerably. If it had served as the basis for the Four Year Plan back in 1936, by 1939 Germany's superiority in armaments would have been more or less invincible. In reality, the programme was on its last legs as early as December 1939.

The working class expressed its opposition to the war and the cut in its living standards in the only way it could: the whole of industry was swept by a wave of passive resistance. The pre-war indiscipline now extended to

---

[41] See especially the labour law decree of 1 September 1939, *RGBl* (1939) I, p. 1683, and the notification to Trustees of Labour, 4 September 1939; Bundesarchiv Koblenz R41, vol. 57, pp. 1–7.

acts which, to one concerned official, seemed to bear the stamp of 'sabotage'.[42] The government, taken aback and deeply worried about the reliability of the home front as well as the supplying of the Wehrmacht, caved in immediately. Of all the proposed measures, only two were left in force, and then only partially: the wartime income tax was modified to the point where overtime would still be attractive, and although pay supplements for the ninth and tenth hours of overtime remained suspended for another year, in September 1940 they too had to be restored. Because of this capitulation it then became impossible to meet the demands of the Wehrmacht, or to restrain consumer goods production by means of plant closures in the winter of 1939/40. The extremely scanty preparations for the attack on France were carried out without any noticeable conversion of productive capacity. Funk, Minister of the Economics, who had to explain this dangerously compromising mood to the generals, also remarked that 'to live through this mess one has to be either mad or drunk: I prefer the latter'.[43]

Meanwhile the internal defeats of the regime were increasing further. To keep up the morale of troops in the field, the government introduced very high levels of support payments for their families. For this reason there was a steep rise in the number of marriages in late summer 1939, and the resulting 'war wives' deserted their jobs *en masse*. Between June 1939 and March 1940 the number of women workers in the German economy fell by 450,000 – and this at a time when the war was causing a drastic worsening of the labour shortage. Worst hit was the munitions industry, where the shortfall in production in early 1940 was most serious: there was a shortage of women to do the mostly unskilled labour. The government reluctantly took counsel over the possibility or necessity of extending labour conscription to non-employed (*nichterwerbstätige*) women. Only the unexpected opportunity to plunder the French economy saved them from that embarrassment.[44]

Even more suggestive, although it did not directly influence the course of events, is the crisis in basic economic planning. If diplomatic tactics were to fail, and a European war be triggered prematurely, the idea was to concentrate all armaments production in the few really big companies. Small suppliers and handicrafts were to be savagely pruned, as was the consumer sector, and their plants and workforces placed at the disposal of

---

[42] Note on the departmental meeting of 10 November 1939, in course of which the government's retreat was decided; DZA, Ministry of Economics, vol. 10401, pp. 85–6. See Dietrich Eichholtz, *Geschichte der deutschen Kriegswirtschaft 1939–1945*, vol. I, 2nd edn (East Berlin 1971), Chapter 2, section 1.

[43] As Schmitt, previously Minister of Economics, reported to Hassell: Ulrich von Hassell, *Vom anderen Deutschland*, 3rd edn (Zürich 1947), p. 121 (13 February 1940).

[44] *Statistisches Handbuch*, pp. 47, 474; Eichholtz, *Geschichte*, pp. 79 ff.; notice of a discussion between Krauch and Thomas, 17 November 1939; BA/MA WiF5, vol. 412.

heavy industry. The labour conscription regulations meant that workers could be compulsorily transferred and redeployed – the very measure that the government had not dared to use fully before the war. We still lack a detailed scholarly examination of these plans. But we already know that on 12 November 1939 Hitler ordered them to be completely rescinded: it was 'impossible' to move workers all over the place; what was needed instead was a policy of broadly distributed contracts which would let them stay where they were. When Major-General Thomas announced this decision in a cabinet conference, the feeling of relief among participants was unmistakable. One secretary of state, for example, talked of how the big industries, with their large numbers of poorly provisioned, crammed-together workers, would have been in danger of becoming 'danger zones'. On the other side, Thomas expressly warned that the policy of distributing armaments orders broadcast could only serve for a short war.[45]

It is easy to conclude that this almost total abandonment of any plans and measures for a war economy was dictated by the unexpected course of the war after September 1939. This hypothesis is, however, untenable. All the essential decisions on wages and labour policy fell between the beginning of October and the middle of November 1939, during which time Hitler was clinging to his plan to conquer France before the year's end with a stubbornness that almost put him in danger of a military coup. The kid-glove policy that was forced on the government remained almost unchanged until the first Russian winter. This is hardly a case of perfect tactical adaptation to the rapidly changing course of the war, nor of a carefully calculated margin of risk. The impression is rather that the whole situation had slid out of control. The only suitable tune to accompany the chaotic retreat on the home front issued from the staff of the quartermaster-general of the armed forces: on 8 October they reckoned that munitions stocks were sufficient only to keep one-third of the divisions combat-ready for another four weeks at the most. On top of this the Luftwaffe's reserves of bombs were almost exhausted, the motorized divisions of the army and the supply system were mostly out of fuel, tyres and spare parts, and the shortage of vehicles for an invasion of France ran into five figures. The level of armaments had only just sufficed for the rapid defeat of Poland.[46]

The subsequent plundering of the conquered areas did a great deal to save the German economy and the combat capacity of the Wehrmacht. Deliveries from the USSR played a lesser, but still important part. The war of aggression failed in one of its purposes: despite the assault on

---

[45] Minutes of a conference of heads of department, 13 November 1939; ibid.
[46] Wagner, *Generalquartiermeister*, p. 142; Hans-Adolf Jacobsen, *'Fall Gelb'* (Wiesbaden 1957), pp. 19 ff., 131–7, 187 ff.

conditions at home which initially accompanied the invasion of Poland, it created no secure grounds for going over to a full-scale war economy in Germany. This made the second purpose – plunder – all the more important. It allowed the regime to stick to its cherished expansionist aims without seriously endangering internal stability. The regime seemed to believe that a hero's death on the battlefield was quite acceptable for German manhood, but that wage cuts or an increase in the price of butter were quite unacceptable for the population as a whole: they could be asked only for occasional sacrifices.

These findings and considerations show clearly enough that Hitler's original strategic conception was impracticable. The Third Reich could not have waited much later than autumn 1939 before breaking out of its internal crisis – certainly not until 1943. Without this 'flight forwards' (*Flucht nach vorn*) there would have been no possibility of increasing repression to the extent required to pursue rearmament and avoid further economic crises. Without this flight forwards there was no chance of filling the gaping holes everywhere in the economy with booty. On the exceptional economic importance of these plundered goods all the responsible German authorities were agreed: they were the decisive margin that saved the Wehrmacht and the armaments industry from total shutdown. In comparison with the whole German gross national product they may not all have carried much weight, but they included transport and production capacity, raw materials (petrol, oil, metals) and manufactured goods (machine tools, lorries, weapons), which were of the greatest value to the German war economy. Their value should be assessed in terms of strategy rather than of national economic statistics. In two areas – conquered agricultural surpluses and manpower – the war of plunder was, from the outset, not only qualitatively, but also quantitatively of decisive economic importance.

If these hypotheses conform to the facts, then between 1938 and 1940 the concept of *Blitzkrieg* underwent a subtle, but decisive change. The pressure of economic crisis and intense social tension ruptured the vital means–ends relationship between the planned annexations and the great European war. Instead of being entirely subordinate to the latter, the annexations became necessary to maintain the ruling regime and keep the war-oriented economy going. The system had needs which had to be fulfilled immediately, and these took precedence. They strengthened the expansionist dynamic of the Third Reich, but at the same time they reduced the room for diplomatic manoeuvre. Out of the *Blitzkrieg* concept there grew a game of hazard which Hitler's speculations in foreign policy were scarcely able to disguise, and which was aimed solely at bolstering the system: the seizing of men, raw materials, foodstuffs, industrial products and plant. That the adventure did not end in failure or catastrophic collapse as soon as it began, in 1939/40, was a result of factors which the Germans could scarcely have counted upon: in particular, the military inactivity on both sides of the Franco-German frontier.

It is still frequently maintained by scholars that Hitler's strategy did not initially need a greater concentration of economic forces on rearmament before 1939. On the contrary, we can now assert that the ruling regime would not have been *capable* of doing this. The redistribution of resources was not – as has often been suggested – a mere administrative procedure which the dictatorial regime was free to adopt as and when it wished. On the contrary, it was the most explosive internal problem that ever faced the government of the Reich.[47] Hitler was relatively well informed about the dimensions and nature of the problem, in the first place probably by Göring, Lammers and the generals. A careful reading of the scanty and scrappy jottings from this period makes it clear that Hitler intended to resolve the matter in his own way. For example, the so-called 'Hossbach memorandum' on the conference of 5 November 1937:

If, in territorial terms, there existed no political outcome corresponding to this German racial core...the greatest danger to the preservation of the German race at its present peak would lie in the continuance of these political conditions. To arrest the decline of Germanism [*Deutschtum*] in Austria and Czechoslovakia was as little possible as to maintain the present situation in Germany itself. Instead of increase, sterility was setting in and in its train disorders of a social character must arise in course of time, since political and ideological ideas remain effective only so long as they furnish the basis for the realization of the essential vital demands of a people.

It was not possible, in a continent sharing more or less the same standard of living, to meet food supply difficulties over the long run by lowering that standard or by rationalization.[48]

Thus, *one* function of the war was to avoid internal dangers. The weakness of the ruling system and its apparent reliance on a political outlook whose internal contradictions could be disguised only so long as it was bolstered by material success; the possibility of a 'decline of Germanism' and of 'sterility'; the political impossibility of lowering living standards – these became the proposed grounds for military expansion. The same peculiar logic lay behind Hitler's words in May 1939 concerning Germany's economic position. It was precisely the difficulties in this sphere that made the war necessary:

The ideological problems have been solved by the mass of 80,000,000 people. The economic problems must also be solved. To create the economic conditions

[47] The first standpoint is represented by Klein, and the second by Petzina, *Autarkiepolitik*, e.g. p. 161; also by Albert Speer, *Erinnerungen* (Berlin 1969), p. 546, n. 1.

[48] *Akten zur deutschen auswärtigen Politik (ADAP)*, ser. D: 1937–45 (Baden-Baden 1950), vol. I, pp. 26–7.

necessary for this is a task no German can disregard. The solution to the problems demands courage. We must not allow the principle to prevail that one can accommodate oneself to the circumstances and thus shirk the solution of problems. The circumstances must rather be adapted to suit the demands. This is not possible without breaking into other countries or attacking other people's property.[49]

After the occupation of the rest of Czechoslovakia two months earlier – if not before that – this last thought had already become a reality. This was noted by a leading officer on the staff of the army's quartermaster-general:

Considerable quantities of military equipment of all kinds...already on their way to Germany, an enormous increase in strength . . . Up to now thousands of serviceable aircraft . . . The Führer is glowing . . . Very large supplies of raw materials . . . Up to six weeks' worth of fuel supplies, coal sufficient . . . Lots of money and foreign currency . . . The Führer can hardly wait to get a summary of the war *matériel* and is constantly pressing us.

And indeed, the '500 trainloads of war *matériel*' were sufficient to arm five new German divisions.[50] But they could not satisfy the demand. On 22 August 1939 Hitler bestirred himself to convince the top generals of the need to attack Poland. He made use of the following argument, among others, which reads as if he was concerned to take the sting out of the bad news that had been presented to him by military and economic authorities over the last few months, and indeed to twist its meaning to suit himself: 'We have nothing to lose. We have everything to gain. Because of our limitations our economic situation is such that we can only hold out for a few more years. Göring can confirm this. We have no other choice, we must act.'

According to another version, what Hitler said was: 'Göring has said that the Four Year Plan has failed and that it is all up with us, unless we have victory in the coming war.' Here, and again in a later address to a similar audience on 23 November 1939, Hitler returned to the overall problem of the relationship between the conduct of the war and internal political stability, which he had already touched on at the end of 1937. His contradictory assertions on this point betrayed an uncertainty that led him into an unjustified decisionism (*Dezisionismus*). If at one moment he saw the German people in danger of getting out of condition through a 'long period of peace', at another he saw them as the guarantee of victory, however unaccustomed they might have become to 'hardships and burdens': 'our people are the best'. Here Hitler stressed the 'spiritual

---

[49] International Military Tribunal, *Trial of the Major War Criminals at Nuremberg* (IMT), vol. XXXVII (Nuremburg 1949), Doc. 079-L, pp. 546–56.
[50] Wagner, *Generalquartiermeister*, pp. 82–3; Jacobsen, *Fall 'Gelb'*, p. 20.

prerequisites for endurance' which 'are of the essence'.[51] In the following weeks the labour administration observed few if any traces of these qualities. Then, on 6 October, Hitler said that the conquest and exploitation of France had become urgent; otherwise it was to be feared that the 'spiritual attitude [seelische Haltung]' of the German people might come to harm.[52] But what he said on 23 November 1939 again had an ambiguous ring: 'Behind me stands the German people, its morale can only get worse.'[53] Of course, Hitler normally expressed anxieties of this nature only to his closest associates. To Speer, in 1939, he explained the necessity of building the planned new government quarter as a fortress with the remark, 'It is not out of the question that I shall some day be forced to take unpopular measures. These might possibly lead to riots.'[54] Morale would be further sustained by the establishment of colonies of Polish agricultural workers and prisoners of war, who were just then beginning to take over some of the worst-paid jobs in the German economy. Also relevant was Hitler's programmatic declaration that Poland must remain a poor country so that Germany could draw on it for labour. Here was a precarious path to skirt 'unpopular measures'.[55]

Despite the monolithic casuistry of Hitler's thought, despite the tactically conditioned and irrational confusion of his arguments at this time, a single red thread runs through his recorded remarks and reactions which is not to be found in his comments on foreign policy in 1938–9: the more uncertain he became about the precarious situation at home, the more he tried to stabilize it through success in war. From beginning to end, the war of plunder was its own justification.

My conclusion will attempt to fit the above arguments and analyses into a wider historical framework. I am not, of course, trying to say that the governmental and economic crisis I have briefly described was in any way the primary cause of the Second World War. Historians prefer to use the concept of 'causes', if at all, for the slowly developing, underlying impulses behind historical developments: in this case it could be used for the inexorable racial and anti-communist aims of the Nazi leadership – to dominate Europe as far as the Urals – and the economic imperialism of German industry with its drive to expand its markets and resources. These two fundamental factors, whose relationship to each other has not

---

[51] *ADAP*, ser. D, pp. 168, 171; see IMT, vol. XLI, Doc. Raeder-27, pp. 16–25, and the excellent source study by Winifred Baumgart, 'Zur Ansprache Hitlers vor dem Führern der Wehrmacht am 22. August 1939', *Vierteljahrshefte für Zeitgeschichte*, vol. 16, no. 2 (1968), pp. 120–49.   [52] Jacobsen, *Fall 'Gelb'*, pp. 16–17.

[53] IMT, vol. XXVI, Doc. 789-PS, pp. 327–36.   [54] Speer, *Erinnerungen*, p. 173.

[55] See Eva Seeber, *Zwangsarbeiter in der faschistischen Kriegswirtschaft* (East Berlin 1964). On the pillaging of the Polish economy see Wagner, *Generalquartiermeister*, pp. 124–5, 131. Polish agricultural potential and railways were also of great importance. Hitler's interest in the war as a war of plunder was increasing all the time. See Andreas Hillgruber, *Hitlers Strategie. Politik und Kriegführung 1940–1941* (Frankfurt am Main 1965), pp. 256–7, 264 ff., 521, 548.

yet been fully explained, determined the basic orientation of German policy after 1933. Since they inevitably constituted a challenge to the British Empire and the USSR, they already implied the possibility of a second world war. My remarks bear principally on the *consequences* of that policy, the crisis which arose out of the preparations for that war. My perspective here is therefore deliberately short term.

There is more than one reason for this choice of emphasis. First, the internal politics of Germany immediately prior to the Second World War have hitherto been insufficiently closely examined. I have attempted to demonstrate that the *course* of events and decisions was strongly influenced by Germany's internal crisis: further, that this crisis was an inevitable consequence of the structure of society and government. Certainly, much depended on the course of international disputes: it is hard to be sure how Britain and France would have reacted to a further (short) period of 'peaceful' German penetration of Central Europe after September 1938.

Second, this study offers the possibility – which has not been exhausted here – of making a cross-section through the political and economic system which would depict the links, well recognized by those in power, between different areas of public life. It also allows us at least to indicate the possible relationship between their intentions and the tendencies in state, economy and society which were beyond their control. Connections and interactions between these two areas can perforce only be suggested; it is clear, however, that diplomacy did not take place in a vacuum. For the Third Reich especially, foreign policy was also social policy.

The third point is also the most significant. A short-term sectional analysis seems particularly suited to Nazi foreign policy, since it was the nature of this system to destroy long-term, rational political perspectives, even – or especially – where it was itself involved. The ultimate cause was the capitalist economic system, but a second reason for this self-destructive element was Nazi ideology itself. For one thing, its adepts found long-term, practical political thought quite beyond them. Their political thought and action moved on two associated, and quite irrationally connected, planes: superficial calculations about the use of force, and commitment to unrealistic, ideologically determined aims of human conditioning. These reasons, and the special role of the charismatic Führer, left scarcely any room for pragmatic discussion of political alternatives. Causes and effects, means and ends, methods and goals, preparation and realization, became increasingly confused in the political thinking and behaviour of the ruling clique. The longer the Nazi regime lasted, the harder it becomes to say what their policies were actually meant to achieve. This underlying irrationality was the root of their total rejection of economic and social realities in deference to a weird idealism which fed the notion that terror and empty rhetoric could evade the rules of a class-based society and the relationship of forces in the world economy. That was the basic, founding concept of Nazi domestic and foreign policy, and the *Blitzkrieg* strategy simply put it into effect. It was this founding concept that ran into trouble in 1938/9, when the very rules and realities which National Socialism was determined to invalidate once again took centre-stage: the people were *not* eager for sacrifice, and the room for diplomatic manoeuvre was decreasing all the time. With this huge question mark over the assumptions behind their politics, the leadership was left wide open to the influence of *immediate* necessity. The original concept turned into a 'flight forwards', in which the link between the shortest of short-term necessities and the old, glittering and distant goals was guaranteed only by force. The capitalist economic system then had a great deal to do with the destruction of all long-term political perspectives. If the fundamental aim of the modern bourgeois state is to restrict the nihilistic tendencies of private capital accumulation and technological management, then the Nazi regime took the brakes off this desire for limitless expansion without meeting any noticeable opposition from industrial circles. The basic question about the costs – human and financial – of economic and territorial expansion was no longer asked. All things were possible through conquest, murder and pillage – even in the economic sphere. To adapt their practical politics to the needs of a self-perpetuating society would have been a sisyphean task for the ruling elite: they did not even attempt it. On the contrary, the unrestrained and therefore barbaric natural growth of economic development, once it was turned loose, answered to the short-term dynamics of Nazi aggression. German policy through the Second World War had a correspondingly chaotic appearance. At least three different directions can be discerned: the economic imperialism of German industry, the war of pillage necessary to the survival of the regime and the continuation of the war, and the striving after illusory long-term goals. The relationship of these three tendencies was entirely contradictory and they did not add up to any reliable concept of political power. The resulting primacy of short-term needs, calculations and improvisations is thus the third justification for the ideas which I have brought forward in this study.

Hitler himself pointed out this particular constellation. 'We are not fighting the same battles as we were a hundred years ago. Today we can speak of a racial battle. Today we are fighting for oil fields, rubber, ores, etc.'[56] In 1939 the war he referred to could not be long delayed. From this viewpoint, it is clear that the temporarily successful military execution of the *Blitzkrieg* in 1939/40 rested on an unholy alliance of internal coercion, external coincidence and outrageous adventurousness on Hitler's part. The successes lent the whole an air of careful preparation which it did not, in fact, possess.

[56] On 23 November 1939. See note 53 above.

5

❧

WOMEN IN GERMANY, 1925–1940.
FAMILY, WELFARE AND WORK[1]

*If we say the world of the man is the state, the world of the man is his
commitment, his struggle on behalf of the community, we could then perhaps say
that the world of the woman is a smaller world. For her world is her husband,
her family, her children and her home. But where would the big world be if
no-one wanted to look after the small world? How could the big world continue
to exist, if there was no-one to make the task of caring for the small world the
centre of their lives? No, the big world rests upon this small world! The big
world cannot survive if the small world is not secure.*

Adolf Hitler, speech to
the National Socialist Women's organization,
Nuremberg Party Rally, 8 September 1934[2]

IN THE winter of 1939/40 the Nazi regime faced a major internal crisis.
The mobilization of resources for war was inadequate in every respect;
the German people, in particular the industrial working class, showed no
enthusiasm for a war of aggression, no willingness to make further
sacrifices in the interests of imperial expansion. Discontent and anxiety
were apparent in all walks of life, and the conservative resistance to Nazi
rule developed briefly into a serious political and military conspiracy. A
large part of Poland had been conquered, but Britain and France were at
war with Germany. In the armed forces and among the civilian
population morale was low; rationing, blackouts, overtime, shortages of
all kinds and the evacuation of people from frontier areas heightened the
general sense of foreboding and insecurity.

It was against this background of pressing external and internal
dangers that the leaders of the Third Reich discussed the question of
conscripting women into war industries. The issue was very much a part

---

[1] This essay started life as a paper at the two Ruskin History Workshops on Women in
History in 1973. Whatever merits it may have in its recent form are due in large measure to
the discussions at the workshops and to the constructive criticism of numerous friends
and colleagues, in particular to the unstinting assistance of Jill Stephenson, University of
Edinburgh.   [2] Max Domarus, *Hitler. Reden und Proklamationen* (Würzburg 1962), p. 450.

of the overall domestic crisis for the need to get more women into regular work was no longer questioned – of all the shortages, the shortage of labour posed the most severe threat to the German war effort. The need demanded to be met at once, and so conscription seemed the only practical measure. After long deliberations the government decided against conscription. It was an important decision which had far-reaching consequences for the population of Germany and of German-occupied Europe in the following war years.

The decision was not easy to understand at first; it seemed initially unnecessary and in some measure untypical of Nazi policies. The need to make sense of it was one of the reasons why I became interested in the position of women and the family in German society in the 1930s. This particular question has retained its importance and it will be discussed in some detail in the second half of this chapter. The attempt to answer it, however, led backwards and outwards to a range of new topics and problems, for the government's decision had a long and difficult history.

In respect of its attitudes and policies towards women, National Socialism was the most repressive and reactionary of all modern political movements. And yet it seems that the overtly anti-feminist policies of the regime after 1933 were at least partially successful, in that they secured the approval, perhaps gratitude, of many German people, men and women alike; partially successful too in blocking and turning back the social, economic and educational pressures which had been conducive to gradual progress towards emancipation in the preceding decades. At the very least, there is scarcely any evidence that the policies adopted on the family and on women's work were unpopular, despite the fact that they ran directly counter to basic liberal, democratic and socialist principles, principles which seemed to have been widely accepted during the 1920s.

Why was this the case? And what was the significance of these developments? These two deceptively simple questions cannot be answered in isolation. They each raise a large number of further questions, both about the position of women in German society in the inter-war years and about basic features of National Socialist rule. This chapter is thus concerned with a series of large, complex and inter-connected themes: with the nature and political function of Nazi anti-feminism; with the forms and consequences of the regime's anti-emancipatory welfare policies; with the role of women and of the family in the political economy of German imperialism before 1945; with the contradictions inherent in the attempt to combine the protective repression of women with a policy of war and territorial expansion; and, most important of all, with the social bases of National Socialist power after 1933/4. Such general themes do not lend themselves easily to discussion in a brief historical essay: they call for a long and detailed book. But it is not only on account of the need for brevity that at many points in the following pages the argument is perfunctory and speculative, or the evidence adduced remains incomplete, or the relationship between the descriptive and the interpretative sections becomes uncertain. It is to some degree unavoidable, for, since Clifford Kirkpatrick published his thoughtful and detailed empirical study in 1938, *Nazi Germany. Its Women and Family Life*, very little new research has been done into this aspect of modern German social history. Much important work is being done at the moment – interestingly enough all of it, as far as I am aware, by women scholars – but, with the exception of Jill Stephenson's thesis 'Women in German Society 1930–1940', few results are yet available.[3] And my own research has not been systematic enough to warrant an attempt to write a book.[4]

The chapter is also tentative in a second sense. While it does not address itself to the theoretical problems, now much debated in Britain and the United States, of constructing a 'women's history', it is inevitably – but indirectly – of contemporary relevance: it was actually prompted, not to say demanded by socialist members of the women's liberation movement in England, and it is to their insistent encouragement that I owe the necessity of rethinking many of my ideas on the structures of National Socialist domination. Attempts to account for the durability and efficiency of the Nazi regime, attempts to understand its capacity to enforce the dynamic integration of a conflict-ridden society, which simply ignore the position of rather more than half the members of that society and make no reference to the family as a public institution, are unlikely to possess much explanatory power. My own previous work has been weak in this respect.

The women's movements in Britain and the USA, which are significantly stronger and more active than their counterparts in West Germany, have helped decisively in the past six years to revive the theoretical and historical discussions of the 1920s and 1930s on the role of the family and of the sexual division of labour in modern capitalist societies – discussions which, on account of their debts to Marx and Freud, were obliterated in the epoch of fascism, together with the many movements of the period for the emancipation of women.[5] The study of

---

[3] I have used the typescript version, Edinburgh 1974. The book appeared after this chapter was completed: *Women in Nazi Society* (London 1975). Dörte Winkler-Schnurr is preparing a detailed study of women industrial workers in the years 1933–45. Helen Boak is writing a thesis on the position of women in south-west Germany during the world economic crisis. Louise Willmot is investigating the organization of adolescent girls within the Hitler Youth. All of them have given me helpful advice and references.

[4] Some of the weaknesses of this part of the essay and some of the openings for further research will be discussed in the concluding notes.

[5] For example Wilhelm Reich, *The Mass Psychology of Fascism* (Harmondsworth 1975, first publ. Denmark 1933), and the as yet untranslated writings of Max Horkheimer, Erich Fromm, Herbert Marcuse and other members of the Frankfurt school, *Studien über Autorität und Familie* (Paris 1936). Paul A. Robinson, *The Sexual Radicals* (London 1970), and Martin Jay, *The Dialectical Imagination* (Boston/Toronto 1973), Chapter 4, give good summaries and discussion of the theoretical issues.

anti-feminism is one of the directions which these discussions can now take. There is no shortage of source materials, and this line of enquiry may help to fill out, modify and give historical context to general theories on the role of the family under industrial capitalism. In a comparative context, the oppression of women in Nazi Germany furnishes the most extreme case of anti-feminism in the twentieth century. Quite apart from the fact that the social, economic, medical and cultural conditions which define the position of women in Western Europe have changed decisively since 1945, it is the extreme character of National Socialism which makes it unhelpful to draw any direct parallels with the present. But it is arguable that the antagonistic pressures to which women were subjected in Germany in the 1930s, the extraordinary contradictions in the policy of the Nazi regime towards women and the family – the multiple exploitation and the simultaneous repressive protection – reveal, *precisely because of* their exceptional character, some fundamental and general features of the problem, which are less visible in times when the crisis of modern capitalism has been latent rather than manifest.

The results, which are highly provisional, also draw attention to one social-historical point, which is perhaps of direct contemporary relevance: the general predominance of the *specifically modern*, urban/suburban, small family, in which the woman either does not work outside the house at all, or works as a regular wage- or salary-earner, is a much more recent phenomenon than critical social scientists have tended to assume. The growth and spread of this type of small family in Western Europe was a trend above all of the period since 1900, and the real (as opposed to the demagogic) achievement of National Socialism was merely to accelerate this trend in Germany. The proportion of adults in the population who have remained unmarried has decreased steadily and rapidly over the last one hundred years. In the short period between 1910 and 1939 the proportion of adult men (over eighteen) in Germany who did not marry at all fell from 33.8 per cent to 26.7 per cent, the proportion of adult women from 28.2 per cent to 23.1 per cent. The absolute number of married couples rose by almost 6 million over the same period. A large part of this increase was concentrated in the years 1933–9.[6] The archaic

---

[6] Richard M. Titmuss, *Essays on the Welfare State* (London 1958; 6th edn 1966), Chapters 5 and 6, gives a brilliant introductory survey of this theme. Figures from *Statistisches Jahrbuch für das Deutsches Reich*, Statistisches Reichsamt (comprehensive series of detailed official statistical publications; hereafter *Stat. Jhb.*) *1941–2*, p. 25; widowed and divorced persons are counted as having married. The high birth-rate in the late nineteenth century, its decline thereafter and the consequent shift in the age-structure of the population after 1918 meant that the change appeared even more marked than it anyway was: the proportion of the whole population who were married rose from 41.6 per cent to 53.9 per cent between 1910 and 1939 – figures which tell us little about the marriage-rate, but a great deal about the changing shape of society.

imagery of the fertile, dutiful, harmonious peasant or artisan household invoked by conservative and Nazi propaganda, and the endless verbiage about the blessings of motherhood served to obscure the fact that the most significant changes which took place after 1933 consisted in the option of an increasing number of young people for the type of small family which is now an almost universal social institution. The women's movements of today are thus confronting social structures, conventions and attitudes which are in many respects of comparatively recent origin, and it is in this context, at least as much as in respect of its distinctive, reactionary–utopian ideology, that National Socialism is of a certain contemporary relevance.

The chapter is constructed around the treatment of two main topics: the first two sections deal with the policies and attitudes of the regime towards women, the family, the birth-rate and the welfare of children; the third section discusses the employment of women outside the home. This division of the subject permits a juxtaposition of Nazi ideology with the social realities, and it also reflects the real change in emphasis in the regime's policies which took place in the later 1930s, when the labour shortage made industry increasingly dependent upon women workers. Although it does have these advantages, such a division of the material can be defended only if it enhances the clarity of presentation – in substantive terms it is a schematic and artificial device, for it is exactly the interrelations of the two topics which raise the important issues of interpretation.

THE POSITION OF WOMEN AFTER THE FIRST WORLD WAR

First, however, it is necessary to give a brief sketch of the social structure of the female population of Germany in the 1920s, for the picture which emerges contains a number of remarkable features which need continually to be borne in mind in all discussions of the Nazi period. The first such feature is the numerical preponderance of women over men. Nearly 1.7 million German soldiers were killed in the First World War. Throughout the inter-war years there were roughly 2 million more women than men; in 1925 there were over 2.25 million more women than men aged over twenty, 1.25 million more women in the age-group twenty-five to forty. Of the male population aged over twenty 67 per cent were married, but only just 60 per cent of adult women. The census of 1925 showed that there were 2.8 million widows, 500,000 more than there had been in the same territory in 1910, and single women accounted for almost three-quarters of the 1.03 million single-person households. Many women who wished to marry could not do so, and the consequences of the First World War undoubedly *forced* many widows, spinsters and fatherless daughters who would otherwise have stayed at home, to seek regular employment.[7]

The number of economically active women seems to have increased steadily from the 1870s on, but the census statistics for the late nineteenth and early twentieth centuries probably understate by a wide margin the extent of part-time and non-contractual labour carried out by women, and thus exaggerate the rapidity of the rise in the number of working women after 1914, which may well have been as much due to better counting by the census-takers as to real changes in the labour market. The rate of increase in women's employment during the main period of industrialization was certainly not faster than that for men.[8] By 1925 there were 22.06 million men aged fifteen and over, of whom 20.53 million were economically active; and 24.28 million women aged fifteen and over, of whom 11.48 million worked for their living in one way or another. Thus a clear majority of adult women lived either from unearned income, or from pensions, or – the greatest number – from the earnings of their husbands or children: *they did not work at all outside the house.* The socially useful labour of almost 13 million adult women was confined to caring for present and future members of the active labour force.[9]

It is vital at this point to clarify the categories used in the German census and labour statistics. 'Economically active' (*erwerbstätig*) is a census category which comprehends all persons who performed, part-time or full-time, productive work of any kind, except housework, whether they were employed, self-employed, or the so-called 'family assistants' (*mithelfende Familienangehörige*). It is particularly helpful for the study of women's work that the German censuses, unlike the British, tried to

---

[7] *Stat. Jhb. 1934*, pp. 12, 26. A very small number of women married before they were twenty. The difference between the proportion of women and of men who were actually married was due to the fact that women tended to live longer than men. Over this whole period there were thus always more widows than widowers, and their numbers continued to increase to 3.2 million in 1939 (pre-war): *Stat. Jhb. 1941–2*, p. 25.

[8] See comments on the 1939 census later in this chapter (pp. 186ff.), and Renate Bridenthal, 'Beyond *Kinder, Kirche, Küche:* Weimar Women at Work', *Central European History*, vol. 6, no. 2 (1973), pp. 149–51. This point is often missed, for example by Jürgen Reulecke, 'Veränderungen des Arbeitskräftepotentials im Deutschen Reich 1900–1933', in Hans Mommsen, Dietmar Petzina and Bernd Weisbrod (eds.), *Industrielles System und politische Entwicklung in der Weimarer Republik* (Düsseldorf 1974), pp. 90 f. Although Bridenthal's reading of the statistical evidence is in places hard to follow and her conclusion is both abrupt and contestable, her article is a really valuable contribution to our understanding of the subject. I have gained much from her argument and in some respects am trying to carry it forward through the 1930s.

[9] These and the following figures are taken from *Stat. Jhb. 1934*, p. 12, and *Statistisches Handbuch von Deutschland 1928–1944*, Länderrat des Amerikanischen Besatzungsgebiets (Munich 1949), pp. 32 f.: hereafter *Stat. Hdb.* There were in fact rather fewer than 13 million housewives in the strictest sense of that vague term, since the figure includes many aged women with no dependants, and some women who in fact worked as family assistants but were not categorized as such.

count the 'family assistants', though they had no contract of employment, no insurance, and often worked for irregular periods of time without a regular wage. Reliable figures covering these three categories are available only for the census years 1907 and 1910, 1925, 1933, 1939. The category of the 'employed' (*Beschäftigte*) is much narrower, since it comprehended only those whose work was of such a kind that they had to join the state sickness insurance schemes, i.e. almost exclusively wage- and salary-earners who either were in regular employment or were registered as unemployed. These distinctions are of great importance in quantitative terms: in 1925 for example there were 11.5 million 'economically active' women, but of these only 4.2 million were 'employed' (or unemployed); thus only just over one-third of all 'economically active' women were wage- or salary-earners. In this essay I have kept to these definitions. They are not satisfactory, but it is not possible to recategorize the statistical source materials. Thus when the text refers to 'women workers' or to 'the employed population' the remarks are confined to those whose work (when they had any) was regular, paid, contractual and subject to sickness insurance.

The years from 1916 (mobilization for the war effort) to 1929 (onset of the world economic crisis) were a period of intense and rapid transition in the employment patterns of those women who did work outside the home. Older types of work, many of them pre-industrial in kind, persisted alongside a proliferation of new employment opportunities in commerce, administration and industry, and in the 1920s women had a remarkably wide range of different roles in the economy. This diversity of occupations reflected in an accentuated form the unequal development of German capitalism as a whole, and the tensions within a social and economic structure in which some of the world's biggest and technically most advanced industrial monopolies co-existed uneasily with large numbers of primitive peasant farms and economically precarious corner-shops.

The figures cited above from the 1925 census show, however, that despite the cumulative and on-going changes wrought by industrialization, bureaucratization and the growth of towns, in the later 1920s a clear majority of all economically active women were still engaged in menial tasks in the least modern sectors of the economy. No fewer than 4,133,000 female family assistants were counted in 1925, and later censuses showed that this figure was itself too low. These women worked on the farms, in the shops, bars, cafés and workshops of their husbands, fathers or other male relatives. Though their work was often irregular – many of them also had to look after the family – it was frequently essential for the survival of these enterprises, most of which were very small family undertakings.

Family assistants enjoyed no contractual rights, they were in practice left unprotected by labour legislation, and it is likely that many of the women received no money wages at all. They formed a crucial part of the agricultural labour force. There were 3,578,000 female family assistants on Germany's farms in 1925, that was, on average, just over one for every holding of more than 1.25 acres. Practically nothing appears to be known about the lives of these women, nor about the female agricultural labourers (wage-earners), of whom there were also still just over 1 million in 1925, but their lot was certainly hard: the wives of farmers, agricultural labourers and rural craftsmen had more children than women whose husbands had urban occupations (in Prussia on average twice as many), and their double burden of work and family was thus that much heavier;[10] also, much of the work on the small under-mechanized holdings was back-breaking manual labour. The number of economically active women in German agriculture declined steadily in the 1920s, partly, it seems, because the available employment was limited and it was the women rather than the men who came under pressure to try their luck in the uncertain labour markets of the towns.[11] Yet the figures were still very high: taken together, farm family assistants and agricultural labourers constituted the largest single group of women in the labour force in 1925 – 4.63 million persons.

The lot of the 450,000 female family assistants in other sectors of the economy was probably less harsh – most of them were behind the counter in the family shop. But the element of male domination in peasant farming, the retail trade, handicrafts and other trades in which there was still room for minuscule enterprises, is brought out clearly by the fact that in 1925 only 1.3 million men still had to escape from ill-paid and non-contractual employment as family assistants: it was a distinctively female economic role, an attractive proposition probably only to those men who stood to inherit the farm or business. Men formed, of course, the overwhelming majority of the proprietors of such small enterprises. The number of female proprietors in agriculture, handicrafts and retailing declined rapidly from the 1900s to the 1940s, despite the fact that there were so many more widows and spinsters in the post-war years; they appear often to have been excluded from inheriting and/or running family enterprises of this kind; or perhaps those who did inherit were the most eligible candidates for remarriage. We do not know. It is clear only that many German war-widows found employment as wage- or salary-

[10] Friedrich Bürgdorfer, *Volk ohne Jugend. Geburtenschwund und Überalterung des deutschen Volkskorpers*, Zeitschrift für Geopolitik, 2nd edn, Appendix 9 (Berlin 1934), p. 61.

[11] Bridenthal, 'Weimar Women', pp. 151 f. This situation was transformed by the armaments boom of the later 1930s – the men then wanted to leave: see pp. 178ff.

earners in trade, transport, public administration and domestic service. Their history has yet to be written.[12]

The number of women wage-earners increased during this same period; the First World War temporarily accentuated this trend. In 1925, almost 5 million women were employed regularly for a weekly wage, a larger number than the category of family assistants; but as noted above, over 1 million of these women wage-earners were employed on the land, and a further 1.3 million were domestic servants. Several hundred thousand more women were still employed in domestic outwork.[13] In industry and handicrafts there were only 2.2 million women manual workers, and they were concentrated to a very great extent in a few branches of industry – above all in clothing and textiles and in the food processing industries – and in badly paid unskilled or semi-skilled jobs. One effect of the rationalization movement in German industry in the later 1920s was to increase the demand of large modern firms for unskilled female labour. In an effort to restore the competitive position of their exports and to offset rising wage costs, firms in the clothing, footwear, chemicals, electrical goods and light engineering industries went in for big investment programmes, which led either to the displacement of skilled male labour from older trades or to the installation of entirely new and highly mechanized production processes. In both cases employers hired unskilled women where possible, on account of their alleged docility and their low wage-rates.[14]

The most significant and rapid change in the employment of women was taking place in the sector of non-manual employment: in 1925 there were almost 1.5 million women white-collar workers, three times as many as in 1907. The growing bureaucratization of public life and of industrial enterprises, together with the rapid development of large-scale trading and retailing organizations, created in the cities a rapidly increasing number of subordinate jobs for young women as clerks, typists, salesgirls and minor administrators. These jobs appear to have been eagerly sought after – the work was clean, less strenuous than factory work, and some, though not all of the occupations carried at least vicarious membership of the middle class with them, together with relatively high earnings, and better social insurance protection and job security than wage-earners enjoyed. The expansion of this respectable sector of women's employment

[12] Bridenthal, 'Weimar Women', p. 153; Ludwig Preller, *Sozialpolitik in der Weimarer Republik* (Stuttgart 1949), p. 120. There was a brief increase in the number of female proprietors during the world economic crisis.

[13] Bridenthal's figures for domestic outworkers are too low: 'Weimar Women', p. 160. Compare *Stat. Hdb.*, pp. 480 f.

[14] Judith Grünfeld, 'Rationalization and the Employment and Wages of Women in Germany', *International Labour Review*, vol. 29, no. 5 (May 1934), esp. pp. 612–31.

was a product of long-term changes in social, economic and administrative organization, but this development too was speeded up by the rationalization movement in industry, with its frequently absurd emphasis on administrative procedures, supervision, filing systems and the general convenience of managers.[15]

Very few women rose to positions of independence, responsibility or high professional status during the years of the Weimar Republic, and those who did do not seem to have gained easy acceptance. The decade between the revolution of 1918/19 and the world economic crisis was too short and too unstable a period for the new constitutional guarantee of equal rights for women to be translated into far-reaching changes in social and occupational structures; and liberal principles were rarely matched by liberal practice in the upper classes of society. Some changes were perhaps beginning to take place by the late 1920s and early 1930s – there were over 19,000 women students in German universities in 1931 – but it was only in the medical profession and in public administration that middle-class women had succeeded in establishing themselves in significant numbers. There were some 3,500 women doctors and a considerably larger number of female public officials, but most of them were characteristically concerned with women's illnesses, social welfare, women's affairs, etc.; and women civil servants did not enjoy the same job security as men.[16] The numbers of women in responsible positions in the legal profession and in the universities rose slightly, but remained derisory.[17] Overall, the pressures, conventions and prejudices which professional women had to defy in order to pursue their careers proved to be strong and tenacious. Thus the most important single source of employment for educated women remained school-teaching; the numbers of women teachers rose slowly but steadily to almost 100,000 in 1925, but they were mostly in less-well-paid posts than men and relatively few women

[15] Grünfeld also makes some interesting comments on this point. See further in Preller, *Sozialpolitik*, pp. 130–8; Robert A. Brady, *The Rationalization Movement in German Industry* (Berkeley, CA 1933). The above figure for women in non-manual employment includes civil servants (mostly teachers) who were not counted as a separate category until the 1933 census: *Stat. Hdb.*, p. 33; Preller, *Sozialpolitik*, pp. 132 f.

[16] The statistical evidence on these groups is incomplete and imprecise, but the overall upward trend of women's employment in them is clear. A majority of the women categorized as civil servants were schoolteachers. See Bridenthal, 'Weimar Women', p. 164; Clifford Kirkpatrick, *Nazi Germany. Its Women and Family Life* (Indianapolis/New York 1938), p. 249; Jill McIntyre, 'Women and the Professions in Germany, 1930–1940', in Anthony Nicholls and Erich Matthias (eds.), *German Democracy and the Triumph of Hitler* (London 1971), p. 200; Michael Kater, 'Krisis des Frauenstudiums in der Weimarer Republik', *Vierteljahresschrift für Sozial- und Wirtschaftsgeschichte*, vol. 59 (1972), pp. 207–55; Jill Stephenson, 'Girls' Higher Education in Germany in the 1930s', *Journal of Contemporary History*, vol. 10, no. 1 (January 1975), pp. 41–69. Under the terms of a retrenchment decree in force from 1923 to 1929 women civil servants were eligible for compulsory retirement. I am grateful to Jane Caplan for this point.

[17] Bridenthal, 'Weimar Women', p. 164; McIntyre, 'Professions', pp. 178, 201.

teachers advanced to senior positions: they were thought to be best suited to instruct infants and girls, while boys were to be taught by men. The only other large group of non-manual women workers, the 130,000 nurses, enjoyed the customary combination of high prestige with subordinate status and poor pay and working conditions.[18]

The trends of future development *appeared* relatively clear in the late 1920s: the level of women's employment in agriculture would continue to decline quite rapidly; the number of women industrial workers would continue to grow steadily as the rationalization movement and technological advance generated more and more routine, light and unskilled jobs for which women were thought to be suitable; and the ranks of the typists and salesgirls, who enjoyed a brief and falsely glamorized interlude of personal independence in the urban centres, would continue to expand at a fast pace.

These do indeed seem to be the lines along which social change took place in the four years after the 1925 census. In fact the number of insured women with regular employment increased very rapidly in the short period of relative stabilization in the later 1920s: it rose by just 20 per cent from 5 million to 6 million between the late summer of 1925 and the late summer of 1929 – a remarkable change, when one remembers that these were not years of all-round full employment.[19] Many women, of course, continued during this period in their dependent roles as domestic servants, family assistants and domestic outworkers. More detailed information on the patterns of women's employment in the later 1920s is not available, since the next census was not taken until 1933, and by then the economic situation was very different. It looks, however, as though it would be worth investigating the hypothesis that the growth in the employment of women wage-earners and white-collar workers between 1925 and 1929 was sufficiently sharp to activate the anti-feminist resentments which were so powerful during the subsequent years of economic crisis. This crisis brought to an abrupt and violent end the trend towards the increased employment of women in insured occupations, though it did not thereby quieten the anxieties and resentments of men.

[18] The number of women teachers must be estimated, since the official statistics do not distinguish the sex of some 58,000 teachers in a variety of private and vocational schools: *Stat. Jhb. 1934*, pp. 528 ff.; Bridenthal, 'Weimar Women', p. 163. On nurses, see Bridenthal, p. 164; *Deutsche Sozialpolitik. Bericht der Deutschen Arbeitsfront* (DAF) *Zentralbüro, Sozialamt*, 30 June to 31 August 1937 and 1 January to 31 December 1938 (Berlin 1937, 1939), 2 vols.: *1936–7*, p. 215. (The Labour Front was the party organization of all workers and employers; its main task was to further the cause of class harmony.)

[19] In the late summer of 1929 there were 7.5 million women in insured employment, but the *real* increase since 1925 was about 1 million, since 1.5 million women workers were brought into the sickness insurance scheme for the first time in October 1927, through a change in the regulations; *Stat. Jhb. 1926*, p. 376; *1929*, p. 270; *1930*, p. 215.

And the effects of the depression in constricting economic opportunities for women were to some extent reinforced by the policies of the Nazi regime in 1933 and 1934.

The most striking feature of this picture of women's employment in the 1920s is its diversity. Whereas in Britain the female agricultural labourer had, accordingly to the doubtless inaccurate official statistics, all but disappeared by the end of the nineteenth century,[20] in Germany in 1925, 4.6 million women did work of this kind, either paid or unpaid: not a few of them laboured in close geographical proximity to cities in which there were large numbers of fashion-conscious young typists and clerks, some women doctors, civil servants and headmistresses, to say nothing of the film stars, actresses, dancers, politicians and writers, on whom so much public attention was focussed. The existence of these latter groups demonstrated in turn that the typical roles of working women were changing at a comparatively rapid rate: it was a highly dynamic diversity, in which the ever expanding demand for women clerical staff was the main motor of transformation. The subject still has to be investigated in detail, but it seems most probable that the extraordinarily unequal development in the social and economic position of women during the 1920s was a cause of deep social tensions, which finally found political expression in the Nazi movement.

The city of Berlin for example, comprehended and most effectively symbolized everything that German conservatives and reactionaries hated and feared about the development of public life under the Weimar Republic. As if it were not enough that the capital city should be a stronghold of the political left, the cosmopolitan centre of liberal and socialist journalism and of radical modern experiments in entertainment and the arts, Berlin was *the* city where bright young women went out to work and demonstratively enjoyed themselves. It had by some distance the lowest birth-rate of all regions in the country, and by far the highest divorce rate; the birth-rate was indeed the lowest for any city in the world: in 1933 just over 35 per cent of all married couples in Berlin were childless, nearly twice the national average, a fact which was attributed – not without evidence – to the high abortion-rate in the city. In short, in the eyes of right-thinking citizens in the provinces, Berlin had become a threateningly large wilderness of sterile promiscuity, hedonism, degeneracy and unnatural progress. The – much exaggerated – new independence of

[20] Even if the British statistics were wildly inaccurate, the contrast with Germany would remain very sharp. For this point, and many other suggestive remarks, see the bold article by Eric Richards, 'Women in the British Economy since about 1700. An Interpretation', *History*, vol. 59, no. 197 (October 1974), p. 349. There were still a large number of peasant holdings in France in the inter-war years, and the development of women's employment there was more similar to that in Germany: Evelyne Sullerot, 'Condition de la femme', in Alfred Sauvy (ed.), *Histoire économique de la France entre les deux guerres*, vol. III (Paris 1972), p. 421.

women appeared to have a prominent part in the insidious development of this 'asphalt culture', as Goebbels was to call it.[21]

As already noted however, the majority of German women did not work outside the home in 1925 and most of these 13 million women were married. Except in one respect it is impossible to generalize briefly – or, for that matter, at length – about their position and about German family life in this period. Family law, which gave the husband almost exclusive rights over his wife's property and their children, remained unchanged in the 1920s, and many observers, of whom the most noted in our own day is perhaps Talcott Parsons, expressed the view that German women were in general more deferential to their menfolk than women in Britain or the United States.[22] The large numbers of family assistants and the small numbers of female proprietors suggest that this idea was not entirely without foundation, at least as far as the economically independent middle classes were concerned; and the very success of the anti-feminist campaigns after 1929 also indicates that this notion would be worth investigating futher. But in the absence of comparative studies, little weight can be attached to the hypothesis; the evidence is still indirect and impressionistic, no more.

Whatever the nature of their relations with their fathers and then with their husbands, the position of married women did change quite drastically in the one respect which probably mattered most to them: the size of families declined at an exceptionally rapid rate. This change was common to practically all European countries in the later nineteenth and twentieth centuries, but in Germany it was compressed into a much shorter period than in France or Britain and the extent of the change was probably greater.[23]

---

[21] At this point the temptation to refer to Christopher Isherwood's Berlin novels must be resisted! See instead Bürgdorfer, *Volk*, pp. 32–8, 95 f.; *Stat. Jhb. 1934*, p. 50; R. R. Kuczynski, *Childless Marriages* (London n.d. (1939?) – pamphlet reprint of three articles from *The Sociological Review*, vol. 30 (1938), pp. 45–9; D. V. Glass, *Population Policies and Movements in Europe* (Oxford 1940; reprint. 1967), pp. 278 ff. On reactionary hostility to the growth of cities see Harold Poor, 'City versus Country: Urban Change and Development in the Weimar Republic', in Mommsen, Petzina and Weisbrod (eds.), *Industrielles System und politische Entwicklung*, pp. 11–27; Klaus Bergman, *Agrarromantik und Grossstadtfeindschaft* (Meisenheim am Glan 1970).

[22] Talcott Parsons, 'Democracy and Social Structure in Pre-Nazi Germany', *Essays in Sociological Theory* (Glencoe 1954). It is noteworthy that this is the only idea in this little-read essay by Parsons that Ralf Dahrendorf does not try to develop at length in his *Society and Democracy in Germany* (London 1968). See also Richard J. Evans, 'German Women and the Triumph of Hitler', *Journal of Modern History*, vol. 48, no. 1 (March 1976), on the attitudes of the women's organizations.

[23] The following figures in the text are an attempt to provide a substitute for an index of changes in the mean size of families since the 1890s – I have not been able to find the appropriate series. Bürgdorfer estimated it at approximately 2.6 children per married woman in 1927, 2.1 in 1931: *Volk*, pp. 18, 65. John E. Knodel, *The Decline in Fertility in Germany, 1871–1939* (Princeton 1974), pp. 121 ff., shows that it varied between 3 and 6.2 in different parts of the country and in different classes at the turn of the century.

In the early 1890s there were each year 303 births per 1,000 married women of child-bearing age; in 1932, 101.

Of those couples who had married before 1913 and were still together in 1933, 47.1 per cent had had four or more children; of those who married in 1913 or after, 11.6 per cent.[24]

At the time of the 1933 census 62.8 per cent of all married women had fewer than three children.

In 1910, 22.1 million out of a total of 64.6 million German citizens were children aged under fifteen; in 1933, 15.8 out of 66 million.

The number of households containing six or more persons fell by 524,000 in the fifteen years between 1910 and 1925; in 1910, 46.5 per cent of the population lived in households of this size, in 1925, 35.4 per cent.

By the 1920s the trend towards smaller families among the urban population had become overwhelmingly predominant. In every German town the mean size of household had fallen below four persons by 1933. Only in agricultural districts did households of six or more persons account for more than one-third of the total number. The proportion among households in which the breadwinner worked in industry, trade or administration was very much lower – in the latter case one-ninth. The breakdown of these figures according to social class both confirms and amplifies the picture, for households in which the breadwinner was self-employed (that is, in the main, peasant farmers, craftsmen and shopkeepers) were on average larger than those in which the breadwinner was a wage-earner, and very much larger than those in which the breadwinner was a white-collar worker.

Despite the slaughter of the war, the number of separate households in the Germany of 1933 was 39 per cent higher than in the same area in 1910 (the population increase over the same period was 12.8 per cent), and this expansion was massively concentrated among the small household units:

The number of households consisting of two persons rose by 98 per cent in these twenty-three years, of those with three persons by 92 per cent and of those with four persons by 52 per cent.

By 1933 well over one-half of the population of the country lived in small households of one to four persons; in 1910 it had been just over one-third.[25]

---

[24] This calculation of course exaggerates the fall in family size, since those who married *after* 1929 would not have had time to have four children by 1933.

[25] Sources: *Stat. Jhb. 1934*, p. 26; *1936*, pp. 7, 11, 13, 28–34; Bürgdorfer, *Volk*, pp. 17 f., 53 ff.; *Statistik des deutschen Reichs*, Statistischen Reichsamt (comprehensive series of detailed official statistical publications, henceforth *SdR*), vol. 470/1, p. 20. The problem with using *household* size as an index is that these figures include non-family members – lodgers, domestic servants, journeymen, apprentices and agricultural labourers who

These pallid statistics bear terse witness to changes in the lifestyle of a large proportion of the population, which, in their scale and their suddenness, were little short of revolutionary. They had been compressed into a single generation. The parents of the typical small families of the 1920s were themselves typically offspring of the large families of the 1880s and 1890s. In the 1920s more and more people were getting married, and they were having fewer and fewer children. This amounted to a fundamental change in the life-situation of adult women.

Yet Renate Bridenthal is certainly right to insist that the degree of social and economic emancipation achieved by German women in the years of the Weimar Republic has been very greatly exaggerated; and, to her observations on the evidence of the occupational statistics, one can add the generalization that there was probably nothing especially emancipated about the lives of the growing numbers of young housewives and mothers in all social classes, who stayed at home to look after their husbands and their one or two children. It was a highly restricted role, which perhaps involved less independent responsibility in sustaining the family than had often been exercised by the wives of farmers, craftsmen and workers in an earlier industrial era; and for an anxious possessive mother, whose ambition is displaced on to her child, a single son or daughter can be quite as much of a burden as four or five children may have been to a woman who also had to work the fields or help in the workshop, and thus left her children to their own devices.[26] In the post-war years, with their crises of civil strife, inflation and depression, these new constraints upon the role of the modern housewife in the working and the lower middle classes were not often compensated for by the contemporary benefits of creature comforts and security: boredom, safe routine and enforced inactivity, which figure largely among the charges against marriage made by women liberationists today, were not, one imagines, among the major problems of housewives who were responsible for bringing up children and managing a narrow family budget during the years of revolution and hyper-inflation, 1919–24, or in the period of mass unemployment after 1929. Furthermore, in Germany, as in all European countries, the housing situation remained in the 1920s a cause of acute anxiety and

---

lived in. In 1939 over 2 million households contained one, and over 100,000 two or more non-family members. These figures are given here in an inexact form because the source refers to Germany within the boundaries of mid-1939: *Stat. Jhb. 1941/2*, p. 29. See also the highly positive correlation between family size and the amount of land owned by a family, calculated on the basis of the 1933 census: *SdR*, vol. 470/1, p. 18. The marriage-rate among professional middle-class people was much lower than that of the rural and working-class populations. Class and urban/rural distinctions were not the only source of variation in family size – in most parts of the country Roman Catholic families still tended to be larger than Lutheran or Jewish families: Bürgdorfer, *Volk*, pp. 45 ff.

[26] I owe this perspective to the work of Raphael Samuel on changing patterns of family life in nineteenth-century England. See also Richards, 'Women'.

suffering for most of the population – a burden which fell especially upon women. And for the 800,000 women (1925) who *both* worked away from home *and* managed their households, little was done in the 1920s to relieve this crushing double burden. The number of married women who bore this double burden was increasing steadily – among female industrial workers the increase was over 300,000 (129 per cent) from 1907 to 1933.[27]

Yet when all of these qualifications have been made, the rapid extension of birth-control and the growing preference of married couples for small families, both such marked features of the 1920s, were beginning to create conditions under which the social and economic emancipation of women could, perhaps for the first time, realistically be discussed and fought for. The characteristic pre-industrial life-cycle of poor women – heavy manual labour from an early age, punctuated after marriage by repeated pregnancies which often ended in early death – this cycle had been decisively broken. More precisely, it had been confined to parts of the country and to sectors of society which were shrinking in both absolute and relative terms. Yet these sectors were still comparatively large, and their customs and values, which so recently had been those of the whole society, still exercised wide public influence.

The many public battles over family policy and the status of women in the 1920s tended to end in stalemate situations, in which progressive forces gained only small or insecure concessions. Thus the law on abortion was not materially relaxed, although the vocal and well-organized proponents of family planning fought an impressive campaign on this issue. And family allowances were not generally introduced – only higher civil servants received them as a matter of course (they tended to have particularly small families!), but for the rest the state confined its action to encouraging public and private employers to pay a family wage. The legislative protection and insurance benefits given to women wage- and salary-earners in the event of pregnancy were greatly extended in 1927, but the provision of day nurseries and other facilities necessary in order to encourage women to try to reconcile family and work or career remained patchy. Vigorous propaganda was conducted on behalf of modern methods of birth-control, a number of family planning clinics were established and some local branches of the state sickness insurance scheme began to offer advice on contraception, but the number of illegal abortions remained exceptionally high. The constitution of the Republic guaranteed equality between the sexes, but the government itself could continue to defy with impunity an explicit constitutional guarantee of equal treatment for men and women civil servants. The parties of the left never gained unequivocal power over the state in the Weimar Republic, and it was not least for this reason that changes in policies, institutions

[27] Preller, *Sozialpolitik*, p. 121; Bürgdorfer, *Volk*, p. 209.

and ideologies of central importance to the 'woman question' were *much less definitive* than the contemporaneous changes in the birth-rate, family size and occupational patterns – these latter were much less directly subject to the distribution of political power.[28]

The fall in the birth-rate, for example, provoked a major ideological onslaught from the extreme right in which many of the themes of later Nazi policies were clearly prefigured. Social scientists saw the prospect of imminent demographic disaster; they began to discuss the margin by which the number of births was falling below the level necessary to replace the existing population, and to argue about the precise future date at which population decline in absolute terms would set in. The overtly reactionary school of writing on this subject exhibited a wondrous blend of technical expertise and racial imperialist hysteria, of scholarly diligence and unthinking axiomatic hostility to the emancipation of women. The most respected of the prophets of power politics and high fertility was Friedrich Bürgdorfer. He systematically translated his statistical tables into the language of alarmist journalism. He described the declining birth-rate among the German minorities of Eastern Europe, for example, as a 'bio-political struggle'. He wrote of the growing preference of German parents for small families as though it were the Red Army advancing from the East: 'the two-child family system is on the march'. 'Our people', he proclaimed, 'is like an obsolete fleet, for not enough new keels are being laid down to replace it' – echoes of the Dreadnought-race with Britain before 1914! 'In biological terms the German people is pressing forwards towards the precipice.' In order to make sure of terrorizing his readers, Bürgdorfer printed large black diagrams which showed what would happen if the trends of the 1920s continued unchanged: by AD 2075 the descendants of the 4 million Berliners (1925) would number 100,000; and if every married couple produced only two children, after 300 years the descendants of 1,000 adults would number exactly eight! He also made great play of the reluctance of the educated ruling class to have large families, and so he then went on to demonstrate that this class could extinguish itself in six generations, and thus leave the country in the hands of rough, ignorant and prolific workers.

What was needed? 'A religious-moral revival, a spiritual transformation ... which will restore to the people the morally serious will to live.' And,

---

[28] These incomplete and rather general comments are based on Glass, *Population Policies*, pp. 271–92; Preller, *Sozialpolitik*, pp. 353 f.; and Werner Thönnessen, *The Emancipation of Women. The Rise and Fall of the Women's Movement in German Social Democracy, 1863–1933* (London 1973), Chapters 6 and 7. Thönnessen, pp. 91 f., also emphasizes the indifference of the male leaders of the Social Democratic Party and the trade unions to equality of employment opportunities for women in the months after the revolution and the armistice, 1918–19. Evans, 'German Women', emphasizes the lack of enthusiasm of all major political parties, except the Communist Party, for further emancipatory legislation after 1919.

his voice rising to a strident pitch of tautologous paranoia, 'For us today it is a matter, no more and no less, of the self-assertion of the German people and of German culture by the German people and for the German people.' A fit of dedicated idealism, Bürgdorfer seemed to think, would solve Germany's population problems and make her a great power again, just as Nazi propagandists pretended that idealism would also obliterate class conflict. Bürgdorfer achieved success by prostituting his scholarship in the cause of national aggrandisement. A note to the effect that even on the most pessimistic reckoning the total population of Germany would continue to increase until the later 1940s was hidden away in his flood of pejoratives about 'dwarf-families' and their opposites, 'child-happy parents'. Bürgdorfer's technical virtuosity was matched only by the insatiable quality of his desire to gain public attention for his new method of calculating the replacement rate of populations. The lurid manner in which he prosecuted his case was grist to the eager mills of Nazi propagandists. The work of creating fear and anxiety, the work of confusing the issues and of linking the movement of national fortunes to the movement of the birth-rate had all been done for them by men of high scholarly repute. It goes without saying that Bürgdorfer and his fellow prophets were quite oblivious to the interests of women in having smaller families; this he saw mainly as a financial problem, and advocated family allowances.[29]

There was in Germany in the 1920s no fundamental sea-change in social attitudes of a kind which is perhaps beginning to take place in Britain and the USA today, and which promises to make a re-imposition of cruder forms of discrimination and stereotyping simply inconceivable

---

[29] Bürgdorfer, *Volk*, pp. 30, 36 f., 66–9, 72 f., 140, 143, 429. This book, first published in 1932, was just one (probably the most comprehensive) in a stream of similar works which the author produced in the inter-war years. It is sanctimoniously dedicated to 'My dear wife, the mother of my children'. Unlike some lesser colleagues, he did not push his irrational doctrines to their ultimate inhuman political conclusion: he pointed out in 1936 that war was bad for racial hygiene, peace essential to the goal of population growth and breeding, but this was a logical, not a self-consciously political judgement, quite at odds with the whole drift of his earlier argument. In *Volk* he repeatedly makes, in a purely decorative manner, and presumably in order to protect his scholarly reputation, the crucial distinction between substantive predictions in demography and statistical projections of existing trends, *but* he gives great space in his analysis to the *projections*, all of which were intensely gloomy. Even today demographers are almost completely unable to predict accurately, a point made at that time by Glass, *Population Policies*, Chapter 8, which is a model of caution, modesty and rigour. With the exception of many British writers, demographers in the inter-war years appear to furnish a further example of the way in which professional groups have used nationalism and imperialism as vehicles for advancing their own status. Most of the arguments of the 1920s and 1930s had already been worked out in the spate of patriotic birth-rate propaganda before and during the First World War: Glass, *Population Policies* pp. 272 ff.; Anna Davin, 'Imperialism and Motherhood' (typescript) [later publ. in *History Workshop Journal* no. 5 (1978), pp. 9–65].

in the future. Those opposed to and disturbed by the progress of women towards equality of rights in German society in the 1920s suffered a series of minor defeats, but the interests and attitudes to which they were committed never suffered a decisive reverse on any issue in which they could influence the outcome. Indeed they seemed to gather strength from the accumulation of diffuse challenges – ideological, political, economic and 'biological' – which partial liberalization and on-going social change furnished to male domination of German society during this turbulent decade. And whereas the cause of women's emancipation was necessarily, on account of its complexity and its ramifications in every sphere of social and political life, promoted by a very wide range of small and normally uncoordinated groups with different partial goals and conflicting political outlooks, the cause of the restoration of men's pre-eminence could be made to appear a relatively simple single issue and could be pre-empted by a single political movement of incomparably greater power.

WOMEN AND FAMILY 1933–1940

National Socialism and women to 1933

The Nazi regime had a more clearly defined and more self-conscious attitude towards women than perhaps any other modern government. It was avowedly illiberal and protective in its aims. Although its practice was more illiberal and less protective than its declared intentions, some important welfare reforms were enacted, and the political leaders clearly regarded women as a very special category among the ruled. In their eyes *women were that part of the population on whom, if it was at all possible, novel, major and general hardships should not arbitrarily or continuously be inflicted*. What did or did not constitute a hardship in this respect, was of course decided upon by the political leadership alone, but, although they appear to have taken little advice on this question even from the party's own women's organizations, Hitler and his colleagues were demonstrably sensitive to popular prejudices, fears and interests in the formulation of their policies towards women. More precisely, they were sensitive to what they thought popular attitudes were.

Thus although the regime *initially* adopted its protective line, its emphasis on motherhood and the home, out of paternalistic and eugenic conviction, the leadership group *later* came to think, probably rightly, that German men would deeply resent the imposition on women of the sorts of hardship which they were being called upon to bear themselves. This was not just a matter of paternalistic 'altruism' among German men, of fixed notions concerning the proper division of roles between the sexes, though such attitudes were probably widespread in all classes.[30] More important was perhaps the fact that in a variety of ways, not least in a material sense, men were the direct, perhaps the main beneficiaries of the regime's policies towards women. Family allowances increased the income of the whole household; after 1939 it was both comfortable and reassuring to workers and soldiers to know (where this was in fact the case) that their wives were at home with their children, and not being forced to work in factories; and in many parts of the country it was also a matter of social status and prestige to be the head of a household in which the women did not need to take employment. Thus the Nazi regime's policies towards women were in fact policies towards the family, policies towards the whole population. They constituted arguably the *only* new and comprehensive social policies which the regime implemented in the 1930s. The question of the position of women in the Third Reich was thus a question of the broadest political significance.

A variety of different sources convey the impression that in the later 1930s the Third Reich enjoyed a large measure of active and passive support from among German women, a larger measure than it gained from among men. This is a very vague and uncertain judgement, and it may be that the political attitudes of women in these years can never be the subject of exact or confident generalization – the source materials are not very helpful. The evidence of movements in the birth-rate and of attitudes to the often conflicting roles of housewife and worker, discussed below, offers indirect support to the hypothesis, as too does the even less secure evidence of newsreel films and of diaries and memoirs. All manner of qualifications have to be made with respect to women in different age groups, women of different social classes, women of different religious confession (or of none) etc. The issue is too complicated and too little researched to be discussed in detail at this point. The low level of women's participation in resistance groups of all political persuasions, in particular in the conservative resistance, also points in the direction of a high degree of passive acceptance of the regime by German women. (This may have been no more than a continuation of the relatively low level of political activity among women before 1933).[31] By and large, however,

---

[30] These prejudices and interests were not uniform or socially homogeneous. For evidence that working-class men resented the fact that middle-class women were contributing too little to the war effort in 1940–2, see Heinz Boberach (ed.), *Meldungen aus dem Reich* (Neuwied/Berlin 1965).

[31] I know of no investigation of the role of women in the various resistance movements; it would be very difficult to carry out, but worth doing. Some working-class women were active in communist and social democratic resistance groups, not many; the wives and female supporters of the conservative and military groups appear to have played hardly any active role at all. In this, as in so many respects, the so-called Red Orchestra (a communist group led by a senior civil servant and an airforce officer) was the exception which proves the rule. There are some indications that older women who had clear

although the latter part of the war imposed the most frightful sufferings on women on the 'home front' – bereavement compounded by air-raids, evacuation, food shortages and growing pressures to take work in the war industries – most German women fulfilled to a remarkable degree the role assigned to them by Göring in his speech on 9 September 1939: 'the silent sufferers'.[32] There appears to have been much less unrest and opposition among women in 1944/5 than in 1918.

It is at first sight a little surprising that the Nazi leadership should have had any success in winning the loyalty and confidence of women. The anti-feminism of the movement before 1933 was notorious and extreme. This stance was an integral part of the Nazi Party's general rejection of liberalism in all its aspects, but it was less opportunistic and less superficial than some manifestations of the movement's anti-liberalism. First, it derived to a considerable degree from the party's militarism, an organizing principle of social life which necessarily magnified the distinctions between the sexes and was predicated upon overt and total male supremacy. Second, all racialist movements which take the biological, pseudo-scientific elements in their ideologies seriously are bound to attach particular importance to women's procreative role. A hysterical protective anxiety on behalf of guileless German women was one of the hallmarks of Hitler's fantasies on the subject of 'Jewish pollution of the German racial stock' in *Mein Kampf*, and it formed one of the most persistent themes in later Nazi anti-Semitic propaganda. The purity of the blood, the numerical power, the vigour of the race were ideological goals of such high priority that all women's activities other than breeding were relegated in party rhetoric to secondary significance.[33] Third, it is noteworthy that before 1933 the Nazi Party gained support especially among those social groups and classes where the question of the position and rights of women was a live issue: that is, on the one hand, in those sectors where emancipation, in the liberal sense of the word, was *farthest advanced* and, on the other hand, in those where women were *least emancipated*. The programmatic Nazi demand, that in the new Germany a woman's place should be in the home, appears to have been well received by men in those types of employment – clerical, administrative

memories of the First World War were much less enthusiastic about the regime and its wars than younger women. The Gestapo regarded Roman Catholic women as a distinct source of support for parish priests during the 'Church Struggle'; the opposition of the Lutheran Confessing Church seems on the other hand to have been carried by men. Some biographical materials on resistance by women have been edited by Gerda Zorn and Gertrud Meyer, *Frauen gegen Hitler. Berichte aus dem Widerstand 1933–1945* (Frankfurt am Main 1974).

[32] This major programmatic speech at the start of the war was made to an audience of Berlin armaments workers: extracts in Timothy W. Mason, *Arbeiterklasse und Volksgemeinschaft. Dokumente und Materialien zur deutschen Arbeiterpolitik 1936–1939* (Opladen 1975), Doc. 174.   [33] Adolf Hitler, *Mein Kampf*, Book I, Chapter 11.

and professional – in which women had made the most headway in the 1920s, and where there was in consequence a measure of sexual competition for jobs during the depression. Civil servants were laid off in considerable numbers in the course of attempts to balance the budget in 1931 and 1932, and the census of 1933 showed that the total number of male white-collar workers, employed and unemployed, had actually *fallen* in the preceding eight years, whereas the number of women white-collar workers had continued to rise, despite the economic crisis.[34]

On the other hand many of the country's approximately 5 million peasant holdings, artisan workshops, small retailing units, hairdressing salons, restaurants, pubs, etc. were family undertakings, in which the head of the household was the head of the enterprise and in which his female dependants combined household duties with largely unpaid and unregulated work in the fields, behind the counter, etc. Nazi propaganda attacks on the 'degeneracy' of childless, educated, decorative city women who smoked and drank probably struck some deep chords in rural and small-town Germany, where the long-term trend towards the economic emancipation of women posed an indirect but much publicized threat to the dominant value system and to the whole social structure.[35]

The basic elements of anti-feminism were not, of course, the exclusive property of the Nazi Party – the outlook was shared by many other socially and politically conservative groups and parties. It was especially strong among those many influential nationalists who harked back to the Wilhelmine Empire and the manly days before 1914 when the monarchical constitution and the hierarchical social order were supposedly intact, the civil service ran the country and Germany had the highest birth-rate and the strongest army in Europe. And it was of course on this issue, above all others, that the teachings of the Roman Catholic church and the ideology

---

[34] *Stat. Hdb.*, p. 32. On men's efforts to restrict women's access to white-collar employments see Grünfeld, 'Rationalization', pp. 613 ff.; and pp. 158f. below.

[35] On the attitudes of the economically independent, see Jeremy Noakes, *The Nazi Party in Lower Saxony 1921–1933* (London 1971); Heinrich August Winkler, *Mittelstand, Demokratie und Nationalsozialismus. Die politische Entwicklung von Handwerk und Kleinhandel in der Weimarer Republik* (Cologne 1972); Martin Schumacher, *Mittelstandsfront und Republik. Die Wirtschaftspartei Reichspartei des deutschen Mittelstandes 1919–1933* (Düsseldorf 1972); Annette Leppert-Fögen *Die deklassierte Klasse. Studien zur Geschichte und Ideologie des Kleinbürgertums* (Frankfurt am Main 1974). Only Chapter 3, section 3 of this last work attempts a *systematic* discussion of the relationship between family structure and political ideology in this social class, but the author has very little source material to back up her marxist–freudian theories. The other works cited contain passing references to anti-feminism. Further research is urgently needed. It seems possible, for example, that anti-feminism was of especially great political importance in the industrial areas of Saxony and Thuringia, which were the only such areas in which Nazism seems to have gained a significant degree of working-class support. This was a poor region, with a large number of small and middle-sized enterprises and, on account of the textiles industry, a high rate of women's employment. The birth-rate was also abnormally low.

of the Catholic Centre Party most nearly approximated to the propaganda tenets of the Nazi Party. The Centre Party's Chancellor Brüning, for example, introduced higher tax rates for single persons in 1930, and the Papal Encyclical of 1931 restated the virtues of traditional family life. The bitter political rivalry between the two parties for the votes of the Catholic peasantry, artisans and shopkeepers has tended to disguise the extent of their common ground in such social matters. This type of partial or apparent consensus on a basic issue among different sectional interests and elite groups was one of the most important foundations of Nazi rule. The political implications of such common positions, of which this is an interesting example, did not always become clear until after the seizure of power in 1933. (Compare the parallel attitudes of Hitler and the army to rearmament, of the Nazi leaders and industrialists to trade unions.) The effect was to accelerate the reconciliation of such established groups with the new regime and to broaden its popular appeal after 1933. The forces which resisted the emancipatory processes and measures of the 1920s thus eased the path of an extreme reaction.

Anti-feminism is an interesting and important political ideology in this respect, for, although it has been much less carefully studied than various forms of racism, it seems to share with these violent types of prejudice the capacity to appeal to groups who are not in any way *directly* 'threatened' by (and perhaps even have no first-hand experience of) the phenomena to which they object. Just as Jews or Negroes often become objects of the hatred or fear of people who have no contact with the minority against which they are prejudiced, and thus serve as a focus for general resentments and anxieties which have in origin nothing at all to do with Jews or Negroes, so also can emancipatory changes in the roles and position of women excite an opposition among men whose own dominance is not immediately challenged. The woman question becomes a man question and a political question insofar as it arouses *general* passions, and is felt to raise *general* questions about the 'moral', 'natural' and 'biological' order of society. Much more research needs to be done on these issues, but there are some reasons for thinking that anti-feminism did realize its latent capacity to arouse such *generalized* sentiments in Germany between 1928 and 1933: much publicity was given to the career woman, so that men who had never seen such a creature could form their own views about the desirability of her existence. One of the most distinguished victims of this type of vilification, Toni Sender, a member of the national parliament (Reichstag) who laboured bravely under the triple burden of being Jewish, a social democrat and a woman, has left a memorable account of the personal attacks on her by nationalists and Nazis during the violent election campaigns of 1932. They culminated in the repeated assertion that she was a high-class prostitute who only donned proletarian clothes when she went to address workers' meetings. In the poisoned atmosphere of the Nazi struggle for power there were few defences against this salacious campaign of defamation – the courts declined to convict those responsible.[36]

For these reasons, and for others which social psychologists have analysed and speculated about, anti-feminism was not a minor or opportunistic component of National Socialism, but a central part of it, and a part the importance of which in the years 1929–33 has probably been underrated. This anti-feminism amounted to much more than the notorious demagogic attacks on the 'subversion of traditional moral standards by the Jewish–marxist advocates of free love'. David Schoenbaum scarcely exaggerates when he speaks of a 'secondary racism'.[37] And yet the relationship between the party's reactionary propaganda on the woman question on the one hand, and the fact that women were markedly underrepresented among its electoral supporters on the other, was far from simple.

In the last years of the Weimar Republic some liberal women's organizations recognized the dangers of Nazi anti-feminism, and warned women not to vote for the party. For rather different reasons, and perhaps with greater effect, working-class women's organizations took the same line. The influence of the women's organizations, both in general and in this particular respect, is difficult to assess. It was widely thought that the various women's movements made relatively little progress in changing public and private attitudes during the 1920s, and at the end of that decade the liberal women's organizations appear to have become weak, disunited and increasingly conservative.[38] As Gabriele Bremme has shown, however, there was no clear correlation, either positive or negative, between the attitude of the political parties to the woman question and the political preferences of women voters in the last five years of the Weimar Republic. Fewer enfranchised women actually voted in elections than men, though the proportion of women who did exercise their new constitutional right grew slowly in the later 1920s and early 1930s; the lowest turnout was among women in rural areas. Those who voted showed a marked preference for parties which, in the local or

[36] Toni Sender, *The Autobiography of a German Rebel* (London 1940), pp. 280–3. The early chapters of this book on Toni Sender's childhood and her work in the international socialist movement up to 1919 are also of great interest. On the social psychology of anti-feminism, see Hans Dieter Schmidt and others, *Frauenfeindlichkeit. Sozial-psychologische Aspekte der Misogynie* (Munich 1973).

[37] David Schoenbaum, *Hitler's Social Revolution. Class and Status in Nazi Germany 1933–1939* (New York 1966), p. 187.

[38] See Parsons, 'Democracy and Social Structure'; Kirkpatrick, *Women and Family Life*, Chapter 2; Thönnessen, *Emancipation*. On the background to the role of the liberal women's organizations: Richard J. Evans, *The Feminist Movement in Germany, 1894–1933* (London 1976), Chapter 8; and Evans, 'German Women'.

regional context, occupied conservative positions, in particular for parties which were favourably disposed towards the major churches. This latter point probably goes a long way towards explaining the very high women's vote for the anti-feminist Centre Party and the relatively low women's vote for the anti-feminist Nazi Party. (Aside from the rising level of electoral participation, the only notable change in women's political preferences in the last election before 1933 evidently resulted from the abandonment by some working- and middle-class women of their picture of Social Democracy as a party of violent revolution and atheism – but even this change was probably more apparent than real, for there are strong grounds for supposing that the rising *proportion* of women among social democratic voters merely reflected the desertion of the reformist party in favour of the Communist Party by male working-class voters.[39]

Thus the new party of the radical right did not fit at all easily into the German political scene in this respect: to women voters (and not only to them) it did not represent a typical conservative party. Up to 1930 and to a lesser extent afterwards, it perhaps suffered from a further electoral disadvantage, in that there appears to have been a widespread if inconclusive reaction among German women against the slaughter of the First World War, and a reluctance, encouraged by the women's movements of all colours, to support programmes which would condemn further generations of women to the loss of their husbands and sons in war.[40] These factors should not be overemphasized, however, for the proportion of women's votes in the total Nazi vote seems to have been rising slowly but steadily after 1928, and in 1932 a large number of women clearly *did* vote for the Nazi Party; in doing so they were almost certainly acting as most, though by no means all, German women did, and following the political lead of the head of their household.[41] It remains nonetheless significant that men were substantially overrepresented among Hitler's

[39] Gabriele Bremme, *Die politische Rolle der Frau in Deutschland. Eine Untersuchung über den Einfluss der Frauen bei Wahlen und ihre Teilnahme in Partei und Parlament* (Göttingen 1956), pp. 73–7; Thönnessen, *Emancipation*, pp. 108–16. The Communist Party received very little electoral support from women, less than any other party.

[40] See the interesting, partly autobiographical book by Katherine Thomas, *Women in Nazi Germany*, (London 1943). The solid electoral support among women for the revanchist German National People's Party in the 1920s, however, points to the limits of this reaction against militarism: Bremme, *Rolle der Frau*, pp. 68–73.

[41] Bremme, *Rolle der Frau*, p. 74. The statistical evidence on this point is very fragmentary, since by no means all local and regional authorities made a separate count of men's and women's votes: Herbert Kühr, *Pärteien und Wähler im Stadt- und Landkreis Essen in der Zeit der Weimarer Republik* (Düsseldorf 1973), pp. 289 f. The fact that the Communist and Nazi parties appealed predominantly to male voters does not invalidate the view that the head of the household customarily set the political tone for his wife, since these parties were supported above all by *young* men in the towns and the countryside respectively – many of them were unmarried.

supporters in the presidential elections of 1932, and women even more markedly overrepresented among those who voted for the incumbent President, the conservative Field Marshal von Hindenburg, who was supported by the Centre Party and the Social Democrats. Women did *not* rush in overwhelming numbers, as has frequently been asserted, to the support of the movement which promised to envelop them in primordially feminine protective subordination. In January 1933 the new regime thus had some leeway to make up in gaining the confidence of German women.[42]

Women's place

That it was able nonetheless to implement with impunity a wide range of anti-feminist policies in the years 1933–6 was perhaps due less to its usurpation of dictatorial powers than to the comprehensive dislocation of the social order caused by the world economic crisis. The eugenic and procreative emphasis of these policies was firmly stated from the outset: in June 1933, for example, Wilhelm Frick (Minister of the Interior) called on middle-class women in particular to be sensible of their duty to the race and to produce large numbers of healthy and intelligent children.[43] But at this stage such talk was overshadowed by a comprehensive attack on the employment of women, in particular of married women. The disruption and uncertainty of social life, the widespread poverty and disorientation, the pervasive sense of crisis, had created conditions in which *any* governmental initiatives of this kind were bound to produce a variety of different effects at the same time, and thus to appeal to different people in different ways, to be open to a variety of different interpretations and propagandistic justifications. Nazi policies towards women in the years 1933–4 furnish an excellent example of this ambiguity, of the way in which the multipurpose character of the regime's early measures derived from the fact that the self-regulating mechanisms of economic and social development had ground to a halt: for the long-term and basic racial, military and population goals of the movement both matched with and were disguised by short-term policies to cope with the crisis of unemployment, which had done so much to accentuate antagonism between the sexes in the labour market. Thus the slogan 'work for married men' could be justified in crude 'sexist' terms, in terms of social equity and

---

[42] Karl Dietrich Bracher, *Die Auflösung der Weimarer Republik*, 3rd edn. (Villingen 1960), p. 476, n. 132. (Compare Kirkpatrick, *Women and Family Life*, p. 156, on the relative popularity of Hindenburg and Hitler as godfathers to the children of large families!) Dahrendorf is probably the most influential author who still insists, despite the evidence, that women voted in disproportionately large numbers for the Nazi Party: *Society and Democracy*, p. 116; the point is not discussed in the earlier German edition of the book. Bridenthal's formulation, 'Weimar Women', pp. 149, 169 f., is more cautious but still misleading – the change in women's political attitudes seems to have come *after* 1933.

[43] Quoted in Glass, *Population Policies*, p. 282.

utility (reducing *family* poverty) and in terms of population policy (areas with the highest level of women's employment had the lowest birth-rates).

However, the Nazi attempt to reduce the numbers of working women in fact gave no more than insignificant reinforcement to a trend in the labour market which was already very strong indeed before January 1933, for the crisis had already pushed a large number of women out of the workforce entirely. This trend was visible even in the census of economically active persons, the broad category which included all those who worked irregularly and/or without payment. In 1925, 51.5 per cent of the female population of working age was economically active in this sense, in 1933 only 49.3 per cent; in absolute terms, a decline of over 300,000. This figure had been rising steadily over the long term: *the rise was not merely checked, but actually significantly reversed in the crisis*. The figures for the insured labour force, that is those who worked regularly for a wage or a salary *and* those who registered themselves as unemployed when they could not find such work, are even more revealing. While the number of men who were in the labour market in this sense fell from September 1929 to January 1933 by 950,000 to 13.23 million, *the number of insured women was cut by almost 2.5 million* to 5.4 million – a reduction of 31.6 per cent. And of this 5.4 million over 1 million were unemployed.[44]

But since only 1.13 million women continued to register at the labour exchanges as unemployed in January 1933, the overall insurance statistics nurtured the illusion that the crisis had hit women wage- and salary-earners much less hard than it had hit men: 57.2 per cent of all *insured* men had a job in January 1933, 73 per cent of all *insured* women. The source of this illusory discrepancy lay in the fact that the most important public relief schemes imposed a *family* means test during the years of mass unemployment. The unemployment insurance system, in which unemployed working women had an individual *right* to benefits, had all but collapsed by 1932. This meant that unemployed women who lived with their fathers or husbands received little or nothing by way of dole payments, and so had little incentive to make the weekly trip to the labour exchange and register as unemployed. Thus they disappeared from the statistics, while the men, except for adolescent dependants, were still counted because relief was distributed through them.[45]

---

[44] Stat. *Jhb. 1929*, pp. 270, 274; *1934*, pp. 297, 307.

[45] Jill Stephenson, 'Women in German Society 1930–1940', Ph.D. thesis, Edinburgh 1974, pp. 123 ff., identifies the source of the illusion, but underestimates its importance as also does David Schoenbaum, *Social Revolution*, p. 190. The only way to calculate the fall in the number of working women in the crisis is to compare the totals of employed and unemployed, since this reveals the extent of what was called 'invisible unemployment'. Expressed as a proportion of those in the labour market in 1929, the total of registered and 'invisible' unemployed women in January 1933 was slightly lower than that of men: 3.6 out of 7.9 million, as against 7.0 out of 14.2 million. But the conclusion that women came better out of the crisis is entirely unwarranted, since most of those without work also received no relief. See Preller, *Sozialpolitik*, p. 120.

The unemployment percentages were accurate in the technical sense but they completely obscured what was in fact happening – a massive degradation of teenage girls and older women workers into the ranks of the family assistants and above all into the ranks of the entirely unproductive. This development undoubtedly set back acceptance of the notion that women should and could work outside the home. Nazi propaganda and policy was parasitic on such statistical illusions, parasitic on the resentments and needs of unemployed men, and parasitic on a socio-economic trend the strength of which was anyway overwhelming. By stressing the priority of unemployed male heads of households, the measures adopted in 1933/4 to increase and re-allocate employment opportunities suggested a plausible concern for distributive social justice (in the exact Aristotelian sense!);[46] they appealed directly to male self-interest; they suggested to people of conservative and Catholic persuasion that the Nazi leadership really did take seriously its rhetoric about the sanctity of the family; and in the form of the marriage loan scheme they met the real economic needs of numerous young couples and at the same time furthered the population policies of the regime.

Competition between the sexes in the labour market was probably most acute among civil servants, white-collar workers of all kinds and in the free professions. Women had gained professional positions in increasing numbers in the 1920s, especially in public service; in 1933 there were many employed men with university and professional qualifications. The Brüning and von Papen governments had already begun to reduce the number of women civil servants in 1931-2, and it was in respect of its own employees that the new government adopted the most firmly and openly discriminatory policies in the following two years. Women, especially married women, were removed from responsible posts in public administration, in the schools men were automatically given precedence for senior positions, and the number of women students was cut back.[47]

---

[46] According to this notion goods, services and rights should be allocated according to ability, and – deriving from this – just need, rather than according to the principle of formal equality. Aristotle regarded women as innately inferior to men, as subordinate members of the family household. He set a very long tradition of discriminatory political theory on its methodological feet.

[47] See Stephenson, 'Women', Chapter 3 and idem 'Girls' Higher Education'; McIntyre, 'Professions', p. 192; Kirkpatrick, *Women and Family Life*, p. 232. In 1989 only 6.2 per cent of women civil servants were married: *SdR*, vol. 556/2, p. 4. The loss of valuable racial stock in the shape of 140,000 highly educated unmarried women (mostly schoolteachers) does not appear to have bothered eugenist opinion! – perhaps keeping senior jobs a male preserve appeared more important. Public employees have always been in the front line of governments' attempts to influence the birth-rate and family patterns: they were the first to receive family allowances in most European states, and, in the case of women, the first to be pushed around in periods of retrenchment. Married women found it very difficult to gain work as schoolteachers in Britain in the 1930s, and in the late 1930s the French government tried to make promotion for senior male civil

Despite loud demands from the rank and file of the Nazi movement, however, the government stopped short of formally compelling women to give up their jobs in other branches of employment. Families in which husband *and* wife or father *and* daughter both had regular work came under great pressure in the years 1933 and 1934 to surrender the woman's job for the benefit of unemployed married men. While the government declined, on the social darwinist grounds that such action would penalize the able and the diligent, to introduce any mandatory procedures for the replacement of such women by men in trade and industry, and while it rejected the denunciations and the more violent forms of agitation which accompanied the campaigns of local Nazi groups, official blessing was given to efforts to 'persuade' women who had male breadwinners to withdraw 'voluntarily' from the labour market. It was presented to them as their duty to do so. The assertion of the priority of men's needs coincided with the reassertion of the virtues of woman's traditional role as housewife and mother. Precisely because these pressures did remain unofficial, it is not possible to say how many women succumbed to them. Some undoubtedly did succumb and were forced by moral blackmail and threats to confine themselves, at least for a time, to domestic routine.[48]

But the census of June 1933 revealed just how closely the stance of the Nazi Party on the question of *married* women's work resembled that of King Canute as he faced the incoming tide. For the proportion of married women among female wage-earners was seen to have risen quite sharply since 1925, and the overall proportion of married women who were economically active in any manner had also increased slightly – *despite* the crisis, and *despite* the assorted discriminatory measures and pressures of the Brüning government and of the Nazi Party.[49]

It must be admitted that the census was taken before the campaign against double-earnings had reached its full pitch of intensity; it must be

servants dependent on their being married. Glass, *Population Policies*, cites much evidence on this point.

[48] For details see Timothy W. Mason, 'National Socialist Policies towards the German Working Classes, 1925–1939', D.Phil. thesis, Oxford 1971, Chapter 4a. The establishment of political control over the labour market at a time of mass unemployment marked a decisive step in the breaking of opposition to Nazi rule. Aside from communists and social democrats (who were sacked in large numbers) and women, the other most exposed group were young unmarried men; however, they were not expected to give up jobs unless there was some alternative for them, such as work on land reclamation in the Labour Service. It must be noted in this context that women had been selectively dismissed in large numbers in a previous crisis – during demobilization at the end of the First World War, then too with governmental support: Thönnessen, *Emancipation*, pp. 91 ff.

[49] See *Wirtschaft und Statistik*, vol. 21 no. 3 (February 1941), p. 50; Preller, *Sozialpolitik*, p. 121. In absolute terms the number of economically active married women increased by 30,000 between 1925 and 1933, an increase of one-seventh. The proportion of married women who were economically active rose in the same period from 28.7 per cent to 29.2 per cent. It was the unmarried and the widows who were being forced out of economic life.

stressed that the increase in the employment of married women would almost certainly have been greater had the crisis been less severe and had there been no anti-feminist reaction; and it must also be admitted that the evidence of the census *could* be interpreted by those who were, for whatever reason, hostile to the regular employment of married women, as renewed proof of the objective need for their campaign.

Yet when all is said and done, the tortuous relationship between the paternalist anti-feminist ideology and the realities of social change in these crisis years remains noteworthy. If the question is first taken as a whole, it is evident that the conservative, Catholic and Nazi attack on the *regular* employment of women in general (whether married or single) was most vociferous at a time (1929–33) when women were anyway leaving the labour market in very large numbers and at a rapid pace for elementary social and economic reasons. On this broad front the anti-feminist reaction was rushing with an impressive display of virile energy through a wide-open door. Exactly the opposite was the case, however, on the narrower front which concerned *married*, economically active women, and in particular married wage-earners. Here the anti-feminist reaction found itself in head-on collision with a long-term process of social and economic change, which was drawing ever more married women into trade and industry; here paternalists, eugenist zealots and misogynists flailed about themselves with an irrational and noisy mendacity, which was powerless to disrupt the nexus of the joint interests of employers and married women workers. The irreducible facts were that more and more married women were working, partly because more and more women of working age were getting married.[50]

This question requires further research with respect to the years of the economic crisis, for it is not yet clear in what types of employment the increased numbers of married working women were concentrated. It is highly probable that a part of the increase is accounted for by a rise in the number of wives who worked as family assistants. It is also probable that employers in the industrial and service sectors of the economy preferred to keep on the payroll during the crisis years those women whose productivity was highest, that is, women who were experienced in their trades and perhaps semi-skilled. These women were more likely to be married than were teenage girls or women over fifty. Strength is lent to the hypothesis by the fact that women in their twenties and thirties were employed in above average numbers in the consumer goods industries (especially in textiles, clothing and foodstuffs), which were less severely hit by the world slump than most other sectors of industry. If one examines the census evidence by age-groups, it is apparent that between

[50] Not even the sharp fall in the rate of marriage during the crisis years held back the trend towards the increased employment of married women.

1925 and 1933 there was a marked decline in the proportion of women who were economically active only among those aged under sixteen or over fifty, that is, among those women whose labour power was least productive for the employers. It was the young and the old who were pushed to the wall in the brutal competitive conditions of the crisis years.[51]

In socio-economic terms, the campaign against *married* women who worked was thus a largely ineffectual and deeply irrelevant exercise in paternalistic and male chauvinist demagoguery, the only significant impact of which, outside the professions and the civil service, was to embarrass and intimidate a large number of families. There were two general reasons why it had little effect in most branches of trade and industry: there were relatively few types of work which unemployed men were normally thought to be suited to or trained to take over from women (some white-collar and some unskilled jobs furnished the few exceptions outside the professions); and women's wages were generally much lower than men's so that either the man who replaced a woman had to accept very low remuneration, or the employer in question had to replace cheap with less cheap labour. Either way, the disadvantages were considerable.[52]

Neither these various pressures, nor the marriage loan scheme under the terms of which women who received a loan on marrying were required to give up their job, can account for the fact that the level of women's employment in trade, industry and administration did indeed remain low during the first three years of Nazi rule. The very slow rate of increase in the insured female labour force – June 1933: 4.85 million; June 1936: 5.63 million[53] – was only to a very limited extent a reflection of policies towards women. It was rather an unintended but inevitable consequence of rearmament and of the related attempt by the government to keep wages, and thus consumer purchasing power, at their low crisis levels. For the rearmament boom created jobs above all in the investment goods sector of the economy, where legislation, tradition and the heavy nature of the work combined to restrict very narrowly the employment of women. Well over one-half of all women industrial workers were concentrated in the textiles, clothing and foodstuffs industries, which

---

[51] *Wirtschaft und Statistik* (1941), p. 50; *Stat. Jhb. 1939/40*, pp. 376 f. I have not yet found separate figures for married women salary-earners, but it is unlikely that the increase in the number of economically active married women was concentrated among white-collar workers, since these women tended to give up their work on marriage anyway – see pp. 189–90, below. They were also subject to greater pressure to leave their jobs.

[52] A few big firms offer women workers redundancy payments and replaced them by men; one of the firms immediately reduced wage-rates: Glass, *Population Policies*, p. 460. The notion that some types of industrial work are essentially women's jobs, calling for especial dexterity, patience etc., is generally an ideological rationalization of social and economic interests, shared in a complicated manner by employers and male workers. In this situation it may actually have helped to save some women's jobs – a superficially paradoxical outcome.   [53] *Stat. Hdb.*, p. 474.

recovered much more slowly from the world economic crisis than did iron and steel, engineering or building.

The attack on the regular employment of women and the campaign for marriage and child-bearing were thus in practice distinct initiatives; they concerned different, though related aspects of economic organization and personal behaviour, both of which were susceptible to direct political influence only insofar as such interventions ran with the tide of social trends. The distinction was blurred in official propaganda, blurred too by the fact that the two programmes were developed simultaneously. Despite the claims made about its impact upon the labour market, the marriage loan scheme was primarily an instrument of family policy; and it is to this topic that the discussion must now turn.

Procreation

Marriage loans were made available from the summer of 1933. They were one of the most ingenious pieces of social engineering which the regime devised. The scheme was also National Socialism's only major innovation in the field of family and population policy, for most of the other steps it was to take had already been tried by other European governments. Under the terms of the scheme young couples were granted an interest-free loan of RM600 (average), provided that the woman withdrew from the labour market.[54] This sum amounted to between four and five months' wages for most industrial workers, and repayment was drawn out over a long period – 1 per cent per month. Some 700,000 couples, that is over one quarter of those who married in the period, passed the various tests of economic eligibility and political and eugenic reliability between August 1933 and January 1937. Loan certificates – made over, typically, to the husband rather than the wife – entitled the bearer to acquire household equipment and furniture, and the scheme thus gave a considerable stimulus to these depressed sectors of industry. A clause under which the sum to be repaid was cut by one quarter for every child born to the couple

---

[54] Women whose husbands were earning less than RM125 per month did not have to give up their jobs at once – this was a low wage for a man, though in 1933/4 there were certainly many workers earning even less. For this and further details, see Glass, *Population Policies*, pp. 287–9; also Kirkpatrick, *Women and Family Life*, Chapters 5 and 6; DAF, *Deutsche Sozialpolitik 1936–7*, pp. 59 f. The scheme gave rise to a new verb in the German language: *abkindern* – to repay-a-loan-by-having-children. The marriage loan scheme was not in fact associated with any systematic effort to place men in women's jobs; the government claimed that it was, but this was just another attempt to curry favour among men. Its main effect on the labour market probably lay in causing a higher turnover than usual among young women workers – an effect which was of no small importance, in view of the fact that the large cohort of children born immediately after the First World War was leaving school in the years 1933–6. There were thus more teenage girls seeking employment, and the marriage loan scheme tended to produce more openings for them by removing young women from clerical and factory employment.

was designed to encourage procreation, and Nazi propagandists attached great importance to the success which they claimed for the scheme in this respect: it was asserted that couples who received marriage loans had on average twice as many children as those who, for one reason or another, did not qualify. Even if allowance is made for the fact that applicants were probably more likely to want to start a family than non-applicants, and that some of the women who benefited were pregnant when they married, the marriage loans constituted the only significant exception to the general rule that financial incentives (or disincentives) had no demonstrable effect upon the birth-rate in Europe in the inter-war years.[55] The scheme was financed in the first instance by the tax on the unmarried, but this propagandistic device was soon dropped on account of the resentment which it caused among working spinsters, who were not reluctant to marry but could find no partner, because of the slaughter of young men in the First World War.

The political gains for the regime from the introduction of marriage loans were probably considerable. Known opponents of National Socialism will not have been impressed by it, since they were excluded from its benefits, but there can be little doubt that for numerous young couples, whose political views had hitherto been characterized by uncertainty or abstinence, the early stages of married life were made a great deal less hard than they would otherwise have been. The poverty and insecurity of the crisis years had caused many people to defer marriage. The provision of marriage loans for working and lower middle-class couples certainly played a part in bringing about an extraordinary increase in the number of marriages after the Nazi seizure of power:

1929	589,600
1932	516,800
1933	638,000
1934	740,200.

The marriage-rate declined a little in the mid-1930s, but throughout the pre-war years it remained well above the average for the 1920s.[56] The new regime thus associated itself closely with an unprecedented outbreak of

[55] Richard and Kathleen Titmuss, *Parents Revolt. A Study of the Declining Birth-Rate in Acquisitive Societies* (London 1942), p. 111, made this generalization. Glass points out that the loans may well have furnished poor couples with a real alternative to abortion or illegitimate birth, and that the recipients came from lower income groups among whom the birth-rate was anyway higher than average. Furthermore, at the beginning some loans were granted to couples who were already married. He nonetheless inclines to the view that the loans did have some effect on the marriage- and birth-rates: *Population Policies*, pp. 308, 461.

[56] *Stat. Hdb.*, p. 47. Full details of marriage-rates by age-group: *Stat, Jhb. 1941/2*, p. 73. The economic recovery was, of course, the major cause of the increase, which occurred in most other European countries too, though it was greatest in Germany.

domestic bliss and appeared to be making good some of its campaign rhetoric about restoring the integrity of the family, giving women an assured and tolerable place within the home, and safeguarding the demographic basis of the German race.

This latter point loomed, of course, very large in official thinking on these topics: the simultaneous assertion that Germany needed living space because the country was over-populated, and that the race was threatened with extinction because of the declining birth-rate, furnished one of the most extreme examples of that 'brutal casuistry', to use Alan Bullock's phrase, which characterized both nationalist and Nazi political thinking on these questions. Prior to 1933 the German birth-rate had indeed declined very sharply: from over 2 million live births at the turn of the century to 1.3 million in 1925 and to 971,000 in 1933. Since there were many more women of child-bearing age in the population in 1933 than before the First World War, mean fertility had in fact fallen even more steeply: from 128 live births per 1,000 women aged fifteen to fifty in 1910/11, to 80 in 1925 and to 59 in 1933.[57] This was a long-term trend common to all Western European countries. It resulted in the main from the increased accessibility of reliable methods of contraception, and the desire of a rapidly expanding urban population for higher standards of living (in towns the restriction of family size made a decisive difference to living standards). In Germany the First World War, the post-war inflation and then the world economic crisis, all of which had a more severe impact here than elsewhere, greatly accentuated this downward trend; in 1930 only Austria had a lower reproduction rate.[58]

Marriage loans were only one of the many instruments deployed by the Nazi regime in a massive campaign to reverse the fall in the birth-rate, and this campaign was in turn one of the major influences upon the social position of women in the Third Reich. Richard and Kathleen Titmuss

---

[57] *Stat. Jhb. 1934*, p. 27; *1941/2*, p. 77. There are a variety of different methods of computing birth-rates and fertility. The most simple index has been chosen here. The more sophisticated calculations – net reproduction rates – are mainly of predictive value, and require evidence which was not always gathered in full in pre-1945 censuses. They do yield slightly, but not significantly, different rates of change in fertility from the crude figures quoted above. Robert R. Kuczynski, *The Measurement of Population Growth, Methods and Results* (London 1935), gives a helpful discussion of these problems. This study contains much statistical evidence from Germany and many other countries, together with a devastating critique of the ways in which such figures and calculations were misused in the 1920s by panic-mongers and imperialist procreation zealots. See also Glass (who acknowledges his debt to Kuczynski), *Population Policies*, pp. 9–14, 270, 305. Knodel, *Decline of Fertility*, gives a detailed and highly technical account of the causes and course of the fall in the birth-rate.

[58] Bürgdorfer, *Volk*. p. 372. The author also rehearses the long, inconclusive discussion among German demographers about the exact extent of the effect of the war on the change in the birth-rate during the 1920s; Bürgdorfer himself claimed that it was slight: pp. 77–81, 101–7.

described the campaign as 'the most tremendous experiment ever attempted consciously to change biological trends'.[59] Financial inducements and compensation were an important part of the experiment, but it also comprised improvements in welfare and maternity services, an unending barrage of propaganda designed to elevate the status and raise the self-respect of mothers and housewives, and repressive measures against birth-control and abortion. The experiment was conducted blindly, for there was no prior evidence that any of these interventions would in fact cause the birth-rate to rise.

By the beginning of the Second World War the cumulative economic effects of welfare reforms in the interests of families with children were considerable. Though the diversity of the measures makes it impossible to compute average financial benefits, the strain on the family budgets of many households – especially of poor urban households – must have been very substantially eased. In October 1934 the income tax allowances for every dependent child were roughly doubled, and voluntary payments by employers to women workers on marriage were freed from tax (provided that the recipient gave up her job). Further tax legislation in 1938/9 extended the allowances and exemptions. These reforms made a substantial difference to family incomes. Maternity benefits for working mothers, introduced during the First World War and codified in 1927, were generally increased after 1933, especially for the period of four to six weeks before confinement; there were no significant changes in the law on these questions before 1942 but the Labour Front brought strong pressure to bear upon employers, and in the increasingly rare cases where they refused to increase the benefits the National Socialist Welfare Organization often stepped in. Such payments were also exempted from taxation.[60] On marrying working women were allowed to claim back 50 per cent of the contributions they had paid into the compulsory state invalidity insurance scheme. The rights of working mothers and of the parents of large families to benefits under the sickness insurance scheme were extended, and nursing payments were introduced, together with

[59] Titmuss, *Parents Revolt*, p. 105; similarly Kirkpatrick, *Women and Family Life*, p. 152. The following highly condensed account of the further welfare measures is based on Kirkpatrick, *Women and Family Life*; DAF, *Deutsche Sozialpolitik 1936–7* and *1938*; Glass, *Population Policies*; Schoenbaum, *Social Revolution*, Chapter 6.

[60] The law of 1927 on paid leave for pregnant women was the major reform: *Reichsgesetzblatt* (German Statute Book), I, p. 187; Preller, *Sozialpolitik*, pp. 353 f.; Friedrich Syrup, *Hundert Jahre Staatlicher Sozialpolitik* (Stuttgart 1957), p. 362. Kirkpatrick, *Women and Family Life*, pp. 226–9, exaggerates the extent of the further governmental reforms in this sphere after 1933. The promised Law for the Protection of Mothers was held up by disputes within the government in 1937–9 and did not reach the statute book until May 1942: *RGBl* I, pp. 321–8. On paper this act did substantially extend protective restrictions and benefits for pregnant women workers, but it is not clear that the new regulations were fully enforced during the crisis of war. On reforms by industrial employeers in the 1930s see DAF, *Deutsche Sozialpolitik, 1938*, p. 51.

periods of paid leave of absence from work for those with infants to care for. School fees were reduced for families with more than one child at school.

The most important reform was undoubtedly the introduction of family allowances. These were made available by stages and in two different forms. As a measure of relief rather than an incentive, large families which were in need became eligible in September 1935 for once-and-for-all grants of up to RM100 per child. Preference was given under this discretionary scheme to families with more than five children: by March 1938 560,000 families had received grants averaging RM330 (= 3 million children at an average of RM62 per head). Very few families of the prescribed size failed to benefit; indeed some of the money must have gone to households in which the eldest children were no longer dependent. It can be safely assumed that this measure was of particular importance to the rural areas, where, as Nazi ideologues never tired of pointing out, the procreative urge was still stronger than in the cities. (In rural areas, it must also be noted, a much smaller proportion of the population was covered by social insurance than in the towns.) The second type of family allowance, the recurrent grant, was inaugurated on a modest scale, but the government soon made it almost universal. It was additional to and did not supplant once-and-for-all grants. From July 1936 RM10 per month was paid for the fifth and every further child under sixteen years of wage- and salary-earners whose income did not exceed RM185 per month; this earnings limit was well above the average industrial wage in 1936, but it excluded some two-thirds of all white-collar workers from the benefits. Fifteen months later the self-employed were made eligible and the income limit was raised to RM200 per month. The self-employed were, however, excluded from the decisive further reform of April 1938, which raised the income limit for wage- and salary-earners to RM650, and granted *RM10 per month for the third and fourth, RM20 for all subsequent children*. The number of children covered by these monthly payments rose from 300,000 in 1936 to 2.5 million in 1938. Public employees – workers and clerks, but not the higher ranks of the civil service – were eligible, although they already received salary increments in respect of some of their children. The money was drawn from the national unemployment insurance fund, which had accumulated a large surplus since 1934.[61]

These more or less general measures to lighten the economic burdens of larger families were supplemented by a wide and intricate range of specific discretionary programmes, designed and financed by both

---

[61] Glass's account, *Population Policies*, pp. 291–6, gives slightly different figures from DAF, *Deutsche Sozialpolitik, 1938*, pp. 182–4. In 1941 public employees were put on the same footing as civil servants and received RM20 per month for each child. I am grateful to Jane Caplan for this point.

government authorities and party and professional organizations, also by industrial firms and the social insurance offices. Their individual impact was slight but taken together they added up to a further noteworthy reinforcement of welfare facilities. In the later 1930s the size of the average marriage loan rose by RM50, and specially advantageous terms were offered to couples who earned their living from agriculture, also to women who worked as auxiliary nurses or social workers – these groups were evidently thought to be likely to produce large or model families. From March 1938 allowances were available for the education or vocational training of politically reliable teenage children from large families. The parents of large families paid subscriptions at reduced rates to Nazi organizations (most notably in the Labour Front, membership of which was virtually compulsory), and they could buy cheap railway tickets for themselves and their offspring. A number of cities followed the example of Berlin, where the birth-rate was exceptionally low, and offered generous children's allowances to couples who would agree to have a third child; and the professional organizations of doctors and dentists followed that of the federation of pharmacists and set up income equalization schemes for the benefit of members with numerous children. The National Socialist Welfare Organization, the Winter Relief programme and the specialist organization Mother and Child all laid great stress upon the relief in kind and cash which they distributed to large families. The latter, a voluntary organization employing over 120,000 full-time or honorary officials and assistants, set up a comprehensive network of 26,000 agencies, which claimed to have given economic assistance to 1.2 million needy families and aid and advice to over 600,000 expectant mothers (one in two) during the year 1935 alone; holidays were arranged for mothers and children who would otherwise have been unable to get away from home, kindergartens set up in agricultural districts during harvest-time, etc., etc.[62]

The Labour Front exerted especially strong pressure for such improvements in welfare policies. This mass organization developed a well-founded scepticism about the capacity of the regime to enforce sacrifices in the interests of rearmament, and a firm, if opportunistic, concern for family incomes and the standard of living of the working population. Unlike other issues on which it pressed for concessions – e.g. wage-rates, hours of work, food prices – the issue of welfare reforms for mothers and children appears to have been relatively uncontentious. The economic and political elite groups were unaminously committed to the goal of population growth and, having accepted the goal, they had to reconcile themselves to what appeared to be the necessary means to

---

[62] Details from Glass, *Population Policies*, pp. 293–303; Kirkpatrick, *Women and Family Life*, Chapter 6; DAF, *Deutsche Sozialpolitik 1938*, p. 215.

achieve it, despite the fact that the cost, in terms of the diversion of resources to non-military purposes, was considerable. Given the peculiar institutional and ideological limits within which discussion about financial priorities *was* possible in the governmental system of the Third Reich, it is immediately obvious that the demand for family allowances etc. should have been irresistible, while open demands for higher wage-rates were ruled out – although in economic terms the effects of the two concessions would have been very similar. Family policy and eugenics furnished the propagandistic framework within which the problem of poverty could be taken up by this regime. Or, to put it another way, in Germany as in most Western European countries it was the forces of the political right which effectively took possession of the crucial issue of family policy, with all its broad practical and ideological ramifications. It was a strategic conquest of the greatest importance. By contrast, in Britain the question of family allowances was integrated into the Labour Party's programme of social democratic reforms and largely dissociated after the First World War from the debate about eugenics and the imperial master race.

Taken together, the new measures certainly fell far short of that general equalization of burdens as between large and small families which had long been called for by demographers, parents' associations, racialist ideologues and political leaders of all parties, and in terms of cost–benefit calculations they provided only a very small compensation for the loss of income and the expense involved in starting a family. Small families, noted Glass, 'have a substantially higher standard of life than large families', and he cited calculations made in England in the 1930s, according to which a working-class family with three children cost 66 per cent more to run than a man-and-wife household.[63] The new benefits conferred by the Nazi regime on a three-child family did not come remotely near to 60 per cent of the average wage. Even if notional values for discretionary benefits which not all families received – such as cheap transport, lower school fees and the non-repayment of marriage loans – are added on to family allowances and income tax reductions, it is difficult to see how this figure could have been higher than 20 per cent.[64] But this must not obscure the fact that the reforms did yield in direct cash terms a clear improvement in the economic situation of millions of households, thus lightening the oppressive burden of trying to make ends meet week by week. It was usually wives who had the responsibility of managing the family budget, and in the mid-1930s the margin between debt, hunger

[63] Glass, *Population Policies*, pp. 371, 206. For more detailed present-day calculations, see Margaret Wynn, *Family Policy*, 2nd edn (Harmondsworth 1972), esp. Chapter 5 and Appendix I.

[64] For comparison, in France, after the reforms of 1938 which put a cash premium on mothers staying at home, family allowances alone amounted to more than this in many regions of the country: Glass, *Population Policies*, pp. 120–3, 206 ff.

and cold on the one hand, and being able to buy the occasional Sunday joint, new shoes or a bottle of beer on the other, was still desperately narrow for most working-class families – every *Pfennig* counted.[65]

These economic measures were accompanied by incessant propaganda and by a variety of organizational innovations, all of which were designed to further the realization of the official ideal of womanhood and to improve the 'professional aptitudes' of mothers and housewives. Only the briefest summary of these developments is possible here.[66] Central importance was attached, of course, to everything associated with pregnancy and birth, and the encouragement of procreation was a major element, though not the only one, in this exercise in dictatorial persuasion. The National League of Large Families, an influential organization founded during the First World War which had 300,000 members and its own periodical, received official recognition and was brought under the direction of the Race Policy Office of the Nazi Party. The number of maternity clinics was increased, and both infant and maternal mortality-rates continued to fall steadily from their already comparatively low levels – this, despite the weakening of the medical services caused by the persecution of the many Jewish doctors.[67] Changes in the law also played an important part in stereotyping women's social role. From 1936 infertility among married women was categorized as an illness and could thus be treated free of charge under the sickness insurance scheme, and in 1938 wilful or premature infertility was declared to be grounds for divorce. However, since the regime was as much interested in the 'racial–biological quality' as in the sheer quantity of children born, laws concerning the sterilization of those with serious hereditary ailments and the enforcement of eugenic tests on those intending to marry were progressively tightened from 1933 to 1935. This legislation resulted in numerous personal tragedies, but far more numerous were the potentially flattering notifications to aspiring parents that they were of sound biological stock.

Secure in this knowledge, pregnant women could then graduate to the Mothers' School, which formed one of the most striking institutional innovations in this sphere. The schools were run on a voluntary basis and offered training courses in the arts and sciences of motherhood and household management which evidently met a real need, for, although a

---

[65] Mason, 'National Socialist Policies', Chapter 4b, presents some of the data on household budgets in the 1930s. Up to 1937 working-class expenditure on such 'non-essentials' as writing materials, travel, entertainment was minimal.

[66] I again draw heavily in the following section on Kirkpatrick, *Women and Family Life*; also Glass, *Population Policies*, pp. 272 f., 286, 303.

[67] Benefits and allowances probably had very little effect on the birth-rate, but by making it possible for parents to improve standards of care and nutrition they may have helped to cut infant mortality-rates.

small fee was charged, they were attended in the mid-1930s by roughly one-third of all pregnant women – such at least was the claim of the organizers. For their part, they tried to convey the high political and social calling of the housewife and mother, stressed the crucial nature of her contribution to the future health and strength of the race, gave instruction in hygiene and baby-care, and pointed out the ways in which a shrewd and careful management of the family budget could help to ease the economic problems of the Reich, in particular the pressing shortage of foreign exchange – buying fish instead of meat, synthetic fats instead of butter, and clothes made from artificial fibres; cooking nutritious simple dishes, etc. Less obviously marked by ulterior political motives and highly realistic in view of the straitened circumstances of most households in the 1930s, was the consistent emphasis on thrift and the avoidance of waste in managing family resources: here too a potentially flattering concordance was suggested between the interests of the individual household and those of the national economy, and the everyday actions of each housewife assumed strategic importance. Women could contribute directly to the prosperity and strength of the Reich. National attention was focused regularly upon the family kitchen by the propaganda institution of the 'One-Pot-Sunday' when a single-course meal was to be eaten as a token of solidarity with those living in poverty.[68]

The essential burden of this campaign was the development of a comprehensive alternative to the emancipation of women. The effort was directed at inducing women to *celebrate* their domestic role as mother and housewife, on account of its allegedly supreme importance in the life of the nation. The status and characteristic life-patterns of women were not to be changed, but a systematic attempt was made to change their perception of this status: drudgery, scrimping and saving, anxiety, self-abnegation and the highly constricted perspective of a life revolving around the household remained, but they were now hallowed by a never-ending stream of compliments from the country's political leaders, attended to by an ever growing phalanx of governmental and party organizations, endowed with the greatest possible general public signifi-cance, and, in the case of the rigours of childbirth, translated through a frenetic vocabulary of adulation into an ideological experience worthy of quasi-religious reverence. The machinery of propaganda and welfare administration appeared to take the problem of married women seriously, and this was to a large degree novel. Specious, insulting, mendacious and wildly overdrawn though a great deal of this attention may have been, the campaign to ennoble the natural and the everyday, allied as it was to a

[68] Ernest K. Bramsted, *Goebbels and National Socialist Propaganda 1925–1945* (London 1965), pp. 102 f.

series of financial compensations, *addressed itself to and fed upon some of the real frustrations of married women.* The Mother's Cross in gold (eight children), silver (six) and bronze (four),[69] the innumerable pictures of the Führer posing with young children, were merely among the more memorable excesses of a reactionary programme, which was, in view of the conservative self-image of many German women and in view of the unattractive character of most employment opportunities for women outside the home, very shrewdly conceived. It was also energetically prosecuted. But was it successful?

One admittedly uncertain measure of the appeal of this brand of women's politics is furnished by the strength of the organizations which carried out most of the helping, advising, schooling, relieving, holiday planning and propagandizing of women and children. These were run by women, and if the official claim that the Frauenwerk, the umbrella organization, had between 6 million and 8 million members, was even remotely accurate, it was already in the mid-1930s the largest non-compulsory organization in the Third Reich. The 'elite' organization, the Frauenschaft, itself claimed 2 million members, few of whom were also in the party. One of the magazines which it sponsored enjoyed a circulation of over 700,000.[70] While a great deal remains to be discovered, about the recruitment, structure, activities and power of these women's organizations, one thing is clear: they offered a wide and politically unexceptionable framework for responsible public activity, on an honorific part-time or a paid full-time basis to a large number of women with the requisite skills and disposition. Women were not entirely eliminated from public life under Nazi rule, rather their role was confined to the relatively broad sphere of what the party leadership considered to be specifcally women's affairs. The element of surrogate emancipation involved in encouraging *some women* to run classes for *other women* in hygiene, baby-care, toy-making and domestic science is unmistakable.[71] Though hard evidence is still lacking, it is probable that the Nazi women's organizations bore a basic resemblance in their social composition and functions to those organizations in late Victorian England, which were dominated by educated upper- and middle-class women with time and energy to spare,

[69] The first awards were made in May 1939, probably in direct emulation of France, where similar crosses had been distributed since 1920: Glass, *Population Policies*, pp. 172, 303. Among the mothers so honoured were probably some who had tried and failed to obtain an illegal abortion – this had been made much more difficult since 1933: Kirkpatrick, *Women and Family Life*, p. 169.

[70] See ibid., Chapter 3.

[71] Many women functionaries pushed beyond the limits of this surrogate emancipation after 1933, and got into conflicts with the party hierarchy for their pains. They were not always unsuccessful: Schoenbaum, *Social Revolution*, Chapter 6; McIntyre, 'Professions'.

women who felt called upon to bring poor families up to bourgeois standards of self-reliance, thrift and cleanliness.[72] It is not easy to imagine working-class wives or the wives of peasant farmers playing an active role in the Frauenschaft on any large scale (though this assumption could well be mistaken); that they played an extensive passive role seems to be beyond doubt.

Precisely in this context it is important to emphasize that Nazi eugenic propaganda was populist rather than exclusive or elitist in tone. The principles of selection invoked were racial and medical rather than social. The upper-class German nationalist stress on the threatening failure of the educated ruling groups to reproduce themselves was overlaid after 1933 by considerations relating to the health and strength of the German race as a whole: all children were welcome, provided that they did not suffer from hereditary defects and were 'racially pure'. Parents' class became a matter of indifference, indeed the low birth-rate of the professional classes served to illustrate their obsolescence as a ruling elite. The Nazi political elite portrayed itself by contrast as a new leadership group, springing direct and supposedly classless from out of the healthy vigorous people, superseding the incompetent and sterile caste of bourgeois nationalists. It betrayed no outward sign of feeling threatened by 'the people' and went to great rhetorical lengths always to appear to take their part. In the sphere of family and population policy social darwinism thus seemed to be overshadowed by a pseudo-egalitarian racial darwinism, which identified the enemy as being outside 'the people'. The potential appeal of this kind of doctrine was much greater than that of the more exclusive variants current in Europe during the age of high imperialism before 1914. The regime spoke to all German citizens (as defined by the Nuremberg Race Laws of 1935). Only to the smallest degree was this propaganda stance matched by real changes in the social order, but this does not mean that it was ineffective.[73]

The increase in the birth-rate after 1933 seems to offer a surer measure of the popularity of the regime's policies towards women and the family than that of the membership, activities and ideology of the women's organizations. In absolute terms the number of live births rose from its lowest point of 971,000 in 1933 to 1.2 million in 1934, and continued to rise almost without a break to 1.41 million in 1939. Expressed in terms of births per 1,000 women of child-bearing age, the increase was only a little less dramatic:

[72] See Brian Harrison, 'For Church, Queen and Country. The Girls' Friendly Society 1874–1920', *Past and Present*, no. 61 (November 1973); also C. L. Mowat, *The Charity Organization Society 1869–1913* (London 1961), Chapter 2.

[73] On changes in the social structure, see Schoenbaum, *Social Revolution*, Chapter 8. Frick, quoted above on middle-class birth-rates, belonged to the conservative–nationalist wing of the Nazi Party.

1933 58.9
1936 77.4
1939 84.8.

Richard and Kathleen Titmuss commented, 'Germany alone in the world has succeeded in obtaining some increase in fertility. This is a spectacular fact when viewed against the background of the trend in other countries peopled by whites.'[74] Aside from the marriage loan scheme, however – and this only to a certain extent – *none* of the regime's *positive* policies for the encouragement of motherhood can be demonstrated in a method-ologically conclusive manner to have played *any* part in bringing about this result. This is not only due to the great intricacy of the science of demography and to the large role played therein by unquantifiable aspects of human behaviour. On a more mundane level, both hostile and impartial observers agreed in attaching great weight to the effects upon the birth-rate of attempts to suppress the practice of illegal abortion: the legal penalties were increased in May 1933, and the law was more rigorously enforced under the Nazis than before, with the result that convictions increased from 5,072 in 1934 to 7,670 in 1938. Furthermore, information about and devices for birth control were made less accessible after 1933, though they were not placed under legal restrictions.[75]

It would be out of place in more than one sense to offer any judgement here upon the debate about the causes of the increase in the German birth-rate after 1933. I am not competent to do so, those who are competent remain undecided,[76] and the issue is anyway of only secondary relevance to the argument of this chapter (though it would clearly be very relevant if the birth-rate had in fact continued to fall, as it did in France and Italy where similar efforts were made to encourage procreation). The important fact in this context is that there were substantially more children and that this access of domesticity was welcomed and assisted by the regime, both factors combining to reinforce the official definition of the social status of women. Yet some remarks on the controversy are called for, since certain aspects of it do relate to the general social

[74] *Stat. Jhb. 1941/2*, p. 77; Titmuss, *Parents Revolt*, p. 108.
[75] *Stat. Hdb.*, p. 635. Glass, *Population Policies*, pp. 284–6, 458 f., gives the fullest account of these points. Kirkpatrick, *Women and Family Life*, pp. 16of., was written before the major police drive against illegal abortion took place. Bridenthal, 'Weimar Women', p. 150, n. 20, is mistaken on the law concerning contraceptives, only the display and advertisement of which was restricted. Reliable evidence on the extent of illegal abortion does not exist. Some German clinics noted a decline in the number of what they took to be self-induced miscarriages after 1933, but the effects of the campaign against abortion cannot be calculated with any degree of accuracy. The suppression of abortion not only increases the number of live births in direct proportion, but also reduces subsequent sterility resulting from the operation being carried out in a crude way.
[76] Again, Glass offers by far the most sober assessment of the various explanations: *Population Policies*, pp. 307–12.

conditions of women's life and to important patterns of women's behaviour.

Aside from the effects of stressing deterrent measures against abortion, demographers and social historians who are sceptical about the impact of the government's policies and propaganda make three valid comments on the evidence. First, although it is indisputable that the birth-rate did rise significantly after 1933, it still remained below the average level of the years 1922–6: the long term trend *was* reversed, for the average did rise above that of the pre-crisis years 1926–30, but not decisively. A considerable part of the increase, it is argued, was no more than a return to 'normality' after the devastating economic crisis had been overcome; mass unemployment and extreme poverty always depress the birth-rate in advanced industrial societies, and the economic recovery of Germany after 1933 was on its own a sufficient explanation of most of the increase in the birth-rate. Second, the fertility of couples who married after the Nazi seizure of power was considerably lower than that of couples who married in the 1920s: of the couples who married in 1929 and were still together at the end of 1934, 25.9 per cent had remained childless in this period and 36.4 per cent had had one child; for those married in 1933 and still together in December 1938, the corresponding figures were 33.1 per cent and 26.9 per cent. Couples who married after 1933 continued to conform to this pattern of starting their families a little later in their married lives and of keeping them a little smaller.[77] This difference is the more striking when one recalls that the period 1929–34 was marked by acute economic crisis and unemployment which depressed the birth-rate. A considerable part of the rise in the birth-rate up until 1939 was thus due to the continued, perhaps increased, fertility of marriages entered upon in the 1920s and the early 1930s. The government acknowledged this fact by introducing in February 1939 special penal tax rates (40 per cent above the standard rate) for couples who remained childless after five years of marriage. This was a most significant measure. Nearly 620,000 of the couples who married between 1929 and 1933 had had no children by 1939 – that was just over 20 per cent. Hundreds of thousands of other couples who married before 1929 were also eligible to pay the new tax.[78] Coming shortly after the police round-up of back-street abortionists, the measure indicates that the government was still anxious about the birth-rate.

Third, the effects of Nazi policies were magnified by one other long-term trend, which had been underestimated by the prophets of demographic doom in the 1920s and which tended to cancel out in part the ineluctably growing preference for smaller families: throughout the

[77] *Stat. Hdb.*, pp. 54 f.; *Stat. Jhb. 1936*, pp. 36, 44; Titmuss, *Parents Revolt*, p. 109. A slight change in the methods of compiling these figures made the difference between the two groups appear a little bigger than it in fact was.

[78] DAF, *Deutsche Sozialpolitik 1938*, p. 174; Glass, *Population Policies*, p. 301; *Stat. Jhb. 1941/2*, p. 74.

inter-war years a steadily growing proportion of the population of marriageable age actually did marry. In 1938/9 the overall *proportion* was around 6 per cent higher than it had been in 1910/11. This figure seems small, yet 6 per cent of the population aged over twenty in 1939 amounted to 2.83 million persons – almost 1.5 million married couples. What is more, the average age of women on marriage was steadily falling.[79] Thus there were more married couples, and married couples were more likely to have children than single people: despite a variety of changes in the law and in taxation policy which eased the lot of unmarried mothers, the number of children born out of wedlock was much lower after 1933 than it had been in the 1920s.[80]

Considered in conjunction with the partial suppression of abortion, these comments seem to indicate that the massive rhetorical, institutional and financial encouragement of motherhood in Nazi Germany had little impact on people's behaviour. Such a conclusion would, however, be premature, for it is also necessary to consider those conditions of life in the country during the 1930s which might have been expected, all other things being equal, to depress the birth-rate – for if they did so, their effects were compensated for by other factors. At least six points must be noted in this context. First, the demographic effects of emigration, murders, executions and imprisonment may have been minimal before the war began – terror must be on a massive scale to affect population trends – but the continual political uncertainty and fear among the many who remained opposed to the regime must have had adverse consequences for their family life. (And perhaps at least a few women were so sickened by the blatantly instrumental biological romanticism of Nazi fertility propaganda, that they decided to have no children!) There is more than polemical point to this consideration, for the government repeatedly cited the rising birth-rate as evidence of popular confidence in National Socialist policies in general, as proof of the rebirth of the nation. By the same token, it must be noted that the police terror and the open drive to prepare for war can scarcely have acted as an encouragement to the many opponents of the regime, whether Jews, Christians, social democrats or communists, to start families. Whether or not to bring children into *this* world must have been a very difficult decision for those who rejected Nazism.[81] Second, owing to the effects of the First World War, the number of women who entered child-bearing age after 1935 was

---

[79] *Stat. Hdb.*, pp. 28, 47, 51; *Stat Jhb., 1936*, p. 40; and *1941/2*, p. 25.

[80] Just over 100,000 illegitimate children were born each year, 1933–9, that is just under 8 per cent of all births. This was *one-third less* than the average for the 1920s. The numbers began to increase again in 1938 and 1939: *Stat. Hdb.*, p. 47.

[81] I have no evidence on this point yet. However, the birth-rate clearly is influenced by changes in political circumstances: the number of births began to fall in Britain in the latter half of 1939, probably as a result of the Munich crisis. A very large proportion of the German people was unenthusiastic about the Nazi regime.

unusually small, and this fact was widely expected beforehand to reduce the total number of births very sharply.[82] Of greater general importance, third, was the relationship between living standards and size of family. The real incomes of many German workers *continued to fall* until 1936 on account of price increases for foodstuffs and clothes, and in that year about one-third of the working class (those employed in the consumer goods and service sectors which were at first left on one side by the armaments boom) was still living in much the same poverty which had been the major cause of the sharp fall in the birth-rate during the world economic crisis.[83] The living standards of the majority of workers did improve quite rapidly after 1934, yet a Labour Front newspaper which invited readers' letters on the theme 'reluctance to have a third child', was told in no uncertain terms by many of its correspondents that they simply could not afford it.[84] The welfare measures outlined above, together with the accelerated increase in real incomes after 1936 weakened these constraints somewhat, but the improvement in living standards was largely confined to consumption and did not touch one problem which was most relevant to patterns of marriage and family limitation: house-building, fourth, did not remotely keep pace with the rate at which new households were founded in the 1930s, because the government concentrated both the necessary financial resources and the capacities of the building industry on the rearmament programmes. The ministry responsible estimated that there was a deficit of 1.5 million dwellings in 1939. Rents for new homes (though not for those built before 1914) were high. These problems were widely acknowledged to be causing great difficulties for young married couples in the main urban and industrial centres, delaying both marriage and the decision to have children.[85] By simultaneously encouraging people to marry and breed and failing to provide them with homes, the regime furnished a clear measure of its humanity, clear evidence too of the economic contradictions on which its policy rested. Fifth, a further self-imposed obstacle to Nazi population policies was the introduction in 1935/6 of compulsory labour and military service for young men. This appears to have slowed down quite markedly the general trend towards earlier marriage among men, because conscripts earned very little during their total of two-and-a-half years' service and

[82] Figures are given on pp. 187–8 below.

[83] Details in Mason, 'National Socialist Policies' Chapter 4b. Women workers were strongly concentrated in these sectors of industry; insofar as they lived with parents or husbands, the effect of the stagnation or fall of their real earnings on family budgets was mitigated by the increase in men's earnings. This question is discussed in more detail on pp. 183–4.   [84] *Angriff*, 2 February–2 March 1937.

[85] Minute by Minister of Labour, 2 March 1939: Bundesarchiv Koblenz, R43II, file 1171; report on economic conditions in Berlin in the last quarter of 1938, Mason, *Arbeiterklasse*, Doc. 151; Glass, *Population Policies*, p. 302.

thus needed longer to save up in order to found a household.[86] Finally, it can probably be assumed that a development to be considered further below, the increase in women's employment from 1936 on, also had a slight tendency to depress the birth-rate. The obstacles in the way of the increase in the birth-rate were thus neither few nor small – and yet it did rise.

The argument about the weight which should be attached to these various considerations cannot be resolved here. The questions involved are complex and encrusted with ideological thesis and counter-thesis. Thus Nazi writers went to great lengths actually to *minimize* the effects of the regime's individual measures, so that as large a part as possible of the increase in the birth-rate could be attributed to the 'psychic rebirth of the nation', to the supposed restoration of national self-confidence and unity of purpose.[87] The problems of interpretation can be set into clearer focus if Germany is compared with other similar countries. The much more protracted attempts to raise the birth-rate in Italy and France in the inter-war years remained completely unsuccessful,[88] while in Britain, whose governments took no steps whatever to encourage population growth and whose official delegate at the International Congress of Demographers in Berlin in August 1935 defiantly announced that small families were a fine thing since these small islands were anyway overcrowded,[89] the marriage-rate rose significantly from 1933 and the birth-rate slightly from 1934 on.[90] What grounds can there be for arguing that the German measures had any effect?

The main reason concerns the monolithic and comprehensive nature of the effort in Germany. Whereas in France the government remained in the background until 1938/9, paying for a wide range of decentralized incentive and relief schemes but leaving propaganda to private associations and tolerating various forms of counter-propaganda and activity,[91] and whereas in Italy there were strict financial limits on the scale of government intervention, the Nazi regime was altogether more systematic:

---

[86] Figures on the marriage-rate for men aged twenty-one to twenty-five; *Stat. Hdb.*, p. 51; *Stat. Jhb. 1941/2*, p. 73.

[87] While he takes the component parts of this corrupt argument to pieces with a remorseless analytical skill, Glass does allow it a residual plausibility – national aggrandisement and military victories evidently can help to raise the birth-rate: *Population Policies*, pp. 307–12.

[88] Of course it may well be that French and Italian policies did arrest the rate of decline; this too cannot be proved.

[89] Address by Close, reprinted in Hans Harmsen and Franz Lohse (eds), *Bevölkerungsfragen. Bericht des Internationalen Kongresses für Bevölkerungswissenschaft* (Munich 1936), pp. 93–8.

[90] B. R. Mitchell and Phyllis Deane, *Abstract of British Historical Statistics*, 2nd edn (Cambridge 1971), pp. 30, 46.

[91] French pro-natalist ideology and policies were on the whole conservative and defensive in tone, and lacked the imperialist racial-darwinist edge characteristic of Nazism. In 1938/9, however, the government became both more aggressive and more anti-feminist, as the catalogue of previous failures in population policies grew longer and as the German threat loomed larger: Glass, *Population Policies*, pp. 120–3, 213 ff.

it drew fully on its great resources of dictatorial power and influence over the German people. By the late 1930s exhortations, deterrents, partial compensations and obstacles in the way of non-conformist behaviour had been orchestrated into a massive campaign of manipulation. People are not infinitely manipulable, but if the factors which inhibited the continued rise in the birth-rate after 1933 are given full weight, the changes which occurred in these pre-war years perhaps regain something of their remarkable character.[92] If the seriousness of the Nazi claims to have changed people's attitudes towards parenthood – and therewith to have effected a partial redefinition of women's self-image and behaviour – is not fully borne out, it perhaps appears at least worthy of careful discussion and further research. Some further light can be thrown on the issue by a brief consideration of women's work.

WOMEN, THE LABOUR MARKET AND THE STATE IN THE LATER 1930S

In the late 1930s the question of women's work came to pose one of the most intractable and embarrassing sets of problems which the Nazi regime faced in internal affairs. The immediate cause of these difficulties was straightforward and obvious – women's employment was essential to the rearmament programme and the war effort – but their resolution called for measures which were diametrically opposed to the direction of all earlier Nazi policies. Attempts to mobilize women for war production also came up against many of the irreducible facts about the nature of women's work in the capitalist system of that epoch, and they threatened to destroy a large part of the regime's basis of popular support. The regime found itself impaled upon a set of contradictory imperatives.

From 1936 on the rearmament boom caused an unforeseen and increasingly acute shortage of labour, which rapidly spread to all sectors of the economy – industry, agriculture, services, trade and administration.

[92] Some of these inhibiting factors were, of course, also at work in France and Italy too, but most of them were less marked than in Germany; and in Italy the birth-rate was declining from what had been a comparatively high level in the early 1920s. Perhaps one last speculation might be permitted here: there is some inconclusive evidence that in this century generations tend to react as adults against the circumstances and conventions of their own childhood. It may not be altogether far-fetched to suggest that those in their twenties and thirties in the Germany of the 1930s were rejecting by their own preference for marriage, family, privacy and the home the exceptionally turbulent and insecure experience of their and their parents' life in the years of war and revolution, 1914–23. The narrow security of the clear division of sexual roles within the family perhaps appears most desirable to those who never really knew it as children, constricting and repressive to those who knew nothing else.

By the end of 1938 the labour exchanges had 1 million vacancies on their books. It was painfully clear to the government that the some 3.5 million women who neither had children under fourteen nor were in regular employment formed the main potential source of additional labour.[93] The labour shortage was critical. It was not only slowing down production, retarding the preparation of war and thus jeopardizing the regime's fundamental policy of future military expansion. It was also bringing new and dangerous elements of disorder into the social, economic and political system. Workers began to exploit their own scarcity value and employers began to compete with each other for their services: wages rose, productivity and work discipline fell. Production schedules could not be kept to, and stoppages resulting from the labour shortage reduced the efficiency of industry and raised production costs. The pressure of inflation on both industry and government grew more intense as a result, and, under these accumulating strains, bitter rivalries for power and economic advantage broke out within the complex structures of government, business and administration. The labour shortage was not an isolated economic problem of supply and demand – indirectly, it affected the whole conduct of public life. In losing control over the labour market, the government felt that it was losing control over workers and employers in general and surrendering control over the allocation of economic resources to an increasingly anarchic competitive process. It was both administratively unprepared and, out of fear for its popularity, reluctant to impose comprehensive restrictions on the mobility of workers or on their wages. Unlike the previous crises which the regime had surmounted, this one seemed to be here to stay, indeed certain to get worse as long as the government remained set upon further rearmament for future military conquest.[94] And yet, despite the severity of the crisis, the efforts to mobilize women's labour power were hesitant, half-hearted and relatively unsuccessful.

The extent of the failure to draw upon women's labour in the later 1930s can be presented in fairly exact general terms. It is essential in these calculations to distinguish between changes in the absolute or gross figures, and relative or proportional changes – the latter are normally more significant. In May 1939 there were 1.94 million more women of working age than there had been in 1925, and there were, according to the

---

[93] Figures from a report by the Minister of Labour to the Reich Chancellery, 17 December 1938: Mason, *Arbeiterklasse*, Doc. 149; and from a paper for the Reich Defence Council by Syrup, State Secretary in the Ministry of Labour, 23 June 1939: International Military Tribunal, Nuremberg, Doc. 3787-PS (*Trial of the Major War Criminals . . .*, vol. XXXIII (Nuremberg 1949), p. 153).

[94] I have discussed these issues in detail in my thesis; for a brief sketch see 'Labour in the Third Reich 1933–1939', *Past and Present*, no. 33 (April 1966), pp. 112–41.

census, 1.22 million more economically active women.[95] The proportion of women of working age who were in fact economically active rose very slightly in the same period from 48.2 per cent to 49.2 per cent, while the proportion of the adult male population who were economically active fell between 1925 and 1939, because of conscription into the armed forces and the Labour Service (*Arbeitsdienst*). The increase in the proportion of women who did work of one kind or another (aside from housework)[96] was, in the opinion of the statisticians who evaluated the census, partly due to the more accurate counting of family assistants in agriculture – it did *not* reflect a significant real increase in the mobilization of women's labour power. Of the 12.7 million women who were economically active in 1939, 4.62 million were family assistants: 36.3 per cent. And a further 1.33 million were domestic servants: 10.5 per cent. Insofar as these groups worked in agriculture – and most of them did so – their labour was of great economic importance, even though it was not being efficiently exploited on many of the smaller farms.

In the context of rearmament and preparation for war, however, by far the most important category of economically active women was the wage-earners. Their numbers increased by 278,000 between 1925 and 1939, *but* this total represented a *diminishing* proportion of all employed women: 43.5 per cent in 1925, 41.5 per cent in 1939.[97] This category of women wage-earners also included a large number whose work was not productive in the narrow sense: for example, there were 820,000 women whose employment – office cleaning, etc. – was like that of domestic servants, although they were not classified in this way in economic terms.[98] In order to assess the extent of the mobilization of women for the production of manufactured goods, the decisive figure is that of the number of women workers in industry and handicrafts: in absolute terms, this figure increased between 1925 and 1939 by 127,000, *but* wage-earning women in industry and handicrafts accounted for a *diminishing proportion* both of economically active women taken as a whole, and of the total labour force employed in this sector of the economy. This impression of

---

[95] These and the following statistics are taken or computed from *Stat. Hdb.*, pp. 32 f.; *Wirtschaft und Statistik* (1941), no. 3. Girls working in the Labour Service are not included in these and the subsequent figures. There were about 50,000 of them in 1939. I am grateful to Jill Stephenson for this point.

[96] For the categories used in the censuses and by the social insurance authorities, 'economically active', 'workers' etc., see pp. 136–7 above.

[97] To put it differently, the total number of economically active women increased by 10.6 per cent between 1925 and 1939, while the number of female wage-earners rose by only 5.6 per cent. All of these percentages are slightly distorted by the more complete counting of family assistants in the 1939 census.

[98] In the *economic* census category 'domestic service' there were 1.33 million women, but in the *occupational* category 'domestic servants and related types of work' 2.15 million women were counted: *Stat. Hdb.*, p. 32; *Stat. Jhb. 1939/40*, p. 376.

the *relative failure* of the regime to mobilize women's labour is confirmed by the figures concerning the insured labour force, that is, those who were in regular dependent employment. The number of women manual and white-collar workers who were covered by the compulsory sickness insurance scheme – and their work was of greater importance in the efficient preparation of the war than that of the rest of the economically active women – did indeed rise much more rapidly in the later 1930s than in the first three years of Nazi rule – from 5.71 million in October 1936 to 7.14 million in July 1939 – *but* it still remained significantly below the levels of the later 1920s – 7.41 million in October 1928.[99] Since the total number of women of working age increased by some 2 million between 1928 and 1939, the *proportion* of women in *regular* work fell quite markedly – despite the rapidly growing demand for labour in all sectors of the economy after 1936.

These figures point to a number of different questions and conclusions, some of which will be discussed below. At the most general level, however, they reflect directly upon the inadequacy of the scope, scale and type of women's emancipation achieved under the Weimar Republic. While it had been generally accepted that the provision of well-paid, responsible and appropriate employment for women was one of the cornerstones of any emancipatory programme, whether liberal-democratic or socialist, the reforms of the 1920s did not in fact reach beyond the sectors of civil rights and welfare provision: employment, wages, education, vocational training and career structures were left to the uncertain, slow-moving and often contradictory influences of market forces and pressure-group interests, of custom and conventional attitudes. Working conditions did not improve much for women wage-earners, few careers were opened up to women and little was done to ease the lot of women who were both housewives and also held down a job outside the home. Compounded as they were by the adverse effects of violent economic crises, these failures and omissions meant that no general expectation that women could and should have regular and satisfying work was ever established in Germany before 1933. In a wide variety of ways, and for some very good reasons, the role of the housewife really did seem preferable to most women who were not forced by their economic circumstances to seek regular employment in the modern capitalist sectors of the economy – such employment brought few rewards and many additional strains.

Thus the drive for domesticity in the years 1933–6 had fed on the inadequacies and superficialities of the liberal theory and practice of emancipation. The socio-economic structure had remained largely

---

[99] *Stat. Hdb.*, p. 474. The insurance categories were changed again after 1928, but not, it appears, to a degree which rules out direct comparisons between the years.

impervious to liberal reforms in the 1920s: more dramatically and less obviously, the socio-economic structure had also accommodated the early Nazi policies *only* where these policies met the needs and aspirations of large numbers of people. The point of the evidence and of this argument, however, is that the emphasis on domesticity, in conjunction with the economic recovery which came with rearmament, really did meet the needs and aspirations (and aversions) of *at least some* of those women who had no wish to work in factories, offices and shops, and run a household as well. This was probably the ground on which the regime gradually began to win general recognition and support among German women. Whether they had no children or two or six, whether they subscribed to any part of Nazi ideology at all or not, their own experience (reinforced no doubt by the wishes of their husbands) told them that regular work under the prevailing conditions was little more than an unpleasant necessity and that their 'pre-ordained' place in the home was altogether more comfortable. Hitler's injunctions on this point were reassuring, encouraging, but not necessary to the decision. In 1939 there were at least 3.5 million women who had taken this decision to stay at home even though they had no young children. But in the face of the growing labour shortage, the early policies of the regime had to be rethought.[100]

In 1936 the National Organization of Industry (Reichsgruppe Industrie) first became seriously anxious about the future supply of labour. It commissioned a detailed investigation of the structure of the industrial labour force which devoted close attention to the employment of women. The picture which emerged was that of female workers eking out a precarious existence in the margins of the economic life of the country, many of them carrying out indispensable tasks which men would not accept, in return for very poor remuneration.[101]

There was only one partial exception to this generalization: the demand for women white-collar workers (sales and clerical staff) grew steadily in the 1930s, and, in consequence of earlier trade union action to safeguard the employment of men, the salary differentials in jobs open to both men and women were slight. Opportunities for women to be promoted into higher salary groups were, it is true, rare, for they were not generally

---

[100] In addition to the important perspective opened up by Bridenthal, 'Weimar Women', see the brilliant essay by Ernst Bloch, 'Die Frau im Dritten Reich', written in February 1937 and republished in Bloch, *Politische Messungen, Pestzeit, Vormärz* (Frankfurt am Main 1970), pp. 106–13, and in Bloch, *Vom Hasard zur Katastrophe. Politische Aufsätze aus den Jahren 1934–1939* (Frankfurt am Main 1972), pp. 129–36.

[101] This very detailed report was never published. Typescript entitled 'Die Facharbeiter- und Nachwuchsfrage in der Industrie': Bundesarchiv–Militärarchiv, Freiburg im Breisgau (Military Department of the West German Federal Archives; henceforth BA/MA Freiburg), files of the War Economy Staff of the High Command of the Armed Forces, WiLF5, file 1917.

expected to make a career of their work. Many though by no means all of them were, however, *relatively* well paid, enjoyed tolerable working conditions and received some vocational training. Employment of this kind was clearly sought after; it was a desirable alternative to the factory and to domestic service. Thus the relatively few complaints about shortages of such women employees came from public authorities, which paid their typists badly – on the whole, supply kept pace with demand and the number of women clerks, typists and sales-girls increased by almost 300,000, over 19 per cent, between 1933 and 1939. The increase was especially marked in industry as the bureaucratization of the larger firms proceeded apace. As in the 1920s, the expansion of non-manual occupations remained the most important single agent of change in the structure of the female labour force. This was the only sector in which the employment of women increased rapidly and steadily throughout the inter-war years, and it accounted for a large part of the total increase in the numbers of working women.[102]

Women wage-earners were of much greater concern to the National Organization of Industry. In October 1936 only just under 1.5 million women were employed as workers by industrial firms; they amounted to only 13 per cent of the total number of women who were economically active in any manner, and to only 6.1 per cent of the female population of working age (fourteen to sixty-four in this case).[103] There were more women non-manual workers than women industrial workers, and about the same number of female domestic servants. Of all women industrial workers roughly two-thirds were employed in the consumer goods industries, only 200,000 in the various branches of the engineering industry and 90,000 in the production of electrical goods. Furthermore the overwhelming majority of women industrial workers were either unskilled (45.3 per cent) or semi-skilled (49.8 per cent); there were *only 71,000 skilled women workers in the whole of industry* – only 4.8 per cent of women industrial workers were skilled, as against 37.5 per cent of the male industrial labour force. In this respect practically nothing had changed since the 1920s.[104] This heavy concentration of women in dead-end jobs was only in part a consequence of the production methods

---

[102] *Stat. Hdb.*, p. 32; Arbeitswissenschaftliches Institut der DAF, 'Beiträge zur Beurteilung des Frauenlohns', (typescript 1938, copy in Deutsches Zentralarchiv Potsdam). The number of women civil servants fell a little between 1933 and 1939.

[103] This enquiry covered only firms which were members of the National Organization; it did not cover craft enterprises, domestic outwork, etc. A comparison with the 1939 census suggests that there were a further 500,000 or more women engaged in manufacturing production outside the larger firms which reported in 1936. The same applies to male industrial wage-earners: the National Organization counted 5.45 million in 1936, the census recorded 8.74 million in 1939, by which time, of course, employment levels were anyway higher.

[104] This section of the 1936 report can be compared with Preller, *Sozialpolitik*, p. 118.

peculiar to the textiles, clothing and foodstuffs industries. It also reflected what was evidently a typical life-cycle for many working women, derived from mutually reinforcing experiences: on the one hand, there was little attraction in or possibility of making a career out of industrial work and, on the other hand, they would anyway marry in their early or mid-twenties, start a family and become housewives. The age-group which was most heavily represented in industry was the eighteen to twenty year-olds (17.4 per cent of the female population of that age in 1936); in 1938 there were as many women wage-earners under the age of twenty-five as there were between the ages of twenty-five and forty-four.[105] Marriage was not least an escape route from highly routinized, boring and underpaid labour, and as long as it appeared in this light to women, employers had little economic incentive to offer women vocational training facilities and opportunities for promotion. It was a very vicious circle.

For those women whose husbands' earnings gave them the economic freedom to choose, the unattractiveness of industrial labour was compounded by very low rates of pay. In 1939 the weekly pay-packet of a skilled or semi-skilled man was *on average just over twice* that of a skilled woman; an unskilled man earned 50 per cent more than an unskilled woman. A number of factors combined to produce so unequal a distribution of earnings. First, women were concentrated in industries where wages were anyway low. The domestic market for consumer goods did not recover from the depression until workers in other sectors of the economy began to earn high wages again in 1937/8 – until then, the demand for labour in the consumer goods industries remained slack and wages stagnated as a result. For women workers the situation was made worse by widespread short-time in the textile and clothing industries up until 1937, which was due to shortages of imported raw materials. The real weekly earnings of many workers in consumer goods industries actually fell from 1933 to 1936.[106]

Second, differentials between the wages of men and women were wide, ranging in 1939 from 21.5 per cent in the electrical goods industry to well

---

[105] The first of these figures is taken from the report 'Facharbeiter- und Nachwuchsfrage', and is unsatisfactory in that no separate calculation was made for the age-group twenty to twenty-five or twenty to twenty-nine, in which the proportion of women industrial workers among the whole female population was probably higher than that of those aged eighteen to twenty. It is supplemented by figures for *all* women wage-earners, derived from a census carried out by the labour exchanges in 1938: *Stat. Jhb. 1939/40*, pp. 376 f.

[106] Earnings statistics: *Stat. Hdb.*, pp. 469 ff.; Mason, *Arbeiterklasse* (Appendix II), and 'National Socialist Policies', Chapter 4b; Gerhard Bry, *Wages in Germany, 1871–1945* (Princeton 1960), pp. 242 f. Earnings in the consumer goods industries did increase quite rapidly after 1936, but the 1939 figures only serve to emphasize the enormity of the gulf before they began to rise. Unskilled women in other branches of industry earned on average more than semi-skilled women in the distinctively 'women's industries'.

over 40 per cent in the pottery, glass, printing, clothing and baking trades; the differentials were *not* reduced between 1933 and 1936/7. An investigation of this subject by the Research Institute of the Labour Front reached the conclusion that there was no rational justification of any kind for so profuse a variety of wide differentials: they could be accounted for only as the outcome of decades of local trade and industrial practices. Piece-work was sometimes paid at the same rates for men and women, and sometimes not.[107] The standard case for differentials was that a man had to keep a family, while a woman did not. This outlook was reflected in one of the few detectable regularities within the system of unequal remuneration: the differential was often wider for older than for younger workers doing the same job – in many trades men *began* to earn substantially more than women at the age of twenty-two. One other recurrent feature, both punitive and supremely hypocritical, was the way in which the differentials tended to be widest in precisely those trades in which there was *least* difference between the severity of the work-effort and the unpleasantness of the working conditions of men and women, and narrowest where men's work really was marked off by the heavy character of the tasks performed. This shrewd observation cast doubt on the conventional argument that men were paid more because they did harder work, and pointed to the conclusion, not spelled out in the report, that differentials had considerable symbolic importance and that they constituted a mechanism for influencing the distribution of available work between the sexes. Women's earnings were also kept low by protective restrictions on overtime and night-work – longer hours and the attendant bonuses contributed in considerable measure to the increases in men's earnings after 1936.

These disincentives, inherent in the character of women's industrial work and its remuneration, were not new in the later 1930s, but the *social context* in which they operated *was beginning to change* in these years: the material well-being of the majority of working-class households began to improve quite markedly. It seems reasonable to suppose that most married women worked only if they had to. Necessity in this connection is of course culturally and economically determined – prosperity in Germany in 1936/9 did *not* approach those post-1945 levels, which, by placing expensive consumer durables within the aspirations of working-class households, have provided a major incentive for married women to seek employment. But in the immediate pre-war years, the earnings of men in the boom industries – engineering, mining, some building trades, etc. –

---

[107] For these and the following points, see Arbeitswissenschaftliches Institut der DAF, 'Beiträge'; Bry, *Wages*, p. 248. The differentials are calculated on the basis of hourly wage-*rates* (*not* earnings) and the women's rate is expressed as a percentage of the men's rate.

did rise to such an extent that many families could meet the customary modest needs of this period out of the one wage-packet. By the summer of 1939 the *average* weekly earnings of industrial workers were about 30 per cent higher than they had been six years earlier, and were in real terms probably a little higher than they had been in the later 1920s. For skilled men the increases were considerably greater.[108] Improved welfare provisions, in particular the monthly family allowances, reinforced this trend in the working class, where families still tended to be larger than in the middle class.[109]

These formidable obstacles in the way of an intensified mobilization of women were in several respects raised even higher by the consequences of the government's earlier policies. The effects of propaganda about the 'honour attaching to the status of housewife and mother' in actually deterring women from seeking employment were no doubt minimal – there were anyway sufficient practical deterrents. But the rhetoric and practice of welfare does seem to have created expectations on the part of married women that they would be looked after if they were in need. These expectations were not to be disappointed. The government was also faced with the more tangible outcome of its campaign to sell a domestic idyll to the German people. The higher marriage- and birth-rates of the years after 1933 undoubtedly limited the number of women of working age who needed or were in a position to take employment. Contemporaries speculated with great interest as to whether the number of *married* working women was rising or falling during the later 1930s, for the answer would clearly have thrown interesting light on the validity of the claims which the Nazi leaders were making for their family policies. Clifford Kirkpatrick found it impossible to discover conclusive evidence on the issue, and it does indeed seem that no such evidence was published until some preliminary results of the 1939 census were made available in a little-read technical periodical early in 1941.[110] If Kirkpatrick was right in supposing that in 1937 the government would have been embarrassed by the publication of any figures showing an increase in the number of

---

[108] Kirkpatrick, *Women and Family Life*, p. 205, quotes impressive sources on the overwhelming importance of family poverty and economic need in motivating women to take regular employment. It is very difficult to calculate accurate figures for *real earnings* in this period, since the statistics worked out at the time are defective and incomplete. There are quite good figures on money wages for the period from December 1935; according to them the average earnings of skilled and semi-skilled male workers in industry rose by 19 per cent between then and June 1939: Bry, *Wages*, p. 243. See also note 14 above.

[109] For welfare reforms and family allowances, see pp. 164–9 above.

[110] *Wirtschaft und Statistik* (1941), no. 3; the following calculations are based on this source. Kirkpatrick, *Women and Family Life*, pp. 204, 227 ff. It is noteworthy that the otherwise detailed and comprehensive publication of the Ministry of Labour, *Schutz der werktätigen Frau* (Berlin 1941), gave no figures for married women workers and failed to discuss their particular difficulties in combining the two roles, although these issues were of decisive importance for any new wartime labour policy.

married women at work, by 1941 there was a second and contradictory reason for such embarrassment: married women's employment had in fact increased, despite all the propaganda, but the census statistics also showed that the furtherance of marriage and child-bearing had greatly inhibited the mobilization of women's labour. The developments were themselves contradictory.

Between 1933 and 1939 the number of married women in Germany aged between fourteen and sixty-five increased by 1.5 million to 14.9 million, an increase of 11.5 per cent; at the same time the number of married women who were economically active rose by 1 million to just over 5 million, an increase of 24.8 per cent. This was a big change, but the figures also need to be looked at from another angle: if the total number of married women is taken as 100, the proportion of married women who were economically active rose from 29.9 per cent in 1933 to 33.6 per cent in 1939. Put in these terms, the change appears less dramatic, though it is still significant. Now these figures mean no more and no less than that the number of married working women was increasing steadily: they do not in themselves say anything abut the *relationship* between the fact of being married and the fact of working. Different calculations must be made in order to establish this relationship.

Common sense suggests that young mothers with small children were less likely to hold down a job in a society which did nothing to help them do so, than unmarried girls or older women, and this was in fact the case. Taken as a whole, the proportion of all women of working age (fourteen to sixty-four) who were economically active in Germany rose from 46.9 per cent to 49.2 per cent between 1933 and 1939. For the economically most important age-group, however, *those between twenty and twenty-nine* (that is, who were old enough to have gained working experience and a minimum of training but were still young enough to cope with demanding jobs), this proportion *fell*. It fell only by a small margin, 4.5 per cent, it is true, but it fell at the same time that the corresponding figures for all other age-groups except the over-sixties were rising sharply. And the twenty to twenty-nine year-olds normally furnished the most important single cohort among women workers.[111] This fall in the percentage of women aged between twenty and twenty-nine who were economically active was very largely due to the increased rate of marriage. In 1933 41.6 per cent of

---

[111] To be precise, in May 1939, 21.6 per cent of all economically active women were aged between 14 and 19, 21.8 per cent between 20 and 29 – thus the younger age-group was numerically more important. However, in this year the cohort aged between twenty and twenty-nine was unusually small on account of the low birth-rate in the First World War; and teenage girls normally had economically less important occupations than young women, on account of their relative lack of experience and physical strength. The decline in the proportion of economically active among the over-sixties was very marked and would bear further investigation. It can probably be interpreted as evidence of gradually rising living standards.

this age-group as a whole was married, in 1939 56.3 per cent – an extraordinary change. What would have happened if the number of marriages had not increased in this manner? This type of quantifiable what-would-have-happened-if-not . . . question can be answered in hypothetical terms. A crude but suggestive counter-factual conditional calculation shows that, if the marriage-rate had remained unchanged from 1933 to 1939, there would have been 722,000 more single women aged between twenty and twenty-nine in the latter year. Almost 90 per cent of single women in this age-group were economically active, but only 31.3 per cent of married women: thus, all other things being equal, there would have been 445,000 more women in the labour market in 1939 than there actually were, if the rate of marriage had not increased so sharply. That was roughly twice as many women as were employed as wage-earners in the whole engineering industry.[112]

The seriousness of this change with respect to the size of the labour force at the disposal of the German economy was enhanced by the fact that the cohort aged twenty to twenty-four in 1939 was exceptionally small: these were the women born during the First World War. There were about 1 million fewer of them than there would have been but for the war, a 'loss' of almost one-third of the age-group; there was a similar 'loss' of men of this age. Seen in this light, and in view of the labour requirements of the armaments economy, the increase in the frequency of marriage could not have come at a worse time for the Third Reich.

Before the response of the regime to this dilemma can be discussed however, the above figures must be analysed in class terms, for the relationship between marriage and employment among women varied very widely among the different social classes. In 1939 on average 41.4 per cent of all economically active women were married, but for women civil servants (mainly teachers) the figure was 6.2 per cent, for white-collar workers 11.4 per cent, for wage-earners 28.2 per cent and for family assistants 70.1 per cent. This last group was overwhelmingly concentrated in agriculture and the retail trade, so that the total number of married women who worked for a wage or salary in industry, handicrafts and

---

[112] This figure is reached by subtracting 10 per cent from the 722,000 women who would have been single in 1939 if only 41.6 per cent of the age-group had been married, in order to cover those who did not work anyway; and then subtracting 31.3 per cent to take account of the fact that this proportion of the women who did marry continued to be economically active. The marriage-rate among women of this age in 1933 was, of course, unusually low, on account of the economic crisis. It is interesting that the position in respect of the age-group thirty to thirty-nine was quite different: the increase in the marriage-rate in this case went hand in hand with a marked increase in the proportion of economically active women. In this context, widows and divorcees are classified as single women.

administration was rather small – just over 1.5 million in 1939.[113] By far
the most typical form of married women's work involved assisting the
husband on the farm or in the shop, and women were still much more
likely to remain economically active if they married a farmer, publican,
artisan or shopkeeper, than if they married a factory worker or a clerk.

The contrast between blue-collar and white-collar families, however,
calls for comment. Although the work performed by female white-collar
workers was perhaps less difficult to reconcile with the simultaneous
burdens of running a home (no shift-work, less physical strain, less
difficulty in finding time to do the shopping), *a remarkably small number*
stayed on at their work after they married, or returned to it after they had
brought up their children. Only a minute number of married women
white-collar workers had dependent children. The behaviour of women
manual workers in this respect was very different, for all that their work
was in many ways more demanding, and for all that they tended to have
more children; it was nearly three times more probable that they would
continue in employment after they married. A number of reasons may be
tentatively suggested to explain this difference. First, the work done by
female white-collar workers was not in itself much more attractive or
more interesting than that done by women manual workers; it may have
been less tiring, but there were few career opportunities and thus the
nature of the work did not give much of a positive incentive for married
women to return to their desks or counters. Second, employers probably
did not encourage them to do so, for the salaries of white-collar workers
rose with age, and there was a plentiful supply of teenagers and of young
graduates of typing academies.[114] Third, they probably tended to marry
husbands whose income was higher than that of the typical husband of a
factory girl, and thus there was less economic need for them to continue at
work. And *their* husbands would also be likely to set more store by having
a wife who did *not* work, than would an engineering worker or a tram
driver: this was an important question of social status. Finally, it seems
possible that all of these different factors converged around the differing
family and neighbourhood structures of the manual and the non-manual
working population. In order for young working-class mothers to
maintain their jobs – and over 500,000 did so in 1933[115] – it was obviously
essential that someone should look after their children while they were at
work. Further research may well show that the availability of grannies

---

[113] These figures are not strictly comparable with those for 1933, since they refer to the
population within the boundaries of May 1939, that is, including Austria and the
Sudeten German area ('Greater Germany'): *SdR*, vol. 556/2, pp. 2 ff.

[114] It is also possible that the anti-feminist reaction among the salaried middle class
persisted into the later 1930s and that it was still made difficult for married women
employees to retain their posts. I have no evidence on this point yet.

[115] *SdR*, vol. 470/1, p. 21.

and aunts was much greater, the inhibitions against handing over an infant to a friend or neighbour for the day much less strong among the industrial working class than among the aspiring bourgeoisie of the new surburbs and city flats. It is certainly not easy to imagine a female bank-clerk leaving her new town house in Köln-Holweide, Märchenstrasse, early in the morning with her schoolteacher husband, and taking her two-year-old child to the old lady round the corner for the day – and paying her for the service. Yet such scenes must have occurred daily in the working-class quarters of the big textile towns.

Must have . . . These remarks are necessarily speculative, but the question has a wider importance, for, as the numbers of female white-collar workers grew, so the number of married women normally available to work diminished. White-collar workers were by far the fastest growing group among the female working population in the 1930s, but, paradoxically, they were also being pushed out of economic life at a much faster rate than any other occupational group. They were creating the new type of the house- or flat-bound housewife and mother. In fact, *this was the form of domesticity which National Socialist rule really was encouraging – middle-class, home-centred and indifferent both to the appeal that women should work for the national cause and to the appeal that married women should have large families!*

There is a further dimension to this paradox, for it appears that a substantial number of middle- and upper-class women did not wait for the arrival of their first child after marriage before giving up their jobs. There are no statistics on this question, but a rough juxtaposition of the figures on the fertility of marriages in the 1930s with those which categorize the gainfully employed women by marital status and age-group makes it clear that *many married women who had no children at all chose or were persuaded not to work outside the home in any way.* Of the women who were married at the time of the 1939 census, 2.2 million had married in 1929 or later and had had no children by their present husband.[116] It is certain that not all of them had a job. Thus the 3.5 million women with neither dependent children nor employment who were counted in rapacious hope by the Ministry of Labour in 1939, included not only fifty-year-old war-widows and women who looked after the young children of working neighbours and relatives, but also a sizeable number of young, mostly middle-class, wives whose life was spent looking after their husbands alone. In September 1941, the Labour Front asserted that many such women, together with well-to-do spinsters and the daughters

---

[116] *Present* husband is an important qualification, since the marriage and family statistics take no account of children brought by their mothers (or fathers) into second marriages. In 1939 nearly 90,000 women married for the second time ('Greater Germany'): *Stat. Jhb. 1941/2*, p. 72.

of rich parents had retreated to Germany's spas for the duration of the war.[117]

The encouragement of marriage and of child-bearing, then, was fundamentally at odds with efforts to increase the numbers of working women, and there was indeed a very considerable potential labour reserve among married women in 1938/9.[118] The question was, could the regime mobilize and exploit this labour. The need fast became desperate: by the summer of 1939, before the invasion of Poland, a number of major armaments firms had begun to turn down all new contracts from the armed forces, on the grounds that the labour shortage was so severe that they could not even estimate delivery dates.[119]

The change in policy on women's work, such as it was, was not made any easier by the fact that the people most fully persuaded by Nazi propaganda on the domestic role of women and their inferiority to men, were those who peddled it. The official attitude to the competing demands on married women was often one of embarrassed resignation:

the state stands helpless before many things. The scornful smile, expressing the sentiments of the childless in regard to the 'stupid' people with large families, cannot be forbidden or restricted. The state cannot completely eliminate the manifold dangers of the large city and it cannot deprive mothers of their employment. At first it can only honour the mothers of children and remove from the fathers of large families part of their extra burden by reducing their tax-rates.[120]

This was scarcely a clarion-call to action from a government confident in its approach to the problem! The regime made few practical or propagandistic preparations for the expansion of the female labour force in war industries. There were appeals to young women, but governmental directives on the allocation of labour for the event of war were still cast in the language of discriminatory paternalism, even at the height of the Munich crisis in September 1938, when mobilization seemed only days away:

women should not be given work which calls for special presence of mind, powers of decision or a capacity for swift action . . . women should not in general be entrusted with work which calls for special technical competence or knowlege.[121]

---

[117] Childlessness varied markedly with social class. In 1933, 16.4 per cent of families headed by self-employed men, 19.5 per cent of families headed by workers and 28.6 per cent of families headed by white-collar workers were childless: *SdR*, vol. 470/1, p. 14. On the flight to the spas, which were not priority targets for Allied bombers, see Ley to Reich Chancellery, 10 September 1941: Bundesarchiv Koblenz, R43II, vol. 652.

[118] There was also a considerable reserve among domestic servants, insofar as they were not employed in farmers' households. I have not been able to find statistics on the employers of domestic servants.

[119] Mason, 'National Socialist Policies', Chapter 6d.

[120] Frick, Minister of the Interior, in June 1937, quoted by Kirkpatrick, *Women and Family Life*, p. 278 (amended translation).

[121] Ministry of Labour directive, 16 September 1938, reproduced in Ursula von Gersdorff (ed.), *Frauen im Kriegsdienst* (Stuttgart 1969), p. 287.

As late as 1940 even the well-informed and opportunistic technocrats of the Labour Front's Research Institute dilated at length upon the *essentially different nature of 'women's work'*, upon the fundamental incapacity of women to cope with things technical or to plan a series of work-processes, upon their 'basic indifference to the factory', their lack of 'any inner bond to industrial labour' and upon the alien character which 'not only machines but industrial tools in general' possessed for them.[122] These last two texts were not propaganda documents – they record the holders of power talking to each other. Such attitudes influenced policy, at least in a wide variety of acts of omission; even small omissions were important, because the task of persuading large numbers of women to take up employment in industry was anyway so difficult. Short of naked coercion (which was not seriously considered before 1939), the limits of effective governmental intervention in this question were very narrow, for the authorities were now asking some women to make quite fundamental changes in their expectations and in the organization of their own lives and of that of their families: they were asking those who had no pressing need to work to do so. Even for a ruthless and inhumane dictatorship, this was a major undertaking. Nothing less than a wholehearted and insistent campaign of propaganda pressure and inducements had any prospect at all of success. Every tergiversation, every ambiguity in the stance of government and party spokesmen was bound to undermine the effort and to reinforce doubts, fears and resentments among the women whom they addressed. There were many such ambiguities and hesitations.

By the same token, any campaign to secure a major increase in the number of women in regular employment needed a long time to take effect; numerous deep-rooted and interlocking resistances had to be worn down. There was in fact no room in National Socialism for the politics of the long haul; the absence of such a middle ground of political practice, a middle ground between dramatic and brutal improvisation on the one hand and the pursuit of visionary final goals on the other, was one expression of the total irrationality of the social and political system of the Third Reich. In this question, as in all others of similar complexity, time was in practice very short. None of the elite groups had given any serious thought to the matter before mid-1936: industry and government alike had been preoccupied with overcoming unemployment; rearmament was proceeding apace, but it was at this juncture by no means clear that the country's economic position in the world was secure enough to sustain the limitless expansion of production and employment, which actual preparation for war would entail. A general shortage of labour thus seemed a fairly remote possibility and the regime was content at first to sit back and congratulate itself upon the success of its family policies. When

[122] Arbeitswissenschaftliches Institut der DAF, *Jahrbuch 1940/1*, vol. I, pp. 376, 383, 392, 394.

it did come, the problem thus came suddenly, and it very quickly became acute. Meanwhile the momentum of earlier policies remained considerable, not least because they were thought to be popular, and the contemptuous paternalism of the ruling groups also stood in the way of any far-reaching reappraisal. And then, on the invasion of Poland, a new and decisive dimension of the question emerged: the attitudes of men, whether soldiers or workers, to the enforced employment of their wives in industry.

The positive measures taken to get women into regular work before September 1939 were few and hesitant. Between June 1936 and November 1937 the government gradually whittled away the condition that women receiving marriage loans should give up their jobs; in the end, however, it still discriminated against those who did not do so, since they and their husbands had to pay back the loan at 3 per cent per month rather than 1 per cent.[123] After February 1938 the cost of employing a domestic servant ceased to be a tax-deductible expense for the employer. There were over 1.3 million domestic servants working in private homes in June 1938, 160,000 more than there had been in 1933; nearly all of them were women.[124] It is difficult to reconcile the intention of this reform – indirectly pressing women workers into industrial employment – with the simultaneous introduction, and later extension, of a 'Year of Duty' for young women before they started certain types of regular industrial or office work, for this year was supposed to be spent either in agriculture or in domestic service. The government probably hoped that the scheme would relieve the crushing burden on farmers' wives – if so, it was disappointed, for the Year of Duty does not seem to have been enforced at all thoroughly: there were a great many exceptions and limitations in the original decrees, and industrialists in the textile and clothing trades were quick to voice their dismay at this threat to their supply of labour.[125] Yet the industrial employers themselves made no serious attempt to improve the technical qualifications of women workers or to build up career structures for them. The number of apprenticeships open to women almost doubled between 1934–6 and 1938–9 but the overwhelming majority of them were for clerical and sales staff.[126]

Wage differentials did become a little narrower in the later 1930s and

[123] DAF, *Deutsche Sozialpolitik 1936–7*, pp. 60 f.; *1938*, p. 181. On the form and purpose of marriage loans, see pp. 162–4 above.

[124] See note 6 above. During the war these women were to a large extent replaced by conscripts from the German-occupied territories.

[125] See Stephenson, 'Women in Nazi Society', pp. 168–72; Mason, 'National Socialist Policies', pp. 616 f. It is possible that the government hoped that girls doing their Year of Duty would replace older women, pushed out of domestic service by the new tax legislation. For further details, see Frieda Wunderlich, *Farm Labor in Germany 1810–1945. Its Historical Development within the Framework of Agricultural and Social Policy* (Princeton 1961), pp. 329 ff.

[126] *Stat. Hdb*, p. 482. Of the apprenticeships for women 72 per cent were in white-collar occupations, the rest mainly in the textiles and clothing industries.

early 1940s, but on this vital and hotly debated issue the government felt its hands to be tied by the substantial wage increases which had been *generally* permitted (i.e. mainly to men) up to the invasion of Poland in 1939. These had had a marked inflationary effect, and the purchasing power thus created was sustaining consumer goods production at an undesirably high level: capital and raw materials, both in short supply in the armaments sector, were going in increasing quantities into the production of consumer durables. Any big general increase in women's rates could only have exacerbated these problems – and nothing less than this would have brought women into industry in large numbers. Thus a formidable new argument was added to the battery of justifications for wide differentials, but it was an argument which deprived the government of any employment policy based on monetary incentives.[127] The Labour Front lent its weight to the cause of wage-increases for women, but the only successes which it could boast about in this connection had nothing to do either with egalitarianism or with an effort to attract women into industry – wage equalization was used by the government in the late 1930s only as a means of *deterring* employers from using women in some especially heavy jobs in brick-making and pottery, etc. (This did not inhibit the Labour Front from hailing such regulations as victories for its pressure on behalf of women.)[128] And in the shadows of this specious propaganda, extremes of degradation and exploitation persisted in some parts of the country: in 1938 there were still women working in the iron-ware trades in Iserlohn (Westphalia) for starvation wages of 20 *Pfennig* per hour (less than one-half the average women's wage, less than one-quarter of the average men's wage), and in the Waldenburg area of Silesia women textile workers who earned even less than this were reportedly forced by their poverty into prostitution.[129]

Although wage-rates were not generally raised as a means of recruiting women into industry, the Labour Front did meet with some success in its drive to improve the general social conditions of work for women in industry. In the course of the Model Factory Competition between firms for the honour of flying the Golden Flag of the Labour Front (1937 on), considerable emphasis was placed on such matters as medical facilities, rest rooms, the availability of nurses and social workers, additional maternity benefits, extra holidays, etc. Many employers co-operated, not least because of the labour shortage.[130]

[127] For details see Bry, *Wages*, p. 248; Mason, 'National Socialist Policies', Chapter 8a and c.
[128] DAF, *Deutsche Sozialpolitik 1938*, pp. 51 f., 120–3.
[129] Reports of the Trustees of Labour for May–June and October–December 1938: Mason, *Arbeiterklasse*, Docs. 108, 137.
[130] See Mason, 'Labour in the Third Reich', Kirkpatrick, *Women and Family Life*, pp. 222 f.; DAF, *Deutsche Sozialpolitik 1938*, p. 51. I am grateful to Dörte Winkler-Schnurr for further information on this point.

All in all, the Labour Front propagated an attitude of extreme protective superiority towards women in industry, portraying them in their advice to managers as fragile, valuable and responsive to personal attention on the one hand, unreliable, feckless and uninterested on the other. According to this diagnosis, the good manager required a superhuman combination of technical and administrative foresight and personal sensitivity in order to induct new women employees successfully and to keep morale high. By making the task of women-management appear so formidable, the ideologues of the Labour Front both furnished a subtle reinforcement of male superiority *and* demonstrated their care for the well-being of women.[131]

The real world of industry was, no doubt, very little affected by such programmes, but the activities of the Labour Front after 1936 probably did marginally ease the daily routine of working women, as too did the re-opening of kindergartens, many of which had been closed down during the depression or turned into maternity clinics in the first flush of Nazi enthusiasm for domesticity. But the regime could do nothing to lighten decisively the double burden borne by all working housewives, and this was acknowledged by the Labour Front. Before 1940 surprisingly few firms experimented with half-shifts or part-weeks for women workers, and even in the war such arrangements appear to have been rather infrequent, though a number of firms did offer married women regular time off for shopping and housework. (A general introduction of part-time work for women in industry might well have had the consequence of inducing many full-time women workers to go over to part-time work!)

Little time need be lost over the outcome of these non-policies. In October 1938, two years after the original survey had been done, the National Organization of Industry checked up again on the composition of the industrial labour force. While the number of male wage-earners in industrial enterprises had increased in the intervening period by 13.4 per cent, the number of women workers was up by only 11.6 per cent (172,000). A higher proportion of the new recruits than of those employed in October 1936 was unskilled. The overall number of women wage-earners increased a little faster, but the important point was that not many of them were going into large-scale industry as manual workers.[132]

The anxious inactivity of the regime with respect to this group of women workers threatened to become self-destructive. With respect to another, the largest single group, its inactivity was marked by callous neglect. *German farming became more and more dependent upon female*

---

[131] Arbeitswissenschaftliches Institut der DAF, *Jahrbuch 1940/1*, vol. I, pp. 373–6, waxed especially eloquent on these themes.

[132] Supplement to report 'Facharbeiter- und Nachwuchsfrage', BA/MA Freiburg, WiLF5, vol. 1917.

labour during the 1930s. Almost 400,000 men, most of them agricultural labourers, disappeared from the land between 1933 and 1938; this represented a decline of 25 per cent in the number of male wage-earners. The men went off into better-paid jobs on building sites or in manufacturing industry – and the women stayed. The number of female agricultural labourers did fall off a little, but this was more than compensated for by an increase of 360,000, over 10 per cent, in the number of women family assistants (though it must be noted that part of this increase was apparent, not real, in that it merely reflected a more careful collection of census data).[133] In 1939 3.83 million women worked on Germany's farms in this capacity – an average of more than one per holding. In 1933 there had been 50,000 more men than women employed in one capacity or another in agriculture; in 1939 there were over 800,000 more women than men. What little is yet known about the lot of these women indicates that it was hard, and that it got progressively worse. In 1939 the labour shortage in agriculture was even more acute than in industry. Small farms could not expand and contract their activities as could business firms – the amount of work to be done remained much the same, regardless of how many people were available to do it – unless, that is, proprietors went over from labour-intensive dairy-farming to grain-production, as some were forced to do by the labour shortage; but this was no answer for the small farmers, and it was dairy produce, not grain, which was in especially short supply and had to be imported in large quantities. The increased burden of work fell to a great extent upon the women, especially upon farmers' wives. In the last twelve months before the invasion of Poland in September 1939 the Reich Food Estate, which controlled all agricultural production, became thoroughly alarmed about this development and circulated to ministers a great deal of evidence, admittedly impressionistic, according to which the strains of overwork were having a drastic effect upon the health of women in the countryside. The number of miscarriages suffered by farmers' wives was alleged to be increasing rapidly, and the role of farmer's wife had come to appear so unattractive that the sons and heirs of small farmers were having great difficulty in finding women willing to marry them: they had to act as housewives, mothers and labourers. Total exhaustion was the only possible outcome.[134]

[133] For these and subsequent statistics, see *Wirtschaft and Statistik* (1941), no. 3; *Stat. Jhb. 1939/40*, p. 379; *Stat. Hdb.*, pp. 32, 84 f. There were a further 340,000 part-time women family assistants. The number of male family assistants fell sharply after 1933. This whole trend marked a reversal of that of the 1920s, when women were leaving the land at a faster rate than men. Wunderlich, *Farm Labor*, pp. 297–301, gives a good description of the flight from the land.

[134] See the numerous reports and proposals, some of them sent by Minister Darré personally to Hitler during 1938 and 1939: Bundesarchiv Koblenz, R43II, vol. 213b, 611; also reports by the Trustees of Labour, reprinted in Mason, *Arbeiterklasse*; and Wunderlich, *Farm Labor*, pp. 299, 322 f.

The bitter irony of these reports ought not to have escaped those readers who had been so loud in their praise of the healthy attitudes to the family and to child-bearing in the farming community; and yet the government felt itself unable to take effective action. Industry was critically dependent upon the flow of male workers from the countryside, and young men conscripted into the armed forces swelled the ranks of the migrants; attempts to bind farm labourers to their jobs by the force of law had been given up as hopeless in 1936; in the later 1930s the government considered both plans to force those who had recently left the land to return to their old jobs, and plans to replenish the agricultural labour force through civil conscription, but rejected them all on the grounds that they would be too unpopular and thus administratively impracticable.[135] And improvements in wages and working conditions on the land, which the Ministry of Agriculture was demanding as an incentive for men to stay there, would have had the supremely unpopular result of raising food-prices in the towns – and were rejected for this reason by Hitler.[136] The women on Germany's farms thus had to wait for the arrival of columns of prisoners-of-war and of conscript labourers from the conquered territories of Eastern and Western Europe, before their burden was lightened. Their real social and economic status, as opposed to their legal rights, had been little different from that of those who took over from them. German agriculture was saved from collapse by forced foreign labour.[137]

Thus through the first phase of the war, 1939–42, the old male-dominated order in industry lived on, unchanged by the growing crisis; the new suburban paternalism of the party tended to keep married women out of regular work, or, failing this, to confine them to appropriately female occupations in the service and administrative sectors; and in the countryside the old patriarchal order reserved to men the right to take advantage of the new possibilities of industrial employment and thus intensified the subservience and exploitation of women.

In 1939 the crisis in industry came to a head. In terms of policy-making, the crisis arose out of two interrelated issues, which pushed the government in diametrically opposed directions; the contradictory arguments were equally compelling. While the armed forces pushed with ever greater vehemence for measures to conscript women who were not working into the war industries, it also became essential to decide upon a policy for the financial support of families whose breadwinners were to be called up when war commenced. As the military and some senior civil servants realized, the latter issue presented the government with a lever for solving

---

[135] Mason, 'National Socialist Policies', pp. 682–91, 720 f.   [136] See note 42 above.
[137] See Edward L. Homze, *Foreign Labor in Nazi Germany* (Princeton, NJ 1967), pp. 16, 46–49, 234 f; Wunderlich, *Farm Labor*, pp. 343 ff.

the labour problem: allowances for the wives of soldiers could be introduced at a level so low as to compel many of them to take a job. (A very tentative experiment of this kind was made in the spring of 1939 with the dependants of men drafted to armaments firms away from their homes, but it was dropped after a few months.) In the first instance this approach was decisively rejected. Many of the details of this controversy are still obscure, but it is clear that fears about the effects of such a scheme on the morale of the troops in the field were a predominant consideration – more important than the often cited ideological purism of Hitler on questions relating to motherhood and the protection of women. In the event, the separation allowances for the wives of soldiers were set at a maximum of 85 per cent of the husbands' previous earnings, a very high level, higher than in any other country during the Second World War. (In only one respect was the government inhibited in its generosity, and here the demands of budgetary economy were at odds with the needs of industry: wives who were already working received a much lower allowance! – they expressed their indignation at so unjust and so discouraging a ruling by working less and less well. The government raised their allowance in May 1940.)[138]

This solution to the problem of maintenance, the propaganda value of which the government exploited to the full, played no small part in producing a catastrophic situation in the labour market during the winter of 1939/40. The imminence of war anyway induced more people to get married, but it is probable that the separation allowances accentuated this trend. In 1939 130,000 more couples were married than in 1938 – 774,200 in all, the highest figure ever! The number of women in insured employment declined from July 1939 to March 1940 by 540,000 (6.3 per cent); this fall was far greater than the seasonal average, it started earlier and lasted longer than the normal seasonal swing, and it was due only in small part to new wartime restrictions upon the consumer goods industries, for these restrictions were slight and ineffectual during 1940. The military authorities were in no doubt that the separation allowances had induced many women to marry and give up their work.[139] The conjunction of this development with the conscription of numerous men from industry into the armed forces placed war production in extreme jeopardy. By February 1940 armaments plants alone, strictly defined, were short of 250,000 workers according to an authoritative estimate.

---

[138] Source materials in BA/MA Freiburg, WiLF5, vol. 319, 420/1, 420/2; and WO8, vol. 110/8. Bundesarchiv Koblenz, R41, vol. 161; and R43II, vol. 648. Wunderlich, *Farm Labor*, p. 323.

[139] *Stat. Hdb.*, pp. 47, 474. Jill Stephenson points out that a temporary relaxation in the eugenics regulations played a part in the increase in the number of marriages.

The forces' reserves of munitions were so low that military aggression in the months after the fall of Poland (October–December 1939) was completely out of the question – yet Hitler was pressing for an immediate invasion of France. This problem was sufficiently acute for the head of the War Economy Staff himself, Thomas, a top-ranking general, to take part in a search for 300 additional women munitions workers in Berlin. He noted in February 1940 that 'the labour shortage has become the crucial issue of the war'.[140]

Women who did not work and had no young children were the only large and immediately accessible reserve of labour. And by this stage nothing less than methods of compulsion would get them quickly into industry; in the view of General Thomas, cutting the separation allowances would no longer suffice. But industry was ill-prepared for an influx of women workers, particularly if they were to be reluctant conscripts rather than eager volunteers. Even those firms where they were already employed in large numbers made, it seems, little allowance for the severity of wartime conditions; and many women workers responded to blackouts, rationing, shortages, queues and, in some cases, the burden of running a household alone, by taking time off without permission. There were many complaints in the winter of 1939/40 about absenteeism and declining work-discipline among both men and women in industry, but women where thought to be especially unreliable. Morale and productivity fell off especially among those women who had not given up their jobs although their husbands had been called up, and who thus forfeited a part of the separation allowance; and married women whose husbands were on good wages had long been counted among the least enthusiastic and least reliable members of the industrial labour force. This indifference to the pressing needs of the war effort furnished a further occasion for the regime to exhibit its dedication to double standards in the treatment of men and women: after the invasion of Poland, men who repeatedly breached the rules of industrial discipline were handed over in increasing numbers to the Gestapo, which incarcerated them for short periods in concentration or labour camps; but women 'offenders' were not considered to have the same degree of responsibility for their actions (or were perhaps thought not to need such stern measures of deterrence) and customarily got off with a warning.[141]

Despite these difficulties the government had no option but to press on

---

[140] Minutes of a conference on 22 February 1940: BA/MA Freiburg, WiLF5, vol. 103a. See the detailed discussion in Dietrich Eichholtz, *Geschichte der deutschen Kriegswirtschaft* (Berlin 1971), vol. I, Chapter 2d. On the background relationship between economic and social policy on the one hand and the prosecution of the war on the other, see Tim Mason, 'Internal Crisis and War of Aggression, 1938–1939', pp. 104–30 above.

[141] Details in Mason, 'National Socialist Policies', Chapter 7; Wunderlich, *Farm Labor*, p. 327.

with plans for a measure of conscription of women. This was done with the utmost reluctance, and represented by and large a capitulation on the part of the civilian ministries to the urgent demands of the military. The Minister of Labour had foreseen both the need for and the unpopularity of this policy as early as July 1938, and had laid down at the time of the invasion of Poland that women were not to be conscripted into industry.[142] In the face of the extreme shortages of the winter of 1939/40 this position could no longer be maintained. Top level discussions about the number of women workers needed and about the details of a conscription scheme began in earnest in February 1940. By the end of April, a consensus was emerging in favour of the Ministry of Labour's plan to restrict the victims, in the first instance, to women aged between fourteen and forty who were no longer at school or university and who had no small children; but the talks dragged on through May without a firm decision. The Minister of the Interior could not deny that there was an emergency, but he was very worried about the effects of conscripting women on 'the mood both within Germany and on the fighting front'; he insisted that fourteen and fifteen year-olds be left out of the scheme entirely. All of the ministries concerned were perplexed by the problem of the soldiers' wives who had given up regular employment since September 1939 and were living on their separation allowances. On 16 May 1940 the High Command of the Armed Forces peremptorily demanded that these women be compelled to return to work; its spokesman asserted that unless such a clause were included, the Minister of Labour's draft decree would not be adequate to the crisis in the armaments industry, and one *Gauleiter* intervened to suggest that they be allowed to receive their allowances in full, on top of their wages, if they returned to work.

It was all in vain. On 4 June 1940, over a fortnight before France capitulated, Göring announced that he was not going to sign any such decree: this step would cause 'far too much unrest among the population at the moment', and there would anyway be sufficient prisoners-of-war to meet Germany's manpower needs, without the government having to drag women out of their homes!'[143] The history of the Second World War contains many illustrations of the element of social imperialism in Nazi policies, but few as clear as this.

[142] Minister of Labour to Reich Chancellery, 14 July 1938: Mason, *Arbeiterklasse*, Doc. 144; *Reichsarbeitsblatt*, 1939, Part I, p. 502; Bundesarchiv Koblenz, R41, vol. 279.

[143] In addition to the analysis by Eichholtz, *Geschichte*, Chapter 2d, see the full collection of papers on these deliberations, 1940–1, in: Bundesarchiv Koblenz, R43II, vol. 652. These are quoted above and drawn upon for the following paragraph. After June 1941 women who received allowances and had no dependants were interviewed and asked to return to work; if they refused without reason, they were threatened with conscription under the terms of an unpublished (!) decree. Well over 80 per cent found good reasons for refusing.

The matter did not end there; for, despite the plunder of labour from occupied territories, acute shortages arose repeatedly throughout the war, and on each occasion the demand for the conscription of women was raised again. In 1941 it was rejected twice by Hitler, and he did not give way until January 1943, when the Red Army began to move on to the offensive. Women aged between seventeen and forty-five were then required to register so that the authorities could check whether their family responsibilities allowed them to be drafted into war work of one kind or another. In the first few months this decree seems to have been enforced with some vigour, but momentum soon lapsed as women conscripts proved themselves adept at fulfilling conditions for exemption. By December 1943 Speer's Armaments Ministry was again in despair: 'We must record a total failure to mobilize German women for work in the war effort.'[144]

The main reason for this hesitancy was *not* of an ideological order, but was rooted in the well-founded fear that civil conscription for women would be extremely unpopular, both with women and with men. The eugenic argument against forcing women to work – that it would weaken the racial stock, slow down population growth, cause miscarriages, disrupt the delicate balance of male supremacy – was, it seems, merely a piece of ritualistic rhetoric, behind which embarrassing domestic political considerations arising out of the weakness of the regime and its fear of the people could conveniently be hidden. When for example, Sauckel, the new head of the labour administration, was forced to announce on 20 April 1942 that Hitler had yet again refused to permit the conscription of women, he ran through all the eugenic clichés and then, adopting Hitler's standpoint as his own, significantly added, 'I cannot enumerate all the reasons which have made me come to this decision.'[145] He went on, following Göring's line, to invoke a barbaric utopia, in which Germany's ultimate victory in the war would give her control over such large numbers of foreign workers that 'we shall be in a position to remove all women and girls from jobs regarded as unsuitable for women'. Meanwhile

[144] Quoted by Gregor Janssen, *Das Ministerium Speer. Deutschlands Rüstung im Krieg* (Berlin/Frankfurt/Vienna 1968), p. 226; see also pp. 130, 282. Dietmar Petzina, 'Die Mobilisierung deutscher Arbeitskräfte vor und während des Zweiten Weltkrieges', *Vierteljahrshefte für Zeitgeschichte*, vol. 18 no. 4 (October 1970), pp. 454 f., gives a brief survey of the effects of the conscription decree.

[145] International Military Tribunal, Nuremburg, Doc. 016-PS (*Trial of the Major War Criminals . . .*, vol. XXV (Nuremberg 1947), p. 63). See also Jeremy Noakes and Geoffrey Pridham (eds.), *Documents on Nazism 1919–1945* (London 1974), pp. 647 f. Petzina, Janssen and most other authors attribute the failure of the regime to force more women into industrial employment entirely to Hitler's ideological preconceptions. I find this account wholly unconvincing. The sources make it quite clear that much bigger issues were at stake, and the vacillation of the government on this question was all of a piece with its attempt to bribe the German people into passivity on other major questions of social policy.

the utopia had to be partially anticipated, for the regime thought that it was a very popular programme, good for morale. Many sections of the party organization, which was, in the view of the Gauleiters, responsible to the Führer for the mood of the population, considered the conscription of women into industry to be quite out of the question; the most that should be done was to use the party and the propaganda machine to ask for volunteers. Not until 1941 did the number of women in regular employment exceed the figure for 1928. At least until 1943 many women enjoyed a *relatively* protected position in the wartime social and economic system. It must have seemed to them – and to their boyfriends, husbands, fathers – that they had something to thank the regime for. The mobilization of women for war production remained much less efficient in Germany than in Britain, and British policies were often held up as an example and a warning by those Nazi leaders who were prepared to risk the enforcement of stronger measures.

A comparison with Britain is instructive at this point.[146] The increase in the number of jobs available, combined with a government campaign to persuade women to volunteer for war work, led to a 10 per cent increase in the number of women in regular employment in the United Kingdom between June 1939 and June 1940; in Germany the number fell during this period. By the spring of 1941 it was clear beyond all doubt that an enormous manpower shortage would develop within twelve months, both in industry and in the armed forces. The compulsory registration of women was introduced in March 1941 and, on the basis of the register, women were selectively conscripted into industry, the administration and the armed forces from December 1941 on. These decisions were resisted at the highest level by Conservative members of the government and the civil service, including Winston Churchill himself, on the ground that they would be bad for the morale of men, but the Minister of Labour, the trade unionist Ernest Bevin, successfully insisted that the measures were necessary and practicable, and that they would not be bad for morale. The similarity with the debate in Germany is striking, but the outcome was quite different. In Bevin's view it was so different because the people in general and the working class in particular trusted him and recognized the strength of the Labour representatives in the cabinet; they accepted the legitimacy of the parliamentary system and accepted the defensive goals for which the war was being fought at this time. The Conservative opponents of the conscription of women could not, for their part, deny

---

[146] The following remarks are based upon Alan Bullock, *The Life and Times of Ernest Bevin*, vol. II: *Minister of Labour 1940–1945* (London 1967), pp. 27, 47, 56, 62 f., 117, 122, 138–44, 172 f., 253 f., 266; and Angus Calder, *The People's War. Britain 1939–1945*, rev. edn. (London 1971), pp. 85, 309, 382–7. See also the survey by Mass Observation, *People in Production. An Enquiry into British War Production* (Harmondsworth 1942).

the urgent need of the armaments industry for more labour. On every single one of these counts, the position of the Nazi government was weaker. Bevin also set great store by the efforts to secure the *voluntary* enlistment of women before December 1941, so that he could claim that compulsion was only introduced when the need for labour could no longer possibly be met by the number of volunteers – the population had thus been prepared for the measure. And after December 1941, compulsion was used only to reinforce and guide voluntary enlistment: by May 1942 fifteen women had been gaoled for refusing to do work allocated to them, no more, but no less. Conscription was confined at first to young women, but soon extended so that, 'by 1943 it was almost impossible for a woman under forty to avoid war work unless she had heavy family responsibilities or was looking after a war worker billeted on her'.[147] Between September 1939 and May 1942 the number of women working in industry alone increased by over 1.1 million, and it went on rising throughout the war; in September 1943, all women aged under fifty-one were required to register; by December 1943 there were 1.5 million women in the engineering industry, 1.46 million more than in 1939! In practice the conscription of women raised very few political or industrial problems, and there was very little popular resentment or resistance. Employers were forced to go in for factory welfare schemes and scientific management on a large scale, in order to hold on to their new female labour force and secure high rates of productivity. The most bitter resistance came from a few groups of skilled male workers who wished to defend their jobs and the status of their trades.[148]

No conclusion can be more than suggestive. The Nazi regime consistently attached a peculiar importance to family, domesticity and child-bearing. The political leaders did not, to be sure, consider this as a separate autonomous sphere in their policy-making, and the goals of their family policies were anything but ends in themselves: the removal of women from political life and the attempts to restrict their employment were an integral part of the general attack on liberalism, and in the eyes of the ideologues the raising of the birth-rate had an important place in the strategy for the racial supremacy of the Germanic people. Further, if the cost of the welfare reforms in the interests of large families is set against armaments expenditure, the reforms appear positively mean, even trivial. Housing needs were almost totally neglected. And, as the promiscuity of

---

[147] Calder, *People's War*, p. 383.
[148] Further interesting comparisons are suggested by Thomas R. H. Havens, 'Women and War in Japan, 1937–1945', *American Historical Review*, vol. 80, no. 4 (October, 1975), pp. 913–34; and Robert O. Paxton, *Vichy France. Old Guard and New Order, 1940–1944* (New York 1972), pp. 165 ff.

the political leaders became public knowledge, as the divorce-rate steadily rose, as children were encouraged to inform on the political attitudes of their parents, as the demands of the armaments drive forced more and more male workers to live away from home for long periods of the year, and as unmarried women began to get official encouragement to bear illegitimate children, so the official shining ideal of the integrated, stable and prolific family began to look more and more like a monstrous deception.[149] Yet it would be a serious mistake, even in the light of these important facts, to dismiss the family policies of the regime as so much manipulative verbiage and gesture.

For these policies do *seem* to have had a considerable resonance; if they had not, it would be hard to account for the consistent concern of the leadership with them. Hitler and his civilian advisers thought that the German people were particularly sensitive to political and economic impositions on married women and the family. At their inception, the family policies of the regime may indeed have been strongly influenced by extreme, irrational and impractical fantasies of a eugenic and racialist order, which could never be of more than sectarian appeal. But it can perhaps be argued that their import was very much wider, because they addressed themselves, almost by accident, to some general and deeply felt needs engendered by the social order of modern industrial capitalism: 'almost by accident', because the success of the policies lay *not* in persuading more married couples to have large numbers of children and all mothers to stay at home, but in persuading (or more exactly, assisting) more people to marry, to have no children or one or two, and in reinforcing the distinction between men's and women's spheres of responsibility.

In the era of the large-scale organization of industry, services and administration, the family household has been deprived of most of its original functions as a unit of property ownership and production, and its economic role is to an increasing extent defined in terms of the organization of consumption. (In this context the small family household is certainly indispensable to business interests, precisely because it is outstandingly inefficient and wasteful.) Some of the older welfare and educational functions of the family have also either lapsed or been taken on by public authorities. And the moral foundations of its claim to be the primary social institution are beginning to be questioned and undermined in a

---

[149] The reform of the marriage laws in 1938 led to an immediate increase in the divorce-rate of over 20 per cent: *Stat. Jhb. 1941/2*, p. 92 f. (Divorced women always found it much harder to remarry than divorced men.) The legal and financial position of single mothers was improved in the later 1930s. The atavistic element in the sexual morality of National Socialism was institutionalized in the war years through the building of 'B-Barracks', in which women from the occupied territories served the males of the master race as prostitutes: Bundesarchiv Koblenz, R43II, vol. 1186; R41, vol. 69.

wide variety of ways. Whatever its utility to the economic structure of capitalism, the family may be on the way to becoming an anachronism.[150] But until very recently the increasing industrialization and bureaucratization of economic and public life has gone hand in hand with a *steady growth* in the popularity of marriage and of the separate family household as private institutions. For the period under consideration, it is probably more appropriate to think of this modern form of domesticity as a specific *reaction to* industrialization and bureaucratization, than as just another example of the persistence of anachronistic forms of social organization in advanced industrial capitalism. In the first half of the twentieth century the small closed family unit is not a remnant of a bygone peasant/artisan economy, but in many important respects a novelty with its own distinct history.

The evidence that can be offered for this suggestion is sketchy in the extreme, and I am aware that there is a good deal of work on the subject with which I am not familiar.[151] However: the conventions customarily used to describe public life on the one hand (politics, administration, work) and family life on the other, form sets of polar opposites. According to these conventions, the public sphere is cold, impersonal, competitive, insecure and often arbitrary or opaque, usually enormous in scale, demanding, geared to efficiency and, perhaps above all, tending to reduce the person through the progressive division of labour to a function, so that work becomes instrumental. In popular imagery the family is *both*

[150] I have dealt only obliquely with the question, much discussed by socialists and feminists, of the appropriateness of modern family organization to industrial capitalism, because I am not yet at all clear what the issues in this discussion are. It is particularly unclear to me *by what specific means* industry has suggested, required, enforced on an almost universal scale this form of family organization, which appears to suit its interests. This way of posing the question seems to me to underestimate drastically the latitude which people have had to respond in different ways to the transformed social-economic order of the later nineteenth and twentieth centuries, and to suggest – but not to demonstrate – that capital has exercised an enormous direct influence in this sphere.

[151] The introduction which I have found most helpful is Rose Laub Coser (ed.), *The Family. Its Structures and Functions*, 2nd edn (London 1974); see in particular the imaginative and well-documented essay by Judith Blake, 'Coercive Pronatalism and American Population Policy', which deals with basic sociological aspects of the problem, aspects which I have largely neglected, and makes suggestions for a causal analysis. Karin Hausen, 'Familie als Gegenstand historischer Sozialwissenschaft', *Geschichte und Gesellschaft*, vol. 1 no. 2/3 (1975), is an excellent discussion of the historical literature. The three-part review essay by Christopher Lasch, 'The Family and History', *New York Review of Books*, vol. 22, nos. 18–20 (November–December 1975), contains a wide range of incisive and thoughtful judgements. The work of Lutz Niethammer on the housing market and changes in working-class dwelling patterns in Germany since the 1870s is opening up a new dimension of empirical and theoretical enquiry into the history of the family, which also brings out the novelty of the modern family unit; before 1900 many working-class families had no place where they could constitute themselves in a stable and defined manner: 'Wie wohnten die Arbeiter im Kaiserreich?', *Archiv für Sozialgeschichte*, vol. 16 (1976).

the *compensation and* the *justification* for this anxious and alienated toil, both the refuge from the compulsions of work and the unquestionable good for the sake of which the public sphere is endured: the family is warm and supportive, individual, intimate and secure, it encompasses the whole person and is small and manageable – motives are rewarded, not just performance. (That these conventions themselves constitute a distorting ideology is less important in the present context than the fact that they are very widespread.) In this most bourgeois of bourgeois ideologies, the boundary between the realm of necessity and the realm of freedom is not a distant and difficult future divide between historical epochs, but a line across which people believe that they commute daily.[152]

It can perhaps be argued that the romantic nostalgias and the eugenic fantasies of the Nazi movement led the regime to tumble upon the immense potential of this dichotomy. In extolling the virtues and the importance of the private sphere, of family life, the Nazi leadership was not just engaged in a cynical trick to distract people's attention away from politics and to underpin legal disenfranchisement with a psychological self-disenfranchisement – though they were certainly trying to do this too. Whether they realized it or not, their propaganda and their policies magnified the much more fundamental *reconciliatory function* of family life, and people were responsive to this because the campaign spoke to long-established and almost universal mechanisms of self-protection against the alienated rigours of life outside the home. If this speculation is well founded, then we have to do with a 'higher cynicism', embedded in the structure of modern industrial and bureaucratized societies, and articulated only in a peculiarly extreme form by National Socialism: for the more intense the economic and political pressures became in the 1930s, the greater the exploitation of labour and the concentration of capital, the more arbitrary, inaccessible and incomprehensible the sources of public power – *the more important was the reconciliatory function of the family.*

The nightmare world of dictatorial government, huge industrial combines, all-encompassing administration and organized inhumanity was parasitic upon its ideological antithesis, the minute community of parents and children. The regime propagated both elements of this

---

[152] I use the term ideology here in Marx's sense, to denote a set of bedrock assumptions, responses and notions, not in the more trivial sense of specific public ideals, deliberately propagated. Reverence for the family on these counts cuts across most political alignments today, though different parties and regimes may adopt different types of family policy in recognition of their commitment. To remain with Marx, it is interesting that the family as an ideal has survived the decline of one of its strongest supports, organized religion – perhaps it has even become a substitute, a new 'opium of the people', again in Marx's exact sense.

pseudo-contradiction simultaneously, with great energy and, perhaps, to considerable effect.[153] Women may have been more open than men to the blandishments of such a policy, not only because they were normally responsible for house and home, but also because the public roles and the types of work which were available to them were so very restricted. Men benefited, not only in that their masculine pride was flattered and their protective instincts encouraged, but also directly: for it was, as Hitler indicated at Nuremberg in September 1934, nice, comforting, relaxing and reassuring to return from the brutal struggle for survival, wealth, land and power, to return from muder and carnage, to the enclosed warmth of a supportive family: 'the big world rests upon this small world! The big world cannot survive if the small world is not secure.'[154]

POSTCRIPT

One of the ways in which historians characteristically keep their readers at a distance is by leaving only the most discreet and delphic clues as to the position which any one piece of their work occupies in relation to their past and future writing. Impersonality is one of the costumes worn by authority, and it is in the same spirit and with the same results that historians are reluctant to draw attention to what they regard as the weaknesses of their own work. In *History Workshop Journal* we hope to break down conventions of mystifying reticence. While the subject of enquiry will always remain more important than the writer, some studies may be made more intelligible if the author tries to place them and discusses briefly the main problems faced in writing them.

I resisted for a long time the idea that it was possible or necessary to investigate the position of women in society as an undertaking distinct from any other form of social historical enquiry. I was bemused and depressed by the scholasticism of much methodological left-wing writing on the subject, which elaborates with impeccable logic the necessary relationships between production and reproduction and vice versa, but which never promises to reach any goal beyond unimpeachable definitions, and of course does not reach that non-existent goal either – militancy congests into clamorous categories, producing works which might be the offspring of a proud union between a prayer-wheel and a sausage-

---

[153] These tentative concluding remarks were suggested by Sheila Rowbotham's work, in particular by *Woman's Consciousness, Man's World* (Harmondsworth 1973), Chapters 7 and 8.

[154] See the quotation from Hitler at the start of this essay, p. 131 above. The emotional patterns which I have tried to sketch in here in general terms are perhaps most clearly documented in the memoirs of Rudolf Hoess, *Commandant of Auschwitz* (London 1959).

machine.[155] More important, however, was the difficulty which I experienced in deciding what the enquiry could really be about, if it were not to be of a general theoretical kind. Historians are brought up and accustom themselves to write about people's actions, that is, about the people who acted in public.[156] By this criterion women were barely present on the historical stage in Nazi Germany; individually they played little role in politics after their – admittedly incomplete – expulsion from public life in 1933; and collectively their active presence was very hard to discern except when the women's organizations of the party were carrying out one propaganda campaign or another.

What was there to write about? There was something to be said on the subject of the policies of the regime towards women, but this would not amount to a discussion of the position of women of a kind similar to that which could be written about peasant farmers, who lost their labourers and complained about prices; or workers, who refused to do overtime; or Jews, who organized (or collaborated) in response to persecution. Women were not a collectivity in this sense. Women workers were paid less well and were concentrated in certain industries, and the number of women clerks and typists was increasing, but this was much the same in all Western European countries, and appeared almost self-evident. Part of the problem arose from the fact that Germany in these years was a male-dominated society, which meant that it was men who decided what the important political issues were and who wrote most of the documents on which research has to be based, but this second-hand bias and indifference was far from being the whole reason why women appeared not to be *doing* things in the manner in which historians customarily expect the subjects of their research to make their presence felt. The relative subjection of women really did manifest itself in a lesser degree of activity in this sense.

This issue thus raised a more fundamental question of historical method, a question about the presuppostions of a discipline which is still narrative in its basic structure, and thus emphasizes and revolves around activity of any kind. (This is as true of much socialist writing about working-class movements, as it is of liberal or conservative writing on political and economic history.) The question can be resolved in a variety

---

[155] Chris Middleton, 'Sexual Inequality and Stratification Theory', in Frank Parkin (ed.), *The Social Analysis of Class Structure* (London 1974), might, on reflection, be a parody. The discussion in *New Left Review*, no. 83 and 89 (1974–5), did not leave me much wiser.

[156] Although this is not true of some recent social history which aims to elucidate social structures and processes, it seems to me to be true of the discipline as a whole. The notion of what constitutes a significant public action is, of course, being broadened all the time by the work of social historians. But it remains the case, for example, that women's movements furnish the only aspect of the history of women which has been widely researched into.

of ways. It would certainly be possible and desirable to find out a great deal more about the non- or semi-public actions of women in Germany during the inter-war years than I (or any other historian) have yet done, and to construct a densely documented picture of the way in which at least some women lived in the 1920s and 1930s. It would be a very laborious piece of research which I did not want to undertake, and I am not certain at the end how much light it would actually shed on the main developments and crises of the period – the rise of Nazism, the consolidation of the Third Reich, the Second World War; I did not want to lose sight of these points of reference.

A second possible resolution of the problem, revisionist rather than innovatory, gradually forced itself on to my attention as a result of looking again at the materials which I had already gathered together. It became clear that practically all historians who have written about Germany in this period had simply taken the family and the division of roles between the sexes for granted, and had written about the men who did act publicly *without examining this essential context of their public behaviour*, much as the men they were writing about usually took it for granted too. Thus as the chapter developed, it became more and more clear that the study of the non-actors provided an exceptionally fruitful new vantage point from which the behaviour of the actors could be – indeed, had to be – reinterpreted. By setting their actions in this broader *factual* framework (for it is not in the first instance a question of a new theoretical approach), hitherto neglected aspects of the policies of the regime took on a new significance and old questions about its durability gained a wide new dimension. It was possible to come a lot nearer to seeing things in the round. Even an unsuccessful or incomplete attempt to study those who had no voice and who, for the most part, suffered passively, can throw the actions of those with property, power and an easy hold on the historian's ear into much sharper relief. What was surprising was the time and difficulty it had cost to break the tyranny of the foreground actors over my historical perspective. They had seemed so self-evidently more important.

This is, of course, by no means the only resolution to the problem of method posed by writing about women, but I think it does bring out one of the major difficulties, and indicates one of the major rewards to be gained. In order to begin with this approach it was necessary to make some concessions to a different type of resolution of the problem. The methodologically least complicated way of writing about people in the past who appear to have been largely passive in public affairs, is to assume and emphasize their passivity by subjecting them as far as the source materials allow to entirely impersonal analysis – birth- and death-rates, nutrition, land tenure, income, social stratification, migration, legal controls, etc. Valuable though all such sociological data is, it cannot *on its own* do much to enhance our understanding of the past; it has to be organized around a discussion of the relations of the group in question with other groups in society and with the state.

These are the main reasons why this essay is shaped as it is. And they are also among the reasons why I do not intend to do any further detailed research into the position of women in Nazi Germany in the near future; I want to go back to finishing a book about the German working class during this period. It will be a different book from the one which I would have written if I had not done this work, and I hope a better one.

Concentration upon those aspects of the position of women and of policies towards women which shed most light upon the general character of the Nazi regime has its own numerous drawbacks, and these account for some of the weaknesses of this essay. Most of these weaknesses reflect my lack of detailed knowledge about the everyday life of women. The chapter is very thin on relationships within the family, a subject which the techniques of oral history could open up. Its silence on prostitution and on unmarried mothers bears witness to my ignorance about these subjects, not to a belief that they were unimportant or are uninteresting. It seems in general difficult to avoid being either anecdotal or wildly speculative in writing about sexual relations between men and women in this period, and here too I have preferred to remain silent. My reticence in using the categories of social psychology has rather different reasons, for some very interesting work is being done in this field.[157] But active Nazis were mainly men and so the experts write mainly on male psychology; furthermore, I have a simple-minded belief that these explanatory categories should be used only when other types of account manifestly fail to do justice to a subject – that is, when more mundane explanations simply do not match the extreme character of the behaviour under discussion. By implication I have suggested in this chapter that one can get a long way with mundane explanations. I fully expect to be proved wrong.

Perhaps more serious is the amateur quality of my forays into demography. I do not think that I have mistaken the essential lines of change in population and family structure, but in this complex and fascinating discipline important points of interpretation can hang upon seemingly minor and technical questions regarding the statistics and the calculations done with them. I wish I were more confident, and can only draw small consolation from a recent remark of Germany's leading historical demographer: 'The demographic history of the Weimar Republic

[157] For example, Peter Loewenberg, 'The Psychohistorical Origins of the Nazi Youth Cohort', in *American Historical Review*, vol. 76 no. 5 (December 1971), pp. 1457–502; Henry V. Dicks, *Licensed Mass Murder. A Socio-Psychological Study of some SS-Killers* (London 1972); Norman Cohn, *Warrant for Genocide* (London 1967), esp. the Conclusion.

has hardly been studied hitherto.'[158] A great deal of work remains to be done on all these aspects of the subject of this chapter.[159]

[158] Wolfgang Köllmann, 'Bevölkerungspolitik in der Weimarer Republik', in Mommsen, Petzina and Weisbrod (eds.), *Industrielles System und politische Entwicklung*, p. 76. Since he wrote these words, one highly technical monograph has appeared, which is a contribution to a discussion among demographers rather than a study in social history: John E. Knodel, *The Decline of Fertility in Germany 1871–1939* (Princeton, NJ 1974).

[159] Since the first half of this chapter was completed, Peter H. Merkl's study, *Political Violence under the Swastika. 581 Early Nazis* (Princeton, NJ 1975), has been published. It contains some interesting evidence (pp. 117–37) on the motives and attitudes of thirty-six women who joined the Nazi Party before 1933.

6

∾

INTENTION AND EXPLANATION: A CURRENT CONTROVERSY ABOUT THE INTERPRETATION OF NATIONAL SOCIALISM[1]

FOR THE past eleven years or so a subterranean debate has been going on among German historians of National Socialism. It has been growing increasingly bitter, and yet it has not really come out into the open, as a debate with a clear literary form. One has to trace its erratic public progress through a series of book reviews and odd passages within articles in journals and anthologies. The debate has reached such a pitch of intensity that some historians are now accusing other historians of 'trivializing' National Socialism in their work, of implicitly, unwittingly, furnishing an apologia for the Nazi regime.[2] This is perhaps the most serious charge which can be made against serious historians of the subject. Since the historians so accused have not the least sympathy for fascist causes, past or present, but are on the contrary progressive in their political positions, the debate is not a political slanging match (although in a strange way it is that too) – it raises in an acute and bitter form fundamental questions about modes of historical understanding and methods of interpretation, and fundamental questions about the moral and political responsibility of the historian.

The purpose of this essay is to draw attention to this partly hidden debate; to put forward in the form of theses (rather than of extended and documented historical arguments) a critique of both positions in the controversy; and to suggest that the terms of debate can be and should be transcended. It is not an easy subject to write about. The issues concerned are both abstract and highly emotive, at once theoretical and personal, scholarly in one form and the engine of harsh professional in-fighting in another. It is beyond the scope of this essay to give an

---

[1] I am deeply grateful to Jane Caplan and Wolfgang J. Mommsen for their detailed advice and criticism in the revision of this essay.
[2] Thus among others, Karl Dietrich Bracher, 'Tradition und Revolution im National-sozialismus', in Manfred Funke (ed.), *Hitler, Deutschland und die Mächte* (Düsseldorf 1977), p. 18. The customary German term is *Verharmlosung*.

historical account of the origins and development of the controversy and the purposes which it has served: although it is a somewhat artificial procedure, the positions adopted and the arguments deployed will be abstracted from their context of the pressures within (and acting upon) the German historical profession. This does not make for good intellectual history but it does guide *our* concern away from the purely polemical uses to which the charge of 'trivializing' National Socialism has been put, and towards the central theoretical conflicts – the argument is worth confronting at its most serious and difficult level, which should not be lost sight of amid the grape-shot and the imprecations. It is still going on and the issues are not closed.

Unike the debates of the 1960s on theories of fascism, debates in which marxist concepts were the main focal point, this more recent German debate is not in any straightforward sense political or ideological in character. We have to do with two different schools of *liberal* thought about historical work and about the responsibility of the historian, rather than with a confrontation between two antagonistic views of history which entail or grow out of totally opposed political commitments. And yet the differences are fierce, sometimes also sharp. Although the debate about 'trivialization' is different in kind from and owes no overt intellectual or political debts to the preceding controversies over marxist theories, in both cases the role of impersonal forces in historical development, the role of collective processes as opposed to self-conscious decisions in determining political outcomes, is at the centre of the argument. If for no other reason than this, marxists cannot afford to ignore the current dispute among liberal historians.

The historians under attack for offering an unwitting apologia for National Socialism have been called functionalists.[3] The label is not strictly appropriate since, unlike the schematic writings of self-consciously functionalist authors, those of Hans Mommsen and Martin Broszat do not pass over human agency in politics and do not assign historical and moral responsibility for Nazi policies to blind forces and pressures.[4] However, the label is worth retaining as a rough form of shorthand: it indicates the emphasis which these historians have placed on the machinery of government and its effect upon decision-making in the

---

[3] See Klaus Hildebrand, 'Monokratie oder Polykratie? Hitlers Herrschaft und das Dritte Reich', in Gerhard Hirschfeld and Lothar Kettenacker (eds.), *The 'Führer State'. Myth and Reality. Studies on the Politics and Structure of the Third Reich* (Stuttgart 1981), pp. 17–29.
[4] Contrast on this point the emphasis which Martin Broszat does allow to agency in 'Soziale Motivation und Führer-Bindung des Nationalsozialismus', *Vierteljahrshefte für Zeitgeschichte*, vol. 18, no. 4 (1970), pp. 329–65, with the full-blown functionalism of Ludolf Herbst ('Die Krise des nationalsozialistischen Regimes am vorabend des Zweiten Weltkrieges und die forcierte Aufrüstung', *Vierteljahrshefte für Zeitgeschichte*, vol. 26, no. 3 (1978), pp. 347–92) in which the sub-systems have taken over from the people.

Third Reich, on the dynamic interaction of the different component institutions of the regime and of the different forms of political power on the structure of Nazi politics. The 'cumulative radicalization' of Nazi policies which ended in total war and genocide, the progressive selection for implementation of only the destructive elements within the regime's *Weltanschauung*, are portrayed not as the work of a deliberate dictatorial will, but rather as the consequences of the way in which the Nazi leadership conceived of political power and of the way in which political power was organised in the Third Reich: the dominant tendency was a striving towards 'politics without administration', or towards the substitution of propaganda for administration.[5] The traits of systematization, regularity, calculability inherent in the construction of a comprehensive administrative base for the dictatorship, were perceived, particularly by Hitler, Himmler and Goebbels, as limiting factors, as constraints, actual or potential, on their power as they understood it. The regime thus characteristically produced both non-policies or evasions which were of great political consequence at a later date (civil service policy; economic policy in the late 1930s; treatment of the Jews 1939–40), or sudden and drastic decisions which had not been prepared in the governmental machine and thus both disrupted existing policies and practices and had quite unforeseen administrative and political results, which latter in turn called for further ill-considered decisions (Reichskristallnacht, occupation policies in Poland). These characteristics of the political system were enhanced in the late 1930s by the consequences of earlier decisions to establish special new agencies and jurisdictions directly responsible to Hitler, whenever political tasks of especial urgency or interest arose (Himmler's career to 1936, DAF, Ribbentrop's Office, Todt (autobahns), Four Year Plan, Speer (cities)). This trend was symptomatic of the disintegration of government into an aggregation of increasingly ill-coordinated special task-forces; it also reinforced the fragmentation of decision-making processes, since lines of political responsibility became increasingly blurred as ministerial and party jurisdictions expanded, were fractured, eroded and contested. That ministers learned of important decisions from the newspapers is significant less of their personal (or collective) dispensability, than of fundamental changes which were taking place in the processes and procedures of government and administration. There was less and less co-ordination.

It is argued by those suspected of 'trivializing' Nazism that Hitler was the beneficiary rather than the architect of the increased powers which necessarily devolved upon the institution/person of the Führer in step

---

[5] These points have been repeatedly emphasized by Hans Mommsen, 'National Socialism. Continuity and Change', in Walter Laqueur (ed.), *Fascism. A Reader's Guide* (Harmondsworth 1976), pp. 179–210.

with these changes. Hitler certainly did not encourage his subordinates to collaborate politically with each other (unless it was a case of their resolving a disagreement which he did not wish to adjudicate); he personally had a decisive preference for creating new organs of state to carry out specific projects, for choosing 'the right man for the job' and giving him powers to carry it out, regardless; and there is no doubt that he carefully sought out men who were loyal to/dependent upon him for all top positions in the regime. But it does not follow from this that his power grew out of consistent application of the maxim 'divide and rule'. The relevant political and institutional divisions needed no nurturing – they had been present in the Nazi movement before 1933 and had been greatly augmented by the 'legal' seizure of power. Within the regime they took the form of conflicts for particular powers, in which Hitler was generally recognized as arbiter, a role which he more often found tiresome or awkward than profitable. Göring became convinced that he wished to take as few decisions of this kind as possible.

More important as a source of power was his personal popularity, but while this shielded him against ultimative contradiction by ministers and generals, it was not much help in the practical business of selecting goals, reaching decisions and making policy. It may on the contrary have been a real obstacle to policy-making. Hitler's sense of dependence upon his own popularity was so great and the possibility that that popularity might be sharply diminished by specific decisions was so difficult to assess in advance, that the cult of the Führer may well have been conducive to governmental inaction in internal affairs: Hitler was certainly careful not to associate himself with any measure which he thought might be unpopular, and to prevent the enactment of many such proposals, put forward by government agencies.[6] In this sense Hitler can be said to have been a 'weak dictator':[7] dependence upon his personal popularity for the political integration of German society under the dictatorship circumscribed the regime's freedom of action.

His power to co-ordinate policy in an effective manner was further limited by his characteristic deference to the senior leaders of the Nazi movement. It was not just that he enjoyed their company and trusted their political instincts: he continued to consider himself an agent of the movement, and, in that sense, dependent upon/beholden to it. The dissolution of governmental policy-making procedures marked out a political space around Hitler which the movement's leaders were able individually to occupy – their advice was usually taken seriously, and

---

[6] I have pointed to some of the evidence for this in *Sozialpolitik im Dritten Reich. Arbeiterklasse und Volksgemeinschaft* (Opladen 1977), Chapter 6.

[7] Hans Mommsen first used this term in *Militärgeschichtliche Mitteilungen*, no. 1 (1970), in a review essay which helped to start the present controversy.

their requests for the extension of their own particular jurisdictions or for specific policy initiatives were frequently granted, quite regardless of their (usually problematic) relationship to existing institutional arrangements or policies. It is of decisive importance in this connection that the leaders of the movement were in no way united among themselves; they were neither an organized group with regular functions, nor were they pursuing practical common goals. Their policy concerns were limited to their own jurisdictions, and they were frequently in competition with each other. In no sense did they furnish a possible basis for general policy-making. They were agreed only on the desirability of making Germany, in particular the country's government and administration, 'more National Socialist'.

This latter goal was intrinsically and irreducibly vague; in practice it could at best be defined negatively in the persecution of the designated enemies of the cause. More importantly, the anti-practical nature of the *Weltanschauung* meant that the most radical steps on any issue were always those which could be presented as 'most National Socialist' – there was no practical yardstick for judgement. Thus *radicalism*, and, in society at large, continual political *mobilization*, became ends in themselves, substitutes of a kind for policy goals. While Hitler was clearly not antipathetic to this trend, he was not, it is argued, its self-conscious or purposeful author. The decay of policy-making institutions combined with the specific contentlessness of the ideology to generate a larger historical process, which, once firmly in motion, was not fully in the control of those who held power – not, because the (dis-)organization of political power, the manner in which decisions were reached and the normative power of the demand for the most radical solutions all limited the effective range of choice. In the absence of policies, political improvisation, especially in occupied Eastern Europe, rested upon the deployment of extreme physical violence, which handicapped the prosecution of the war. There were no coherent war aims, only a number of mutually contradictory ones (race war/military conquest). There was no way within the regime to resolve the contradictions.

The central point in this 'functionalist' position is an insistence upon the fact that the way in which decisions are reached in modern politics is vital to their specific outcomes, and thus vital to the historian for an understanding of their meaning. Only in retrospect and without consideration of decision-making do policies appear to *unfold* over the years with a necessity which is *coherent*. Nor, given the high degree of interdependence between all sectors of public life, can this be a matter of individual decisions to be taken as 'case studies' or 'models': uncoordinated, unprepared and arbitrary decisions, decisions taken with regard only to a single project or goal (e.g. the Siegfried Line 1938; the battle fleet 1939) and without reference either to side-effects or to their impact upon other imperative projects, always further fragmented the processes of policy-making, making them cumulatively more arbitrary in their character, more violent and radical in their implementation, more conducive to competitive struggle among the executive organs of the regime. Policy-making on this analysis is simply not comprehensible as the enforcement of consistent acts of dictatorial will – the view that it can be so comprehended is superficial and does not do justice to the available evidence on the conduct of politics in the Third Reich.

'Intentionalism' is the name which has been given by 'functionalists' to the position of those historians who regard the consistent dictatorial will as being of the essence of National Socialist rule.[8] The difference between the two schools of thought was first and most clearly exemplified by the controversy over responsibility for the Reichstag Fire, a controversy which has engaged an enormous amount of time and energy, although the significance and consequences of the event are not a matter of dispute. In the absence of conclusive evidence about the identity of the arsonist(s), two different hypotheses have been constructed which rest upon and reinforce two fundamentally different interpretations of Nazi politics. For intentionalist historians (who on this issue, as on others, are a politically most heterogeneous group) the Reichstag Fire is a part (a very important part) of the deliberate erection of a bestial dictatorship, a necessary preparation for war and for crimes against humanity: it is in alleged conformity with these later acts that the arsonists should have been Nazis. There is thus a presumption of intention and responsibility on their part. To deny this is to underrate the capacity of Nazi leaders for premeditated evil and to run the risk of making the regime appear less monstrous than it was. If, on the other hand, the opposite inference is drawn from the inconclusive evidence, if there was no Nazi arsonist, the fire and its consequences stand in alleged conformity with that swift and ruthless opportunism, with that capacity for violent improvisation and for seizing the main chance regardless of wider consequences, which, it is argued, was the hallmark of all later Nazi decision-making. And it is these traits, not calculated intention, which offer the key to the cumulative radicalization of the regime towards world war and genocide. This particular controversy is thus about fundamentals.

The 'intentionalist' position appears to be less difficult to summarize than that of the 'functionalists', if only because these historians have been less explicit about their methods. They are in essence those of classical liberal and conservative historiography. Intentionalist writers are far from rejecting all of modern political science, but in this controversy it is

---

[8] See Hans Mommsen, 'Ausnahmezustand als Herrschaftstechnik des NS-Regimes', in Manfred Funke (ed.), *Hitler, Deutschland und die Mächte* (Düsseldorf 1977), p. 33.

the most basic elements of their historical understanding which are at stake. In their recent essays Karl Dietrich Bracher and Klaus Hildebrand are largely concerned with the intentional actions of Hitler, which, they believe, followed with some degree of necessity from his political ideas.[9] They formulate the question: why did the Third Reich launch a murderous war of genocide and the destruction of human life on a hitherto unprecedented scale? They come in the end to the conclusion that the leaders of the Third Reich, above all Hitler, did this because they wanted to do it. This can be demonstrated by studying early manifestations of their *Weltanschauung*, which are wholly compatible with the worst atrocities which actually occurred in the years 1938–45. The goal of the Third Reich was genocidal war, and, in the end, that is what National Socialism was all about. From this it seems to follow that the regime is 'unique', 'totalitarian', 'revolutionary', 'utopian', devoted to an utterly novel principle for the public order, scientific racism. The leaders, in particular Hitler, demonstrably wanted all this, and it is thus, as Hildebrand has recently suggested, wrong to talk of National Socialism; we should talk of Hitlerism.

This approach does not lead its advocates to concentrate narrowly upon Nazi race and occupation policies, nor upon Hitler himself. They range widely in their writing, but the above point is their central point of reference. And having identified the problem in this way, intentionalist historians then appear to stand back from their subject and to meditate on the enormity of the regime's crimes, on the enormity of the destruction of human life. This entails trying to *understand* National Socialism, for an intentionalist historian *must* understand (in the German sense of *verstehen*). In this case understanding is possible only through an empathy born of hatred. This probably yields a less sure type of understanding than does an empathy born of respect or admiration, but given the historical personages concerned, there is no choice but to take those risks. They then invite their readers to hate and abhor too. This is where the political and moral responsibility of the historian comes in: it is clearly implied that it is the historian's public duty to write in this way. Faced with genocidal war, historians should not emphasize decision-making procedures, administrative structures or the dynamics of organizational rivalries. These things were at best secondary. To make them a vital part of a general interpretation of National Socialism is to trivialize the subject, to write morally incompetent history. What really matters is the distinctive murderous will of the Nazi leadership.

[9] See Bracher, 'Tradition und Revolution', and idem, 'The Role of Hitler. Perspectives of Interpretation', Laqueur (ed.), *Fascism*, pp. 193–212; Klaus Hildebrand, 'Weltmacht oder Untergang? Hitlers Deutschland 1941–1945', in Oswald Hauser (ed.), *Weltpolitik II, 1939–1945. 14 Vorträge* (Göttingen 1975), pp. 286–322; idem, 'Hitlers programm und seine Realisierung 1939–1942', in Funke (ed.), *Hitler, Deutschland und die Mächte*, pp. 63–93.

Since the historians who write from this vantage point have, in a tactical sense, taken the offensive in the controversy, their position should be subjected to a critique first. Two general comments seem to be called for, and then a number of specific criticisms will be raised.

First, the intentionalist attack on the incorporation of functionalist types of explanation into our understanding of National Socialism proposes, implicitly but clearly, a retreat by the historical profession to the methods and the stance of Burckhardt. On the evidence above all of his *Reflections on World History* (a book which greatly impressed anxious conservatives when it was re-issued in the late 1930s) Burckhardt saw the historian's task as to investigate, to classify and to order, to hate and to love and to warn – but *not*, except upon the smallest of scales, to explain. This approach had almost no explanatory power at all. The attempt at explanation in any and all of the various different traditions of rationalist historiography seems to be put on one side in intentionalist writing on National Socialism. The view that Hitler's ideas, intentions and actions were decisive, for example, is not presented in these works as an argument, but rather as something which is both a premise and a conclusion. It can perhaps be said that historians have a public duty to attempt to explain, and that informed explanatory reasoning about the past (however indirect or surprising its routes may be) has its own moral purpose and power. This is not generally questioned with respect to other topics in modern history, however much argument there may be about specific types of explanation.

The second methodological point concerns the role of individualism in ethics and the social sciences. Following the arguments of Steven Lukes, methodological individualism simply cannot work as a way of giving a coherent account of social, economic and political change.[10] Marx, Weber, Durkheim and their successors buried this approach with a variety of different funeral rites, and still it lives on, on borrowed time – a commodity with which historians are especially generous. Unless virtually the whole of modern social science constitutes an epochal blind alley, 'Hitler' *cannot* be a full or adequate explanation, not even of himself. To dismiss methodological individualism is *not*, of course, to abolish the category of individual moral responsibility in private or public life: explanation is one thing, responsibility something else. As Isaiah Berlin points out, even advocates of determinism continue to *behave* as if individuals were fully free and responsible agents: it is a necessary assumption for human interaction.[11] But it is an impossible *basic* assumption for the writing of history, for it would require us to concentrate upon the actions of individual free agents in such a way as to elevate them to the status of prime cause, and to deny that we can in some respects better

---

[10] Steven Lukes, *Individualism* (Oxford 1973), esp. Chapter 17.
[11] Isaiah Berlin, *Four Essays on Liberty* (London 1969), pp. ix–lviii.

understand the significance of the actions of people in the past than they themselves could. Such a history would banish all processes of change and constitute the subject as 'one damn choice after another'.

Thus to argue that the dynamic of Nazi barbarism was primarily institutional and/or economic does not entail any denial that Hitler was a morally responsible political leader who made choices which were inspired by distinctive malevolent intentions – it is only to insist that his will cannot carry the main burden of explanation. And by the same token, to insist in detail upon the unique character of his political will and intentions does not of itself establish an argument about the importance of these attributes in an account of National Socialism. That requires a comprehensive social, economic and institutional history.

In addition to these general observations there are a number of specific objections to the intentionalist position. The first is both technical and obvious, but it must be continually restated. The hypothesis that Hitler was the sole author of all the crimes of the Third Reich cannot be proved in the most mundane sense – the source materials are inadequate both in quantity and in quality to prove it. At this elementary level we know less about Hitler's control over German policy, much less about his motives and calculations, than we know about the conduct of most other nineteenth- or twentieth-century political leaders. For this reason alone, an analysis of his choices and of his influence is exceptionally difficult to execute. Caution is always called for, areas of inescapable ignorance emerge everywhere. It is particularly difficult to assess how far subordinates were able to bring influence to bear upon him, how suggestible or complaisant to insistent requests or proposals he was. The inadequacy of the sources in this sphere (which is of vital concern to an intentionalist interpretation) is a direct consequence of the fragmented and informal character of the decision-making procedures referred to above, as well as of Hitler's personal aversion to the written word: motives were rarely formulated, reasons rarely given, policy options rarely recorded as such, the origins of policy initiatives rarely disclosed. Concerted policy-making would have produced more and better records of calculations and intentions.

Second, even before radically different methods of interpretation are considered, it must be pointed out that, at a very simple level, the sources which we do possess on Hitler's goals and intentions can be read in very different ways, depending upon the different kinds of other historical knowledge which is brought to bear upon these texts. To come to the very few good records of Hitler's policy statements between 1936 and 1941 from the papers of the Ministries of Labour and Economics and of the War Economy Staff is a very different intellectual experience from coming to the same texts from the papers of the Foreign Office or of the Frankfurt Auschwitz Trial. Ideally one ought to come at the texts from all of these angles, and more, but in the meantime there are legitimate grounds for provisional disagreement about the meaning of the evidence concerning what Hitler thought he was doing. There are different, sometimes contradictory emphases in the evidence. Disagreements on these points will be clarified by further contextual research (why did Hitler make the speech to the press in November 1938? why did his Reichstag speech of 30 January 1939 take that particular form?), rather than by further philological research. Meanwhile these sources can be interpreted in different ways, even if one confines oneself to a literal reading.

There is however, third, no reason why sources should be read *solely* in a literal manner. Intentionalist historians tend to do so – they identify the goals and choices of their historical actors by reading the words on the page in the archive and assuming that they can only mean what they appear to mean on a common-sense reading. Intentions are established by taking the relevant sources at their face value (at least wherever a literal reading yields internally coherent sense). This is one of the reasons why Martin Broszat's designation of *Lebensraum* as an ideological metaphor has aroused such indignation.[12] (Insofar as he is thought to be belittling what happened in German-occupied Russia, he has simply been misunderstood.) He was attempting a partly functional analysis of Hitler's stated intentions, arguing that the full political significance of his words on this subject is of a different order from their literal meaning: that the goal of *Lebensraum* served as a focus for boundless political mobilization. Broszat may or may not have clinched this particular argument, but that type of approach to the interpretation of ideas and sources is not only legitimate; it is essential. Notions of symbolic meaning are commonplace in psychology and literary criticism, and a variety of efforts have been made in order to systematize techniques for eliciting symbolic or hidden meaning – and thus for redefining the 'intentions' being studied. While work of this kind is not easy and seldom yields indisputable conclusions, it can, as Klaus Theweleit has shown, greatly enlarge our understanding of motivation and human agency.[13] And it is precisely the exceptional quality of Nazi politics, the compulsive repetitiveness and the extremes of violence, which make non-literal interpretations seem so urgently necessary and literal readings so unsatisfactory, simplistic. What *were* Hitler's intentions in his hate-filled outbursts against 'the Jews'? Various suggestions have been made of motives and meanings which perhaps lay behind or went beyond the anti-Semitic words on the page, but which do comprehend these words.[14] To deny in principle or to disregard the possibility of analysing evidence

---

[12] Broszat, 'Soziale Motivation', p. 407.

[13] Klaus Theweleit, *Männerfantasien*, 2 vols. (Frankfurt am Main 1977).

[14] The suggestions which seem most helpful and most capable of further development detect strong elements of self-hatred in Hitler's anti-Semitism. See Norman Cohn, *Warrant for Genocide* (London 1967), pp. 251–68. The weakness of much other psychological work does *not* invalidate this approach to the texts.

of intentions in a complex manner and of thus identifying intentions which are not explicit in the sources, to say, that is, that Hitler ordered the extermination of the Jews and instigated other racial policies because he wanted to, is a form of intellectual surrender. Intention is an indispensable concept for historians, whether they are determinists or not, but we do not have to take people in the past at their own word concerning their intentions. The realm of their self-consciousness as presented in historical sources is not trivial, but it does not define the limits of our understanding. It is a starting point; it constitutes a problem, not an answer.

   This point can perhaps best be illustrated from that branch of historical enquiry which has hitherto been the pre-eminent stronghold of intentionalist research and writing – the study of foreign policy. Klaus Hildebrand's book, *Vom Reich zum Weltreich*, is in parts sensitive to the effects of pressure-groups on policy-making, but it concentrates very strongly upon the evolution of Hitler's intentions and it eschews functional analysis of foreign policy. Hitler is presented as an uneasy amalgam of two character-types: the ruthless, aggressively calculating strategist, and the obsessive doctrinaire ideologue. This dual personality havers during the decisive stage of Nazi foreign policy, 1938–41, between two quite different paths of conquest. Why? I cannot find in Hildebrand's work a satisfactory answer to this question. My failure to find explanations may well be due to my own shortcomings as a reader, but for the moment the extended re-enactment of Hitler's restless strategic intentions in these years does not make sense. Alternative goals and tactics crowd in on each other; means and ends change places at bewildering speed; and all changes in policy can be comprehensively rationalized. In the course of a single day, 21 May 1940, for example, Hitler is recorded as making two completely different statements about fundamental strategic priorities to two different military leaders; the inconsistency is allowed to pass without comment by the historian.[15] Elsewhere Hildebrand suggests the possibility of knowing Hitler's mind almost on a week-to-week basis. There are, it seems, in principle reasons for everything the Führer does or says (or omits to do), reasons which are usually reconstructed in the interrogative mode by an elaborate process of intuitive/empathic speculation. But one is very little the wiser. There are many reasons why Hitler is and is not interested in overseas colonies . . . The outcome is a detailed picture of confusion.

   A literal reading of the sources on Hitler's strategic intentions leaves several dimensions and questions out of account. It lacks insight into the real anxieties, confusions and uncertainties of Hitler himself. (Would this detract from his responsibility?) By treating every recorded utterance as

---

[15] Klaus Hildebrand, *Vom Reich zum Weltreich* (Munich 1969), p. 643.

though it were carved in marble it makes his foreign policy seem more confusing than it would if at least some utterances were read as *evidence of confusion* (and not of intention). A literal reading also lacks insight into Hitler's habitual, though not universal, deference to the interests and views of his immediate advisers and subordinates while he was talking to them. For this reason alone he was unlikely to hold out the same strategic prospects to both Halder and Raeder in their separate discussions on 21 May 1940. This pervasive and evasive complaisance was, for all that it was non-committal and revokable, an important part of policy-making in the Third Reich. That is, Hitler's latent, as opposed to manifest, intention in making many pronouncements was probably to avert dissension within the regime, to encourage or mollify his subordinates. Last, an intentionalist diplomatic history skirts around the question of the basic expansionist dynamics of the regime – economic and military dynamics, the dynamics of political mobilization, forces which made it impossible for the Third Reich to stop anywhere short of total defeat. While it is possible to identify the decisions and the reasoning behind them which originally set these dynamics in motion (1933–6), one must ask whether they did not later emancipate themselves from their creators. If it is true, or even only a useful hypothesis, that the process of Nazi territorial expansion created its own momentum, and that this momentum could at best be guided but not held under control by the leadership, then the relative importance of Hitler's musings on alternative goals, strategies and power constellations is diminished. While it was clearly not a matter of indifference which territory and which people the Third Reich at any one point in time devoured next, the history of the years 1938–42 strongly suggests that there *had* to be *a* next victim. Perhaps the ambivalences of Hitler's foreign policy and strategy in these years, the changes in emphasis and direction, the promiscuity of aggressive intentions can be seen as a product of, or response to this expansionist imperative. The appearance of control and of historic choice may be in large part appearance, the practised posture of the dictator. This loosely functionalist approach suggests that much of the source material, which in the intentionalist account is presented as reasoning prior to action, is better understood as symptom of the internal and external pressures for further aggression and conquest. If none of the above criticisms have any weight, it is difficult to see how historians of the Second World War can talk about the causes of developments, as well as about the reasons for policy decisions.

The fourth criticism of intentionalist writing concerns decision-making processes and the power structure. It seems to me simply wrong, mistaken, contrary to the evidence to argue that enquiries in this field shed little light on the great facts about the Third Reich. The methodological principle that it is essential to study policy-making processes in order to understand any specific outcome or decision has been brilliantly stated and illustrated by Hans Mommsen; and its value has been demonstrated beyond doubt and in a wealth of detail by Wilhelm Deist and Manfred Messerschmidt in their new study of rearmament and foreign policy, a study untouched by functionalist theory but full of general implications for our understanding of the power structure.[16] It is true that there are pitfalls in this type of analysis: in the study of decision-making processes it is possible to get entrapped within the fascination of that subject, and to fail to place the results in a wider context of interpretation; and, more importantly, if the debate about polycracy is reduced to a discussion of how polycratic or monocratic the Third Reich was, if polycracy is understood as a *static* concept which will help only to produce a cross-section of the complex layer-cake of power structures, then this concept will indeed be of little use to historians. But the work of those attacked for trivializing National Socialism has *not* fallen into these pits. Hans Mommsen has moved the discussion about polycracy into its proper dynamic political context. He has shown, though not yet in an extended historical account, how this discussion illuminates the formulation of policy and the selection of goals in the Third Reich – and not just the regime's secondary goals.

If this point is correct, it must be concluded that the study of institutions and decision-making processes and enquiry into the polycratic nature of National Socialist rule form an essential part of a liberal/moral history of the regime and its crimes. They are not in themselves alien considerations or factors, nor are they morally neutral. To introduce them into a moral historical enquiry is simply to insist that the responsibility of political leaders needs to be and can be more widely defined than reference to their policy intentions alone will allow, defined to include the workings of institutions. From this it follows that the moral responsibility of the historian can be more widely defined too. The monstrous will and administrative dilettantism were, at the very least, necessary to each other. It seems trivial to resist this line of enquiry.

Finally there is one immanent argument against the intentionalist case. Hitler can be demonstrated to have known that a great deal depended for the Nazi regime upon his own capacity to exaggerate his personal domination: his capacity to exaggerate it *both* to the elite in the closed meetings where policy was announced or debated, *and* also to his popular audience. Hitler well understood his own function, the role which he *had* to act out as 'Leader' of the Third Reich. He was good at the street theatre of dictatorship; it is arguable that he transformed himself into a function,

---

[16] Wilhelm Deist, Manfred Messerschmidt, Hans-Erich Volkmann and Wolfram Wette, *Ursachen und Voraussetzungen der deutschen Kriegspolitik*, vol. 1 of the series *Das deutsche Reich und der Zweite Weltkrieg*, Militärgeschichtliches Forschungsamt (Stuttgart 1979).

the *function of Führer*. Several aspects of his behaviour in this respect are well documented: his aversion to identifying himself in public with any specific policies (other than the major foreign policy decisions); his reluctance to refuse requests or reject suggestions from the old guard of the party leadership; his calculated use of his own personal popularity in conflicts within the regime; his evasiveness when faced with conflicts which were hard to arbitrate. He always appeared more ruthless, more cold-blooded, more certain than he actually was. This role-playing aspect of Hitler's power, his instrumental attitude to his own person, is not, of course, the whole Hitler-story. But it is a very important part of it. However one may read his intentions, there is no doubt that Hitler was *also* a 'good functionalist'. And this is, at *the level of 'Verstehen'*, an important fact about the personality to whom intentionalist historians would attach such overriding importance: that personality was in large measure a self-consciously constructed role, the nature of which was conditioned by the nature of the regime.

The present weaknesses of the 'functionalist' position are not, I believe, those held up for disapprobation by intentionalist critics. They are quite different. The first is a vulnerability rather than a weakness. We do not yet have a full-length historical study along these lines. Aside from Martin Broszat's *Der Staat Hitlers* (which, because it could touch only lightly on foreign and military affairs, does not fully meet the points now raised by Bracher and Hildebrand), the position has been worked out in essays and articles. An unambiguous demonstration of the fruitfulness of the approach will be achieved by a large-scale study. But this is an extremely difficult intellectual undertaking, much more difficult than to give an account of this or that policy in its development and implementation. It requires a sustained analysis of the (shifting) relation of interdependence between the human agents and their power structures, a relation of a peculiarly complex kind. Aside from conceptual precision, aside from source materials the significance of which is often overlooked in conventional studies, this work also needs a language which is capable of conveying clearly the complexity of its findings – it cannot get by with the vocabulary of intention, calculation and consequence, and the mechanistic vocabulary of functionalist sociology is positively unhelpful.[17] Thus the promise may take some time to be fulfilled.

Second, and more importantly, there are ambiguities and difficulties in the formulation of the liberal functionalist position. Hans Mommsen writes, for example, of the dynamic expansive power of the Third Reich: 'The root of these forces lay in the movement's own apolitical and

---

[17] *Der Staat Hitlers* (Frankfurt am Main 1969). The difficulty of Broszat's prose in 'Soziale Motivation' clearly reflects the intellectual difficulty of specifying the relationships which he is analysing.

millenial dynamics and also in the antagonistic interests among the various groups in the National Socialist leadership.' While this is a suggestive sentence, it is not an analytically clear statement of a hierarchy of determining causes, nor does it specify a non-causal relationship between the two 'roots'. A passage on the bases of Hitler's position as Führer raises similar difficulties:

> Playing off rival power blocks against one another was not so much a matter of securing his own omnipotence, but rather done for the satisfaction of an instinctive need to reward all and any fanatical pursuit of an end, no matter whether institutionally fixed competences were ignored or whether, an advantage having been gained, its bureaucratic safeguards were sacrificed to over-dynamics.[18]

There are, so to speak, too many things going on in that sentence for one to be quite sure what importance the author is attributing to the different factors. What was the relationship between the existence of the rival power blocks and Hitler's 'instinctive need'? – Were the rival power blocks a condition for the articulation of the instinctive need? Had the need contributed decisively to their creation in the first place? Or can the two in the end not be distinguished in this way? Indistinctnesses of this kind grow out of real difficulties of historical interpretation, but they also point to a continuing uncertainty about the explanatory power of the approach. If the presentation is not *analytically* clear it tends to become just a description of a particular mode or style of the exercise of dictatorial power.

Third, the so-called 'functionalists' have written rather little about the German economy, and have not integrated this theme into their overall schema. Given their concern with the dynamics of dictatorial power and expansion, this is, to say the least, surprising.

As indicated at the start, marxist historians and political theorists seem to have paid little attention to this debate between two schools of liberal historians; they have also written rather little about Nazi genocide, the subject which raises the question of agency and cause in its most acute form. There is no compelling reason for this. Marxism offers a dynamic theory of the development of all modern industrial capitalisms, which incorporates, or rests upon, a structural (some would argue 'functional') analysis of these systems. The dynamic element introduces human agency, and human agency is central to Marx's writings: 'Men do make their own history, but they do not make it as they please, not under conditions of their own choosing, but rather under circumstances which they find before them, under given and imposed conditions'.[19] This sentence ought to introduce all biographical studies of Hitler! It formally

---

[18] 'National Socialism', pp. 183, 198.
[19] Karl Marx, *The Eighteenth Brumaire of Louis Bonaparte* (1852).

encapsulates intentions and structures, and suggests the necessity of relating the two in historical writing. However, if intentionalist writers all too often ignore or misunderstand the 'given and imposed conditions', marxists have paid too little attention to 'men do make their own history' when they have been concerned with the ruling class and the holders of power. This deficiency in giving an account of intentions and actions is a weakness in marxist work on fascism; but the weakness is not inherent in the theory as such, for the challenge can be met by further research along the lines of the various non-literal ways of reading sources referred to above.[20] It is an urgent task, for studies which exhaust themselves with the conditions which 'permitted' certain developments, or made certain policies 'possible' or 'necessary' fall short of historical explanation; they cut off before reaching those human actions which actually require explanation – mass murder. But it is the stopping short which is mistaken, not the original effort.

What was permitted by conditions, or was possible, must be analysed, and it is here that marxism offers a more comprehensive framework than an approach which concentrates heavily upon political institutions and decision-making processes. We need to understand how it is decided what the available options are, which political leaders can choose among. Which alternative possibilities in the Third Reich were never even entertained as such by the leadership? Which got lost in the lower ranks of the bureaucracy or party and were thus never presented as policy options?[21] These non-decisions are an important part of any system of power. They define the parameters of possible intentions at the top of the system, which are almost always narrow at that level. It is in this analytically difficult area that the economy and the state need to be taken as a whole in the study of the Third Reich, for the dynamic of economic development played a primary role in the filtering out of impossible options, in determining what it was that could be decided in terms of policy.

I cannot develop this argument in detail here, either in the form of a specific historical analysis or in that of a theoretical discussion. A few historiographical remarks must suffice. A marxist approach, which attaches pre-eminent weight to the processes of capital accumulation and class conflict is neither outflanked nor contradicted by some of the more important conclusions of liberal functionalist writing. It can on the contrary broaden their scope by identifying background economic determinants and conditions of state action. David Schoenbaum, for

---

[20] See above, pp. 221 f.

[21] Joachim Radkau, 'Entscheidungsprozesse und Entscheidungdefizite in der deutschen Aussenwirtschaftspolitik 1933–1940', *Geschichte und Gesellschaft*, vol. 2, no. 1 (1976), pp. 33–65, makes a first, stimulating but empirically unsatisfactory attempt to ask questions of this kind.

example, has developed an influential argument around the contradictions between the provisional achievements of the regime and many of the movement's original declared aims and policies:[22] in the late 1930s autobahns, Salzgitter, intensive technological innovation, concentration in industry and rapid urbanization stood as consequences of a programme which had included the corporate state, rural settlement, some degree of de-urbanization and, at a political level, notions of the liberation of a nationalist citizenry among its serious goals. It must be insisted upon that the points which were not achieved (were filtered out) ran strongly counter to the most elementary processes of capitalist accumulation. And these processes should not be reduced to the formula 'requirements of rearmament'. In this instance the workings of the economic system can be seen in a broadly determinant role, which can be exemplified in part by the activities of the heads of leading industrial concerns. With respect to the 'selection of negative goals', to the emergence of the race war as a dominant part of Nazi political practice, it is a question rather of economic conditions and constraints than of determination. The genocidal tendency in the original programme was one of the few which the regime did pursue with extreme logical rigour. It was also probably less disruptive of the capitalist system than, for example, a fully fledged attempt to 'return' to a small-scale artisan/peasant economy would have been. This is *not* to argue that genocide was enacted for that reason, nor to imply that there is little more to be said about it. It is to make a suggestion concerning the background processes of the selection of negative goals, of the practical definition of what was and what was not possible. The mass destruction of life in the extermination camps and in occupied Poland and Russia does not seem to have had really serious negative effects upon the German economy in the short term. Would it all have been different if there had been large numbers of skilled engineering workers and technicians among the Jews of Germany? Questions of this kind are necessary in order to identify limiting conditions as precisely as possible.

At one level the argument concerning Nazi foreign policy can be put less tentatively than the above remarks. In anticipating and accounting for the war of expansion in the late 1930s, the explanatory power of pressures which in their origin were economic was apparent to many actors and observers. Thus the argument that the decisive dynamic towards expansion was economic does not in the first instance depend upon the imposition of alien analytical categories on a recalcitrant body of

[22] David Schoenbaum, *Hitler's Social Revolution. Class and Status in Nazi Germany 1933–1939* (New York 1966). In anticipation of the present controversy, this book was immediately attacked in exactly the same way that the work of Mommsen and Broszat is now being attacked. See the superficial, moralizing review by Heinz Lubasz, *New York Review of Books*, vol. 11, no. 11, (19 December 1968) p. 33, who failed to understand that one can attempt to explain mass murder without actually writing about it at length.

evidence, nor in the first instance upon the theoretical construction of connections between the 'economy' and 'politics'. For the years 1938–9 a very wide variety of different types of source materials discuss explicitly and at length the growing economic crisis in Germany, and many of the authors of these memoranda, books and articles could see the need to speculate then about the relationship between this crisis and the likelihood of war. The view that this was a major urgent problem was common to many top military and political leaders in Germany, to top officials in Britain, to some German industrialists and civil servants, to German exiles and members of the conservative resistance, and to non-German bankers and academics. The nature of the relationship between economic crisis and war is not easy to specify precisely. I do not for the moment see a need to modify my own view that the timing, tactics and hence also the strategic confusion of Hitler's war of expansion were decisively influenced by the politico-economic need for plunder, a need which was enhanced by the very wars necessary to satisfy it.[23] This appears to me to have been the basic logic of Hitler's foreign policy and strategy in the decisive period 1938–41; without a firm conception of it, the institutional dynamics of the regime and the various specific intentions of Hitler remain less than comprehensible. This is, of course, *not* to argue that Hitler was 'forced to go to war' in the sense of not wanting to, but rather that the wars which the Third Reich actually fought bore very little relation to the wars which he appears to have wanted to fight: and that this was so, because of domestic pressures and constraints which were economic in origin and also expressed themselves in acute social and political tensions. Human agency is defined or located, not abolished or absolved by the effort to identify the unchosen conditions.

But then the will and the intention still have to be specified. It may be helpful here if we can find ordering concepts for the analysis of National Socialism, which *both* capture objective processes (capital accumulation, institutional darwinism, expansionism) *and* also relate clearly to the self-consciousness of the political actors. One such bridging concept is 'struggle', which incorporates notions of both competition and war. Competition and struggle were of the essence of economic and institutional processes, and they furnished one context of social life in general – the individual struggle for advancement and advantage, social mobility. In war too struggle appeared as an inexorable process. Struggle was also for the Nazi leaders a basic intention, the title of Hitler's book. Struggle was, in a distinctive and extreme manner, what their politics was all about,

[23] See Mason, *Sozialpolitik*, Chapter 6. I understand Jost Dülffer's criticism as, rightly, adding a further dimension (the arms race) to this analysis, not as offering a substitute interpretation: 'Der Beginn des Krieges 1939. Hitler, die innere Krise und das Mächtesystem', *Geschichte und Gesellschaft*, vol. 2, no. 4 (1976), pp. 443–70.

struggle against certain enemies but not struggle for any clearly perceived ends. Politics is struggle, as Hitler says in *Mein Kampf*. That one remark *does* perhaps have to be taken literally. But from this distance in time it can legitimately be, must be, related back to wider contexts than its author had in mind – to the highly competitive economic, social and institutional order over which he came to preside and which went under his leadership to destruction.

It might be suggested that just beneath the surface the Nazi leadership sensed that their particular struggle was a hopeless one. The enemies were too numerous, and, in the case of 'the Jews', they were by Hitler's definition too clever and too powerful *ever* to be beaten, even by the Third Reich. The crucial problem for National Socialist politics was to destroy as many enemies as possible while going down fighting to the very bitter end. Genocide was the most distinctively Nazi, the most terrible part of an over-arching politics of struggle. And these were the politics of a whole capitalist epoch.

This suggests in conclusion the need for a materialist history of social darwinism, a history which sees that subject in terms of economic forces and institutional power, in terms of social and economic practice and individual behaviour (intentions), and not just as a peculiar set of ideas which were influential around the turn of the century. It was that too, but it was also capitalist economic competition, economic and territorial competition between states, ethnic, national and cultural conflict, the struggle for eugenic improvement, the struggle on a group and individual basis for material advantage, respectability, virtue and God's grace. Only then in Germany did it become struggle as war and race war. In this broader sense of an interlocking pattern of structures, forces, ideologies and motives social darwinism was, of course, not peculiar to Germany. There are British, American and French versions; liberal conservative, fascist and Nazi versions. Maybe there is the framework for an enquiry here which is both structural and dynamic, and within which the specifically distinctive features and force of the National Socialist political will can be precisely identified.

The precision of the identification matters. Contrary to the implication in the charge that 'functionalists' or marxists trivialize National Socialism, it is logically and morally possible to hold a system responsible for terrible crimes, as well as those persons who exercised power within the system. While systems of domination and exploitation cannot be represented as individual moral actors can, it can be demonstrated that they generate barbarism. The demonstration of exactly how they have done so is often complex, but complex historical arguments are not indifferent to moral issues just because they are complex. If historians do have a public responsibility, if hating is part of their method and warning part of their task, it is necessary that they should hate precisely.

7

———— ❧ ————

THE CONTAINMENT OF THE WORKING CLASS
IN NAZI GERMANY

THIS INTRODUCTION to the essays collected in *Angst, Belohnung, Zucht and Ordnung*[1] does not conform to any standard pattern or formula. It is not an editorial preface, for the collection has no editor, but is the product of individual and collective work by its four authors. The Introduction is not a brief guide to, or historiographical scene-setting for, these four monographic essays, since they do not need an introduction of this kind. They can all stand on their own, as rounded and critically self-aware contributions to the study of Nazi labour and social policies. My introduction has a different function. It aims to furnish both a counterpoint to and one possible interpretative framework for these four exact analytical studies of labour law, wage policies, leisure organizations and factory welfare: to suggest one *general* context (and it is not the only one) in which these four essays, together with some other recent research and criticism, may be read; to suggest possible approaches for new research; and to think out loud about whether I and other historians have been asking all of the right questions concerning the political economy of National Socialism in the past ten years.

What follows is thus long and essayistic. Unlike the four contributions, it is not a scholarly study; references have been kept to an absolute minimum. It is a product of uncertainty and reflection, rather than of sustained and purposeful work. It is as much a response to the work of these four historians as an introduction to it.[2]

———

[1] *Angst, Belohnung, Zucht und Ordnung. Herrschaftsmechanismen im Nationalsozialismus* (Opladen 1982); the four authors and their essays are Carola Sachse, 'Hausarbeit im Betrieb. Betriebliche Sozialpolitik unter dem Nationalsozialisten'; Tilla Siegel, 'Lohnpolitik im nationalsozialistischen Deutschland'; Hasso Spode, 'Arbeiterurlaub im Dritten Reich'; Wolfgang Spohn, 'Betriebsgemeinschaft und innerbetriebliche Herrschaft'. [Editor's note: The text published here is based on Mason's original text, written in English, and varies slightly from the German translation.]

[2] The text has benefited greatly from the criticism of the four contributors, especially from that of Tilla Siegel. I would also like to thank Jane Caplan, Ian Kershaw and Karin Hausen for their constructive criticisms of a earlier draft.

The contributions to *Angst, Belohnung, Zucht und Ordnung* help to advance and to systematize our understanding of the social policies of the Nazi regime. Like many of the previous studies of this general theme, they concentrate upon the position of the industrial working class in the German capitalist system between 1930 and 1945, and upon Nazi policies towards this sector of society. This is, of course, only one aspect of the social history and political economy of the Nazi dictatorship, but it has some claim to be considered the most significant aspect, and also that which is most difficult and important to interpret. At the present stage of research and analysis, the position of other classes and groups in German society seems much less problematic. It was the working class which caused the regime the greatest difficulties and this is a strong justification for focusing attention upon this aspect of class relations and of Nazi social policy and rhetoric. That the dictatorship was ultimately able to contain these difficulties only adds urgency to the enquiry.

Given the conditions under which the Nazi movement seized power, given the social structure of its mass and elite basis in the years 1930-4, it is not wholly surprising that the regime should have enjoyed the active or passive consent of most sections of the middle class and of the power elites for most of the time until the last twelve months of the war. The picture is far from complete, and much research remains to be done on the relationships between the evolving dictatorship and, for example, the independent peasantry, white-collar workers and the professional bourgeoisie; the political attitudes of some groups of employers and bankers also still require clarification. But, aside from the conspiratorial resistance activities of high civil servants and military officers, it is hard to see that middle-class Germany ever could have brought forth a direct political threat to Nazi power, even if it had wished to. Big capital certainly did have the leverage and the framework of largely independent organizations necessary to challenge Nazi rule, but it never showed any interest in using its power in this way, and only very few big industrialists gave support to the conservative military and political resistance. The middle class as a whole did not have such potential power. And there were many strong positive reasons for sections of the bourgeoisie to identify with the regime at least to some considerable degree, once the SA had been deprived of all influence on public life in June–July 1934. One can speak here of a dynamic process of political integration which rested basically upon commonalties of interest and political outlook and only secondarily, or at different brief junctures for different groups, upon terror and manipulation. This integration was never stable or unproblematic and certainly never complete – one thinks of the acute problems of farmers 1938-40, the widespread disgust among the educated middle class at the pogrom of November 1938, or of the bitter conflicts of interest within big capital over the armaments and trade policies of the Four Year Plan, to say nothing of the church struggle. But these marked only temporary or partial shifts in alignment: they cannot be understood as stages in a cumulative process of disintegration. Setbacks for the regime in one quarter were usually compensated for in another, an unpopular policy (for example, the Hitler Youth) overlaid by a popular one (military service). On the whole, there was a broad, if shifting base of active co-operation between the dictatorship and its middle-class subjects. If not all felt enthusiasm, most enjoyed unprecedented economic and social opportunity.

The position of the working class was radically different. Its historic organizations were brutally smashed and declared to be one of the principal enemies of the 'new Germany'. Workers (*das Arbeitertum*) were intimidated and subjected to an intensive, but utterly mendacious and shallow campaign of political re-education, yet they remained until 1944 the main source of political anxiety for the holders of power – they were seen as the sole threatening collectivity by a regime which could otherwise identify only very specific groups as dangerous (Jews, priests, freemasons): the Gestapo showed no interest in clerks or civil servants as a collectivity, and not much in farmers. This was not without reason. It was not just that the underground political organizations of the working-class parties furnished the most consistently active resistance to Nazism. The class as a whole derived few benefits from the regime, and, unlike most of the middle class lost all forms of meaningful corporate organization.[3] Its leadership was physically eliminated; and the regime mounted a sustained, ingenious and multi-faceted effort to destroy the basic solidarities of working-class life, with the aim of transforming labour from a social activity into a political duty of the individual. For some four years after 1933 the only tangible benefit for the working class was the increase in employment, the diminution of insecurity in the labour market. Though this no doubt came as a huge relief to many who had suffered from the disorientation and acute loss of self-esteem engendered by long-term unemployment, the issues which had always made work in capitalist industry the mainspring of class conflict had not disappeared in the mid-1930s – on the contrary, exploitation and inequality of rights and power had been intensified since 1933. If unemployment produces one form of alienation, regular employment may soon produce another. The living standards of only a few groups of

[3] As the organized representative of workers' interests, the German Labour Front (DAF) was far less important and effective for its members than most of the other affiliated and occupational organizations in National Socialist Germany. At least for a time, the associations of farmers, lawyers, civil servants and artisans seemed capable not only of exercising some control over their members but also of advancing some of their demands.

workers increased significantly between 1933 and 1936; the earnings of many merely kept up with price increases, and some were even worse off in material terms than they had been in the depths of the depression. There were a great many small-scale acts of resistance and opposition,[4] which were clearly marked by the history and situation of the working class and its organizations. In the workplace and as working citizens the workers and their organizations were exposed to extensive new repression, which initially looked not much different from what the working-class movement had faced during the previous five decades. The supremacy of capital in the sphere of production was enormously strengthened; the detested political enemy of the crisis years between 1930 and 1933 had come to political power. The self-respect and collective pride of workers who had been active in the movement were systematically insulted and ridiculed; those who were arrested or murdered left many horrified friends and comrades behind; highly prized rights and organizations were destroyed. The challenge was direct and bitter. It is therefore not surprising that all kinds of efforts at resistance were made, however difficult it was for workers to act against the Nazi regime. And yet the working class was largely contained, so it seems.

Why, then, did it stop at only individual, scattered acts of protest and resistance? Why was there not more mass protest from within the working class? Why was underground resistance to the Nazi regime not more militant or widespread? Why did that class in German society which suffered greater disenfranchisement, greater persecution and greater oppression than any other not mount at least one major challenge to the regime?

It is hard enough to explain what did happen in the past, in principle impossible to give conclusive reasons why an event did not happen, a major development not take place. But it can be conducive to analytical clarity to pose the question in this counter-factual form. 'Why did this not happen?' This question has already been implicitly raised in recent research into the National Socialist regime, and I think it would be helpful to formulate it more explicitly.

The main difficulty of such a project lies in identifying exactly *what* did not happen yet might have happened: this has to be plausible in terms of the actual situation. Here it is tempting to look for comparisons in order to construct possible events or forms of behaviour. But although all situations of extreme repression, extreme injustice and desperate resistance

---

[4] Further details in Timothy W. Mason, *Sozialpolitik im Dritten Reich. Arbeiterklasse und Volksgemeinschaft* (Opladen 1977) (trans. *Social Policy in the Third Reich. The Working Class and the 'National Community'*, Providence/Oxford 1993), Chapter 4; idem, 'Arbeiteropposition im Dritten Reich', in Detlev Peukert and Jürgen Reulecke (eds.), *Die Reihen fast geschlossen. Beiträge zur Geschichte des Alltags unterm Nationalsozialismus* (Wuppertal 1981). See also Martin Broszat et al. (eds.), *Bayern in der NS-Zeit* (Munich/Vienna 1977–83), 6 vols.

may appear to share a common anthropological core, this temptation should be resisted. (I shall give in to it in only one respect: see below.) For acts of resistance *in extremis* (and their absence) are always dependent on specific local conditions: different historically developed forms of solidarity and organization; different provocations and opportunities; different causes for or against which people may be willing to put their life at risk. For this reason it would be wrong, when we try to work out what did not happen in Nazi Germany, to refer for example to the massive and sustained strikes by Dutch workers during the Second World War, or to the various forms of rebellion mounted by Black nationalists in South Africa in recent years (the bombing of a major industrial plant, armed attacks on police units, unarmed attacks on police cars and military vehicles). The same is true for the numerous assassinations of leading politicians in tsarist Russia; and even the uprisings by the German workers' movement itself between 1916 and 1923 took place in an entirely different period of economic and political development. Perhaps the great strike wave in northern Italy in 1943 could be a starting point for comparisons and contrasts,[5] though the repression of the Italian working class under fascism was far less extreme than in the German workers' case.

A comparative perspective is directly valuable in only one respect, and even that is quite superficial. It is almost axiomatic that the degree of integration of the working class stands in inverse proportion to its need and ability to rebel in any significant fashion, whether through conspiracy or open revolt. With the exception of Fascist Italy, none of those who held power in the cases mentioned above had detected any need or made serious efforts to encourage the political integration of the groups and classes they were repressing and exploiting. The National Socialist regime in Germany, by contrast, saw precisely the necessity for this, and attempted to do it. I shall return to this point in the last section of this essay.

This observation apart, if we want to define more clearly what did not happen, it is certainly more appropriate to start from the actual forms of resistance and opposition by the German working class. We should start by asking why these were not more extensive, more radical, more aggressive than they were. Why did 300 workers (a whole department in a big plant) go on strike, but not 3,000 (an entire factory, a mine, a dockyard)? Why were there enough cases of refusal to work and indiscipline to amount to 'a genuine wave of sabotage',[6] and also many individual acts of sabotage, but no deliberate mass destruction of production machinery? Why could the attempted assassination of Hitler

---

[5] See G. Bertolo et al., *Operai e Contadini nella crisi italiana del 1943/1944* (Milan 1974).

[6] Timothy W. Mason, *Arbeiterklasse und Volksgemeinschaft. Dokumente und Materialien zur deutschen Arbeiterpolitik 1936–1939* (Opladen 1975), Doc. 224. It was certainly not very easy to get hold of weapons and explosives by illegal means in Germany after 1933, but by no means impossible. See Peter Hoffmann, *Hitler's Personal Security* (London 1979), pp. 105 ff.

be planned and carried out in November 1939 by a single German worker, Johann Georg Elser, but not by an organized group of activists?[7] Why was the profound hatred of the working class for party and police officials vented in expressions and gestures of disgust and in clandestine opposition, yet not in the form of collective outrage and violence against the oppressors? German workers made considerable efforts to support the family members of concentration-camp prisoners, yet they never attempted to storm a single Gestapo office or attack Gestapo functionaries, i.e. the very institutions and men who had thrown communists and social Democrats into the camps. Workers often enough displayed their lack of enthusiasm for the mass demonstrations of the Third Reich, but they never translated a May Day assembly into a street battle. All this is perfectly plausible: so why did none of it happen?

These observations (and the reference to the highly aggressive and determined campaigns of resistance in South Africa) are intended here only to formulate a question which can be posed in a more orthodox way: Why did the Nazi regime, which abused a large part of its subjects in such an unexampled way, survive through the last year of a war which it was obviously losing without any major mass challenge to its power?

The regime held together into absolute defeat. This basic fact is empirically secure. Serious research into wartime resistance and opposition in the working class is only just beginning, but if there had been a large-scale strike or a serious mutiny by German soldiers we would surely know of it by now. Equally surely, there was much more small-group defiance of all kinds than we yet know of. There were many 'treasonable' local initiatives to speed and facilitate military surrenders and to preserve basic installations. But is precisely the specific forms and limits of resistance and opposition which, in this context, require explanation. They are not the only thinkable forms and limits. That is why it is worth asking: 'Why did it not happen?' or 'Why not in a different form?'[8]

This question is not asked in any spirit of judgmentalism, given that working-class resisters *wanted* to harm the regime far more than they knew how to or could. The power-holders themselves persistently expected more difficulties from the left opposition than they actually faced. The question is, rather, immanent: in other words, it is derived from the consciousness of the actors.

One of the many difficulties in posing it is to decide *of whom* the question is being asked. Of the working class as a whole? Of the party political and trade union activists? Of particular occupational groups?...

---

[7] See Anton Hoch and Lothar Gruchmann, *Georg Elser. Der Attentäter aus dem Volke* (Frankfurt am Main 1980).

[8] Barrington Moore Jr's book, *Injustice. The Social Bases of Obedience and Revolt* (London 1978), stimulated me to rethink the issues in this new way.

In what follows the focus shifts in a rather unsatisfactory manner from the class as a whole, to the old supporters of the SPD and the KPD, to the activists of the illegal underground, and back again. This constant shift of focus is not (at least, not only) the child of methodological confusion. It simply reflects the basic fact that a real potential for outraged protest, defiance and hatred clearly did exist both in the class as a whole and in its persecuted organizations. The potential was realized in different ways, which represented different forms of moral and political consciousness. The Gestapo did substantially isolate the illegal cadres from their class in all questions of tactics (see below), but in both the political and the industrial struggles against Nazi oppression new recruits were repeatedly drawn in from the class of wage-earners. But the industrial unrest of 1936-9 and the large-scale communist resistance organizations of 1942-4 were borne to a significant degree by people who had had no, or very little, political experience before 1933, and this is without even mentioning the oppositional youth groups.[9] That is to say, even under these extreme adverse circumstances, the class struggle reproduced itself in its various forms; its sources of strength were renewable, not finite. In this sense the division between the class and its organizations or spokesmen was far from complete. Different major acts of defiance or insurgency can be thought of as real possibilities: a big assassination by illegal groups; a strike by thousands of workers in the mines or shipyards; a riot against hated agents of the regime. These are very different types of political action; had they taken place, they would probably have been carried out by different groups of people with different positive or negative goals. The few direct armed attacks mounted by German resistance fighters against the hated Gestapo were the achievement of scattered gangs of 'Edelweiss pirates': groups of young people, utterly cut off from the inherited organizations and values of the working-class movement, who in the last year of the war spontaneously developed into violent anti-fascist assault troops.[10] But they have enough in common – above all, the enemy, and also shared interests and traditions – for it to be useful to consider them together. My way of discussing them is not intended to conflate them or to blur differences, rather to emphasize that they can only be

[9] On the latter question see especially Lutz Niethammer, Ulrich Borsdorf and Peter Brandt (eds.), *Arbeiterinitiative* (Wuppertal 1976); Detlev Peukert, *Die KPD im Widerstand. Verfolgung und Untergrundarbeit an Rhein und Ruhr 1933–1945* (Wuppertal 1980); idem, 'Der deutsche Arbeiterwiderstand 1933–1945', *Aus Politik und Zeitgeschichte*, vol. 14, 14 July 1979.

[10] See Historisches Archiv der Stadt Köln, *Widerstand und Verfolgung in Köln 1933–1945* (Cologne 1974), pp. 394 ff.; Daniel Horn, 'Youth Resistance in the Third Reich', *Journal of Social History*, vol. 7 (1973, pp. 26–50); Detlev Peukert, 'Edelweisspiraten, Meuten, Swing', in Gerhard Huck (ed.), *Sozialgeschichte der Freizeit* (Wuppertal 1980). The new study by Alexander Goeb, *Er war sechzehn als man ihn hängte* (Reinbek 1981), is somewhat trivializing in tone.

understood as strands of one single history: that of the German working class.

In order to achieve a degree of clarity, the following considerations on the containment of the working class in the Third Reich are arranged according to four general themes: containment through terroristic repression; the willingness of the regime to make concessions to discontent and unrest; the neutralization of resistance potential by divisions within the working class; and, finally, possible elements of integration of the class within the system of domination. This separation of the major strands of interpretation from each other does, however, have a major disadvantage, in that it draws attention away from the central fact that all four categories of constraint and inducement were operating simultaneously for most of the years between 1933 and 1945. It was their *combination* – a combination in which the balance of the different elements was different at different times – which made it so difficult for the working class to challenge Nazi rule. Each different form of containment was dependent for its effectiveness on the others and upon other factors (manipulation of the media, etc.) to which only passing reference can be made. Thus my aim is not to produce a rank order of the causes of containment of the kind, say: 'Rising wages were more important than patriotism but less important than police terror.' This would be absurd. The aim is rather to define and enquire into the main components of a successful pattern of domination: as an object of enquiry the overall pattern is more important than any one of the parts – the latter only have significance in relation to the whole, and their relationship to each other must be understood functionally and not in terms of relative weighting. Themes are an analytical device: a forty-year-old male metal worker, ex-union member, who got a wage increase the month after his brother had been stuck in a concentration camp, then found his eldest son called up for Labour Service, in the middle of his apprenticeship, who received family allowances for the first time, felt that the incorporation of Austria was a good thing, took time off work to try to secure his brother's release and thus became politically suspect himself, then got an offer of a cheap holiday on the North Sea while also being asked to do eight hours' overtime instead of four . . . that is the stuff that themes and analyses are made of.

Scholars working in the various socialist traditions of research and analysis have always emphasized the overwhelming importance of police terror in the containment of the German working class. After 1934 the Gestapo system was indeed refined and ruthless, also relatively unobtrusive. Few underground groups survived more than two years, links between groups were extremely difficult to establish and maintain, informers were numerous and their services were reinforced by the systematic torture of suspects. Furthermore, the Gestapo was immediately present at strikes, and from 1938/9 on exercised terroristic surveillance over workers who were 'unreliable' at their jobs: miniature concentration camps (*Arbeitser-ziehungslager*) were attached to major industrial firms.[11] This system of terror was in large measure pre-emptive. Its aim was not the draconian repression of mass protest or unrest, but its prevention by the continual arrest and incarceration of people whose behaviour made it seem likely that they would organize or lead such unrest, if the opportunity should ever arise. Some degree of organization was essential to most (not all) possible forms of resistance and protest, and it was in this respect that the Gestapo was most effective. Up to 1941 left groups hardly presented a serious political threat to the regime: the potential was there (the will, the numbers and to a lesser extent the organization), but the Gestapo made deliberate efforts to anticipate their future development and worked specifically to prevent this capacity for resistance from being translated into action. Tactically and strategically the police state was always on the offensive. The National Socialist regime had established this powerful position for itself from the very beginning, by eliminating the working-class parties and trade unions. At every decisive point the Gestapo commanded the initiative and was able to retain it. This focused form of terror is certainly more effective than open violent repression.

The technical efficiency and intensity of the Gestapo terror were so great that one of the principal goals of the underground became simply to keep their organizations in existence. There was a tendency for the double process of clandestine organization and successful political education to become an end in itself: distributing literature, collecting membership contributions, recruiting new members, maintaining links with the upper levels of the resistance in Germany or abroad – all this was already so difficult and dangerous that after 1934 demonstrative 'public' protest came to seem increasingly foolhardy or even irresponsible. Open political opposition only put the best resistance fighters in danger of being thrown onto the rubbish-heaps of the dictatorship along with the books they used to read. First for the SPD and then for the KPD resistance began to mean above all the maintenance of their organizational and ideological presence, to be activated when, and only when, the regime itself brought about some major political crisis. (Between 1934 and 1939 this seemed perfectly possible.) This strategy was basically defensive, a waiting game. The successive waves of first populist terror in 1933 and then police terror had thrown the working-class resistance decisively

[11] Up to the middle of the war there were 165 of these labour camps. See Heinz Höhne, *Der Ordern unter dem Totenkopf* (Hamburg 1966), p. 372.

onto the defensive.[12] Aside from the Rote Kapelle the most resilient and skilled working-class resistance organizations played a tenacious waiting game between 1935 and 1943. It was the prudent, professional thing to do. But prudence was defined by the Gestapo.

Intelligent and prudent resistance required a high degree of solidarity, skill and courage, but although its characteristic forms (for example, distributing illegal pamphlets, circulating information about real political developments, maintaining contacts with leading exile groups, supporting the relatives of the murdered and persecuted) were no doubt preconditions for effective political action sometime in the future, they hardly presented a direct threat to the regime as such. By 1936 at the latest the Gestapo's endless claims to the contrary (the deadly 'bolshevik threat' and so on) served simply as legitimatory rhetoric for its strategy of preventive terror.

In common with all terroristic bureaucracies, the Gestapo set out to act pre-emptively in a second sense – intimidation through the creation of fear, anxiety and uncertainty, the vague whispered horrors of the concentration camps. It is very difficult to say how far this tactic was effective in working-class circles. Fear for themselves and their families surely did deter some from working underground, but the number of recruits to the resistance organizations continued to be quite large. (It should be noted here that the regime's notorious basic strategy of creating discretionary powers and legal uncertainty in order to produce caution and anxiety in its subjects was of little relevance to the oppositional sections of the working class: educated conservatives might worry about what was, or was not, an offence against *gesundes Volksempfinden* (healthy common sense), and newspaper editors might be perennially uncertain about what they could or could not publish; but there was never any doubt that collecting KPD dues or distributing *Sozialistische Aktion* was a serious political crime.) The cause for anxiety was fear of what would happen to one if arrested, not whether one might get away with it. Dictatorial pressure on the working class was designed to create fear, not uncertainty. Until 1938/9, however, the position in respect of industrial protest action was a bit different: it was by no means certain that strikers would be gaoled or put in concentration camps, and the Gestapo sometimes agreed that working conditions were indeed intolerable, and only issued warnings. Here the consequences of defiant action were to some degree unpredictable – never pleasant, for arrest was certain, but not always lethal. The regime did, however, try to convey the impression that strike actions would always be severely punished, and after 1938 it was, as too were individual acts of industrial indiscipline, absenteeism, defiance. Fear superseded uncertainty.

[12] Conclusive evidence that the strategy of preventive and exemplary terror was quite deliberately developed includes for example the statements by leadings SD and Gestapo officials cited by Höhne, *Ordern*, pp. 162 f., 170.

Fear was thus certainly a vital constraint upon protest and resistance; and fear of informers, of a stealthy secret police and of concentration camps may well be a more insidious and paralysing kind than fear of armoured cars and submachine guns – the latter are at least visible and constitute potential objects of hatred and rage. But the German working class of the 1930s was not a conspicuously timid body of people. Many were clearly prepared to die in a civil war in 1933, had one broken out. Anyway, common sense suggests that there are limits to the degree to which, or time for which, people – in this case 20–25 million people – are prepared to be ruled by their fear. The achievement of the Gestapo in intimidating German workers was no doubt significant, and it was heavily reinforced by a propaganda which consistently cast all communists and 'marxists' in the role of traitors, dangerous subversives who were beyond the pale of normal treatment by the authorities. But its achievement in actually breaking up resistance groups, eliminating successive formations of cadres, incarcerating and killing activists, preventing the development of large-scale underground organizations was probably much more significant in the containment of working-class opposition and discontent.[13] The isolation of small groups of workers from one another was a very marked feature both of the many strikes of the 1930s and of the underground political resistance. This isolation, compounded by the recurrent need to reconstitute shattered groups and contacts, was perhaps the most important single component of the powerlessness of the working class.[14] To use the formulation of Barrington Moore Jr, the Nazi regime reduced to a minimum the political space available for the expression of moral outrage.

One quite concrete way in which the political space of the left in Germany was radically curtailed was the fracturing of the tactical relationship between the underground organizations and the class which they strove to represent. Opposition and resistance by the working class was always and necessarily public, hence immediately detectable: strikes, go-slows, demonstrations in the workplace, mass absenteeism, epidemics of 'sickness', sudden falls in productivity, etc. The political underground had to be very careful not to be associated directly with protests of this kind, for they automatically attracted interrogations and political persecution. As a consequence of such scattered public acts, numerous activists, especially communists, were dispatched directly from the factory to the concentration camp between 1933 and 1935.[15] Later, in

[13] According to Arnold Sywottek's estimate, over 100,000 communists were victims of the Gestapo during the twelve years of Nazi rule; see also Niethammer et al. (eds.), *Arbeiterinitiative*, p. 34. (Editor's note: I have been unable to locate the reference to Arnold Sywottek in his study *Deutsche Volksdemokratie. Studien zur politischen Konzeption der KPD 1935–1946* (Düsseldorf 1971); this figure is, however, given in Niethammer.)
[14] See for example the *Deutschlandberichte der Sozialdemokratischen Partei Deutschlands (Sopade)* (1934–40, reprinted Frankfurt am Main 1980), pp. 744 ff.

1938/9, this kind of opposition and non-cooperation in the workplace was more broadly supported by workers and presented a real threat to the regime. Clandestine organizations encouraged such mass initiatives in their propaganda in the late 1930s, but they understood well that they themselves had to keep in the background: their political role, which to them was more important, would have been hopelessly compromised, destroyed, if they were identified as strike leaders. The Gestapo thus succeeded in separating through terror the opposition of the working class to its immediate repression and exploitation, from the resistance of the underground class organizations to the whole system of Nazi rule. Prudent communists steered clear of strikes by their fellow workers. The organization was secret and had to remain so – this was a matter of life and death, a matter of political purpose. Thus the political channels between leaders and their constituents in the working class were few, narrow, fragile and informal. This obliteration of political space was primarily an achievement of the Gestapo (there were some other minor contributory causes), and it was another of their most important achievements.

The effectiveness of terror was heightened by the intense speed of political change from 1932 to 1945. The organized working class was called upon to adapt its outlook and tactics to a succession of radically different situations. Confronting the Prussian police was one thing, confronting the SA on the streets another, confronting the SA decked out with police armbands yet another, and confronting the Gestapo was something quite different again, something for which only the slightest mental and material preparation had been made. By the time the Nazi regime had become to some degree familiar, many cadres were dead, imprisoned, crippled or in exile. Then war began (accompanied by the Nazi–Soviet pact), which changed the situation yet again. If there was little political space for resistance and opposition there was perhaps even less political time – the time necessary to discover and invent the most appropriate and damaging forms of resistance, the time necessary to choose the most appropriate occasion for demonstrative action. One possible appropriate form of resistance to this regime might have been clandestine armed struggle, meeting terror with terror. The KPD's 'AM-Apparat' (anti-military unit) was one attempt at this. But it would have required more time to reach the decision to act in this way, more time and space to organize, than was available to the resistance. (That is not the only reason why this approach was scarcely adopted, but it is an important one.) The novelty of the Gestapo's meetings and the speed of political change were a potent source of confusion to opponents of the regime; they made learning and political adaptation much more difficult.

---

[15] Numerous good examples in Broszat et al. (eds.), *Bayern in der NS-Zeit*, vol. II.

One further comment on the relative importance of police terror is necessary. Those scholars who question its significance and assert that there are at least prima facie reasons for believing that processes of integration were more important than repression, overlook the fact that we still have no really detailed study of the normal activities of a Gestapo post. The breaking-up of some specific resistance groups has been recounted and there are some statistics on the total arrests of leftists in the mid-1930s, and of 'undisciplined' workers during the war. But the day-to-day surveillance techniques, the ordinary run of arrests, beatings, warnings, the evolving pattern of denunciation and of the work of civilian informers, the increasingly close administrative relationship between the Gestapo and business management, the practical use made by the police of the enormous sets of personal files concerning dissident individuals which had been compiled by the late 1930s – all of this is familiar only in the most general outline. Further research may well show that the system of police terror against the working class was in fact more elaborate and more effective than we have supposed hitherto. That it was ineffective against the conservative resistance is a quite different matter.

The subjection of the working class to the National Socialist system cannot, however, be explained solely by the specific Nazi forms of police and Gestapo terror. For one thing, there was never any lack of new fighters to take the places of murdered communist and social democrat resisters, especially before 1937 and after 1941. For another, people simply do not let themselves be ruled in the long term by terror and fear alone. But before I proceed to some of the specific strategies by means of which the Nazi regime attempted to integrate the working class into its 'national community', I want to discuss two other matters: the significance of the regime's material concessions to the workers, and the divisions and structural differences within the working class.

It is clear that at several critical junctures, especially after the conquest of Poland, the regime made major material concessions to wage-earners and did so in the face of growing discontent and passive resistance. I have dwelt at length in my own earlier work on these concessions and on the considered (and related) refusal of the government to implement policies which were necessary for rearmament but which would have been most unpopular among workers. These issues concerned the whole range of working conditions and labour law, wages, food-prices, and the social position of women and the family. I see no reason to attach less importance now to this strategy of macro-economic bribery than I did when I completed my research. There is little direct evidence that this (incomplete and erratic) regard for working-class living standards acted in a positively integrative manner. But it did pre-empt and defuse moments of possible breakdown, of potential mass unrest. The question

'Why was there not more resistance and unrest?' cannot be asked in a uniform manner of all twelve years of Nazi rule. The dangerous expression of political anger and defiance requires a conjuncture of circumstances and an occasion – it is not possible at just any time during the rule of a regime which consistently inflicts repression and extreme exploitation upon its working class. In my view, the Nazi regime made its most important concessions at the conjuncture which was most dangerous to it – in the years of peacetime full employment and during the 'phony war', in particular between September 1939 and April 1940. These acts and omissions prevented the full development and articulation of a general, nation-wide sense that government and business were imposing intolerably unjust policies. The issues at stake did not affect only particular groups of workers, and the sacrifices which the regime threatened to impose were not narrowly circumscribed: wage cuts for normal overtime hours, total control over job-changing, suspension of paid holidays, more civil conscription . . . What is more, they came on top of six years of repressive controls. By giving way on most of the issues, by not yet asking for sacrifices, the regime did something to placate the working class at a crucial juncture. Otherwise the spontaneous uprisings feared by Hitler could have occurred. Warned by some organizations of the party, the regime showed that it did occasionally possess some understanding of the most elementary material interests of the working class (and some prudent fear of it).[16] Warfare on a continental scale then came to act as a further constraint upon oppositional thinking and acts by the working class. After the first Russian winter the regime had new opportunities to extend its work of disciplining, containment and intimidation.

The neutralizing effects of concessions and tactical retreats by the state were conjunctural, but the accentuation of differences and divisions within the working class constituted a continuous structural process of neutralization. This is a theme which has only begun to be investigated and the following remarks are necessarily very tentative. The term 'neutralization' itself is vague, looser even than 'integration', a metaphor rather than a concept. It is intended to cover the various ways in which both social processes in capitalism and the policies of state and management may have inhibited the formation of class solidarities, or may have furnished some workers with limited compensations for their degradation and exploitation, compensations which blunted the edge of their resentment, or set them a bit apart from their fellow workers. The notion is counter-factual; it presumes a thwarted potential for action, and suggests the question 'What would have happened if...?' Its utility rests on the

[16] In this context, for details about changes in policy in 1938 and 1939 see Mason, *Arbeiterklasse*, Chapters 6, 20, 21.

assumption that all types of deep division within the working class, whether viewed nationally or in a neighbourhood or factory context, constituted a serious obstacle to the formation and expression of collective resentment and anger; on the assumption that workers, or indeed any other repressed group, need to feel that their anger and sense of injustice is probably shared by very many others in order for them to be able to take the risk of expressing it under such adverse conditions. Divisions prevent the development of a sense that support for resistance will come from quarters unknown.[17]

First and most obviously, the political and cultural divisions within the working class were very great before 1933, greater perhaps than in any capitalist state in the twentieth century (with the possible exception of France in the late 1930s). Catholic, social democratic and communist organizations competed bitterly with each other and with smaller conservative and fascist groupings; and very large numbers of wage- and salary-earners, especially in the provinces, were not organized at all. These divisions persisted to a great degree after 1933. The regime did not need to further them or play on them; it could even pose as the great reconciler! There was little support from the left, for example, for Catholic worker organizations when they were persecuted;[18] a German Popular Front was never constructed and collaboration between communist and social democratic underground groups was for years sporadic and uncertain. Awareness that these divisions had been (and still were) a crucial source of weakness was especially acute in the trade union underground in the mid and late 1930s; more so, for obvious reasons, than in the illegal (or semi-legal) party and confessional organizations. But by 1933 the damage had been done. It was too late and too difficult to constitute unitary trade union organizations of real power under conditions of illegality.[19] The will was there, but the past divisions had presented the dictatorship with a decisive initiative in 1932/3. This loss could not be made good. The lack of unity was debilitating. During the war, though, these divisions among resistance organizations and groups did begin to lose significance, especially among the younger anti-fascists whose political experience barely reached back to 1933 if at all. Terror and war summoned up new perspectives and new common experiences of action

---

[17] Barrington Moore Jr, *Injustice*, emphasizes that divisions and structural differences are especially likely to hinder latent tendencies to revolt or resistance from coming to fruition. I find this suggestion entirely convincing.

[18] This is the indirect conclusion from the detailed but extremely narrowly conceived study by Jürgen Aretz, *Katholische Arbeiterbewegung und Nationalsozialismus* (Mainz 1978). A contradictory example can be found in Detlev Peukert, *Ruhrarbeiter gegen den Faschismus* (Frankfurt am Main 1976), pp. 243 ff. The calls issued by the KPD to Catholics in the years 1935–7 seem empty and formulaic in tone and bear little relationship to reality.

[19] See for example the very instructive evidence presented by Peukert, *Ruhrarbeiter*, Chapter 9.

and constraint. The new ideological and organizational flexibility of these later resistance groups cast a cold light on the crucial structural weakness of the working-class movement in the years before 1933.

Beyond this, there is no doubt that Nazi organizations did increase their membership among wage-earners after 1933. The Nazi presence on the shop-floor in industry was never very strong or reliable, as the elections to the Councils of Trust (*Vertrauensrat*) show, also the failure of the work brigades (*Werkscharen*) to attract numerous recruits, and indeed the occasional participation of party members in strikes. Nevertheless, considerable numbers of industrial workers did join the party or the SA after 1933, and there can have been few large industrial plants which did not have a substantial nucleus of active or nominal supporters of the regime among their manual labour force; furthermore, a proportion of the large body of lowly honorary functionaries of the DAF were certainly industrial workers. These people often enjoyed very little respect or confidence among their fellow workers. Whether they also acted as honorary Gestapo agents within the factories, combining divisiveness with terror, is not yet at all clear. It is unlikely that the mass of them normally acted in this role, partly because informing in this context would have been so invidious as to be dangerous, partly because the DAF wished to keep its own information services separate from those of the Gestapo. It seems to have been management rather than shop-floor Nazis who maintained the links between the factories and the Gestapo; but this is a generalization to which there were surely many exceptions. The very existence of shop-floor Nazis constituted a further important division within the working class, and at least something of a threat to their less opportunist or less gullible work-mates.

These divisions were not just of a political order. Divisions between male and female workers were accentuated by the regime's ostentatiously protective posture towards women. The fate of family members of arrested resisters was nevertheless grim (protectiveness did not go this far), and this was a deterrent factor for many men. Of the differences between generations within the working class very little is yet known: there are some indications that younger workers were less willing to accept fascist industrial discipline than older workers and that the latter frequently retained a pride in their crafts, central to the historic labour movement, which inhibited them from undertaking various forms of industrial sabotage, even in the armaments industries. (However, all age-groups in the working class were represented in the political underground.)

Then, social mobility may have acted as a divisive force. It is mistaken to think of this process only in terms of mobility between classes: mobility *within* the working class cannot be charted accurately, but between 1933 and 1939 there was a huge increase in the absolute number of skilled and better-paid jobs in German industry. Hundreds of thousands of men (though very few women) must have advanced their careers in this way, especially in heavy industry, engineering and the building trades. Many must also have gained promotion to the position of foreman – a position which carried considerable prestige and social and political influence. There is no way of knowing how far social mobility of this kind also involved processes of political co-optation or reconciliation: it was certainly not an automatic cause-and-effect relationship – overt discontent was frequently observed among skilled workers in 1938/9. But it does seem at least likely that the new broad opportunities of career advancement, and of migration from badly paid to well paid employment, helped to neutralize or to divert attention from the lies, exploitation and repression of which everyday working-class life was composed. Furthermore, there certainly was some general mobility from the working class into the lower middle class. The trends of the 1920s and earlier decades reasserted themselves after 1933/4 and white-collar employment expanded rapidly. It expanded more for women than for men, and for women this work was often menial and badly paid. Still, in 1939 there were certainly many more working-class households in which the daughter did not skivvy but went to work in a shop or an office than there had been in 1929. For the families concerned this must have appeared as evidence of a certain social progress. Could they hope that their children might have a better life than they had had (even though the young men were being trained for war)?

There remains the question of economic divisions within the working class, which forms one part of Tilla Siegel's essay 'Lohnpolitik im nationalsozialistischen Deutschland'. Differences in working conditions, earnings and social status within the German working class had always been great. At certain times and in certain sectors of employment these differences were magnified still further by developments after 1933. Not all of the relevant developments were consequences of calculated policies: the inability of workers in many consumer goods industries to raise their earnings in the years 1933-7, years in which skilled engineering and building workers were achieving substantial wage increases, was above all a result of the increasingly uneven distribution of unemployment. The difference in earnings between the two groups did grow much greater, but only because (and as long as) workers in the consumer goods sector could not exert effective pressure upon their employers – from 1937 on they could do so, and the gap began to narrow again. The government was aware that during 1936 this discrepancy in earnings was causing bitter resentment among impoverished textile workers, among others, but there are few indications that discontent took the form of jealousy of better-paid workers – it seems rather to have been a resentment against employers and the state. That is to say, it did not obviously further divide (and thus neutralize) the working class in the social and political sense; it is hard to see these trends as factors which reduced the capacity of the class to undertake militant protest action. In any case, many lowly paid male workers could and did move from the consumer goods industries into the rapidly expanding armaments sector.

Divisions of this kind were the 'natural' divisions of a capitalist labour market. The regime and many employers undoubtedly also made a conscious effort to foster and impose new forms of social fragmentation. After 1933, there was a new intensity and coherence about those aspects of industrial social policy which aimed at dividing individual workers from each other, at stimulating competition among workers in the same firm, or city, or branch of industry. The most obvious manifestation of this was the National Vocational Competition (*Reichsberufswettkampf*). While it is clear that quite large numbers of mostly younger workers took part in this competition, we have no means of assessing the quality or duration of their enthusiasm for this ingeniously divisive selection process. Those who got through to the last rounds of the competition must be presumed to have been politically loyal and individualistic careerists, but their later biographies are largely unknown. Overall, the impact of the competition upon basic social attitudes and solidarities was probably slight. On the other hand, it should be remembered that competition was the guiding principle of all Hitler Youth activities. The entire younger generation was supposed to be brought up in an ethic of competitiveness, through which among other things the inherited solidarity of the working class was to be undermined and replaced.[20]

Then there is the question of the form of wage payments. From the start (with the Law on the Organization of National Labour (*Arbeitsordnungsgesetz*, or AOG, of January 1934) the regime was firmly and publicly committed to the much wider use in industry of wage systems which involved large components of 'payment by results' (*Leistungslohn*) – piece-work, bonuses and a wide range of different incentive schemes for individual workers. Remuneration by the flat hourly rate was denounced as a typical example of marxist 'levelling-down', a typical socialist denial of the positive significance of differential rewards for different degrees of effort and ability, an evasion of the great National Socialist fact, that all of human life was governed by the organizing principle of competition and struggle: workers should compete with each other and with the norms laid down by management in order to increase their earnings; this could only be beneficial to the economy as a whole ... Much of the distinctively Nazi writing on this theme of the *Leistungslohn* was the most dilettantish

[20] On this see especially the very revealing autobiographical observations in Melita Maschmann, *Fazit* (Stuttgart 1963), pp. 143 f.

and superficial kind of propaganda, and there is very little evidence that either the state or the party or the DAF had any effect on the practices of industrial managers in this respect before 1939. The destruction of the trade unions may well have made it possible, however, for some firms to increase the incentive element in their wage systems after 1933, where such a step would have met with organized resistance before; there is some evidence of this occurring in the coal-mining industry, and with negative results for the co-operation of workers underground; but it is still an obscure question.[21] Massive or general changes in wage-forms did not occur before the war. With the extension of detailed state control over levels of earnings and wage formation, a control which became fully effective only in October 1939, there was a more concerted effort to enforce hierarchies of wage-scales based on detailed gradations of occupational skills in certain industries. It seems doubtful, however, that this amounted to an effective engine for the further differentiation of the working class and for the breaking down of solidarities at the workplace. First, only a limited number of industrial occupations or production processes lend themselves to incentive systems of remuneration or to five to seven subdivisions of skill categories; and little was changed in the labour and production processes of German industry between 1933 and 1943 (when a new wave of rationalization, standardization and intensification of work began).

Second, and more important, after June 1938 the state and industry were simply unable to make sufficient money available in order to offer really large wage incentives to individual workers, or to create clear elite groups within the working class. For compelling reasons of general economic policy (curbing consumer purchasing power and controlling inflation), the overwhelming emphasis of state action between 1938 and 1945 was placed on holding down wage costs. This placed very narrow limits on the possibility of using the wage system as a means of recruiting the support of selected groups of workers by systematic bribery, or of offering individual workers the chance to make very high earnings if they collaborated in their own exploitation to the limits of their physical and mental powers. Hitler may have admired Henry Ford, but the regime could not begin to emulate Ford's system of high-wage industrial discipline – in the short term, high wages ran completely counter to the requirements of the arms economy. Thus wage-controls by and large froze the inequalities of pay which existed in 1939 and subjected all occupational groups within the working class to a uniform pressure against further increases – this was a new experience common to all

[21] Background to this section in Gerhard Bry, *Wages in Germany 1871–1945* (Princeton, NJ 1960); Mason, *Arbeiterklasse*, especially statistical appendix. I am grateful to Stephen Salter for information about the wage system for mineworkers.

workers, and it seems, on a preliminary reading of the evidence, to have greatly outweighed the attempts by state and management to divide workers into hierarchical rival groups. Furthermore, in the years of wage-controls, piece-work proved to have a major disadvantage: by skilfully regulating their own efforts and the flow of production, workers on piece-rates could (and did) cause endless friction in the plants, earning either too much or too little. Piece-rates were not conducive to that kind of creative harmony which both management and the state apparatus considered to be essential for high productivity.

To sum up: that the state executive and some major employers did indeed make systematic efforts to fragment the working class through the various instruments of wage policy, and to institutionalize jealousy and rivalry on the factory floor, is now beyond doubt. Tilla Siegel's work both proves this and brings together for the first time a great deal of important information on payment and earnings which will be of enduring value in its own right. I am not convinced, however, that these efforts had a significant degree of success, the sort of success which might have undermined a potential for class solidarity: the policies of wage differentiation were implemented under extremely tight financial constraints, and some of them, at least, could be effectively resisted in the factories. I am inclined to think that the major reasons for the containment of the working class have to be sought elsewhere than in its socio-economic fragmentation. But this provisional judgement in no way diminishes the significance of Tilla Siegel's research – it is rather a question about the political inferences which may be drawn from the economic research. On balance, then, there appear to be few grounds for believing that the socio-economic fragmentation of the German working class was a major factor in the damping down or neutralization of its hostility to the Nazi dictatorship. There already was a very large and complex differentiation within the class in this sense before 1933, and the differences were probably a little magnified by the consequences of the armaments boom between 1935 and 1938, but there were also countervailing trends.

Over and beyond the impact of state wage-controls, it must be noted, first, that both the economic recovery and the rearmament policies of the regime enforced a very high and sustained level of geographical and occupational mobility upon workers: people were forced to take up new jobs in new places. One must suppose that this intense process, which amounted to a partial reconstitution of the class, made the working class not less but more homogeneous (though the same mobility may also have contributed to the break-up of 'red' neighbourhoods or work-groups, which would have weakened potential resistance). Second, due account should be taken of the fact that the party's organizations made a lot of noise about the desirability of reducing, even abolishing, the large and long-standing distinctions between white- and blue-collar workers. The very category 'white-collar' (*Angestellte*) virtually disappeared from the vocabulary of both administrators and demagogues, and the DAF pressed in public for the extension to manual workers of some of the additional labour law and insurance rights enjoyed by those with clean jobs. The details of the real social developments in this sphere have not yet been elucidated; in particular, it is unclear whether the typical male white-collar worker's sense of superior social status was eroded, whether manual workers felt that clerical and technical colleagues were at last being brought down a peg . . . But it is clear that the regime's posture (if not its actual policies) on this major issue was the reverse of a divide-and-rule posture. The rhetoric aimed at blurring differences, at suggesting a sentimental homogeneity or uniformity within the working class, where previously there had been deep antagonisms. In contemporary terminology it was required of salaried workers that they should abandon their corporate arrogance (*Standesdünkel*) and pride – not, of course, in the interests of new and larger class loyalties, but in the interests of creating an undifferentiated mass of labour power, composed of isolated individuals or small groups, all at the disposal of management and the political leadership. The rhetoric may have made little difference to economic practice and social attitudes – we do not yet know. But here at least, dictatorial power was not deployed in order to neutralize opposition by magnifying social divisions within the working population.[22]

In a radically different context it was so used: German workers were systematically separated from those foreign workers who were recruited or conscripted to serve the war economy within the Reich. The discriminatory treatment of foreign workers served not only to reduce the wage costs of war production, but also to suggest that the ideology of racial elitism had a real social and material basis, which every German worker could experience. During the war Nazi racism was presented to German workers as a form of collective social mobility: 'uncultured, brutish' and expendable Slavs would do the heavy, dirty jobs, leaving German workers to perform skilled or supervisory tasks (or to fight in the armed forces). In this provisional, improvised order of the war economy, the ultimate structure of the Thousand Year Reich was temporarily anticipated. Except for the few ideologues and fanatics, the reality of racial imperialism was to be social and economic domination, the transformation of the whole German people, including at least a substantial part of the working class, into an imperial ruling class. Did this programme (briefly, randomly and partially realized) strike chords in the

---

[22] There is a preliminary approach to this issue in Jürgen Kocka, *Die Angestellten in der deutsche Geschichte 1850–1980* (Göttingen 1981), Chapter 6 (in collaboration with Michael Prinz).

German working class? Did the officially encouraged prejudice against 'the stupid Polacks' help to reconcile otherwise disaffected German workers to the prosecution of the war effort? We do not know. It is in the nature of the case that the best available evidence should illuminate the rejection of this Nazi strategy and the various affirmations of solidarity between German and foreign workers, whether these were self-consciously political or (apparently) simply humane. The historical sources left behind by terroristic bureaucracies always document dissent better than they do apathy or consent; the authors of the documents were, literally, paid to produce this emphasis, and they understood their role and their self-interest just as the propagandists and film-makers were paid to produce impressions of limitless enthusiasm. Nonetheless, the number and quality of the cases of defiance of discriminatory rules remains impressive; whatever successes the regime may have had with this policy, they were clearly neither overwhelming nor comprehensive. Yet the fact remains that we know still very little about ethnic prejudice within the German working class after 1914. On this point comparative studies really can be illuminating: the relationship between class formation and ethnicity in the USA from the 1940s, in France since 1919 and especially in the present day, in Britain in the mid ninteenth century and again from the 1950s, in South Africa from the 1890s – all these topics are the subject of much critical research and argument. In the case of Germany it appears to be widely assumed that immigrant workers of Polish origin in the Ruhr had been at least partly assimilated into a stable social and cultural position by the later 1920s, that migrant Polish agricultural labourers were of secondary significance, and that the overwhelmingly important ethnic question in German politics after 1918 was that of anti-Semitism. These assumptions may be right or wrong. Their validity for the working class remains almost completely unexplored. Whether the Nazi policy of elevating German workers above foreign workers, of degrading the latter, made a significant contribution to the stability of the regime during the war remains a genuinely open question. It calls for research which is both empirically difficult and conceptually problematic. But it is an important question.[23]

To sum up this review of some of the many different factors which tended to neutralize the working class's capacity for protest and resistance: of the divisions within the working class, the political and organizational divisions of the 1920s appear to have been more significant than the

---

[23] Christoph Klessmann, *Polnische Bergarbeiter im Ruhrgebiet 1870–1945* (Göttingen 1978), and Richard Murphy, 'Polish In-Migrants in Bottrop 1891–1933', Ph.D thesis Iowa 1977, approach this from a different perspective but offer some evidence about the continuing prejudice against Poles.

regime's attempts to achieve a further fragmentation and hierarchization through new wage systems. Career opportunities within the sector of manual labour probably helped to make life seem less intolerable. How far German workers were flattered and distracted from their own rightlessness by being elevated above foreign slave labourers remains to be explored. The social demagoguery of Nazis has been touched on only briefly in these remarks on political neutralization (blurring the boundary between white- and blue-collar, the mirage of equality and homogeneity). More is said in the following section on integration, but it may well be that the efficacity of the propaganda machine lay more in its ability to confuse, to distract, to focus attention on 'enemies', that is, to neutralize, than in its capacity to command positive sentiments of any kind.[24]

In what ways may the regime have succeeded in temporarily or partially integrating wage-earners into its machine of exploitation, war and destruction? Before discussing the various moments and elements in Nazi rule which may have helped the regime to transcend class antagonism, one central point must be repeated. Repression, neutralization and integration are not mutually exclusive, not even alternative categories of explanation for the absence of massive collective resistance by the German working class. On the contrary, the various different aspects of state policy (Gestapo, wage concessions, egalitarian rhetoric) and the different aspects of the political and economic situation (occupational mobility) were mutually reinforcing, probably mutually dependent. The impact upon workers of authoritarian welfare reforms cannot be assessed in isolation from the general anxiety, fear and political confusion which the Gestapo and the Propaganda Ministry aimed to produce among the beneficiaries of such measures. The presence of secret police agents on mass tourist holiday trips conveys an exact image of the interdependence of the different strategies of containment. Similarly the external manifestations of popular enthusiasm for the regime, by which the rulers themselves set so much store, remain unintelligible without a knowledge of the probable consequences of demonstratively withholding enthusiasm, failing to hang out a flag, declining to volunteer for this ceremony or that collection. Here it was not just a matter of intimidating the sceptical, but also of appealing to the need for identification among deeply insecure and confused people. Enthusiasm and euphoria could take root in all kinds of anxiety. And terroristic repression could never have been so successful had the working class not been so fragmented politically and had it not been offered a number of material concessions and opportunities. Thus, whatever integrative processes did take place after 1933 did so in the

---

[24] Goebbels aimed precisely for this effect. Viktor Klemperer, *LTI. Notizbuch eines Philologen* (Berlin 1947), shows exactly how this propaganda technique worked.

context of, and probably mostly because of, the sustained pressure of police terror, the sustained disorienting effects of the propaganda machine, the divisions within the working class, and the capacity of the regime to relax the economic pressures on industrial workers at the critical moments. Only in this context can the moments of support for or reconciliation with Nazi rule to be discussed below, gain their precise significance; they cannot be seen in isolation from the other structures of containment.

One further preparatory note is necessary. 'Integration' is a loaded term, already occupied by a variety of different meanings and associations. I do not wish to invoke any of the technical connotations conferred upon the concept by sociologists. 'Integration' is used here in a loose and common-sense way. It is a short-hand for those attitudes, policies, social processes and events which may in some way or another have been conducive to an acceptance of the Nazi regime (or some parts of it), or to a partial positive identification with it: the term refers to those facets of public life which may have diminished the hatred and resentment which the regime inspired, or set limits to the alienation which workers experienced.

This is the most difficult and perhaps also the most important part of the discussion of the containment of the working class. The difficulties with the relevant source materials – their paucity and the fact that they are very hard indeed to interpret – are acute, but probably secondary; these difficulties are certainly to some degree soluble in future research. The primary difficulty is ideological, and therefore also methodological. By and large liberal and conservative historians and political scientists have tended to assume that the working class was to a significant degree positively integrated into the political system of the Third Reich: they got jobs again, Nazism appealed to 'the masses', there was no revolutionary uprising . . . The list of bad arguments, non-research, and crude inferences could be continued for pages. On the other hand, scholars on the left have tended to work on themes which bring the repression of the working class and opposition to it into sharp relief. Their work at least implies that the elements and moments of integration were few and not very important. (This is true of my own book.) It is beginning to seem likely that both these positions also do violence to the complexity of the social and political development of Germany under Nazi rule. The fact that the regime maintained control to the bitter end establishes a prima facie need to investigate possible modes of integration of the working class. But because these questions have so far been the object not of debate and analysis but of groundless assumptions on the one hand and of muted passing references on the other, it is not at all clear how the specific lines of enquiry should be formulated.[25] The following remarks are intended to meet this need, and to suggest some of the ways in which the nature and the forms of the positive integration of wage-earners may be identified, defined and conceptualized for further research. The subject is a minefield.

Concrete reflection must start from the working class as it was defeated by the National Socialists in 1933, i.e. with the preconditions of National Socialist rule. Did workers' political organizations or attitudes include elements likely to predispose them to integration into the Nazis' social order? Did the political culture of the working class display specific characteristics that weakened people's capacity to resist Nazi rule? Or that may have made it more difficult for members or supporters of the parties and trade unions to maintain after 1933 that political and organizational self-consciousness which was indispensable for long-term militant resistance and as a defence against the Nazis' arts of seduction? Apart from the important political problem of the consequences and significance of defeat in 1933, which will be discussed further below, most of the questions about the propensity to integration turn on the issue of what can in general be called workers' culture.

One of the most telling criticisms of my own interpretation of class conflict after 1933 is that it almost entirely omits the cultural dimension both of working-class life before 1933 and of the policies of the Nazi regime.[26] The omission is serious, and we still have few studies which illuminate these subjects in any way. There is no work on Germany which is comparable with Victoria de Grazia's study of the simultaneous erosion and destruction of the culture of socialism in Italy during the 1920s – erosion, through the shift towards the mass production and distribution of cultural commodities; destruction, through the violence of fascist gangs.[27]

The sheer size of working-class organizations, the stability of their organizational forms, their capacity to rally support for elections or even for strikes – these are very crude indices of their strength. They say little about the *quality* of the political sentiment or political judgement which grew out of or was a part of membership of a party or union. They say little about the relative importance of politics in the lives of the rank-and-file. This matters in the present context because, after 1933, it

[25] The essay by Alf Lüdtke, 'Faschismus-Potentiale und faschistische Herrschaft oder Theorie-Defizite und antifaschistische Strategie', in H.-G. Backhaus et al., *Gesellschaft. Beiträge zur Marxschen Theorie*, vol. VI (Frankfurt am Main 1976), is one of the few useful contributions to this question. His main line of argument is convincing to me.

[26] See Mary Nolan, 'Class Struggles in the Third Reich', *Radical History Review*, vol. 4, no. 2–3 (1977).

[27] Victoria de Grazia, *The Culture of Consent. The Mass Organization of Leisure in Fascist Italy* (New York 1981).

was precisely the quality of socialist sentiment and of political perception, the relative importance of political commitment among previously organized workers, which was put to the test. 'Worker culture' is a short-hand for this complex of problems. (This is not meant to imply that the unorganized were 'culture-less' in this sense. But the shape of their culture has barely been explored.) The capacity of the regime positively to integrate the working class must, at a very general level, have been in inverse proportion to the strength of worker culture. Only those whose loyalties and judgements were firmly rooted will have been able to withstand all the blandishments of Nazi cultural flattery of workers, and to distinguish consistently, for example, between productionist Nazi icons and the lost representations of worker pride, or between Nazi comradeship and socialist solidarity. At some points (especially perhaps in the division of roles between men and women), the superficial congruences of Nazi and worker culture may have been confusing to the wage-earner targets of Nazi cultural and moral gestures. At the moment it is impossible to assess what kinds of integration may have been achieved through the manipulation of symbols and moral values by party organizations and the Propaganda Ministry, but the question is worth investigating. For the same reason, the quality of worker culture in the social democratic and communist movements before 1933 needs to be reassessed. The very small number of turncoats to National Socialism, the heroic efforts of thousands of activists to reject mentally, morally and politically everything that the regime stood for, form one testimony to its quality, but the evident political uncertainty, caution and withdrawal of many more persons who had been union members and SPD or KPD voters points perhaps in a different direction. (See also my remarks concerning the 'defeat' of the working class, below.)

There are many specific lines of possible further enquiry in this field. Four are perhaps worth mentioning; the first three refer more to the power of worker culture to analyse and resist the pressures of Nazi conformism, than to possible congruences between that culture and Nazi propaganda. First, there is the question of the extent to which a new commercial mass culture had found consumers among the organized working class before 1933. Current research is concentrating strongly upon the successful political organization of cultural activity – the initiatives of Willi Münzenberg, worker-photography, worker-sport, etc. These important stories do need to be rediscovered, but a great many other developments were taking place at the same time and it is by no means clear that all of them strengthened the cultural milieu of the working-class movements. The SPD gave less and less attention to this aspect of party life in the 1920s: the format of its propaganda remained very conservative and was regarded by many members as boring and ineffective.[28] What SPD voters and the ordinary members of the trade unions read before 1933 seems to be largely unknown. That the commercial newspaper press, the light novel and the commercial cinema remained without influence is unlikely. But cultural influences of this kind were not designed to sharpen anti-fascist political consciousness.

The second and third questions both relate to the bonds between members and supporters of working-class organizations on the one hand and the functionaries and leaders on the other. These bonds need to be understood in cultural as well as organizational terms, and the quality of them was probably a significant factor in determining the potential for resistance after 1933. It has often been argued that the SPD and the Free Trade Unions were over-organized, that members and supporters were too dependent upon the decisions of functionaries. Loyalty to the organizations was, on this reading of their history, transformed into respectful obedience and discipline, abstract sentiments which stultified the capacity for independent initiatives and thus bred political impotence.[29] The KPD would clearly have liked to be as over-organized as the SPD, though along Stalinist lines. But it signally failed to achieve that goal in the period of its rapid expansion between 1928 and 1932. That many of its members and supporters created and experienced a real political independence within the communist movement during these years, that they could create new forms of struggle at a local level, probably accounts in part for the fact that communists tended to be more active and demonstrative (also more reckless) than social democrats in the political underground after 1933.[30]

Finally, Nazi propaganda attempted from the later 1920s on to drive a wedge between labour movement functionaries and the rank-and-file. This attack upon allegedly satiated, soft, corrupt, careerist *Bonzen* (office holders, place-men, public officials who owed their jobs to the SPD) was one of the most consistent themes in the Nazi bid for working-class members and voters from 1928 to 1933.[31] In the short run this propaganda does not appear to have been particularly successful among organized wage-earners. It may well have made more of an impression among the unorganized, and it had a superficial similarity to certain motifs in the communist onslaught upon 'social fascism'. Unemployed workers in

[28] See Sergei Chakotin, *The Rape of the Masses* (New York 1940).

[29] In April 1933 the Reichsbanner warned its members against taking part in spontaneous acts of violence against National Socialists; see Karl Rohe, *Das Reichsbanner Schwarz–Rot–Gold* (Düsseldorf 1966), pp. 466 ff.

[30] On the conduct of the KPD see the outstanding study by Eve Rosenhaft, 'Working-class Life and Working-class Politics', in Richard Bessel and E. J. Feuchtwanger (eds.), *Social Change and Political Development in Weimar Germany* (London 1981).

[31] The best study of Nazi propaganda techniques in this context is Max H. Kele, *Nazis and Workers. National Socialist Appeals to German Labor 1919–1933* (Chapel Hill, NC 1972). However, Kele over-estimates the effectiveness of these techniques.

Prussia did indeed have few grounds to feel sentiments of solidarity with or respect for social democratic policemen, housing managers, labour exchange directors and city councillors. The charges of corruption against these people were massively exaggerated, but both they and the party and union functionaries (some of whom also held public office) did have relatively secure and well-paid employment at a time when most of their supporters did not; and their professional task in the years of the economic crisis was to administer the infliction of severe hardship upon the working class. This was an issue that strained the internal coherence of the reformist labour movement and deepened the gulf between SPD and KPD. It was a heavy mortgage to take into the underground struggle.

Comments on the possible integrative effects of the populistic elements in the regime's propaganda must remain equally speculative or inferential, for the source materials on attitudes (more precisely, on the attitudes of those workers who did not act in such a way as to merit entries in Gestapo files) are desperately hard to interpret. I want at this point only to raise a question. It is widely argued, sometimes assumed, in the literature on German working class movements before 1933, that the predominant image of the class enemy was formed at the point of production, that class conflict was, and was perceived as, conflict in and around industry. At times of political crisis this negative image of the capitalist/manager/shareholder was supplemented by a hatred of the executive organs of the capitalist state – the policeman, the food-rationing official, the director of the labour exchange. While this sketch of the aggressive and resentful components of working-class consciousness is clearly not wrong, it is incomplete. It contains no reference to the rest of the middle and upper-middle classes. Nazi populism was directed above all against the educated professional, literary, commercial and financial bourgeoisie – social groups whose 'basic worthlessness' was set in its starkest relief in the Nazi image of 'the Jew.' Now, there is very little evidence that German workers became enthusiastic anti-Semites; and there is no doubt that much of the regime's populism was, both in intention and in the way it was understood, a pure fraud; the post-1933 political biographies of Gottfried Feder, who really did dislike banks and large-scale commerce, on the one hand, and of the directors of the Deutsche Bank on the other, bear adequate witness to this fact. But the issue is not therewith exhausted. How did workers respond to the systematic denigration of the legal and teaching professions after 1933? To the persecution of all independent intellectuals and of 'degenerate' cultural forms? To the harassment and incarceration of priests and pastors? To the consistent, growing disrespect shown by the political leadership at all levels for the interests of the civil service and for the status of its personnel? According to Nazi rhetoric, these people were not part of the *Volk*, but workers (potentially) and employers, managers and engineers were – they were all soldiers of production.

The philistinism, mendacity and arbitrary cruelty of this fascist pseudo-egalitarianism is not at issue. What is unclear, is how far the blend of resentment against these sections of the well-to-do with rhetorical flattery of 'honest toilers' actually spoke to pre-existing components of class consciousness. It is again a genuinely open question, to which there will certainly be no uniform or general answer. But except in those (rather few?) neighbourhoods where doctors, lawyers, teachers, intellectuals and clergy made really systematic efforts to participate constructively in working-class life in the 1920s, it is hard to believe that the professional bourgeoisie was not a part of the worker's image of an antagonistic, privileged and repressive ruling class. It was probably only a minor part of this image, but still the peculiar learnedness and public status of the legal profession may, for instance, have commanded a grudging respect among wage-earners who had dealings with the law; yet it probably also appeared at best utterly alien, almost oppressive, to them – as too did the whole system of secondary and higher education. Then came the Nazi regime, which for quite different reasons had no regard for these sections of the bourgeoisie: the first German state that did not. When the regime did show regard for this class in one case – by not conscripting middle-class women into industrial work during the war – this aroused open discontent in working-class circles. Any conclusion is premature. I emphatically do not want to suggest that there was a real congruence of working-class and Nazi social resentments in this sphere. But the possibility that the rhetoric and practice of Nazi populism did reach obliquely out to elements of a distinctively working-class consciousness, and thus offered one avenue of political reconciliation for some workers, does need investigating. Resentments of this kind probably played a role – especially in Berlin – among those communists who went over to the SA in the spring of 1933.[32] That others stood up for individual priests, artists and teachers who were persecuted, is already well documented, but this knowledge does not exhaust the problem.

It was in the field of social policy that the Nazi regime made the most systematic attempt to present itself as sympathetic to the basic needs of wage-earners. Carola Sachse's 'Hausarbeit im Betrieb' and Hasso Spode's 'Arbeiterurlaub im Dritten Reich' demonstrate convincingly how social policy was prosecuted as 'welfare' (*Betreuung*); so too, in the past few years have a number of studies of Nazi policies towards women. I am now

[32] Cf. Rudolf Diels, *Lucifer ante Portas. Zwischen Severing und Heydrich* (Stuttgart 1950). Diels' description of the Berlin SA in this respect is probably somewhat exaggerated, but nevertheless gives a good description of populist activity as well as the experiences of those threatened by it.

persuaded that my own earlier analysis underestimated the impact of these social policies. It is not just that the number of beneficiaries of the care and attention of the WHW, NSV, KdF, the women's organizations, or of the BDM during the war above all[33] was very large and surely not that the material benefits derived from factory welfare schemes, or even from KdF (see Spode's essay), were in themselves substantial, for they were not. It is rather that recent research has shown more clearly than was apparent ten years ago that the regime adopted a posture of caring about its (rightless) workers, and that this must now be taken more seriously. The significance of this social welfare lay in the great variety and ubiquity of 'caring' schemes and organizations, the incessant propagandistic emphasis upon this aspect of the Nazi national community. Even if some of this propaganda did betray the true aims of the regime's welfare policies (eugenics, productivity), even if some of the schemes took the form of the most degrading or instrumental philanthropy, the general impression created may not always have been negative. The critical responses found their way more easily into the documents than the overtly positive, and much more easily than the private reflections of those working-class parents, who, on receiving their first payment of family allowances, may have thought that Nazism was perhaps not wholly evil after all. The KdF clearly did excite some positive enthusiasm among some wage-earners; what weight and what duration the enthusiasm had is less clear. But it seems probable that the main effect of the welfare policies was to suggest possible real grounds for partial reconciliation with the regime. Workers who felt acutely their loss of rights, both individual and collective, those who in 1939 could still recall with passion their vision of a social democratic or communist order for which they had struggled, those who hated war, will not have been impressed by a holiday at the seaside or extra sickness insurance, but for others with less certainty of purpose these (by now institutionalized) fascist gestures may have blurred their image of the regime as the implacable dictatorship of capital. And those workers who lived from hand to mouth, economically and politically, probably took what they could get, without necessarily experiencing sentiments of gratitude. These are all speculations, but it is obvious that the Nazi posture of 'caring' needs to be taken more seriously – less in itself than for the impression which it made upon those whom the regime exploited, had made rightless and had also put in a state of anxiety and fear. The state also 'cared' for these people. The combination was at the very least confusing, and the confusion was heightened by the

---

[33] For the BDM see the richly documented dissertation by Louise Willmot, 'National Socialist Youth Organisations for Girls', Ph.D. dissertation, University of Oxford 1979; also Maschmann, *Fazit*, pp. 63, 139–42.

extreme difficulty of gaining access to independent critical sources of information, both about the different individual policies of the regime towards the working class (were KdF offerings really a good deal in financial terms?), and about the relationship of these policies to each other and to the (almost completely obscure) overall aims of the leadership. Especially for those workers who had not been thoroughly schooled in parties and unions before 1933, the temptation to take each separate manifestation of state policy at its face value and to dissociate it from the others must have been very great: it may well not have been continually obvious from everyday experience that the very inception of the dictatorial welfare programmes was in practical terms inconceivable without terrorism against those on the left who could have unmasked these schemes. By means of these programmes and their propagandistic isolation from the total context, the regime made it more difficult for industrial workers to sustain a root-and-branch rejection of Nazi rule, more difficult to experience that sense of absolute injustice, and of confidence in one's own judgement and own standards, of which strong mass protest is made.

Here it is worth paying special attention to the socio-historical context of Nazi family policy, which was the core of this welfare strategy. Active opposition of any kind demanded a willingness, irrespective of age or sex, to put one's closest family members at risk. It is true that until 20 July 1944, and even after that date, the practice of arresting family members (*Sippenhaft*) and directing terror against relatives of resistance fighters was less barbaric than in today's Chile and Argentina: even the Gestapo refrained from coercing and torturing wives in front of their arrested husbands or mistreating children in order to weaken their parents. Still, the fate of German resisters' relatives was hard, and there was wide sympathy among working-class circles for the illegal efforts of the communist aid organization Rote Hilfe to mitigate the accompanying poverty, social isolation and discrimination. The price that would have to be paid by parents, children and spouses was well known to resistance fighters. By 1935 it was easy to calculate in advance and figures among the important factors that determined a decision for or against illegal work with the underground.

My wife is still alive, that's all. It's only for her sake that I don't shout it right into their faces . . . You know these blackguards can only do all this because each of us has a wife or mother at home that he's got to think of . . . people have too many things to consider. After all, you're not alone in this world. And these SS devils exploit the fact.[34]

[34] Max Horbach, *Out of the Night* (London 1967), p. 38. Numerous other first-hand accounts in Jochen Köhler, *Klettern in der Grossstadt* (Berlin 1981).

When evaluating and integrating this kind of accidentally surviving account, we have to place the moral problem of family members' suffering in its concrete historical setting. We have to ask ourselves whether the role and quality of working-class family relationships in general might have altered in the years following the First World War. Were typical men and women in the revolutionary movements between 1918 and 1923 plagued by the same dilemmas as voiced in the above comments by a blacksmith in 1943? Was the sense of family responsibility a constant between 1918 and 1945? It seems improbable. It is more likely that the family claimed a larger space in the typical worker's life after 1933 than before 1914. Liberal and socialist social reforms in the 1920s, along with changes in housing design, encouraged this advance into domesticity, which from another angle was also strengthened by the continuing decline in the birth-rate. The 'modern' small family with its three-room flat was more likely to be seen as an institution that needed and deserved protection, i.e. anxiety, than the large, economically insecure, semi-public families of the traditional tenements and workers' quarters. It is possible therefore that National Socialism was running through an already-open door with its vociferous family policy and rhetoric about protecting women. What is certainly true is that the regime simultaneously strengthened people's need for a domestic 'refuge' by making life in the public sphere and the workplace so pressured and threatening. For these reasons it seems important to explore the changing status of the German working-class family in its political context. This research is still in its infancy, but there are some indications that new considerations, new anxieties and feelings of responsibility connected with the family contributed to the dulling and neutralizing of oppositional potential. Similarly, the solidarities of neighbourhood, workplace and political organizations lost strength compared with closer family ties.[35]

In terms of evidence the argument about possible forms of integration moves at last on to firmer ground in respect of the personal popularity of Hitler. Ian Kershaw's research shows that Hitler was not much less admired and trusted in working-class circles than in other sectors of German society.[36] The need to have confidence in the Leader, the need which produced Hitler's charismatic effects, was not class specific. Why many industrial workers should have developed this faith in or identification with Hitler is not clear. It was not a distortion of an existing working-class tradition, for, after Bebel, the political leaders of the working class had

[35] On these aspects of German family history in the period before 1933, see especially the work of Karin Hausen, in particular 'Mütter zwischen Geschäftsinteressen und kultischer Verehrung', in Gerhard Huck (ed.), *Sozialgeschichte der Freizeit* (Wuppertal 1980). For my own first attempt at the Nazi period, see 'Women in Germany, 1925–1940. Family, Welfare and Work', pp. 131–211 above.

[36] Ian Kershaw, *The Hitler Myth. Image and Reality in the Third Reich* (Oxford 1987).

tended to be positively anti-charismatic. Hero worship was not a significant part of left political culture. The need for leadership with a capital 'L' did not appear to have been felt on the left, as it had after 1918 on the right. (Appearances may be misleading, and there may have been a latent need: it is impossible to say.)[37] Aside from all the needs and manipulative techniques which produced Hitler's charisma in bourgeois and provincial Germany, it may be that industrial workers were particularly susceptible to Hitler's mendacious claim, endlessly repeated, that he too had known hunger, acute economic insecurity, the mud of the trenches – that he was almost one of them. This may have been an important variant on the theme of populism mentioned above. But I am more inclined to think that Hitler's popularity had its deepest roots in the conditions of oppression and anxiety which the regime produced. It is not easy to sustain over a long period a strongly negative judgement about the society in which one lives. Where it is difficult and dangerous to express negative judgements, the temptation to find one strongly positive element in the system must be very strong. It may represent a need to feel that somewhere someone or something is right in the world. This hypothesis is, of course, not relevant only to industrial workers in Nazi Germany, but it may be especially relevant to them. Their hostility, scepticism, non-cooperation in political and industrial life is by now quite fully documented. But Hitler was scrupulously careful never to identify himself personally with those measures which were most oppressive of working-class interests; these politically awkward tasks were delegated to Göring and others, while Hitler dealt in vague generalities which evoked social and national progress. He was, he wanted to be believed, in no way responsible for the abuses, shortages, coercive acts, exploitation and anxiety which made up the daily experience of the working class. And many industrial workers, lacking other forms of hope, tended to accept this: the difficulties were the fault of others.

Furthermore, Hitler's foreign policy appeared to be successful until August 1939. Principled pacifism, principled cosmopolitanism had been no more widespread in the German than in any other European working class – perhaps even less so. War was not actively desired, but there is little doubt that most German workers were passive patriots, on balance content to be German, and, whenever they bothered to think about it, unhappy about the territorial settlement of Versailles. Before 1933, the most significant organizations of the working class showed no particular eagerness to do anything about frontier revision, and in this they no doubt reflected the sentiments of their members and voters. But when the Nazi dictatorship did actually succeed in doing something about territorial

---

[37] Both Thälmann (KPD) and Holtermann (Reichsbanner) attempted between 1930 and 1933 to invest themselves with the aura of a Führer.

expansion – in fact, a lot, and rather quickly – it seems from the evidence of police and SD (Security Service of the SS) reports, plebiscites, etc. that the latent national pride of many workers was activated.[38] This effect was achieved by three manipulative means. First, the encouragement of patriotism was reinforced by consistent threats against any unpatriotic mode of behaviour. Second, the propaganda machine was turned up to maximum decibels and deployed with maximum subtlety on the theme of nationalism. And third, if the real goals of the regime (large-scale racial imperialism) were obscure to top army generals as late as 1938, it is small wonder that factory workers could think that Hitler's aim really was to achieve a 'just' revision of Versailles. The extent of this misapprehension was revealed by the widespread despair or active opposition to war in September 1938 and August–September 1939: the desire for peace and non-cooperation with the war effort was, of course, not confined to the working class, but it was especially strong there. Hitler himself clearly recognized the nature of the problem. He could rely upon the patriotic sentiments of most of the population (and the Gestapo could look after the rest), but this was not enough to launch a major war of aggression: the people had to be psychologically prepared.[39]

In the 1930s, patriotism thus formed a sociologically broad but ideologically limited and defined platform for the political integration of the working class. Together with the diffusion of Hitler's personal popularity, the abuse of patriotism probably constituted the most important success of the regime in this sector of domestic politics. After the crises of morale in the winter of 1939/40, the success was then largely sustained throughout the war. It did not become easier to be unpatriotic when continent-wide warfare began. (The contrast with the First World War in this respect, with its munitions strikes, mutinies and insurgent socialist politics is superficial and unhelpful, for both the quite different forms of military conflict and the more comprehensive and less flagrantly unjust management of the 'home front' combined to diminish the anger which wage-earners and foot-soldiers could feel about those who had power over them. This was true of all combatant states.) When the first successes of the Red Army and the first massive bomber raids on German cities allowed the war to be perceived as a war of national defence, patriotic sentiment could again be mobilized and abused. In conjunction with the greatly intensified Gestapo terror and with the cult of the Führer, it must play a significant part in any explanation of why challenges from below did not break down the Nazi order in Germany before the last two or three months of the war.

---

[38] See Kershaw, *Hitler Myth*. There was, however, much support for the Republicans in Spain 1936/7; not all aspects of Hitler's foreign policy found an echo in working-class circles.
[39] Wilhelm Treue (ed.), 'Hitlers Rede vor der deutschen Presse (10. November 1938)', *Vierteljahrshefte für Zeitgeschichte*, vol. 6, no. 2 (April 1958).

The strategic bombing of German cities did not only produce emotions of shock and confusion among the victims (who were mostly working class), nor just a bitter resentment against the Allies – both of which reactions were conducive to the stability of the Nazi regime. It also destroyed institutions and inhibitions, and created space for a degree of social solidarity; in this limited area independent action and discussion was possible again, and circumscribed, 'patriotic' criticism of the regime's conduct of the air war was, to a degree, legitimate. This enforced and partial relaxation of the regime of lies and terror may well have stabilized the dictatorship through 1943 and 1944. As a basic motive force in the determination of political attitudes and action, patriotism requires, even in the twentieth century, a certain space in which people can plausibly believe that they are choosing independently (singly or in groups) and acting voluntarily. The Nazi regime, by contrast, drove towards the total manipulation of its subjects: this is the most constant image in the leaders' perceptions of the German people. That the drive towards total manipulation was only partially realized, was probably one reason why the regime was so resilient – it profited from a partial failure to implement its basic intentions. After 1941 there was some room to feel and express forms of patriotic sentiment which did not rest upon an identity with Nazism and were not just knee-jerk responses to Goebbels' propaganda.[40]

It should be noted in passing that very little is yet known about the German worker as soldier in the years 1939-45. Morale and discipline in the German armed forces have yet to be investigated in detail. If there had been any large scale disaffection or defiance it would probably have come to light already, but both the scale and the quality of individual and small-group protests is unknown. The German army had never exactly been the object of unqualified admiration and enthusiasm in the working class. It is possible, however, that its relative status in the eyes of wage-earner conscripts improved, the more experience these men had of the mendacity, brutality, corruption and exploitation of Nazi civil administration: there were very few DAF or party officials, or organizations, which could command workers' respect on any count, and in the later 1930s the pressures of the rearmament boom were tearing the veil of the capitalist economy and revealing to people on the shop-floor a confused and increasingly cynical war of all against all in pursuit of immediate material advantage. Military service involved all sorts of personal hardship and subjection to strict discipline; for some conscripts it surely also posed hard moral questions. But the German army was not a disorganized, rapacious shambles, built on a foundation of lies, bribery

---

[40] I was helped considerably in the formulation of this and other points in the conclusion of this essay by discussions with Annemarie Tröger about the results of oral history research in West Berlin. Some aspects of virtually all the questions raised in this section can be illuminated only by research of this kind.

and terror. Unlike the Nazi movement in all its manifestations, it could in principle command the respect of its conscripts: it was efficient, clearly organized, purposeful, and it was led by officers who appeared to know whey they were doing. The fact that there were far too few of these officers and that great authority thus frequently devolved upon NCOs no doubt also helped to make the army seem less alien to wage-earners. In this sense it may have compared favourably in the perceptions of some workers with all of the civil institutions of Nazi society.

There are some further strands of possible integration of workers into the 'national community' which could be explored. However, even if the evidence were more conclusive and the argument less speculative we would be considering a collection of randomly varied threads and bonds in the political order, which were of varying importance to different people at different times. The ways in which and the degree to which the working class was positively incorporated into the Nazi system would still appear insubstantial and partial. They do not have the quality of a developing consensus about the basic legitimacy of Nazi rule and policies. The regime could not rely upon the effectiveness of the processes of integration which it tried to set in motion (or stumbled upon unknowingly). The holders of power never felt that they could really trust the working class; this scepticism was probably well founded, not a paranoid fantasy. And in the sphere which really mattered, industrial production, it is quite clear that the regime failed to mobilize the enthusiastic co-operation of wage-earners. This was the acid test of all strategies of incorporation, and the regime failed it – not disastrously, for there were no big strike movements, no large-scale destruction of industrial plant. But there is very little evidence of workers doing more than they absolutely had to, much of them doing less. There is more evidence of finely calculated defiance, of oppositional apathy and demoralization, than there is of joy in work. But work did continue.

Finally, it must always be recalled that the fragmentary paths of integration and the narrow channels through which workers could reconcile themselves with some aspect or other of Nazi rule were all heavily formed by the dictatorial state and its apparatus of terror and lies. This state guaranteed that there could be only one form of welfare reform (authoritarian), one form of social resentment (against 'parasites'), and only one risk-free expression of patriotic sentiment (blind loyalty). Working people were invited to accept this gratefully – or to become enemies of the *Volk*. Without the sanctions the appeal of the offer would have been much slighter.

In reviewing these various suggestions and questions concerning the integration of the working class, the provisional conclusion cannot be that any one single mechanism of any one Nazi policy was stronger or more effective than any other. Further research is necessary before serious arguments of this kind can be conducted.

The surest provisional conclusion about forms of political consciousness, however, concerns not the substance of loyalties, but the mechanism of dissociation. The finely judged division of labour between the propaganda machine and the Gestapo encouraged, indeed forced workers (not only workers, but especially them) to separate off in their minds the few and varying 'positive' aspects of their individual and group experience from the many negative ones. For wage-earners the Third Reich represented a political synthesis of workhouse and supermarket – a remorselessly demanding and threatening construction which generated its own strong pressures upon the inmates both to consume at least a few of the political commodities on display and not to think about the connections between them. The regime incessantly claimed the total loyalty and enthusiasm of the German people, but it in fact throve upon its capacity, peculiar to thorough dictatorships, to present the working class with a large and changing set of totally spurious 'consumer choices': those who hated Himmler and the SS could invent 'their' Hitler, as if they were real alternatives; those who were oppressed by the housing shortage could perhaps approve of the building of the West Wall against the French army, which made the housing shortage worse; the DAF was almost universally unpopular, but not the KdF, which was actually a part of it; even war was on offer as a commodity, and those who rejected it could feel relief, perhaps even pride, at the Anschluss and the Munich settlement – again, as though they were real alternatives; the wage-stop was bad, family allowances helpful, and the fact that they were both integral parts of an overall policy of exploitative social hygiene was not widely advertised. The propensity to consume selected discrete political commodities, without any regard for their meaning for the whole, was heightened by the state of unrelenting anxiety and political agitation and excitement which the regime generated, and made stronger by the secrecy and disinformation which surrounded all of the regime's policy-making.

Points of identification, sympathy or reluctant reconciliation with Nazi rule, however few and random, may thus have been the more effective politically for being isolated in a different corner of mental and moral space from the sense of injustice, resentment or outrage. There was *something* which could command approval amid the lies, chicanery, repression and murder, something which appeared to be quite independent of and unsullied by the general barbarism: it might be the egalitarian rhetoric, the caring posture of fascist welfare gestures, the heroic German army, or a cunningly ill-defined figure called Hitler. Workers could 'choose' among the acceptable commodities, and under that regime it was difficult not to make such 'choices'.

Thus one can advance the hypothesis that, whatever forms of political integration were operative were partial, but were effective for precisely that reason: they were in large measure dissociated from the multiple forms of alienation. This basic attitude to politics is not abnormal; but under Nazi rule it was raised to a peculiar pitch of intensity and assumed a special significance for the stability of the regime. Much of the time in most societies most people's attitude to the public order is expressed in disconnected normative choices: approval and disapproval, enthusiasm and anger over specific issues or acts of state. One of the great historic tasks of all labour movements has been to construct or reveal the connections between ostensibly distinct events or realms of working-class experience, to demonstrate these connections in day-to-day political practice, and to propagate them through newspapers, meetings, etc. In most capitalist states this has been an uphill task, even when it has been a legal activity. In the Third Reich the organizations of the working class could perform this task scarcely at all. Most workers faced management and the regime alone or in small groups, armed – and here only in the case of ex-members and activists – only with the memory of the necessity of making connections in their political judgements. Many did go on doing this, as the remarkable perspicacity of the rumours demonstrates, which circulated in the working class in the later 1930s – rumours about the real intentions of the government, about the real state of the economy.[41] But making connections without organizational support was extremely arduous. The pressure and the temptation to make dissociated consumer choices within the terrifying and garish workhouse/supermarket were both very strong.

In considering the question posed at the start – 'Why was there not more open resistance and mass defiance among workers after 1933?' – it thus seems best to return to the Nazi state and its creation. In 1939, Wilhelm Leuschner described the Third Reich as 'a great prison'.[42] What was the architecture of this prison?

1. The ambiguity of the state system. It is a commonplace that the initial power of the regime depended upon the 'co-ordination' of existing state institutions – their disruption or supercession by the Nazi movement would have created a highly unstable political situation in which the organized working class might have been able to regain the political initiative. As it was, the gradual fusion of the Nazi movement with the machinery of administration and the co-operation of big business and the army with this new political formation put the working class in a position of complete subjection. The new order presented itself *both* as the

---

[41] A number of interesting rumours were mentioned in the monthly reports of the Reichstreuhänder; cf. Mason, *Arbeiterklasse.*

[42] Annedore Leber, *Das Gewissen steht auf* (Berlin/Frankfurt am Main 1956), pp. 97 f.

barbarous terrorism of the SA and the police *and* as the heavy, orderly, remorseless but quasi-legitimate repression of the state machine. On its own, either part would have been a manageable challenge; but the combination was irresistible. It is on the latter part, the legal and administrative repression of the working class by state and capital, that Wolfgang Spohn concentrates in his essay 'Betriebgemeinschaft und innerbetriebliche Herrschaft'. His exceptionally clear and comprehensive discussion of labour legislation delineates one of the walls of the prison. This wall was erected by the state (i.e. civil servants, lawyers and business representatives), not by the Nazi movement; it radically reduced the rights of wage-earners and increased the powers of employers and the state, but it did not appear to be a blank cheque for arbitrary acts of violence or enslavement directed against workers; and it set up a new apparatus of state supervision over wages and working conditions. No politically conscious worker can have doubted that the new 'labour constitution' was extremely reactionary and exploitative. But it did look like a constitution, happily assisted by big business, and the state machine could administer and enforce it. The working class was not just up against the terroristic Nazi rabble, nor only against rapacious employers: it was up against the organized power of an advanced capitalist state, which at this stage still felt the need to impose generally binding legal norms, and had the administrative capacity to enforce them. This made open resistance more difficult, because the new legislation was not simply an act of flagrant usurpation, nor, ostensibly, a recipe for confusion and continued terror – it stood for order, the order of the managers and the state servants. This did not make it popular, but it did make it appear serious.

This appearance was deceptive, for from 1934 on it is clear (in retrospect) that the Nazi system of labour legislation and all its sprawling outworks of precedent, procedural regulations, special courts and ideological rituals was critically dependent upon the Gestapo. Only the constant application of police terror could prevent the outbreak of conflicts which burst open the new 'legal' framework.

Authoritarian repression was parasitic upon terroristic repression. The reverse was also true, as the history of the resistance groups within the concentration camps demonstrates. A regime of pure arbitrary terrorism and degradation, with no veneer of law, order, and stable authority, is in some ways perhaps easier to resist and more likely to provoke moral outrage, than a regime which is systematically ambiguous on this count. Control over the working class at the workplace was systematically ambiguous until 1938/9. On the one hand there was a system of (repressive) positive law, justified in terms of *raison d' état* and efficiently enforced; on the other there was the Gestapo, producing well over 1,000 arrests of working-class activists per month, often with the flimsiest justification. (To add to the confusion, the Gestapo did occasionally arrest an employer for abusing his workers.) It was extremely difficult to strike effectively at this moving enemy target. Who, precisely, was the enemy, the most important enemy – the employer, the Labour Front official, the Trustee of Labour, the police, Hitler? Could the framework of positive law be used against the employers and the regime? Why risk an open confrontation with the employer, if the Gestapo is certain to arrest everyone who takes part? Clandestine organization may elude the Gestapo, but can it contribute anything to the struggle in industry without blowing its cover? The dual nature of the repressive techniques posed a real dilemma to actual and potential resisters. The regime could change and suspend the rules of the game at will, without abolishing the appearance of their importance. The appearances did matter, for the paralysing social and political isolation of working-class dissidents and resistance fighters after 1933 derived in part from the fact that the rest of society was given an utterly one-sided impression of the regime's labour policy – an impression of a strict authoritarian enforcement of duties through the civil service and management, tempered by measures of social reform. This impression of what was happening to the working class seems to have been largely acceptable to all other classes in society. The 'honour of labour', wage and price discipline, industrial relations based on 'trust', the community of productivity in the factory all sounded very nice to those whom they did not affect. The arbitrary police state which underpinned it after June 1934 was much less visible in middle-class Germany, and was presented as relating to a quite separate political and moral issue – the prevention of communist subversion. Not until 1938, with the institution of civil conscription, did the state executive itself appear as the instrument of arbitrary mass violence towards workers, and then only (because of the many protests against the measures) on a relatively small scale. Once the intensely unpopular SA had been put in its place, middle-class Germany could suppose that control over the working class lay where it really belonged. Yet it did not. The dual system of repression and terror thus both held the working class in a vice-like grip, and isolated it from all other social groups. This leads directly to the second wall of Leuschner's prison.

2. *Political isolation.* In general, working-class protest and resistance in the Third Reich could count on no sympathy or support at all from any other social groups or organizations. The only significant exceptions to this were those mostly Catholic congregations which did defy the religious policies of the regime, and did not turn communists away from their demonstrations. For the rest, the anti-Nazi working class felt that it was surrounded on all sides by positive enthusiasm for the regime and by

hostility or indifference to its own economic and political interests. The Propaganda Ministry and the party organizations were undoubtedly very skilled at suggesting, day in, day out, that the regime was much more popular than it actually was – this was perhaps the prime function of the public activities of the mass organizations after 1933 and it may well have had a sustained disconcerting and intimidating effect upon sceptics and opponents: perhaps all the others were right after all? But it was not all done with mirrors: the sense among illegal working-class activists and strikers that they were totally isolated politically, that at any given moment after June 1934 they stood for themselves alone, that their aspirations and interests met with overwhelming rejection in the rest of society . . . this sense of being completely coralled in was well grounded in fact. The regime's effective co-ordination of all bourgeois interests and its orchestration of mass support in rallies, meetings, ceremonies, youth camps, holidays, collections and so on and so forth made it much more difficult for opponents to launch large actions of defiance and protest. It may have seemed to working-class opponents of the regime that their defiance would be directed not only at state, capital, party, but in the first instance against a large majority of the German people. This apparent or real majority included an unknown host of people (hard to identify) who were always ready to denounce any oppositional acts to the Gestapo. The isolation of left resisters was therefore much more than an unsettling ideological experience; it was an important concrete reason for the success of the police terror. The organized and massive hostility of the environment must have made such actions appear as acts of desperation, as futile, suicidal gestures, in Leuschner's words. Yet why workers' outrage at their situation did not explode more frequently into such acts of desperation is not clear. Fear is no doubt part of the answer, tactical concessions and paternalism on the part of the regime another, and the belief that Hitler wanted to put things right yet another. More important perhaps was the fact that, as a whole, the German working class had become politically too sophisticated, too used to organized activities to go in for desperate gestures. Individuals 'snapped'; groups only rarely. In this sense, the Third Reich left less space for Left insurgents than any other regime in history. Here it was dependent upon the great anti-Left consensus in German politics before 1933, a consensus of which the NSDAP had then been only one part, but which it took over, along with the state, after 1933.

3. *Consequences of defeat.* Finally, the foundations of the prison were built by the political defeat of the German working class in 1933, a defeat that acted as a cause of the continuing subjugation of the class throughout the Third Reich. It is easier to state this point than to prove it, but the

defeat was qualitatively different from the defeat of the Russian Revolution of 1905, of the British General Strike of 1926 or even of the Spanish working class between 1937 and 1939. It is not just that the Nazi seizure of power constituted a more comprehensive defeat – though it certainly did. There are defeats that leave cherished memories which inspire future struggles, defeats that give a more precise focus to political hatreds, and defeats that call for and enable the working-out of new strategies of class conflict. The defeat of 1933 had none of these qualities for the German working class – it was too much a self-inflicted defeat.

Both individually and in their relations with each other the SPD, the KPD and the ADGB had shown a catastrophic lack of political judgement. The reformist left had also demonstrated a basic uncertainty of purpose and infirmity of will; and the determined purposefulness of the KPD was mere posture, a rhetorical negation of its real strategic incoherence. All the organizations went down without a fight; even in February 1933 they were still not co-operating with each other; and none of them was tactically prepared for the illegal underground struggle. These were, of course, not the only reasons why the defeat took a form which was so unhelpful for the future of the working-class movement: the Nazi leadership stage-managed the physical liquidation of the class organizations with great tactical skill and also had more than its share of sheer luck in the spring of 1933. But it was a defeat more likely than the others mentioned above to induce scepticism, disillusionment and political withdrawal in the rank-and-file of the parties and the trade unions. We know that many were not disillusioned and went, sooner or later, into the active underground struggle; many social democrats held quietly but unwaveringly to their beliefs, waiting for the opportunity to start again where they had been forced to leave off in 1933; and the underground groups also included during the war years new young recruits to the cause of the left, who had no memories of the disaster of the years 1930 to 1933.[43] There is, however, also some evidence of rank-and-file resentment and anger at the party organizations in and after 1933, especially the SPD and the Reichsbanner. And there are many hints to the effect that members and supporters withdrew, at least for a time, from all political activity. This process is inherently more difficult to document than that of resistance, and motives are very hard to detect, except where it was a matter of people wanting to keep their jobs in 1933. But it is perhaps worth putting forward the hypothesis that disillusionment was widespread, and led to a new distance between sympathizers and activists, and a new uncertainty among the former about the organization and direction of

---

[43] It should be mentioned in this connection that the strong resistance organizations on the left between 1941 and 1944 had far fewer links of any kind to the historic working-class parties than had been the case with the pre-war resistance.

working-class politics.[44] Parties and unions had utterly failed to defend the elementary interests of their members. Were the same organizations and the same political goals appropriate to the future? Workers who had serious doubts on these counts probably tended to concentrate upon their family lives after 1933. Retreat into private life, born of doubt and defeat, is not the stuff of which militant and risk-laden protest is made. Rather, it may have one of the essential building-blocks of a large-scale political prison.

It was only within the walls of this prison that fear and ignorance (terror), governmental concessions to workers, divisions within the class (neutralization) and specific isolated modes of political seduction (integration) could be such effective engines of subordination. And they in turn were effective only in their interaction. This strategy of containment was not a diabolical and conscious overall design of the Nazi leadership. Cynically calculated techniques of domination and befogging were strongly in evidence in the Gestapo/SS, in the Propaganda Ministry, to some extent also in the racket of 'social policy'; 'the Führer' was in some measure a manipulative creation. But many of the other strands of containment were woven despite the intentions of the regime, or at a tangent to these intentions: patriotism and respect for the army were both useful and dangerous to the holders of power; economic concessions to the working class endangered the war effort at a critical juncture in 1939; welfare schemes diverted urgently needed resources, however miserly these schemes in fact were. Still other strands were just lying there in the social and political landscape of 1933, waiting to be picked up, even if the regime did not draw on them deliberately (problems of worker culture, political fragmentation.) The leaders of the various executive apparatuses of the Third Reich never got together to concert their very various strategies of containment. For this regime there was no coherent overall strategy other than the resolve to survive to the end. Every attempt at such a strategy was bound to collapse into contradiction.

The only real certainty was that the gaolers would kill prisoners if they thought it necessary, maybe even before then.

[44] There is a good deal of impressionistic evidence for this. To mention only a few examples: L. Eiber, *Arbeiter unter der nationalsozialistischen Herrschaft* (Munich 1979), especially p. 75; *Deutschlandberichte*, pp. 75 ff., 299 f., 457; Heike Bretschneider, *Der Widerstand gegen den Nationalsozialismus in München 1933 bis 1945* (Munich 1968), esp. pp. 103 f.

8

THE TURIN STRIKES OF MARCH 1943[1]

IN THIS chapter I shall try to answer three questions: what exactly happened on Friday 5 March and Saturday 6 March 1943 in the great factories of Turin; why the most detailed studies to date on the March strikes give such discrepant accounts of those two days;[2] and why these two questions, which may seem both pedantic and insignificant, are actually of some importance. Since I can give a definite answer only to the last of them, I shall tackle them in reverse order, i.e. starting with the conceptual certainties (why they are so important), then passing into conjecture (why the discrepancies), and finally arriving at what we shall perhaps never know: what really happened.

The wave of strikes in March–April 1943 was the first time people subjected to a native fascist regime offered mass resistance. It was,

---

This chapter was translated by Rosemary Morris.

[1] In the course of this research, which has turned out to be unexpectedly complicated and has remained in some ways incomplete, I have received invaluable help from many colleagues. Here I should like to express my gratitude to Aris Accornero, Pierluigi Bertinaria, Nicola Gallerano, Giuseppe Garelli, Carla Gobetti, Liliano Lanzardo, Massimo Missori, Claudio Pavone, Paolo Spriano, and above all Piero Bairati, Raimondo Luraghi and Giorgio Vaccarino. The responsibility for any errors and omissions, of course, remains with me.

[2] Most studies of the problem say that on 5 March, the first day of agitation, there were at least eight or nine strikes. See e.g. Giorgio Vaccarino, 'Gli scioperi del marzo 1943. Contributo per una storia del movimento operaio in Torino', in *Aspetti della Resistenza in Piemonte*, Istituto Storico della Resistenza in Piemonte, (Turin 1950), p. 13, reprinted in G. Vaccarino, *Problemi della Resistenza italiana* (Modena 1966). Umberto Massola, *Marzo 1943 ore 10*, with preface by Luigi Longo (Rome 1950), pp. 60 ff.; and Rome 1963, p. 73; Raimondo Luraghi, *Il movimento operaio torinese durante la Resistenza* (Turin 1958), p. 55; Paolo Spriano, *Storia del Partito comunista italiana*, vol. IV (Turin 1976), p. 175; Gianni Alasia, Giancarlo Carcano, Mario Giovana et al., *Un giorno del '43. La classe operaia sciopera* (Turin 1983), p. 45. However, in his last book Massola speaks only of three strikes on Friday, 5 March and a single strike the next day: *Gli scioperi del '43. Marzo–aprile. Le fabbriche contro il fascismo* (Rome 1973), pp. 64 ff. The latter chronology is adopted by Roberto Finzi, *L'unità operaia contro il fascismo. Gli scioperi del marzo '43* (Bologna, 1974).

274

moreover, a successful act, with the result that there was no great cost in human lives to the strikers. It was in every way the most important act of mass resistance, and not only because it was the first or because it succeeded: the German working class never, even subsequently, defied their Nazi masters in any way even remotely comparable to this.[3] Yet it has been said that for over a decade the Italian working class had grown accustomed to ever-lower living standards and ever-new forms of humiliation and oppression, without having given birth to any sustained and durable protest movement.

The events of March 1943 were thus a fundamental turning point, for at least three reasons: first, because Hitler and Mussolini themselves saw the strikes as a turning point;[4] second, because the far more widely known strikes later in 1943 and in 1944 drew largely on the March strikes for inspiration and practical advice, making them a vital lesson both for the workers and for the underground resistance leaders; finally, and taking a broader view, their success (and the carefully structured image of them which was disseminated) contributed decisively to making the Italian Communist Party (PCI) into the main political force behind the mass resistance to fascism. In other words, if the strikes had never happened, or had been crushed immediately, the role of the PCI in the Resistance after July 1943 would have been much less prominent than it actually was.[5]

Assuming that I am right in attributing such historical significance to the March strikes, as marking a definite break with the 'consensus', it is not so easy to deal with the question of how they began. From Monday, 8 March onwards, the workers engaged in strike action (mostly in the form of a work-to-rule) in dozens of factories in and around Turin, and by the end of March the action had spread to the environs of Milan. All this is

---

[3] I have given a brief analysis of the two working-class resistance movements in my study 'Massenwiderstand ohne Organisation'. Streiks im faschistischen Italien und NS-Deutschland', in *Gewerkschaftliche Monatshefte*, vol. 32 no. 9 (1984), reprinted in Ernst Breit (ed.), *Aufstieg des Nationalsozialismus, Untergang der Republik, Zerschlagung der Gewerkschaften* (Cologne 1984), pp. 197–212.

[4] On the reactions of Hitler and Mussolini see especially F. W. Deakin, *The Last Days of Mussolini* (Harmondsworth 1967), pp. 155–6, 175–6, 205–6 (like all authors of general histories of this period, Deakin adopts the original version of the events of 5 March given by Massola and Vaccarino: see p. 205). On Mussolini's reaction see also the text of his speech to the directors of the Italian Fascist Party on 17 April 1943, reprinted in an appendix to Massola, *Gli scioperi del'43*.

[5] Here I am trying to give a historical judgement on the consequences of the strikes, not an evaluation of the role of the clandestine PCI in organizing and directing the strikes themselves. It is undeniable that, beginning with the accounts in *Unità* on 15 March 1943, communist spokesmen have consistently exaggerated the coherence and effectiveness of the initiative taken by communist groups during the period of agitation; and it is also undeniable that those exaggerations have helped to increase the political capital that the PCI has since made out of the history of the strikes. But the real contribution made by the strikes to the growth of the party does not rest solely on the exaggerations, as is suggested by Romolo Gobbi: see his *Operai e Resistenza* (Turin 1973), and see further below.

well known, at least in broad outline. Spontaneous collective anger on the one hand, and the incitement, encouragement and example of the underground leaders on the other, combined and reinforced each other to unleash a wave of demonstrations and walk-outs lasting over a month.[6] But I must emphasize how important it was that this wave was set in motion by a specific group of people. In other words, it depended to a large extent on the actions of the men and women who first cleared the way: those who on 5 and 6 March not only had the courage to strike, but also rediscovered, through frenetic debate, a form of protest – work-to-rule instead of public demonstrations – which minimized the risk to those involved.[7] Even so the risks were considerable. Who first took action? The initiative was surely taken by isolated little groups, who first raised the banner of defiance so that others could follow their example – without being deterred by the threat of reprisals, such as mass executions. Hundreds of strikers were arrested and imprisoned; some of them were immediately conscripted and sent to the front, while others were sent as slave workers to Germany; but this *relatively* low level of terror could not intimidate the mass of workers. The fascist rulers found that terror was an unreliable weapon against strikes.

In *Injustice. The Social Bases of Obedience and Revolt*, Barrington Moore, Jr argues forcibly that acts of rebellion of this kind are extremely rare in modern history, that they are exceedingly difficult to undertake and that they usually end in disaster.[8] I think this book requires us to reinterpret *ab initio* the history of the anti-fascist resistance movements.[9]

---

[6] The fullest available account of the whole affair is Massola's *Gli scioperi del'43*, but the author's use of archive material is neither exhaustive nor particularly accurate, and the book cannot be used as if it were a collection of primary sources. The studies by Finzi, *L'unità* and Alasia et al., *Un giorno del'43*, give further important information, as do the studies of Claudio Dellavalle, *Operai, industriali e Partito comunista nel Biellese 1940/1945*, Istituto Nazionale per la Storia del Movimento di Liberazione in Italia (Milan 1978); idem, 'Gli scioperi del marzo–aprile 1943', *L'impegno. Rivista di storia contemporanea* (March 1983). See also the special number of the journal *Nuova società* for 1 March 1973.

[7] In retrospect it might seem that no type of protest other than working-to-rule was possible at that time; and some groups of Turinese workers had already tried it, probably on their own initiative, in January and February 1943 (Massola, *Gli scioperi del'43*, p. 61). At that time, however, the tactic was disputed by some communists who inclined to a form of protest which would draw more public attention, and a large number of pamphlets was distributed – almost certainly by underground militants of the PCI – which called on all the Turinese to meet in the Piazza Castello for a mass demonstration on Monday, 8 March. If this demonstration had really taken place and had been violently dispersed, the story of the protest movement would have been very different (see my conclusion, below). Many copies of the pamphlet were found in the pockets of communists arrested in mid-March, and have been kept among the documents accompanying the voluminous records of the trials: Archivo Centrale dello State (ACS), Ministero dell'Interno (MI), *Affari generale e riservati (AGR)*, K 1B/82, 1943.

[8] Barrington Moore Jr, *Injustice. The Social Bases of Obedience and Revolt* (London 1978).

[9] My first attempt to use Barrington Moore's analytical grid was to reinterpret working-class resistance in Nazi Germany: see my essay 'Injustice and Resistance', in R. J. Bullen et al. (eds.), *Ideas into Politics. Aspects of European History 1880–1950* (London 1984).

Moore himself lays great stress on the very first steps of liberation movements: in particular, he says that a movement of this type cannot be explained away with phrases like 'given the circumstances it had to happen one way or another'.[10]

I hope that the foregoing remarks will serve to justify the perhaps slightly pedantic, perhaps purely conjectural, remarks with which I shall now address the first two of my opening questions.

Why is there such uncertainty about what really happened in Turin on 5 and 6 March, and why does this sense persist in the historical reconstructions which have been attempted to date? The following comments are made in a spirit of enquiry rather than inquisition, for the very good reason that many important details of the picture are still somewhat obscure (and this makes it very easy to commit certain errors). As far as I can judge at this point, the traditional, erroneous theory about the origin of the strike wave derives from a dubious interpretation of the first sentence in the 15 March 1943 issue of the then clandestine journal *Unità*, which read as follows: 'From 5 March onwards [*Dal 5 marzo*] more than 100,000 workers struck [were on strike] in the factories of Turin: Fiat Mirafiori, Grandi Motori, Westinghouse, Nebiolo, the workshops of Savigliano, Microtecnica, Pirotecnica, Aeronautica, Villar Perosa and many other establishments.'[11]

In a notable essay of 1950, which has never been surpassed and remains in many respects indispensable, Giorgio Vaccarino, a former member of the Partito d'Azione, seems to have taken this sentence to mean that there were already at least nine strikes and demonstrations in progress in the factories on Friday, 5 March.[12] This reading has become more or less the norm and, so to speak, official, having being repeated (with minor variations) in subsequent years by Luraghi, Spriano, and most recently Alasio, Carcano and Giovana (1983), while Gobbi welcomes it with

---

[10] Moore particularly stresses the very grave risks run by protest movements in cases of isolated and ill-prepared acts of resistance, which were often followed by increased repression and a widening of the gulf between the militants and the oppressed masses; in situations of this kind the former were often accused of 'causing' the increased repression. This view does a lot to clarify the dilemmas of anti-fascist resistance groups.

[11] For an attempt to get at the real meaning of the phrase 'Dal 5 marzo', see pp. 280–1 and note 20 below.

[12] For its balanced and detailed interpretation, Vaccarino's essay still seems to me the best study of the strikes, but I have found nothing to confirm his reconstruction of events on 5 March. The list of disturbances that he gives differs in part from that in *Unità*: he omits Nebiolo, Aeronautica and Villar Perosa and adds (quite correctly) two strikes at the Rasetti works ('Gli scioperi del marzo 1943', p. 13). Before Vaccarino's essay there had only been one brief published account of the strikes: Umberto Massola and Girolamo Li Causi, *Gli scioperi del 1943–44* (Rome 1945). There may be some significance in the fact that in this first essay Massola remained vague about the earliest stages of the struggle and did not allude to any new strikes on 5 March, mentioning only the strike at Mirafiori (pp. 6 ff.).

enthusiasm.[13] Its authority remained unquestioned until 1973, because Umberto Massola, the most important of the strike organizers who survived the war, endorsed and perpetuated it in full knowledge that it was incorrect.

In studies published in 1950 and 1963 Massola, a communist, painted (under Vaccarino's guidance) a picture of a vast explosion of unforeseen mass defiance on 5 March: a movement which, even if it was dependent on the crucial initiatives of small communist groups, *immediately* took on the character of an impressive class struggle.[14] Massola's last book on the strikes (1973), which has a much broader scope than the earlier ones, seems to have received little attention, perhaps because he had already told the story so many times and it had been duly rubber-stamped by professional historians. In fact, this book introduces some very significant differences into the account, though without ever explicitly drawing attention to them. According to this new 1973 version, there were only three strikes on 5 March (Leo Lanfranco's group at Mirafiori, and in two of the Rasetti works); on the next day, the 6th, there was only one, at the Microtecnica. The real 'wave' of strikes began only on the following Monday. Apart from one small but decisive detail, this seems to be the true version of events.

I should like to suggest two reasons (though there must be others as well) why the myth of simultaneous strikes starting on Friday, 5 March has managed to survive long enough to resurface in Giovana's essay, written a decade after the myth itself had been discredited by its own principal creator (albeit with the greatest circumspection). The first reason is that it has never actually been possible to check the accuracy of the story against reliable sources: almost all the original documents which might have given a first-hand account of how the strikes began were destroyed or lost, or perhaps historians have been denied access to them by their present custodians.[15] The only noteworthy exceptions are the

[13] See note 2 above. Gobbi (*Operai e resistenza*, pp. 28 ff.) used Massola's and Vaccarino's assertion that the strikes had started to spread right from the first day as a sort of proof that Massola and the PCI had nothing to do with organizing them: given their character, Gobbi argued, they could not have been other than spontaneous. Thus he accepted the usual version which made nonsense of the political meaning. However, while Gobbi's book was in course of publication (1971–3), Massola was doing his best to clip the wings of that pretty story of working-class dialectic by writing a new account, according to which there had only been four strikes in the first two days. (I am not insinuating that Massola was induced to modify his version so as to parry any blow from Gobbi.)

[14] Massola, *Marzo 1943 ore 10*.

[15] The most important missing document is the customary monthly report by di Suni, prefect of Turin, to the Minister of the Interior, for March. His April report and the reports of the prefect of Milan for both months are also missing from the files (otherwise complete) in ACS, MI, *SCP*, 1943, file 10–11. I have not been able to disinter either these or any other general reports on the political situation in Turin (e.g. from the chiefs of the militia and the Fascist Party, or the regional military commander) from anywhere in the ACS. The total lack of documents at the highest governmental levels, except for the telegrams examined above, may mean that Mussolini had ordered all the documents in

telegrams sent by questors and prefects to the chief of police, Carminé Senise,[16] which Massola was able to read at the end of the 1960s. On 5 and 6 March the prefect di Suni reported three brief protests and walk-outs, demands for salary increases from the workers and arrests by the police in the Mirafiori, Rasetti and Microtecnica works.[17] Massola has proposed a new account of events which in part accepts these sources as trustworthy.[18] The prefect's telegrams may well have made these first strikes out to be much shorter and less important than they actually were,[19] but he would never have dared to pass in silence over a chain of strikes which involved

the case to be put in a special file for his personal use, and that this file was lost during the summer of 1943. No copy of the March 1943 report by the prefect de Suni has survived in the vast collection of papers from the prefect's office now in the Turin state archives; these documents, however, make it clear that di Suni blamed himself for the strikes when he wrote his report, even though this act of self-accusation would inevitably force his resignation (which it promptly did): see the note in the margin of the last of the numerous telegrams sent to him from the Ministry of the Interior, dated 16 April, in which he was reproved for submitting his report late, i.e. three days earlier (ibid., file 134). I have also been told that most of the local police reports quoted by Vaccarino and Luraghi have been destroyed in the course of normal archival weeding practice; this is a grievous loss, because the two versions diverge on a whole series of particulars, and the sources they relate to can now no longer be checked. I learn from reliable sources that there are no papers relating to 1943 in the communal archives of Turin. Up to a short time ago, the archives of the Centro Studi Piero Gobetti in Turin had some original documents from March 1943, which have now, sadly, vanished. A search made at my request by General Bertinaria and his assistants at the Historical Office of the Army General Headquarters has proved fruitless; and Piero Bairati has confirmed that there is nothing of relevance in the archives of Fiat. Although I have not yet consulted some other archive collections (Carabinieri, Procura Generale Militare, Fabbriguerra), it is still quite obvious that since the end of the 1950s the available primary sources have always been extremely sparse; and for this reason alone it is not surprising that Vaccarino's version of events on 5 and 6 March was neither confirmed nor discredited up to 1973. Before the telegrams to the chief of police were made available to researchers, the only other source which could readily be consulted was an inaccurate transcript of an incomplete series of letters and accounts written at the time by employees in the Fascist Confederation of Industrial Workers; this transcript, which is supposed to have been made by an employee of the PCI at the end of the 1940s, and to have been used by Luigi Longo for his prefaces to the first two editions of Massola's book, is now in the Istituto Gramsci in Rome (Archives, box 30). In his last book in 1973, Massola uses this material very selectively; and indeed it is very difficult to apply any scientific rigour to it. One final reason for the lack of available information on the Turin strikes is the fact that many of those who took part were killed in the last two years of the war.

[16] See ACS, MI, UC, 1943, 7, 600 ff.

[17] For the purposes of the present investigation the relevant telegrams are nos. 6185 (5 March) and 6273 (6 March).

[18] The proof of a fourth, very short downing of tools on 5 March, in the Rasetti works on the via Salerno, is given by Massola in the form of a letter written on that day by Emilio Balletti, secretary of the Turin Provincial Union of the Fascist Confederation of Industrial Workers, and transcribed in the collection mentioned in note 15 above, now in the Istituto Gramsci in Rome (Archives, box 30).

[19] For an attempt to evaluate the character of the first strikes, see my conclusion below. It should be noted forthwith, however, that Massola gives a distorted idea of the real content of these telegrams. In Gli Scioperi del'43, pp. 64 n. and 67 n., he quotes from them but omits most of the passages that describe the strikes as very short and inconsequential. Prefect di Suni did have a good many reasons to minimize the events of those two days, but this certainly cannot be proved by rewriting the text of his telegrams.

Grandi Motori, Westinghouse, the Savigliano workshops, etc., all on 5 March. In reality, as Massola duly tells us in his last book (which substantially incorporates the data from the telegrams), such strikes took place only a week later – and in some cases, not at all.[20]

I have not yet found any other sure and certain proof of the exact chronology:[21] the oral testimonies gathered by Giuseppe Garelli are of inestimable value in telling us what it was like to live through the strikes, but (except in the case of the two Riv factories) they are of no help in reconstructing the exact timetable.[22] Moreover, there are almost no sources from the fascist side. The press was effectively gagged, and newspapers were even told to avoid any reference to strikes which may have taken place in other countries.[23] There is also a singular reticence about the strikes in the few government sources that have come down to us. For example, from 14 March 1943 onwards the police arrested more than sixty militants belonging to two PCI cells in Turin. Among those detained was Leo Lanfranco, whose leading role in the strikes at Mirafiori has been recognized by everyone who has studied these events, and along with him other communists who had helped to prepare the strikes. However, the prisoners were interrogated only about the history and organization of the underground PCI, and were asked hardly anything about the actual preparation for the strikes (which were then still in full

[20] According to the list given by Vaccarino and *Unità*, the strikes are supposed to have happened in the following establishments on the following dates: Aeronautica, 8 March; Ferriere Piemontesi, 8–9 March; Nebiolo, 9 March; Savigliano, 11 March (Massola, *Gli scioperi del'43*, erroneously says 9 March); Villar Perosa, 11 March(?) Neither in Massola nor in eyewitness accounts have I found reference to any strikes in the other three factories on the list: Grandi Motori, Westinghouse and Pirotecnica. When he was writing his last book, Massola was so disenchanted with this list that he eliminated it altogether from his citations of *Unità* (ibid., p. 96).

[21] Balletti's letter of 5 March (see note 18 above) is not a completely independent source. The author sent a copy to di Suni, and the prefect seems to have used it that same evening when formulating his own telegram to the Ministry of the Interior. The transcript of Fascist sources makes no mention of a strike on 6 March at Microtecnica.

[22] See Alasia et al., *Un giorno del'43*. The original texts of these accounts are in many cases more substantial than, and slightly different from, the published versions. I am grateful to Giuseppe Garelli for allowing me to read the typescripts. The oral testimony rarely helps to establish exact dates. Moreover, a further chronological problem is raised in the account by Vito Damico (p. 106), who recalls that the communists at Mirafiori originally planned to strike on 1 March (see Spriano, *Storia del Partito comunista italiano*, vol. IV (Turin 1976), p. 174 n.) Piero Bairati (*Vittorio Valletta* (Turin 1983), p. 97) indirectly confirms this when he notes that the management made a small wage concession at the end of February to forestall a strike expected for that date. Massola, *Gli scioperi del'43*, furnishes Lanfranco with plausible reasons for rejecting 1 March and preferring 5 March. I can throw no further light on this question. However, if there was an abortive attempt to organize a strike for 1 March, the two lines of argument proposed above remain intact: that is, there must have been communist groups trying to carry out a planned initiative, and that initiative ran into difficulties.

[23] Telegram no. 17, 765, 9 March, with 'absolute priority', to all prefects etc., in ACS, MI, UC, 1943, b. 18.

swing throughout northern Italy). The detailed records of the interrogations shed no light whatsoever on our present investigations.[24] Another example: during the walk-outs the Turin police arrested hundreds of strikers, eighty-seven of whom were brought before the Special Tribunal on 15 April, but the charge against them was summary and rather imprecise: the local prosecutor (*questore*) made no serious attempt to probe the dynamics of what had happened, or to identify the organizers.[25] These fragmentary pieces of evidence suggest that the fascist authorities were incapable at the time of painting an accurate picture of what had happened at the beginning of the strikes; their disarray and their lack of information (and not just the later destruction and disappearance of documents) have made life difficult for historians ever since 1945.[26]

The lack of evidence to refute it has thus enabled this little myth – that 5 March was the decisive day for the working-class resistance – to persist and prosper undisturbed. One might also suggest that it prospered because its various proponents wanted it to. Throughout the 1950s and 1960s it was a myth laden with political implications. In relation to the political culture of the Resistance in general, the image of a first mass strike spreading in a matter of hours through the leading factories of Turin had an obvious fascination which transcended party lines. It marked the long-sought and at long last definitive breakaway of the working class from the fascist regime; when mass resistance finally broke out, its chroniclers endowed it with a scale and speed such that it acquired a glorious inevitability. This idea of an explosion of democratic aspirations, class consciousness and hatred for the war became a favourite with anti-fascist visionaries after the war; it seemed a great moment in the

---

[24] See ACS, *AGR*, K 1B/82, 1943. It is extremely difficult to explain the reticence of these papers concerning the strikes. It seems clear only that some of the communists arrested had been under police surveillance for any length of time, and that none of them was imprisoned as a direct consequence of their actions during the strikes. Those functionaries (probably from the secret service (OVRA)) who conducted the interrogations were much more interested in the local penetration and the organizational structures of the PCI than in its factory cells (resistance veterans like Lanfranco were naturally active in both sectors); apparently they thought that their own competence was limited to subversion, and was not concerned with mass agitation. However, the interrogators clearly indicate that, rightly or wrongly, the police did not think it possible that the PCI could have inspired and organized the strikes. Those arrested certainly did not rush to supply information on the subject, although some of them were forced to divulge certain particulars of other activities by the PCI.

[25] I am grateful to Giorgio Vaccarino for supplying me with a copy of this document from the Special Tribunal.

[26] One begins to suspect that the machinery of state was not actually prepared to face up to mass agitation on this scale, and lacked the personnel capable of examining and evaluating the events in detail. The arrests seem to have been an attempt at brutal intimidation, or at removing individual alleged 'ringleaders'. In his charge, the prosecutor says he is convinced that underground communist groups were behind the strikes, but he could not supply a single shred of proof.

prehistory of a potential new republic – the democratic republic, based on a broad unity of action among left-wing groups, which was to founder in the late 1940s. As a generalized interpretation of the strikes in March and April 1943 this view was and remains persuasive, but as regards the earliest phase it is no more than a pious illusion: political passion has doubtless given birth to an incautiously triumphalistic interpretation of history. In its own small way, the accepted version of events on 5 March underwrote the political identity of the Resistance as a spontaneous movement of mass unity, at the very time when that identity was becoming fragmented and lost.[27]

Massola's reasons for confirming and perpetuating this story must have been quite different, seeing that he was not an enthusiastically democratic historian, but a high party official of great experience and proven loyalty. We must assume that whatever he wrote was based on specific political choices. It is quite obvious that he was out to emphasize the leading function of the communist groups at every stage during the strikes, but this claim is not furthered in the least by the fictitious exaggeration of the disturbances on 5 March; moreover, his version always risked being contradicted, to the grave detriment of his whole account. What if other initiatives in the struggle, attributed by Massola to the communists, had likewise never happened? He ran the risk of being personally discredited, and seeing his party's role in the event put through a disrespectfully sceptical sieve. That he knew he was walking on thin ice is shown by the fact that he did amend his own account in 1973 – but surreptitiously. Why, then, did he not correct Vaccarino when he brought out his first book in 1950? If the four walk-outs which (presumably) really happened on 5 and 6 March had really been inspired by activists from his party, the PCI's place in the vanguard would have been much more clearly confirmed, to Massola's great advantage.

I can only suggest that Massola's description of these events was inspired by one very precise and urgent priority: to safeguard, at any cost, the account of the Mirafiori strike on 5 March which appeared in *Unità* ten days later, on 15 March. This story, the first and most important of the reports on the strikes which had appeared in the PCI newspaper, had by then become a very familiar, and therefore vital, part of the party's political and historical image. How the management failed to sound the alarm sirens at 10 o'clock in the morning; how the strike started despite the missing signal; how solidarity in the factory was total and how 'the

---

[27] These seem to have been respectively the political argument and the ideological message of the innovative contribution by Vaccarino to the conference on the Resistance in Piedmont in 1948, published in 1950. He gave space to various non-communist Resistance groups operating in Turin in 1943, but without in any way assuming an anti-communist position.

Fiat directors gave in'. Subsequently, in other factories 'the workers, following Mirafiori's example, went on strike'. After the war the account was elaborated when a leading role was claimed for the Mirafiori communists led by Leo Lanfranco, one of Massola's earliest and closest collaborators in the clandestine party in Turin, who later met a heroic death in the partisan war. The idea that the movement started at Mirafiori at 10 o'clock turned into a kind of axiom, a cliché of Resistance storytelling, a lynch-pin for the PCI. As far as I can make out, no doubt was ever cast on *Unità*'s account; its universal acceptance supplied the PCI with political prestige for decades, and of course figured largely in its celebrations in 1963 and 1973. It seems to me logical to conclude that Massola knew that this political myth actually rested on very insecure foundations, and so had no wish to get into any discussion on the exact sequence of events on 5 and 6 March. If Vaccarino and others talked about another series of strikes on 5 March, so much the better, so long as they acknowledged the guiding hand of the Mirafiori workers, and thus the substantial truthfulness of *Unità* – which they did.

At this point it is essential to emphasize the fact that the absolute pre-eminence attributed to the Mirafiori workers in the strikes of 5 March is not the fruit of a historical reconstruction of the movement done after the war: rather, it was a crucial tactical motif in the propaganda that the PCI was using to spread and strengthen the strike *as it was actually happening*. The account was not written by professional journalists; its closeness to events should make us more, not less, cautious in evaluating its real significance. Mirafiori indubitably was the symbol of Italian capitalism, the biggest, most modern and best-known factory in the country, and a vital link in the chain of wartime production. For underground militants and rebellious workers throughout northern Italy, the 'news', arriving in mid-March, that the first big and successful strike had happened there, at Mirafiori, must have come like a thunderbolt – and it certainly was just what was needed to galvanize them into action. At the end of the first week of strikes in Turin, Massola and Negarville, who worked together to print *Unità* in Milan, probably came to the joint conclusion that news of struggles in minor factories would have to be grouped round some kind of 'flagship'. Names like Rasetti, Microtecnica, and even Aeronautica were not exactly household words; they certainly did not have the magic sound of Mirafiori. But if the great bastion of the system, the jewel in the crown, had fallen to the strikers' first assault, then workers everywhere would be encouraged to follow suit. Ten o'clock, the siren . . . The 15 March 1943 issue of *Unità* was a crucial weapon in a great new struggle which was still in full swing: the authors of the article had that fact foremost in their minds. They wanted to spread as effective a call to action as possible, and when we reread the paper we should do it with that key factor in mind. Only thus will it be possible to explain the fact that the first sentence in *Unità* referred to strikes in three famous firms where none had in fact taken place, while saying nothing about the crucial strike which had occurred in a less well-known factory.[28]

The image of Mirafiori as the 'moment of truth' epitomized the fighting mythology inspired by the strikes. And after the war, when the party made Mirafiori the pivotal moment in a period of real and symbolic importance to the working-class communist movement, 5 March became integral to a living tradition of militancy. The propagandistic importance of Mirafiori as the perfect 'example' became a *fait accompli*. Massola (though this is no more than a hypothesis on my part) adjusted his versions of the beginnings of the strike wave quickly and quietly, because any open discussion or investigation would have jeopardized the official story of the role assigned to Mirafiori, which was an integral part of the cultural inheritance of the PCI.[29]

Decisive events, wholly inadequate sources and interpretations loaded with burning political implications . . . But what really did happen on 5 and 6 March? Unfortunately this is not a detective story, with a neat solution in the final chapter: too many clues have been destroyed, or remain undiscovered. Here we shall have to be content with a few approximations. First, however, we must put some background features into clearer focus.

I think it perfectly plausible that the clandestine PCI in Turin made radical modifications to its strategy and tactics during the early months of 1943, adapting an organization which was experienced, and singularly effective, in conspiracy and agitation to a new orientation, one of open mass confrontation with industrialists and with the regime itself. This was undoubtedly a drastic change of direction, which must have provoked considerable resistance within the party; the leaders were obviously aware that if they tried openly to orchestrate a mass struggle they ran a

---

[28] See notes 20, above, and 49, below.

[29] It should be noted at this point that all Massola's accounts of what happened at Mirafiori have remained short, stereotyped and general. The 1973 version offers no new documentation in support of key points and merely repeats the same old sentences, many of them lifted straight from *Unità* (they also appear in most of the books dealing with this period). Other strikes are reconstructed by Massola in a much more vivid and detailed way. I am aware that my explanation of Massola's version may sound tortuous and unnecessarily complicated, but I have been struck by the rather underhand way in which he chooses what to put into his books and what to leave out. There is no question of absent-mindedness or carelessness. Regarding the events at Mirafiori on 5 March, for example, he had already come across Balletti's letter before 1950 (see note 18 above), but he decided to ignore it completely; and in his 1973 book he falls back on the embarrassingly direct witness of Damico (see notes 22, above and 44, below) only in relation to the strikes of the following week. I may also be wrong about the exact nature of his political objective, but that he was consciously pursuing such an objective is beyond doubt.

grave risk, after an unsuccessful strike or public demonstration, of seeing the party discovered and crushed with one blow. We may safely assume that Massola, a past master at conspiratorial caution, disputed and restrained this change in strategy.[30] But circumstances were forcing the party to see the ever-increasing urgency of going onto a large-scale offensive. The most important signpost in that direction – as the PCI knew very well, given that its network of militants, though not large, had infiltrated so widely into the mass of urban workers – was the growing feeling of anger and disillusionment which was creeping into every corner of Turin. The regime had been unable to keep its promises in the matter of prices and food supplies, it had not paid the wage rises promised to the numerous evacuee workers,[31] and it was threatening fresh conscriptions among the workforce.[32] To crown all, it was losing the war, both in North Africa and in Russia. On top of the harsh and unjust material sacrifices imposed on the labouring masses there now came the crushing proof of the obtuse inefficiency of the regime in both the administrative and the military realms. Through January and February 1943 the number of wild-cat strikes slowly increased, and by the end of February a rebellious potential had built up which had not existed at any time in 1942.

By what stages the PCI finally came round to trying to channel and direct this rebellion is not clear. The only certain evidence we have is in the memoirs of Amerigo Clocchiatti, who paints a picture of growing division in the communist ranks after November 1942, over the fundamental strategic question of the risks involved in active revolt and disregard of the rules of conspiracy. Clocchiatti urged, with somewhat ingenuous insistence (and with a rather cavalier attitude towards conspiratorial caution), that they should stir up an open aggressive campaign of mass resistance, guided by the PCI; he favoured organizing public demonstrations. In spite of opposition from Massola, it seems that this new outlook found favour with a fair number of militants who were growing ever more

---

[30] See Amerigo Clocchiatti, *Cammina frut* (Milan 1972), pp. 167 ff. Clocchiatti crossed the Alps on his third attempt and reached Turin, where he worked as a party 'instructor' under (or with) Massola for nearly four months, until mid-February 1943, when for security reasons he had to exchange jobs with Leris and go to Bologna. He and Massola disagreed over the ideology, strategy, tactics and post-war programme of the PCI, and their mutual aversion was still keen in the early 1960s (see Massola's essay in *Critica marxista*, nos. 5–6 (1971)). Clocchiatti's memoirs, though strongly biased, most probably give an accurate picture of Massola's basic political attitude; his position as undisputed leader of the underground movement was already being undermined in the winter of 1942–3 after the arrival in northern Italy of other important officials such as Roasio, Celeste Negarville and Leris. (Having exchanged jobs shortly before the strikes broke out, neither Clocchiatti or Leris was in a position to give an accurate account of them after the war.)

[31] The famous '192 hours' (of paid work per month) were the nub of the strikers' demands.

[32] Vaccarino, *Gli scioperi del marzo 1943*, gives an excellent outline of the social and economic background to the affair.

eager for action.[33] Even Lanfranco, a leader endowed with much more experience and common sense than Clocchiati, seems to have been caught up in this new mood; apparently his replies to the optimistic urgings of the latter were consistently positive.[34] We also have some evidence that discussions and initiatives along those lines apparently took place within the party during the weeks leading up to 5 March 1943.[35]

If I may be allowed a more general comment, this experience is probably one example of a kind of transformation which is perceptible in other long-lived clandestine groups in Nazi Europe: a strong impulse, the moment that political circumstances looked a shade more encouraging, to cast off the rules and habits of clandestine existence and pass to open defiance of the fascist enemy by armed uprising and mass action. From the psychological point of view, the discipline of secrecy was not seen by its adherents as an end in itself, but as the preparation for future struggle.[36] Today's extreme caution was a means towards tomorrow's audacity, and in no way an alternative to resolute action; but for the militants of the Italian Resistance the balancing of the two attitudes, and the right time to switch from one to the other, were terribly complicated

[33] The police found evidence of such initiatives by Clocchiatti (photographs of the execution of a Yugoslav partisan; material aid to Russian prisoners in a concentration camp near Turin) on some of the communists arrested in late March (see ACS, *AGR*, K 1B/82). In *Cammina frut*, p. 178, Clocchiatti maintains that in February 1943 he, along with other party members, printed and distributed 6,000 copies of a leaflet composed by himself, inciting people to strike and to take part in a public demonstration. I have found no evidence to confirm the truth of this assertion, but it may actually have happened; in that case, Clocchiatti and his followers were trying to force Massola and the whole party to adopt a determined strategy: the PCI would have been honour-bound to follow up such a leaflet in one way or another.

[34] Massola, *Gli scioperi del '43*, pp. 60 ff. He says that Clocchiatti had been all for an all-out strike (which could easily have been combined with a mass demonstration), while Lanfranco had pressed for a work-to-rule. Clocchiatti is irritatingly vague on this point (*Cammina frut*, p. 178). I have found no other evidence of the part played by Lanfranco. Massola, for his part, has never explicitly maintained that the strikes were his own idea or his own initiative: the fact is significant, because to judge from his essays in *Critica marxista* (1971, 1976) and his memoirs (which close in 1941), modesty was not his greatest virtue. These essays, along with Clocchiatti's memoirs, also make it clear that throughout February 1943 Massola was intensely absorbed in new and important organizational problems within the party, and engaged in bitter ideological conflict; he spent a good part of his time in Milan and probably did not personally follow the development of the situation on the ground in Turin until the end of the month.

[35] Take, for example, the numerous young apprentices who, suddenly curious and spoiling for a fight, volunteered as messengers and lookouts when meetings were going on: remembered by Giuseppe Pensati (Alasia et al., *Un giorno del '43*, pp. 162 ff.). Talking with Luraghi during the partisan war, Lanfranco apparently said that the high fighting spirit of the young workers had strongly influenced the PCI's decision to foment the strikes. For this information about militants on the ground, and for many other observations, I am very grateful to Professor Raimondo Luraghi.

[36] Clocchiatti's reconstruction in *Cammina frut* (esp. pp. 170 ff.) shows very little understanding of this fundamental aspect, especially with regard to Massola. It was this problem of the form and timing of the future struggle that caused perplexity and discord in the ranks of the underground movement. The form did not bother Clocchiatti much.

questions.[37] We can imagine how the news of Stalingrad must have filled the leading Turin communists with a new and twofold ardour for the fight – a sense of euphoria coupled with a feeling that they had to show solidarity with the Red Army.[38] One more comment on the PCI's position: at that time it was undoubtedly the best-organized resistance group in the ranks of the Turinese working class, but it was not the only one. The history of the other anti-fascist left-wing groups is sunk in almost total obscurity, but we cannot altogether discount the possibility that another reason for the PCI leaders' decision to take the initiative at the end of February was to prevent other groups – Partito d'Azione, MUP, Red Star? – from putting themselves at the head of a mass protest.[39]

Our last peripheral consideration is the state of mind of those facing the strike, i.e. the leading industrialists and the fascist elite in Turin. They knew that the situation was deteriorating and their authority crumbling. They had found out at least two weeks in advance that an organized workers' protest was in preparation, but they had not managed to identify the instigators. Vittorio Valletta was convinced that Fiat and the government should grant wage rises, and in the days leading up to the strike he had gone to Rome in a vain attempt to get the '192 hours' (of paid work per month) for all workers.[40] However, the two elite groups were not so

[37] See, for example, the extraordinary affair of the Wager-Frieb group, which operated around Augsburg and came to an end after eight years of successful clandestine activity through its own impatience to go on the offensive (Gerhard Hetzer, 'Die Industriestadt Augsburg', in Martin Broszat et al. (eds.), *Bayern in der NS-Zeit* (Munich/Vienna 1981), vol. III, pp. 200–5.

[38] On this new upsurge in pro-Soviet militancy amongst the Turinese communists see Vaccarino, *Gli scioperi del marzo 1943*, p. 58. The leaders of the PCI in exile hoped that the clandestine party would put on a show of strength in support of the Red Army, but it seems improbable that any messages or instructions reached Massola in January or February 1943 (see Spriano, *Storia del Partito comunista italiano*, vol. IV, p. 171). Clocchiatti, *Cammina frut*, p. 174, says that he heard a speech by Togliatti over the radio.

[39] On this see Vaccarino, *Gli scioperi del marzo 1943*, p. 8 (and the postscript he added to the same essay in his book *Problemi della Resistenza italiana*); see further Luraghi, *Il movimento operaio torinese*, pp. 38 ff. There may still be time to clarify this delicate matter from the evidence of survivors.

[40] See the prefect's telegram dated 5 March, in ACS, *UC*, 1943, 7, 6.185; Bairati, *Valletta*, p. 47. In his memoirs the chief of police states that the authorities had been warned of the strikes at least three weeks beforehand, but this should not be taken literally; nonetheless Massola maintains that the decision was taken about that far in advance, and Senise himself writes that he did not know the exact predetermined date. See Carmine Senise, *Quando ero capo della polizia* (Rome 1946), pp. 171 and 178. Probably he is enormously exaggerating the significance of a piece of propaganda containing a general incitement to strike (a copy of *Unità*, possibly for January or early February) which reached his desk and which he sent on to Mussolini. Spriano, *Storia del Partito comunista italiano*, vol. IV, p. 174, following an unpublished note by Massola, cites a telegram (undated) from Senise to the prefects, in which strikes and communist demonstrations are said to be imminent. I have still not found the original of this document, nor does Massola refer to it in his books. The question of how far in advance employers and police were informed about the strikes is of some importance. The famous story of the siren that failed to sound at 10 o'clock in the morning gives the impression of a strange combination of previous knowledge and an inability to do anything much about it.

demoralized as to hide the nature of this new challenge from themselves, each other or their superiors in Rome. This is shown by the fact that from 8 March onwards they responded to the strikes with decisive and coherent action; and they were not ashamed to admit to the Minister for the Interior that the situation in Turin had undeniably become very delicate.[41] For the first two days the fascist authorities had every reason to minimize the outburst of strikes, hoping that the matter would resolve itself; but it seems to me that we can categorically dismiss the possibility that they, and Fiat, might have vastly altered, or omitted to include, news of large-scale industrial conflicts on 5-6 March in their official reports. Deception of this kind could never have succeeded. The prefect immediately telegraphed that police units had arrested some strikers; whatever else his telegrams may have said, it was not an ordinary administrative matter. Something was happening, and rapid counter-measures were taken.

What that 'something' was I can only guess. I shall try to make my hypotheses compatible with the general picture of the situation that I have already outlined, and with the few certain facts we know about those days. Maybe they will help to stimulate discussion and research. That is the limit of the merits and their usefulness: they do not, I must repeat, claim to be 'history'.

It seems, then, that on 5 March the PCI tried to launch a wave of strikes and agitation, in which an important part was to be played by a mass demonstration in the Piazza Castello, scheduled for Monday, 8 March and publicized by a large-scale distribution of leaflets.[42] *If such an attempt did in fact take place, it failed by a hair's breadth.*

At Mirafiori, where the PCI was not represented in any great numbers,[43] a demonstration staged by a few militants merged into an

---

[41] See, e.g., the telegram from the prefect dated 14 March, reported in an appendix to Massola's *Gli scioperi del marzo 1943*, pp. 169 ff.; see further ibid., p. 89 and ACS, *UC*, 1943, 7, 6.716 and 6.723 for 11 March.

[42] On the leaflets see note 7 above. My basic hypothesis leads me to set aside two others, as distinctly implausible: (1) the simultaneous beginning of the strikes in different places (Rasetti) and the warnings received by the authorities eliminate the idea that the protests were absolutely spontaneous; (2) the communist leaders neither planned nor expected a wave of strikes such as actually took place. If they had plans, or definite hopes, they concerned the development of a protest movement which would have been more local, less prolonged and perhaps more violent.

[43] Most sources speak of about eighty paid-up members in a workforce of about 20,000, the great majority of whom were unskilled or low-grade. The nucleus of the Turin PCI was composed of highly skilled and specialized workers who were concentrated in two or three departments. It would be worth finding out if the strikes on 5-8 March generally had more success in factories with a high concentration of skilled workers. In 1945 Massola had a different explanation of why Mirafiori was difficult terrain for the PCI: numerous workers had been brought in from the surrounding countryside, they had kept in touch with their own families, and so they had enough to eat (Massola and Li Causi, *Gli scioperi 1943–1944*, p. 6).

episode of violent verbal protest against low wages. There was not enough support among the mass of workers to turn this initial demonstration, or a subsequent protest during the lunch hour, into a strike.[44] There were pretty certainly no successful strikes at Mirafiori on the Friday.[45] In the Rasetti works on the Via Salerno there was a more sustained effort at a strike, chiefly among the women workers, but it stopped as soon as the management promised to revise wages.[46] According to Massola, his comrades at the Aeronautica hesitated to strike on 5 and 6 March, and a communist at Grandi Motori confessed to him that his group had been afraid to come out on strike.[47] It seems likely that the PCI leaders had advised, and expected, walk-outs in these two establishments, and perhaps in a couple of other factories, on the Friday and Saturday, but that the communist section leaders could not do their part (which must indeed have been very difficult).[48] On 5 March the strike movement took off effectively *only* among the 800 workers at the main Rasetti factory on the Corso Cirié: well over half of them downed tools, probably at 10 o'clock in the morning, and stirred up so much trouble in the factory, and

[44] Damico, an eyewitness with communist convictions, speaks forthrightly of 'failure' (Alasia et al., *Un giorno del'43*, p. 107). Pensati's reminiscences (ibid.) are on the same lines. On the stark fact that the strike did not succeed these testimonies are in agreement with Balletti's letter and the prefect's telegram (both of 5 March), cited above. One of the outbreaks of verbal protest, which happened during the dinner hour, may have been a reaction to a notice put up by the management saying (in substance) that the '192 hours' would be paid solely to male workers with families whose houses had been damaged by bombing, after deduction of the advances already paid: see Bairati, *Valletta*, p. 97. Bairati decisively rejects the idea that such a notice could have been the real cause of a completely spontaneous strike movement. If this is true, the interpretation by Gobbi (*Operai e Resistenza*, pp. 20 ff.) is doubly erroneous in that the notice did not provoke a strike, and the strike did not take place anyway. The protests were certainly vigorous enough to induce the police to make an arrest, but a real strike at Mirafiori on 5 March would surely have left some traces in the archives.

[45] Bairati's detailed description of Valletta's wage policy during this period makes no mention of the concessions given on 5 March; he offered an advance to workers distinguished by their good conduct on 15 March, when the piece in *Unità* had already been written (*Valletta*, pp. 96 ff.). If the management at Mirafiori had really given way on 5 March (as claimed in *Unità*), it would be difficult to explain the series of major strikes which actually took place in that establishment from 11 to 13 March (see ACS, MI, *UC*, 1943, 7, 6.715, 6.830, 6.838, 6.894, 6.962, and Massola, *Gli scioperi del'43*, pp. 88 ff.). This is another good reason to think that Fiat did not suddenly yield to the strikers' demands, but the argument is not absolutely conclusive, because in a couple of other factories strikes broke out after the employers had given way (see the prefect's observations on Lancia, in ibid., p. 89).

[46] See Balletti's letter on 5 March in the transcript at the Istituto Gramsci. The prefect said nothing of the matter in his telegram of the same day.

[47] Massola, *Gli scioperi del'43*, pp. 69, 74.

[48] It seems that the party could realistically have hoped to arouse strike action only in half a dozen factories: they did not have the numbers to aim higher. In his 1973 book (*Gli scioperi del'43*, p. 60), Massola describes his aspirations on the eve of the strikes in exactly these terms: a few strikes in the big firms which, he hoped, would have a strong exemplary and propagandistic effect throughout the city.

for so long, that the management called in the police. Ten strikers were arrested.[49]

It was not a promising beginning, and on the next day, Saturday, 6 March, the impetus was kept up only thanks to a single group of workers, the skilled operatives at Microtecnica. The two accounts we have of this strike are mutually contradictory, but in any case the clash was certainly serious enough to bring in the police, who made at least five arrests.[50]

At first sight the successive developments from Saturday to Monday seem pretty clear, if not entirely obvious. The tidings of what had happened at Rasetti, Mirafiori and Microtecnica spread through the working-class districts of Turin, and the militants again pressed their fellow-workers to support the strikes. It is not hard to imagine all the heated discussions, full of fighting spirit but also of uncertainty, perhaps focusing more on the strikes and arrests than on the call for a public demonstration on the following Monday. The lesson of the first two days' struggle was ambiguous: on the one side, there were evidently great reservations and anxieties about going on strike in the big factories, and no wage rises had yet been conceded; on the other, the forces of law and order had not fired on the demonstrators nor made any mass arrests. And the discontent remained. Gathering together his impressions of the conflicts on the Friday, the fascist trade unionist Balletti had come to the conclusion that he was faced with an organized movement, which had got off to a rather sluggish start, but would try again at the beginning of the

[49] On the essential details of this strike Balletti, di Suni and two strikers are substantially in agreement, although the fascists almost certainly present the conflict as shorter and less intense than it really was. See Alasia et al., *Un giorno del'43*, pp. 139 ff., and Massola, *Gli scioperi del'43*, pp. 65 ff.; see also note 19 above. It should be noted that the 15 March issue of *Unità* said not a word about the first really genuine strike: the outbreak actually took place in a medium-sized factory of no notoriety.

[50] The prefect di Suni telegraphed on that day that 450 workers had extended their dinner hour by about ten minutes, demanding the '192 hours'; but something like that could hardly have justified the massive police intervention mentioned in the telegram (ACS, MI, *UC*, 1943, 7, 6.273). The charges against five of the strikers arrested were serious enough to justify bringing them before the Special Tribunal (see the charge quoted above, p. 281 and note 25). However, the evidence of Luciano Rossi on a whole day of agitation, political speeches from the strikers and dramatic moments when the troops refused to fire on the workers also appears somewhat problematic. There are three versions of it: the original account, among Garelli's typescripts (see note 22 above); the published text in Alasia et al., *Un giorno del'43*, pp. 169 ff.; and what Rossi told Massola (*Gli scioperi del'43*, p. 68). Some doubt is cast on the accuracy of Rossi's memory by his original insistence that there were no arrests at Microtecnica on 6 March; moreover, the events which he said happened in the fatory seem more characteristic of the strikes that took place a week later, outside Turin, than of the struggles of those first days. And it seems improbable that a communist would have made the incautious political speech attributed by Rossi to the strikers' spokesman on 6 March: communists did not reveal themselves in that way, and the original platform of the strikes was to do with wages. Rossi categorically maintained that he was not confusing this strike with another one. As things are, the problem remains insoluble. It should be pointed out, however, that in a testimony deposited in the Centro Studi Gobetti in 1983, Carlo Mussa Ivaldi emphasized the strength of the Giustizia e libertà group at Microtecnica over the strike period.

following week.[51] And so it proved. In spite of all the doubts and difficulties, the movement resumed. On Monday, 8 March the anger and self-confidence of the workers broke down the wall of subjection in yet more factories. It was these new and solid work-to-rule actions that turned the first stumbling initiatives into a great wave of working-class protest.[52]

That was the real beginning of the mass resistance. The vanguard in Turin had indeed succeeded, after a fashion, in clearing the road to open defiance by offering the working class a viable way of expressing their anger, an anger that was not provoked solely by their economic situation. However, if we look closely we find that many aspects of the decisive events of 8 March 1943 remain obscure.

The fact that this particular form of resistance was preferred to a violent clash is partly due to the fact that the fascist authorities did not attempt to crush the strikes inside the factories, or give orders to fire on the strikers. Rather they adopted, from the beginning, a strategy of containment which involved barricading the factory gates and – wherever the situation allowed and the management requested – going in to arrest the alleged ringleaders.[53] Groups of workers, police and soldiers sometimes confronted each other, but there were no massacres.[54] It is not clear who decided that the police, militia and army should act in this way, nor when and why such decisions were taken. The ultimate responsibility obviously rested with Mussolini himself, who blustered about shooting the strikers, scolded his subordinates for their lack of vigour, but did not give the order.[55] Regarding the police, we can reasonably believe Senise when he says that he advised against any recourse to *ultima ratio* and concentrated on maintaining public order and preventing the strikers from getting out onto the streets.[56] Among the industrialists, Valletta was probably not the

---

[51] See the transcript of his letter of 5 March, notes 15 and 18 above.

[52] See ACS, MI, *UC*, 1943, 7, 6.409 and 6.472. Massola, *Gli scioperi del'43*, pp. 69 ff., gives a precise outline of the events on these days (in my first essay on the subject, cited in note 3 above, I mistakenly alluded to fifteen strikes). It was after this first day of serious agitation in industry, at dawn on 9 March, that the forces of law and order were put on maximum alert by the chief of police. The first time that he made use of this document, Massola dated it to 6 March: thus it could appear to be the government's response to the many strikes that he and Vaccarino had assigned to 5 March. Spriano, *Storia del Partito comunista italiano*, vol. IV, p. 175, reproduces this chronological framework, which Massola subsequently corrected in his last book, *Gli scioperi del'43* (p. 75)!

[53] Many of those arrested were taken by the police from their homes.

[54] Pensati (Alasia et al., *Un giorno del'43*, p. 164) remembers a single case in which there was shooting.

[55] Cf. Deakin, *The Last Days of Mussolini*; Massola, *Gli scioperi del'43*, pp. 82 and 173 ff.; Senise, *Quando ero capo della polizia*, Chapters 30 and 31.

[56] Ibid., especially pp. 172 ff. The author clearly exaggerates the coherence and precision of the police reaction in order to enlist the sympathies of the post-war reader; contrary to what he says, groups of police did enter factories where there were strikes. We may also suspect that both at the time and when he was writing his memoirs, Senise's anti-communist feelings induced him to exaggerate the PCI's role in the strikes.

only one to urge the authorities, especially the militia, not to engage in any violent repression on factory premises.[57] We know nothing of the opinions of the commanders of the regional militia. The fascist authorities' reactions to the strikes give the impression of being improvised, rather than following a prescribed plan. The result was the formation of a small and unstable barrier to the full exercise of fascist power – or was it only a loss of nerve? In any case, it left enough political free space to allow the various parties to this altogether unprecedented conflict to 'invent', and tacitly accept, certain 'rules' and conventions for its pursuance. In the next few days the strike movement drew strength from those conventions insofar as they reduced the risks that the workers ran by striking[58] – but only as long as they confined themselves to demonstrating inside the factories and took care not to go out onto the streets. Such an outcome had not in fact been ruled out, ever since the very first attempts at a strike. Within certain confines – broad or narrow – it can be said that the margin of self-restraint exercised by the opposing sides was defined – in a sense, 'negotiated' – through the very first phases of the conflict.

These considerations are important both in gauging the intentions of the communist section leaders and in understanding the outcome of their plans on Monday, 8 March. The party leadership, or some of its members, had accomplished prodigies of propaganda so as to persuade the Turinese to demonstrate in the Piazza Castello on that day. The leaflet was specially, but not exclusively, aimed at 'women' and 'young people'. Did the PCI intend to stage a demonstration by the non-employed, parallel to and supporting the work-to-rule by the workers?[59] Or were the striking workers supposed to leave their factories and try to get to the Piazza Castello? These questions remain unanswered.[60] However, it would surely be wrong to suppose that all the thousands of workers who successfully went on strike had, in the excitement of the moment, a firm

[57] See Bairati, *Valletta*, p. 388. Pietro Bairati has kindly shown me a copy of the deposition in which Mario Dal Fiume said that he had been sent by Valletta with an urgent message to the chief of the Turin militia *not* to go into factories; Dal Fiume remembered a long and difficult argument! By about 13 March the prefect was fully aware of the risk of disastrous economic repercussions if there was any attempt to end the strikes by using force inside the factories; he suggested a lock-out, which Senise says he rejected. See Massola, *Gli scioperi del'43*, p. 172.

[58] The risks still remained considerable. Many of the arrested strikers were put into uniform and sent to the front.

[59] 8 March was International Women's Day. Groups of women had already staged a series of militant protest movements over the food situation in the Turin region. At this time I can do no more than mention these points, because I have not found the slightest documentary evidence for the intentions of this demonstration. In 1945 Massola said that there had been a demonstration by women in the Piazza Castello (Massola and Li Causi, *Gli scioperi 1943–44*, p. 7). The fact that Massola passed over the whole question in complete silence in his books distinctly suggests that it embarrassed him.

[60] In practice the question does not apply to the strikes on 5 or 6 March, because no demonstration had been announced for those days.

and disciplined idea of what precise form their protest should take. It would be equally wrong to assume that the communist section leaders were numerous and strong enough to control the movements and actions of all the strikers once the strikes were in progress. Their blood was up, and few of the strikers had a stock of experience in the struggle which they could draw on at such a critical moment. We can gather that two groups of strikers did go towards the exits from their factories, but did not go out into the streets.[61] The big demonstration never took place because, according to Vaccarino, the armed forces had arrived *en masse* to barricade the streets. But many thought that it certainly would take place – such as the Fascist Party member who, passing by two policemen who were taking strikers to prison under arrest, exclaimed cheerfully, 'All off to the Piazza Castello, eh?'[62] The chief of police was very proud of the fact that his men had maintained public order, and the prevention of demonstrations and rioting was probably his main objective at the time. How far the police, in blockading the factory gates, were deliberately trying to thwart the 8 March demonstration is another of the crucial questions to which our sources will allow no clear answer.[63] But if that was their tactical intention, it must perforce have strengthened the hand of those communists who wanted to limit the movement strictly to working-to-rule.

As it turned out, the Piazza Castello was *not* turned into a battlefield. As it turned out, the PCI was unable and unwilling to urge its followers into risking an act of 'pure suicide' – as one of Clocchiati's opponents in the party had put it during a discussion the previous winter on the feasibility of public acts of resistance.[64] But that line had not actually been laid down with absolute rigorous and organizational clarity before the beginning of the strikes.[65]

The literary form of this chapter seems more suited to a study of medieval history than an essay on 1943 – meaning that it is more notes than text. Nevertheless, such a proportion seems appropriate to the nature of the

[61] See Massola, *Gli scioperi del'43*, p. 72 (Aeronautica) and Alasia et al., *Un giorno del'43* (Ferriere). The latter evidence is not very reliable.

[62] ACS, MI, *AGR*, C2A, file 48. The man was arrested and then released after a scolding.

[63] In the far from laconic telegrams exchanged between Senise and the prefect it is not actually said that the police were *primarily* concerned to stop the workers going to the demonstration. Perhaps Senise discussed this choice of tactic with the questor in a form which has left no documentary evidence.

[64] Clocchiatti, *Cammina frut*, p. 171 (quotation marks in the original).

[65] Clocchiatti wrote that he often did things without consulting Massola. Maybe he brought out the leaflet on the demonstration in the Piazza Castello on his own initiative (*Cammina frut*, pp. 171 ff., 178). Maybe the strikes were launched as an alternative to the demonstration, which Massola wished to avoid . . . but there are already too many 'maybes' in this reconstruction.

argument and the historical problems under discussion. Not for one moment, however, would I wish to suggest that the Italian Resistance is now as remote from us as the Wars of the Roses – a theme devoid of emotive connotations that lends itself easily to the abstract procedures of academic investigation.

The events just described (though their outline is still vague and indistinct) may have been grander and more politically significant than any legend of a clear and decisive rupture occurring on that Friday, 5 March – whether the legend of a strike spreading like wildfire, or the legend of a swift and exemplary victory at Mirafiori. Instead, it appears as an action by a vanguard that was just as uncertain and divided as it was eager for the fight; which persevered in spite of initial setbacks; which found the right forms of mass resistance through a risky process of trial and error; which issued some shrewd propaganda; and which managed to win huge popular support and harvest a great political success without sacrificing a single human life.

The accepted versions, which expunge the disputes, the doubts, the false starts and the manipulations that accompanied the struggle, may well weaken the inspirational effect of the Resistance that can still be stirred today; but a painstaking study, such as a medievalist might attempt, can restore these events to their true grandeur.

The version I have just given of the March 1943 strikes still assigns a decisive role to the communist leaders in Turin through the first week of the struggle (though it sees them acting in quite a different way from that suggested by Massola). I have stressed various political interests which seem to have influenced the interpretations made by historians and memoirists. I, too, have my own political concerns: I have been strongly influenced by the marked anti-Stalinist tone of the English Labour movement (*vide* George Orwell). Therefore, my conclusions on the March strikes clash just a little with my instinctive sympathies. But, obviously not even that is enough to guarantee their correctness.

9

THE DOMESTIC DYNAMICS OF NAZI CONQUESTS. A RESPONSE TO CRITICS

THERE IS widespread agreement that the war that began in September 1939 was a disaster for Nazi Germany. This was Hitler's own view, clearly expressed at the time.[1] Contrary to the foreign policy axioms laid out in *Mein Kampf* and frequently repeated by Hitler thereafter, the Third Reich found itself at war with Britain and the British Empire. Contrary to the 'timetable' for military expansion that Hitler elaborated in November 1937, the Third Reich found itself involved in a major European war already in 1939, rather than in the years 1943–5, the period that Hitler seemed to believe would be optimal for large-scale imperial expansion. Hitler's own erratic, confused, and increasingly unrealistic conduct of policy in the ten weeks that followed the British and French declarations of war is but one proof of the extreme seriousness of the new international situation brought about by the German invasion of Poland. The Nazi–Soviet Pact was an expedient that did not make good this damage. The invasion had consequences of an irreversibly damaging nature to the interests of the Third Reich (for example, the future intervention of the USA), which Hitler's prior calculations had ruled out as to be avoided at all costs.

What went wrong? I think it is important to put the question in this way because it is quite conceivable that Nazi domination of Europe and of adjacent subcontinents could easily have been wider, longer and even more destructive than it actually was. The Third Reich's opportunities to consolidate and extend its regime of racial imperialism in the late 1930s were very great; these opportunities were put at extreme risk, and soon (December 1941) destroyed, by the war that Hitler had wanted in 1938, and actually began in September 1939. Why did Hitler force the pace in this way, disregard his own 'timetable', undermine his own continental

---

[1] See Joachim C. Fest, *Hitler. Eine Biographie* (Frankfurt am Main/Vienna 1973), p. 827, n. 295.

and world strategy with respect to the British Empire? Since my argument is much concerned with the timing of events and decisions, it is important to note that he was already willing to take this huge risk in September 1938, and would clearly have preferred a war to the Munich settlement.[2]

In the 1970s I put forward, in various forms, the hypothesis that the accelerating dynamic of Nazi aggression in 1938 and 1939 was strongly conditioned by the *internal* problems of the regime, problems that progressively narrowed the margins for foreign policy choices and made it increasingly difficult for the regime to wait for the right moment to launch its wars of conquest.[3] These internal problems appeared as consequences of forced rearmament after 1936 – of a rearmament drive that required resources far in excess of those available in Germany, given the way in which the regime distributed economic resources. (By 1939 the rearmament targets were far in excess of any conceivable available supplies, but that is a slightly different argument.) I concentrated special attention on the labour market and the working class. By the end of 1938 the overheating of the economy had led to a situation in which there were 1 million unfilled jobs. This had a wide variety of consequences: new workplace wage-bargaining; clear signs of a decline in work-discipline and industrial productivity; a growing drift of workers away from poorly paid into better-paid jobs; and a degree of wage inflation that led to an increased demand for consumer goods. All of these developments impeded the progress of rearmament – just *how* seriously they impeded rearmament is one of the questions under discussion. I originally maintained that these developments did considerable quantitative damage to the rearmament programmes of the later 1930s.[4] I still believe this to be true, although Michael Geyer has pointed to other, different constraints during 1937.[5]

---

[2] The evidence is well summarized by Fest, *Hitler*, pp. 763 ff. and 776.

[3] See my *Arbeiterklasse und Volksgemeinschaft. Dokumente und Materialien zur deutschen Arbeiterpolitik 1936–1939* (Opladen 1975), esp. chapters 13–21; 'Internal Crisis and War of Aggression, 1938–1939', pp. 104–30 above; *Sozialpolitik im Dritten Reich. Arbeiterklasse und Volksgemeinschaft* (Opladen 1977), esp. Chapter 6; 'The Workers' Opposition in Nazi Germany', *History Workshop Journal*, no. 11 (spring 1981), pp. 120–37. The following paragraphs draw in a highly condensed manner on this work.

[4] Without giving evidence or arguments, Ludolf Herbst denies that the developments did quantitative damage: 'Die Krise des nationalsozialistischen Regimes am Vorabend des Zweiten Weltkrieges und die forcierte Aufrüstung', *Vierteljahrshefte für Zeitgeschichte*, vol. 26, no. 3 (1978), p. 390. It is not possible to give precise numerical values to the phenomena under discussion, but those in positions of economic and administrative authority clearly had the impression that the damage done was considerable. They may have been exaggerating a little – see below.

[5] See Michael Geyer, 'Rüstungsbeschleunigung und Inflation. Zur Inflationsdenkschrift des Oberkommandos der Wehrmacht vom November 1938', *Militärgeschichtliche Mitteilungen*, no. 2 (1981), p. 135, n. 105. Geyer points out that during 1937 German heavy industry was limiting output to optimum levels in terms of plant economics and was giving priority to the temporarily flourishing export market.

The Nazi regime responded to these new threats and difficulties in a very distinctive way. It *did* enact counter-measures to control wages and to direct labour, but these measures came a good deal later and were applied with less rigour than was considered necessary by many employers and most experts with practical responsibilities in these areas. The regime used much less dictatorial power than it seemed to have at its command. The main reasons for this tentativeness and uncertainty lay clearly in political fears of a hostile, possibly mass, collective reaction on the part of the working class. Much impressed by the strike movements and by the alleged collapse of the home front at the end of the First World War, the Nazi leaders felt it necessary to purchase at least the passive acquiescence of the much-abused German working class. It was for this reason, I argued, that the labour regimentation of mid-1938 was so late and incomplete, for this reason that there were very few increases in basic tax-rates and food-prices, and so on. The main new burden imposed on German workers was a lengthening of the working week, which resulted in substantial increases in weekly earnings (overtime bonuses). But at the same time, in June 1938 and then again in the winter of 1938–9, the regime vastly expanded its armament programmes, thus making much more acute all of the contradictions inherent in the situation. These were real contradictions, not just technical problems that could be resolved by more sophisticated organizational and administrative interventions (although there were some of these too). In their essence they raised a fundamental problem of the dichotomy between *means* (the regimentation of people and resources) and *ends* (further rearmament), and thus tended to develop into a deep crisis of the power and legitimacy of the whole regime.

The labour market and relations between the regime and the working class were not the only spheres in which signs of acute economic overstrain appeared during 1938 and 1939. Budgetary problems and the threat of inflation became drastic at the end of 1938. Foreign trade and agriculture also came under heavy pressure, the first as a result of the worldwide recession of late 1937, which restricted Germany's capacity to export (and thus to import vital raw materials), the second, agriculture, as a result of a massive labour shortage and of strict price controls on foodstuffs. In both these sectors too, the government did not intervene in a consistent and rigorous manner in order to allocate resources to the armaments industries and to farmers. In both cases such interventions would have meant heavy sacrifices for the mass of the urban consumers. It is vital to observe that all of these four acute new social and economic problems came to a head at the same time – during 1938. They posed a major new set of simultaneous challenges to a regime that, in political, economic, and administrative terms, was not well prepared to meet them.

As far as we can tell (the sources are not very good, given the verbal conduct of government affairs), Hitler was quite well informed of these new and deepening problems – informed above all by Göring, also by the military leaders, and by the head of the Reich Chancellery to whom many reports on the shortages and economic conflicts were addressed. Hitler's advisers did not speak with one voice. Some suggested slowing down the pace of rearmament and of the rush towards war (Schacht, Darré, and sometimes Göring), others favoured forcing through tougher domestic policies (Price Commissar Wagner), and some proposed both of these things at the same time (General Thomas, Göring). Hitler, it seems to me – and this is the crux of my case – stood all of these arguments on their head: to judge from admittedly few recorded statements, he concluded that if the economic and internal political situation really was so strained, this was *in fact* a strong reason for launching military aggression *sooner rather than later*. He began to speak in this sense in November 1937, and half a dozen of his official and informal policy statements between then and November 1939 contain clear allusions to this logic of risking war on account of domestic/economic weakness. There is no space to reproduce all of these statements here.[6] What is striking is their correspondence to the actual situation inside Germany. This reading of Hitler's reasoning fits in with the generally accepted picture of him as a politician for whom defiance and risk-taking were ultimate virtues. The documentation is neither ample nor unequivocal, but Hitler seems to have believed that military conquest would enable the regime to break the chains of immediate domestic bottlenecks and conflicts, and would result in plunder, that is, in the forcible short-term acquisition of resources and manpower that were either not available in Germany, or could be redistributed in favour of the armaments sector only at the risk of great unpopularity for the regime.[7] There is a vital difference between this kind of short-term logic and the long-term goal of *Lebensraum*, to which Hitler was clearly committed.

There was in Hitler's mind a second connection between the urgency of war and the state of domestic affairs, a connection that I did not emphasize enough in my original work: he was constantly worried by the fear that if the period of peace and relative prosperity of the late 1930s were to continue for too long, the German people would lose what he imagined to be their sense of aggressive discipline, militarism and ideological fervour. People could easily forget, he feared, what the true heroic goals of Nazism were and how many sacrifices they entailed.[8]

---

[6] I have laid out the evidence in Mason, *Sozialpolitik im Dritten Reich*, pp. 307 ff. See also Ludolf Herbst, *Der Totale Krieg und die Ordnung der Wirtschaft* (Stuttgart 1982), p. 72.

[7] For early evidence of Hitler's enthusiasm for plunder, see his reaction to the occupation of Prague in March 1939; Mason, *Sozialpolitik im Dritten Reich*, pp. 308 f.

[8] Fest rightly gives emphasis to this point; see Fest, *Hitler*, pp. 738 ff., 831 f., 840, and 924 f. Andreas Hillgruber also quotes two striking examples of Hitler's worries on this account:

Ministers, generals, and senior civil servants gave concrete meaning to this piece of Hitlerian logic in that they saw the beginning of war as the crucial opportunity to put the whole economy in order: to cut wages, lengthen working hours, raise taxes, ration foodstuffs and consumer goods, move workers from one factory or city to another by administrative decree, intensify police terror, and so on. In short, they hoped that the emergency of war would make acceptable to the German people a mass of repressive legislation that had long been necessary anyway; that it would restore discipline, sacrifice, and the Nazi sense of communal struggle – for which Hitler yearned but which he feared to impose – to the everyday conduct of economic life. And, in fact, a large number of decrees of this kind were issued in September 1939. Short of total mobilization, the government made a major effort to use the start of the war in this way.[9]

Thus far, in very rough summary, my argument: in 1938–9 either peace alone or war alone could stabilize (or temporarily save) the politico-economic system. Indefinite further forced rearmament within Germany's existing boundaries was not a practical policy option. And war entailed a wild gamble concerning the response of Britain and France. I want to stress that it is a domestic, social and economic argument about the timing, and thus about the international constellation, of the start of the Second World War that leaves Hitler at the centre of the stage, personally taking the crucial initiatives and decisions. In this sense it differs a lot from orthodox marxist–leninist interpretations, which attach great weight to the economic imperialism of Germany's big financial and industrial combines.[10] In my view it was, rather, the perceived possible breakdown of the whole system of Nazified, militarized capitalism that precipitated events.

Hitlers Strategie. Politik und Kriegführung, 1940–1941 (Frankfurt am Main 1965), pp. 219 and 365.

[9] It has been interestingly argued that there was a close link between Nazi racial thought and Nazi social policies, on the grounds that the quality of the German 'racial stock' depended on a decent level of civilian prosperity, good nutrition, good working conditions, etc. Ludolf Herbst first put forward this interpretation in 'Die Mobilmachung der Wirtschaft 1938/39 als Problem des nationalsozialistischen Herrschaftssystems', in Wolfgang Benz and Hermann Graml (eds.). *Sommer 1939. Die Grossmächte und der europäische Krieg* (Stuttgart 1979), p. 82; see now Herbst, *Der Totale Krieg*, pp. 71, 89, 150 and 163. On the basis of the evidence of the above paragraph, this looks like a typical piece of propaganda or wishful thinking as far as the top leadership was concerned, with the exception of measures that directly affected the birth-rate (marriage loans, child allowances, etc.). The housing conditions of the working class, a key factor in 'racial progress', were badly neglected by the regime throughout. There is certainly no evidence that the regime deliberately tolerated increased living standards in the late 1930s out of eugenic considerations.

[10] I cannot accept this part of the careful critique of my work by Lotte Zumpe, 'Ein Beitrag zur Wirtschafts- und Sozialgeschichte des deutschen Faschismus', *Jahrbuch für Wirtschaftsgeschichte*, Part IV (1979).

Most other historians working in this field have more or less rejected my hypotheses.[11] Direct or, more usually, indirect support for the line of enquiry that I have pursued has come from the research and interpretations of Hans-Erich Volkmann,[12] David E. Kaiser,[13] and Michael Geyer.[14] One part of my argument revolves around the connections that existed between what was going on in German society and what was going on in Hitler's mind, and the importance of these connections for the acceleration of Nazi foreign policy towards war. Most historians, obviously, have focused on Hitler's intentions and calculations, and have argued that not labour shortages, economic bottlenecks, and the risks of mass discontent, but quite other things, were at the forefront of his mind in these years. Three such interpretations call for brief discussion at this point.

I do not want to consider here the school of historiography that sees Hitler as immersed in the relationship between the week-by-week tactics of diplomacy and his final goals, and that thus tends to suggest that the 'wrong' war of September 1939 was in some sense the outcome of a series of diplomatic errors; I simply do not believe that the foreign policy of the major powers, least of all that of Nazi Germany, was 'foreign' policy in this narrow meaning of the term. Much more persuasive is the fundamental foreign policy argument that Hitler *never* understood Britain and the British Empire, that his idea of some kind of a division of world power between a Germanized continent of Europe and a sea-based British Empire grew out of a total misconception of British interests, and that the British government (even that of Chamberlain) was bound to become involved in war with Nazi Germany as soon as that power entered on wars of aggression. This line of argument emphasizes not the faulty application in the 1930s of the strategy that Hitler had elaborated so clearly in *Mein Kampf*, but

[11] For a clear summary with a full bibliography of the first stages of the discussion see Andreas Hillgruber, 'Forschungsstand und Literatur zum Ausbruch des Zweiten Weltkrieges', in Benz and Graml, (eds.), *Sommer 1939*, pp. 340 ff. For some of the later negative judgements (I am sure that this list is not complete), see Alan S. Milward, *War, Economy and Society, 1939–1945* (London 1977), p. 14; Ian Kershaw, *The Nazi Dictatorship. Problems and Perspectives of Interpretation* (London 1985), pp. 78 ff. (with many useful references); and, above all, Herbst, 'Die Krise des nationalsozialistischen Regimes'. Since I believe that Richard Overy's critique, 'Germany, "Domestic Crisis" and War in 1939', *Past and Present*, no. 116 (August 1987), pp. 138–68, rests on a fundamental misunderstanding of what constitutes evidence for the existence of a crisis, I shall make few references to his original arguments. I have replied separately to Overy in *Past and Present*, no. 122 (February 1989), pp. 205–21.

[12] Erich Volkmann, 'Die N-S Wirtschaft in Vorbereitung des Krieges', in Wilhelm Deist, Manfred Messerschmidt, Hans-Erich Volkmann and Wolfram Wette (eds.), *Das Deutsche Reich und der Zweite Weltkrieg*, vol. I, (Stuttgart 1979), esp. pp. 327 ff. and 364 ff.

[13] David E. Kaiser, *Economic Diplomacy and the Origins of the Second World War* (Princeton, NJ 1980), esp. pp. 268 and 282. See also his Comment on Overy's work in *Past and Present*, no. 122 (February 1989).

[14] Geyer, 'Rüstungsbeschleunigung und Inflation'.

the fact that that strategy was itself founded upon a deep misunderstanding of the basic British need for some kind of balance of power on the continent of Europe. This did not rule out the semi-peaceful revision of some of Germany's frontiers, but it did rule out expansionist wars.

This case, that Hitler fundamentally misconceived British interests, seems to be a strong one. What remains difficult to explain, however, is his failure to read the increasingly clear signs from March 1939 on (at the latest) that he was in fact heading for an immediate war with Britain and the British Empire. The British Parliament ratified the military guarantee to Poland immediately after the signing of the Nazi–Soviet Pact. For reasons that remain open to further discussion, Hitler was quite unable to recognize and to adjust to very clear evidence of the collapse of one of the central axioms of his foreign policy. This blindness and inflexibility in the summer of 1939 are hard to account for. It is difficult to accept that he simply did not believe that the Chamberlain government would go to war – at least, any such belief on his part requires a lot of explanation, given all of the evidence to the contrary that was so easily available. There are some hints in the documentation that a concern with domestic and economic problems played a role in producing this inflexibility.

Two further alternative interpretations of 'what was on Hitler's mind' in 1938–9 both stress his sense that the factor of *time* was turning against him. For his biographer Fest, this had the quality of an existential change in Hitler: the collapse within him of the controlled calculating politician, capable of waiting for the right opportunity, and a regression to the impatient, millennarian, and above all violent mob leader of before 1923. The description is sensitive and convincing, but Fest gives no reasons why this change should have occurred in 1938, not earlier, not later.[15] Dülffer at least offers a reason: Hitler, he argues, was increasingly concerned that Nazi Germany was losing its lead in the international arms race, losing its advantage especially from late 1938 on to Britain and the Soviet Union (and he was already casting an eye towards the USA).[16] This trend, it follows, strongly induced Hitler to take great military and diplomatic risks in 1939, to launch a war of conquest before it was too late. (This argument, it should be noted, has less purchase for 1938, when Hitler was already set on war.) That Hitler was preoccupied by the problem of the arms race is beyond doubt, but it brings us back to the question that I posed at the outset: why was Nazi Germany unable to accelerate further the pace of its own rearmament in 1938 and 1939? This had to do, in part, I would insist, with the regime's inability to allocate its

---

[15] See Fest, *Hitler*, pp. 788 and 832–42.
[16] Jost Dülffer, 'Der Beginn des Krieges 1939. Hitler, die innere Krise und das Mächtesystem', *Geschichte und Gesellschaft*, vol. 2, no. 4 (1976), esp. pp. 461 ff.

resources consistently and effectively in favour of the armaments sector of the economy, with its efforts to produce both guns and butter, with its need to produce the biggest army in the world *and* to placate its working population with high real wages. These goals had become incompatible by 1938–9.[17] In my view, Nazi Germany needed war and conquest *in order* to go on rearming at a high rate; the evolution of the international arms race and the changing balance of power cannot possibly be dissociated from the basic conditions of production inside Germany. Thus Dülffer's point adds an important dimension to my interpretation, but does not contradict it.

A different criticism calls for extended consideration: that is that my documentary sources, and the way in which I have used them, tend to exaggerate the acuteness of the social and economic crisis in 1938–9. It has been said that I take the documents that describe the details and symptoms of this crisis too much at face value, and that the real situation on the domestic front was less tense, less fragile than I have portrayed it to be.[18] This is not one single criticism, but an argument that contains a series of different points that must be discussed in sequence.

The first such point is perhaps the easiest to identify and the most difficult to assess. It was always obvious that some employers and some procurement agencies deliberately overstated their needs for resources, in the hope that, by 'making concessions', they would finally end up with roughly the amounts of raw materials and workers that they could actually use. This was a transparent technique in the struggles over shortages, and the decision-making bodies frequently recognized it as such, but the real problems of urgent bottlenecks remained, and indeed grew, even when these inflated demands had been discounted. Less easy to judge is the possibility that those officials in the economic, labour and military administrations who advocated more austere policies *may* have used their regular reports to the government in order to draw an especially black picture of the situation, which was one way to get the government to change policies. Similarly, special reports, like Darré's long letters to Hitler, may have given a particularly dramatic picture of those sectors of agriculture in which the loss of labour and the decline of production were most severe.[19] The authors of official memoranda without doubt used selective emphasis as a regular technique of

---

[17] Dülffer, ibid., p. 469, allows that they would have become incompatible in time, but his own full evidence of the massive state civilian and military projects of 1938–9 suggests that that time would come sooner rather than later.

[18] See Herbst, 'Die Krise des nationalsozialistischen Regimes', pp. 351 f. Without taking account of the contrary evidence, Overy, 'Germany, "Domestic Crisis" and War', asserts that there were no serious problems, just 'frictions' – see esp. p. 148.

[19] For Darré's closely argued demarches, which Hitler refused to discuss, see Bundesarchiv Koblenz, R43II, vol. 213b.

representing interests and of trying to influence policy-making – this is a basic fact of life in bureaucratic infighting. It is very hard to say, however, by how much, quantitatively speaking, the reports really did exaggerate. Industrialists probably tended to exaggerate most of all, but my general impression is that the sources did not overstate the problems by a great deal, and this for three reasons. First, the German civil service and the army had strong traditions of factual accuracy in their paperwork. Second, by 1938 there were a large number of different agencies, some of them purely Nazi, making reports on the same problems and in some degree in competition with each other – serious distortions by one agency could easily be identified by another.[20] If, lastly, there is no way that this issue can be resolved in general terms and in a final manner, the actual breakdown of the accelerated armaments drive of June–October 1938 strongly suggests that pessimistic reports were accurate. Michael Geyer's highly technical investigation of this episode shows in detail the shambles that ensued when constraints on armaments production were lifted at the end of May 1938. Within five months there were insuperable shortages of iron, steel, non-ferrous metals, building materials, workers and cash for the new running programmes of the armed forces. Major cutbacks were then ordered and implemented with Hitler's assent.[21] This is the evidence of real events, not of routine or special reports.

More subtle, and occasionally more telling, is the argument that the reports on the developing crisis were influenced by the ideologies, by the conservative prejudices and fears of their authors; that army officers, civil servants, and industrialists were naturally inclined always to blame the working class for economic problems, and too often to go in fear of its possible subversive action. For this reason, it has been said, they actually misunderstood some of the realities that they observed. While this was not always the case (officials of the Ministry of Labour and of the War Economy Staff showed some verbal sympathy for the growing exhaustion of the industrial workers), two of my critics have pointed to a good example of such a distortion. I gave some prominence to reports, among others, to one from the managing director of a large mining firm, that the per capita productivity of coal miners was falling considerably in the later 1930s. This was attributed at the time simply to diminishing effort, to a decline in working morale, absenteeism, the 'human factor'; and I accepted this upper-class interpretation of working-class behaviour. It was at least partly wrong. One main cause of the fall in output in the mines was the failure of employers to recruit young miners and the growing

---

[20] There are examples of this happening in the excellent article by Klaus Wisotzky, 'Der Ruhrbergbau am Vorabend des Zweiten Weltkriegs', *Vierteljahrshefte für Zeitgeschichte*, vol. 30, no. 3 (1982), pp. 423 ff.   [21] Geyer, 'Rüstungsbeschleunigung und Inflation'.

dependence of the industry on older workers who were objectively less capable of great physical exertion.[22]

The fears, repeatedly expressed by conservatives and Nazis, that there might be another 1917–18, another mass movement against exploitation and war, were, clearly, fixated memories and ideological distortions that were not appropriate to the new situation of the late 1930s.[23] The memories and invocations were certainly dramatic and persistent.[24] While I never thought that they were appropriate in a literal sense to the years after 1938, the issue certainly calls for much more careful analysis than I actually gave it. There was obviously a great deal of discontent and economic ambition among the working population, but the leaders of the class had been killed, imprisoned, or exiled, its organizations smashed. Thus the real danger was not that of mass protest movements or open revolts, but rather, as I originally suggested and as Herbst argues systematically, that of the steady disaggregation, disintegration, of the social order and of the fascist disciplines on which it rested: obedience, sacrifice, the work ethic, intense labour on behalf of a Greater Germany.[25] The real danger was that markets and plans would fall apart under the pressures of economic overstrain, labour shortages and the manifold non-cooperation of the working population. Thus it can be argued that, insofar as they fixed their minds on the open class conflicts of 1917–18, the Nazi elite misrepresented to themselves the problems that they actually faced twenty years later. This is no doubt a helpful addition to and revision of my argument, one that gives greater precision to an important issue. The fact remains, however, that the *outcomes* – in terms of tentative social and economic policies and inadequate rearmament – remained the same, *whatever* the reasons or motivations may have been.

But from this point of criticism there follows a further one. If it is true that the real danger facing the regime was that of a disintegration of the social and economic order, then it must be asked: what was the position of other social groups and classes? Is it correct to define the problem as above all one of the conflictual relationship between the regime and the

---

[22] Wisotzky, 'Der Ruhrbergbau', pp. 427 ff., discusses this problem in a differentiated way. Wolfgang Franz Werner, *'Bleib übrig!' Deutsche Arbeiter in der nationalsozialistischen Kriegswirtschaft* (Düsseldorf 1983), makes the point more bluntly, and polemically attributes the official figures to me, pp. 25 f.

[23] Werner, *'Bleib übrig!'*, pp. 12 and 31.

[24] The theme runs like a red thread through Fest's biography of Hitler. See the cathartic conclusion of Hitler's Sportpalast speech of September 1938, p. 766; also esp. pp. 849 and 924.

[25] Mason, *Sozialpolitik im Dritten Reich*, pp. 312–16; Herbst, 'Die Krise des nationalsozialistischen Regimes', pp. 365 f., 373, and 376, makes this point in a particularly convincing manner. He sees 'disintegration' as a possible prelude to open conflict within Germany, and seems to argue that only the latter would have constituted evidence of a real crisis.

working class?[26] Much research remains to be done on these questions, but it seems fairly clear that many sections of the middle class were also *not* called on to make heavy sacrifices in the interests of the rearmament drive of the late 1930s. Industrial salaries in the private sector (not in the civil service) probably rose faster than wages at this time,[27] and there was a boom in middle-class consumption. On the fate of small entrepreneurs both before and after the beginning of the war the evaluations of the experts seem to diverge somewhat, but the government's attempts to close down small and inefficient workshops and factories in order to release capacities and workers for the big armaments firms were something less than draconian.[28] The upper middle class's most important item of conspicuous consumption, petrol, remained unrationed before the war, although all the armed services suffered from continuing and serious shortages of fuel. And well-to-do young women found it notoriously easy to get around a decree that required them to perform a 'year of duty' in agriculture or in domestic service before entering regular employment or study.[29] It is true that income taxes for the middle classes were raised twice in 1939, and that the corporation tax was steadily increased; and it is true that Germany's farmers were squeezed very hard during 1938 and 1939. But overall it *cannot* be said that the regime paid a special regard to the economic interests of the working class, trying to bribe it alone into passive acquiescence to the drive towards war. Rather, there was a flourishing civilian economy at all levels of society, which put limits to the expansion of rearmament in a whole variety of different ways. In this account the working class was a special case in an overall strategy of political pacification through the means of relative economic well-being. It was a special case because industrial wage-earners were so numerous, because they were in such desperately short supply, and because only they were well placed to take collective disruptive action, but the problem was indeed a general one that encompassed the whole society in its relations with the regime. I accept the need to redescribe the domestic situation in Germany in these terms. But it must be noted that to do so involves listing additional types of intervention (against middle-class

---

[26] See Herbst, 'Die Krise des nationalsozialistischen Regimes', p. 373.

[27] See Michael Prinz, *Vom neuen Mittelstand zum Volksgenossen* (Munich 1986), pp. 165 ff.; Geyer, 'Rüstungsbeschleunigung und Inflation', pp. 157 and 183 n. 204; Werner, '*Bleib übrig!*', pp. 98 and 108.

[28] Two contributors to Benz and Graml (eds.), *Sommer 1939*, seem to differ a little in their assessments: Fritz Blaich, p. 41, and Ludolf Herbst, pp. 96 ff. See also Herbst, *Der Totale Krieg*, pp. 120 f., who points out that the trade sector got off more lightly than small producers (*Handwerk*). Heinrich August Winkler, 'Der entbehrliche Stand. Zur Mittelstandspolitik im "Dritten Reich"', *Archiv für Sozialgeschichte*, vol. 17 (1977), pp. 32 ff., argues that *Handwerk* was indeed being pushed to the wall. On the early war measures, see Werner, '*Bleib übrig!*', pp. 61 f. and 82 ff.

[29] Dörte Winkler, *Frauenarbeit im 'Dritten Reich'* (Hamburg 1977), pp. 57 ff.

interests) that the regime did *not* make in favour of the armaments sector of the economy. In altering it, the point actually broadens my argument, does not negate it.

Building on this observation that the problems of administering the Nazi economy were in fact diffuse and heterogeneous, Ludolf Herbst went on to challenge in a fundamental way my proposition that Nazi Germany was indeed 'in crisis' in 1938–9. Other historians have cast doubt on the appropriateness of the word 'crisis' in general terms, but Herbst threw the whole apparatus of systems theory at the question, demanding that the concept of crisis have a precise, theoretically and empirically verifiable definition. He concluded that the position in Germany did not conform to any such definition, and that my whole argument was thus mistaken. The demand for precise definitions obviously gives rise to a worthwhile, although complex, discussion. I want to confine myself here to four of the component arguments.

First, Herbst insists that the economy was just one of the 'sub-systems' of the whole system of power, and that it is necessary to examine all the other sub-systems in order to assess the extent of crisis. This point can be granted, but I wish to argue for the overriding importance of the economic sub-system. A regime that was about to send its armed forces into war had to be able to equip them properly, and the Nazi regime was not in this position. (See the remarks below on the conflict over strategy in November 1939.) Furthermore, the economy was the arena in which most Germans came into most constant and continuous contact with the demands of the government in these years. But Herbst has in fact very little to say either about the real economy or about economic policy at this time. He denies that the relevant problems were basically social and economic in origin, and he evades the vital question of whether the regime was unable to rearm, or rather chose not to rearm, more intensively.[30] The central fact in my analysis is the *reality* of the massive labour shortage, and of its economic, social and political consequences. Herbst's approach reduces this, and all the other realities of extreme tensions in the economy, to very general problems of social justice and, above all, of politico-economic management (*Steuerung*).[31] Management, however, must be measured against actual problems, as Geyer, Kaiser, and I have tried to do. Geyer leaves no doubt that the real economy was in immediate crisis late in 1938. Based on a detailed analysis of the precipitous developments in industry and finance after the allocations to the armed forces were suddenly doubled in June 1938, he concludes that there arose an 'economic, armaments, and financial chaos'. This took the form of chronic shortages of all the factors of production and of rises in

[30] Herbst, 'Die Krise des nationalsozialistischen Regimes', pp. 365 and 388.
[31] Ibid., pp. 375 and 365 ff.

unit costs, as the armed forces competed with each other for non-existent capacities; this then led to a sudden policy reversal in November, one that gave priority once more to exports and cut the armed forces' demands for steel for 1939 by half. The Reich Treasury was temporarily empty; existing contracts were left hanging in the air.[32] Geyer is unambiguous that in May 1938 'the leadership of the Third Reich quite consciously risked a crisis': 'the precarious armaments boom was transformed into an open economic and financial crisis', and there were no administrative solutions to 'the short-term and deliberate overburdening of German industry'.[33] This was especially acute in the building sector; new munitions and armaments plants remained on the drawing board, and for 1939 the armed forces demanded more building capacity than existed in the whole German economy.[34] Geyer concludes his detailed enquiry thus: 'It was a reproduction crisis [of the economic system] under the conditions of Nazi rule . . . [The] state was not capable of achieving the rearmament of the nation . . . while at the same time guaranteeing private capital formation.'[35] This is in economic and military terms a more comprehensive analysis of the same real developments and actual policy decisions that I have tried to document for the labour market and for class relations. Geyer's repeated and precisely documented use of the term 'crisis' is notable. On Herbst's own chosen ground of systems analysis the term does not seem inappropriate for this 'sub-system' of the Third Reich in the period under discussion.

Second, Herbst strongly advances the view that the regime in 1939 still had unused reserves of power, unused capacities to steer developments and manage problems, and power to intervene with particular new measures or programmes in order to alleviate the most pressing difficulties and to stabilize the system. This was true of budgetary policies and credit creation, a point of actual crisis late in 1938.[36] But in the field of armaments the position in 1939 was characterized by a combination of restraints that were dangerous to the actual military (big delays in programmes, no stockpiling), and the launching of new mythomaniac programmes for the air force and the navy that could only accentuate the basic problems. This creation of new contradictions does not look like successful *Steuerung* through the successful deployment of unused reserves of power.

Arthur Schweitzer has argued that the government did succeed in reimposing some rudiments of administrative order in parts of the

---

[32] Geyer, 'Rüstungsbeschleunigung und Inflation', pp. 129 f. and 143 f.
[33] Ibid., pp. 136, 143 and 146.   [34] Ibid., p. 179.   [35] Ibid., p. 146.
[36] See Fritz Federau, *Der Zweite Weltkrieg. Seine Finanzierung in Deutschland* (Tübingen 1962). Richard J. Overy has recently added some important points on this question: '"Blitzkriegswirtschaft?" Finanz, Lebensstandard und Arbeitseinsatz in Deutschland 1939–1945', *Vierteljahrshefte für Zeitgeschichte*, vol. 36, no. 3 (1988), esp. pp. 391 ff.

economy during the first half of 1939.[37] Administrative order was an important source of power for the system, as the redeployment of manpower on the occasion of mobilization was to show in September 1939.[38] But the state of the real economy mattered more. Although in this respect a detailed analysis of the months prior to Hitler's decision to invade Poland has still to be done, there is no doubt that the yawning gap between strategic needs and mobilizable resources became greater as Germany's international position worsened. To say this is *not* to underestimate the regime's actual achievements in rearmament, but rather to point to the high degree of economic and political instability that this effort generated. Hans-Erich Volkmann's overall picture of 1939 is one of an economy and of the key economic agencies working in highly straitened circumstances; aside from public finance, the one new measure of stabilizing management that could be deployed was the important increase in trade with the Soviet Union.[39]

With respect to social and labour policies the actual events that took place on the outbreak of war *in no way* bear out the view that the regime possessed unused reserves of power (see below). Finally, any attempt to assess the Nazi regime's latent capacities to draw on new powers every time the crisis worsened must come to terms with Göring's exasperated comment in July 1938: the 'Führer wants to take as few decisions as possible'.[40] Hitler, the ultimate source of managerial power, was notoriously indecisive in social and economic matters; he usually preferred the soft, less unpopular options, while at the same time demanding more and more weapons. On this central issue, Hitler contradicted himself all the time, leaving his immediate subordinates in confusion. This was a very important element of 'system destabilization'. The argument, like many in systems theory, must to some degree remain hypothetical, but, contrary to Herbst, I would maintain that the regime had come very near to exhausting its capacities for self-stabilizing interventions, short of war, given the extreme pace of war preparations. It seems to me more likely that the system needed war in order to create new sources of power for itself.

A third point concerning the definition of 'crisis' perhaps carries more weight. Is open confrontation an essential component of a true crisis? Herbst seems to insist that the real lines of potential confrontation in Germany on the eve of war were in fact not very clear-cut, that class

---

[37] See his 'Plans and Markets: Nazi Style', *Kyklos: International Review for Social Sciences*, vol. 30 (1977), pp. 88–115.

[38] I agree with Herbst ('Die Krise des nationalsozialistischen Regimes', p. 369), that the civil service played a very important role in holding the Third Reich together at this juncture.

[39] See Volkmann, 'Die NS-Wirtschaft in Vorbereitung des Krieges'.

[40] See Mason, 'Internal Crisis and War of Aggression, 1938–1939', p. 117 above.

conflict was too muffled to justify use of the term.[41] As examples of the blurring of these lines there can be quoted many cases of employers who gave in to wage pressure from below, improved fringe benefits and the like, and passed on the costs to the consumer who was usually, directly or indirectly, the state; also cases of employers who engaged in open acts of piracy in the labour market, taking over workers from their competitors with offers of higher pay and better working conditions. In such ways industrial conflict was temporarily forestalled. To this evidence of sporadic collusion between the two classes in industry, Herbst adds the correct observation that parts of the Nazi mass organizations (of the party and the German Labour Front (DAF)) were not all all happy about rigorous policies of reallocating resources from the civilian to the military sectors of the economy and imposing heavy sacrifices on the working population. The latter were thus faced with employers, some of whom might from time to time appear as allies on specific matters, and with a political regime of which different sections spoke with different voices.

Where was the real enemy? This degree of muddle and confusion, which was to become greater from September 1939 on,[42] acted, it is argued, as a kind of buffer between victims and oppressors, making the victims' sense of injustice less sharp, less well focused. This historical description is basically accurate in respect of part of the developments in Germany. Concessions to workers, however, did not always lead to satisfaction and greater co-operation; they sometimes made workers more aware of their market power and whetted their appetites for further concessions.[43] And there were clear lines of conflict, too, especially on every occasion that the regime did actually intervene against working-class interests. The formation of clear enemy camps is perhaps too pure a model of 'crisis'; much depends on the precise events that one imagines to be necessary for an actual crisis of the system to break out. In the case of Nazi Germany one must clearly think first of a crisis *within* the regime, such as that of September–November 1939, rather than of the kind of strike movement that took place in Italy in March 1943. At a more general level, not all historical crises manifest themselves in actual breakdown, revolution, or the clear division of society into enemy camps.[44] For all the elements of confusion, the processes of conflict and of economic and social disintegration that were taking place in 1938–9 constituted at least

---

[41] Herbst, 'Die Krise des nationalsozialistischen Regimes', pp. 376 and 383.
[42] This is one of the main themes in the material collected by Werner, *'Bleib übrig!'*
[43] For examples that contradict Herbst's notion that concessions pacified class conflict, see Mason, 'The Workers' Opposition in Nazi Germany', *History Workshop Journal*, no. 11 (spring 1981), pp. 135 f.
[44] Italy in the later 1970s furnishes a good example of this point; by any definition the country was in crisis in these years.

the preliminaries, the basic ingredients, of a crisis in class relations. And to put it in counter-factual terms, I believe that without war in 1939 the regime would have been compelled to make policy choices that would have brought such a crisis nearer.

This argument is incomplete in that it refers mainly to factory politics. Did industrial discontent indicate a wide-scale, hidden political discontent? In my original work I tended to imply that it did, thus reinforcing the notion of a general crisis. I have since revised this view,[45] which rests on the unsustainable proposition that passive loyalty to the class organizations destroyed in 1933 was still widespread in 1938–9. I greatly underestimated the disillusionment and fatalism that the policies of the parties and the trade unions caused among their supporters in 1933, and the depoliticization that followed. More recent local studies and oral history research underline the need for revision on this point. This work has brought out strongly the way in which the subjects of the Nazi dictatorship tended to isolate one sphere of experience from another, to separate in their minds that which was bad from that which was tolerable, and from that which was good. Thus it was perfectly possible that workers who showed bitter resentment against wage cuts, longer hours, or attempts to bind them to their workplace by force of law felt at the same time that Hitler was a good political leader, or that the cheap mass tourism of Strength through Joy was a good thing, or that the regime's foreign policy revived their national pride.[46] It was even possible, it seems, for many people in 1939 to be opposed to the war and to admire Hitler at the same time.

Rejection of Nazi social and economic policies where they hit people's immediate material interests thus did not necessarily imply a disguised rejection of the regime in general, even though partial rejections could be resilient and sustained. This consideration magnifies the importance of

---

[45] See 'The Containment of the Working Class in Nazi Germany', pp. 231–73 above.

[46] For me, by far the most illuminating work on these themes has been the enquiries by Lutz Niethammer and his colleagues into working peoples' memories of their experiences in the Ruhr area. See Lutz Niethammer (ed.), 'Die Jahre weiss man nicht, wo man die heute hinsetzen soll.' Faschismuserfahrungen im Ruhrgebiet (1983); 'Hinterher merkt man, dass es richtig war, dass es schiefgegangen ist.' Nachkriegserfahrungen im Ruhrgebiet (1984); Lutz Niethammer and Alexander von Plato (eds.), 'Wir kriegen jetz andere Zeiten' (1985) = Lebensgeschichte und Sozialkultur im Ruhrgebiet 1930 bis 1980, 3 vols. (Berlin/Bonn 1983–5). For sensitive discussions of workers' opposition, see the editors' Introduction to vol. I, esp. pp. 34 ff., and the evidence presented by Ulrich Herbert in vol. I, pp. 94 f., and vol. III, p. 26. The theme of the compartmentalization of people's consciousness runs like a red thread through all three volumes: see, for example, the cases documented by Bernd Parisius in vol. II, pp. 115, 127 and 131; and the general discussion by Ulrich Herbert in vol. III, esp. p. 29, also pp. 24, 26 and 32. See further Reinhard Mann, Protest und Kontrolle im Dritten Reich (Frankfurt/New York 1987), pp. 42 f. This work underlines the correctness of the criticism in Herbst, 'Die Krise des nationalsozialistischen Regimes', pp. 382 f., and see the earlier critique by Alf Lüdtke in H. G. Backhaus et al., Gesellschaft. Beitrage zur Marxschen Theorie, vol. VI (Frankfurt am Main 1976).

the economic component in my overall argument about the relationship between Nazi domestic and foreign policies.

The final question about the precise meaning of the concept of crisis, and its applicability to pre-war Germany, concerns the degree of diffusion of the consciousness of crisis as such. There is no doubt that most people in Germany did not feel that they were living in the midst of a social, economic and domestic political crisis (as opposed to foreign policy crises). Real crises, it is argued, are always and necessarily characterized by a widespread sense or understanding of the critical nature of developments. Herbst systematically develops an (all too casual) remark of my own, that real knowledge of the crisis, consciousness of it as such, was restricted to relatively few people: to the political, military, and economic elite who were in possession of the facts about the social and economic problems *as a whole*, who knew that the Nazi rulers were set on vastly expanded armaments projects and on war, and who knew that the regime was having the greatest difficulty in finding the human and material resources for these projects.[47] These were the sort of people who wrote the strictly confidential documents on which I based my interpretation. They formed the narrow elite that experienced the collapse of the armaments drive at the end of 1938; or, to take another concrete example, those who were permitted at exactly this time to hear Göring's lengthy and desperate description of the economic situation at the first meeting of the Reich Defence Council on 18 November 1938.[48] (This speech is the clearest evidence that Herbst is mistaken in believing that the top political leadership was not worried about the structural problems of the economy. Unlike Göring, Herbst quite ignores the elite's concern for *future* perspectives and trends.)[49] Their knowledge and understanding, above all their fears of an *impossible future* – Göring used the words 'appears impossible'[50] – were, of course, top secret.

The regime had a monopoly of all relevant information and discussion. People working at lower levels of the economy and administration experienced and knew about only particular symptoms of the general problem – managers had to deal with particular bottlenecks and deadlines; workers found that they could exploit their own scarcity value; train drivers knew that there were not enough railway wagons; farmers knew that they could not restock their farms fully; and so on – but they did not know much more. It is definitely true (unlike 1928–33) that the full dimensions of the economic problems, above all their future implications,

---

[47] See Herbst, 'Die Krise des nationalsozialistischen Regimes', pp. 378 f.
[48] See Mason, *Arbeiterklasse*, Doc. 152.
[49] Herbst, 'Die Krise des nationalsozialistischen Regimes', p. 381.
[50] Mason, *Arbeiterklasse*, p. 917.

were not common knowledge. In this sense the power of censorship in 'stabilizing the system' was very great. It was not even obvious to everyone in the elite that the political leadership was reluctant to impose those austerity measures that its armaments projects demanded, that it wanted to have its cake and eat it too, that it was prepared to risk an unprepared war. Can there be such a thing as a crisis of which so few people were aware, a secret crisis of the system, so to speak? Herbst flatly denies this.[51] It is a serious and open argument. I think that it can indeed be true of a *latent* crisis *in a dictatorship*, of a crisis that had not yet reached an undisguisable breaking point. This crisis was narrowly averted at the end of 1938. However, September–October 1939 did mark such a breaking point insofar as a sense of crisis among industrial workers, faced with the punitive War Economy Decree, was both clear and widespread.[52]

To sum up: does this combination of ignorance and the confusion of different political outlooks, which certainly was characteristic of the mass of the population, greatly attenuate or disqualify the concept of crisis? I think it does only if we imagine crisis to entail the incipient general breakdown of the whole system of rule. I now wish to argue a more restricted case: that the refusal of most of the population to co-operate *economically* in the preparaton of war, and the unwillingness or inability of the regime to cope with this refusal, was by 1938 creating an *economic* crisis. And the fact that the regime nevertheless continued with expansive armaments and foreign policies created a huge contradiction, which amounted to a fundamental crisis of policy choices, and thus to an (albeit hidden) crisis of the regime itself. That is to say, the *economic crisis* was *in itself* serious enough. And it brought in its tow political and then military problems of a basic kind that could only be disguised, but could not begin to be resolved in peacetime.

This proposition needs to be illustrated in more detail, but first there is one final objection to my general picture that has to be considered. It is argued that the yardstick against which I am measuring the equivocations and weaknesses of Nazi social and economic policy is a quite unrealistic, utopian one – that of a total war economy in peacetime.[53] What is more, this yardstick is supposed to have been taken over from the platform of the one general, Georg Thomas (responsible for the economic affairs of the armed forces), who did not share Hitler's view about the possibility of *Blitzkriege* against single smaller states, but had the different goal of preparing Germany at once for a major war against France. My yardstick, my model, for greater austerity and more comprehensive rearmament

[51] See Herbst, 'Die Krise des nationalsozialistischen Regimes', p. 390. He also denies that elite consciousness of crisis is evidence of its real existence. Even as a general proposition I find this unacceptable; the point seems totally out of place in this particular context.
[52] Herbst bypasses these crucial events in his discussion of the extent of the awareness of crisis.
[53] See Herbst, 'Die Krise des nationalsozialistischen Regimes', pp. 385 ff.

does not in fact come mainly from this source, nor is it abstractly utopian, nor is it a *post hoc* model based on the deficiencies that became entirely apparent in October 1939. It is based rather on a very large number of different demands and proposals for specific measures of austerity, which came from many different sources between 1936 and 1939 – proposals by industrialists, the Price Commissar, the Minister of Agriculture, the Labour Administration, the armed forces and many other agencies.[54] That is to say, it is an immanent model, composed of the kinds of legislation and intervention that were thought necessary at the time by *most* of those who held responsibility for labour, economic and armaments policies. Most of these demarches were put into effect in part, with delays, or not at all. My idea of what was objectively necessary in order to concentrate resources on rearmament also tried to take account of the huge new demands placed on the economy by the three massive additional programmes put into motion between June 1938 and January 1939: the building of the West Wall, the headlong rush for war with Czechoslovakia, and then the vastly expanded naval and air force programmes. Thus the yardstick by which the Nazi regime can be said to have held back the progress of rearmament is provided by the Nazi regime itself – both in its documented acts of omission, and in the targets for rearmament that it nevertheless set for itself. No external or invented criteria are involved at all. There were consistent reasons why the regime fell far short of its targets: for one, fear of great unpopularity and discontent kept really rigorous measures off the statute book after 1936.

With the invasion of Poland and the British and French declarations of war we move from the discussion of documents and of the concepts necessary to analyse them to a series of dramatic events that help to give weight to my general thesis about the crisis-ridden relationship between domestic affairs and war in 1938–9. I have already described in detail in print the first of these, the War Economy Decree of 4 September 1939 and the speedy withdrawal of many of its clauses, and must summarize them very briefly here.[55] Right at the start of the war the government imposed a set of draconian sacrifices on the working population: higher taxes for the

---

[54] I published a substantial number of such demands and proposals. See, for example, *Arbeiterklasse*, Doc. 71 ff., Doc. 128, and Doc. 151; also Darré's interventions on agriculture – see note 19 above.

[55] See in brief my 'Labour in the Third Reich 1933–1939', *Past and Present*, no. 33 (April 1966), pp. 112–41; in detail, *Arbeiterklasse*, Chapters 19–21. Werner, *'Bleib übrig!'*, pp. 35–43, 48, 51–4, 66 ff. and 72–9, provides a much more comprehensive picture of this crisis, in that he covers fully the initial response to rationing measures; this response was especially hostile. For additional striking evidence of absenteeism, see Stephen Salter, 'The Mobilisation of German Labour, 1939–1945', D.Phil. thesis (Oxford 1983), pp. 193 f. and 210. Werner is clearly mistaken in arguing that the core of regular industrial workers stood aside from these protests during *these* months (p. 80). Later in the war it is true that women and young workers seem to have been more inclined to protest, take days off, etc.

best-paid wage-earners, a new policy of wage cuts, longer working hours, the abolition of overtime bonuses, a freeze on holidays, the rationing of food and consumer goods, and a big programme of civil conscription.[56] This legislation met with such a degree of passive resistance and manifest hostility on the part of the workers that much of it had to be repealed or revised by the end of November 1939. Hitler himself approved reducing the incidence of civil conscription on 12 November (at precisely the same time as he was demanding the immediate invasion of France!) Even the real emergency of a major war would not induce the working class, dragooned and intimidated as it was, to accept sacrifices of this kind.[57]

These events shed a very clear light upon the pre-war situation. They prove that the regime could under no circumstances have imposed a policy of full austerity in peacetime. They show that the Nazi leaders who had insisted that all sorts of material concessions be made to the working population in order to keep it under control during the later 1930s – that is Ley, Kaufmann and most of the Gauleiters, often Göring, usually Hitler himself – had been *politically* correct. They show that the government had never had much room for manoeuvre on these issues; that, contrary to what Herbst says, in this sector, at least, the regime did *not* possess unused capacities or reserves of power to intervene and stabilize the situation in favour of the armaments drive, not even on the commencement of war. The events of September–November 1939 also show the regime immediately putting the pacification of the working people before the overall (if not the short-term) demands of the war economy, even though Germany was already at war with Britain and France, and was indeed about to invade France.

This domestic retreat was not accompanied by any deceleration in military strategy. On the contrary, at precisely the same time, Hitler, in a panic over the quite unexpected strategic situation, ordered the armed forces to prepare to invade France before Christmas 1939. Once again, contradictions were driven to an extreme point.[58] As late as 6 November 1939 the invasion of France was scheduled for 12 November, one week

---

[56] See Mason, *Arbeiterklasse*, Chapters 19 and 20. Overy, '"Blitzkriegswirtschaft?"' p. 383, is mistaken in describing these measures as 'total economic mobilization'. The mobilization of September 1939 was partial, deliberately incomplete. See Mason, *Arbeiterklasse*, Chapter 18; and Georg Thomas, *Geschichte der deutschen Wehr- und Rüstungswirtschaft (1918–1943/45)*, ed. Wolfgang Birkenfeld (Boppard am Rhein 1966), pp. 129, 154–7, 172 ff., 499 f. and 510 f.

[57] Herbst, 'Die Krise des nationalsozialistischen Regimes', p. 381, and idem, *Der Totale Krieg*, pp. 109 f., cites the retreat by the regime on the domestic front merely as evidence of the shrewd psychological intuition of the leadership. He greatly underplays the element of real conflict that was present in the situation.

[58] For summaries of these events, see Hillgruber, *Hitlers Strategie*, pp. 34–8; and Mason, 'Innere Krise', pp. 180 f. Detailed accounts are furnished by Hans-Adolf Jacobsen (ed.), *Dokumente zur Vorgeschichte des Westfeldzuges, 1939–1940* (Göttingen 1956), vol. I; and idem, *Fall 'Gelb'* (Wiesbaden 1957). On the military opposition and resistance to Hitler see H. Deutsch, *The Conspiracy against Hitler in the Twilight War* (Minneapolis, MN 1968).

later. One of the main reasons why the whole military leadership opposed Hitler's plans on this point grew directly out of the long-term policy of guns *and* butter, which I have outlined above: that is, after the campaign against Poland the German armed forces lacked the munitions, the bombs, fuel, spare parts, trucks, cars and some raw materials that would be necessary to undertake *any* further military campaigns in the near future. On one estimate, the army had enough munitions to permit one-third of its divisions to fight for a further four weeks. The economic policies of the 1930s had left the Nazi Wehrmacht with sufficient resources only to defeat the weak Polish forces. Any immediate confrontation with France would, German generals thought, have led to Germany's defeat. This lack of military supplies then produced one of the turning points of the Second World War, and one of the major military–political crises in the history of the Third Reich: on the agenda was either Germany's defeat on the battlefield or a conservative military–civilian coup against Hitler.

In my original interpretation I did not attach sufficient importance to this conjuncture, for the conflict over the timing of the invasion of France contains in a dramatic manner almost all the elements of the argument. First, Hitler was trying to make good the policy disaster of August–September 1939 by means of a still more adventurous, indeed desperate, step, the invasion of France in November. Second, the armed forces were discovering that, because of past overall policies, they did not have the material resources for such a gamble (they also had no operational plans). Third, as a result, a deeply serious threat was posed to the unity and permanence of the regime. And finally, while all this was going on, the government was dismantling many of its war economy measures against the German population under the compulsion of domestic pressure and discontent.

The regime was splitting at the top and disintegrating openly at the base. If we wish to look for a crisis capable of impeccable definition as such, this seems to be a good place to start. (One element of publicity, thus of public consciousness, was missing, for the conflict over the invasion of France remained a top secret.) It turned out that an open internal confrontation and/or military defeat was averted, it appears, only because Göring found at the last minute a subtle way of persuading Hitler to back down on 7 November; the invasion of France was then postponed some thirty times until May 1940, by which time the German armed forces had been able to retrain, and to restock, thanks in part to supplies from the Soviet Union. Because the invasion of France was then so overwhelmingly successful, I think historians have tended to give far too little weight to the events of October–November 1939. These events shed a lot of light on the ways in which high policy, domestic and military, was made, not only in the critical weeks themselves, but also with respect to war preparations in general. Contradictions led to political–economic crises that at least fuelled military aggression; and when the first act of aggression created an acute strategic danger, Hitler's immediate reaction was to try to launch a second one at once. Throughout, the social and economic situation was at odds with the strategic choices; the two spheres were not co-ordinated, but were connected by a conflictual relationship, in which economic overstrain could be adduced as a powerful promiscuous argument for extreme strategic gambles, and at the same time undermined these gambles, as in November 1939. In describing the drive towards war as a 'flight forward' (*Flucht nach vorn*) I may have been seduced by the need to find a phrase that would put things in a nutshell; but the conflict over the invasion of France leaves no doubt that Hitler was capable of responding to crises in exactly this manner. The politico-economic system of Nazi Germany generated its own impasses, which the leadership consistently attempted to meet by means of violent improvisations.

The invasion of Poland highlighted one such relevant factor about war at this stage in the regime's history – the utility of plunder. Hundreds of thousands of Polish prisoners of war were already performing essential labour in German agriculture in October and November 1939; and to them were added civilian workers, whose recruitment by labour offices operating directly behind the advancing German lines was an early priority. Leaving on one side the conquest of raw materials, industrial plant and rolling stock, etc., here was a way in which military aggression provided immediate relief for the most severe of German economic difficulties, the supply of labour to agriculture. Hitler already formulated this as a basic point for occupation policy in Poland on 17 October 1939; there must be low living standards in Poland, he said, since the Reich must recruit labour there. Ulrich Herbert has brought out well the novelty of this policy.[59] One must insist that it did match perfectly the most urgent needs of the German economy.[60]

To sum up thus far: my argument about the domestic components in the origins and timing of the war of 1939 needs to be refined, qualified, and added to at many points. I have tried to discuss the most important of these points above. I cannot yet see the need to abandon the basic approach. Such debates are not well served by exaggerating the differences between the points of view at issue. I am in full agreement with Ludolf Herbst that the Third Reich tended to use its power and its violence to disguise and postpone the structural problems of Nazi rule, and that these problems tended therewith to become more acute, potentially more

[59] See Ulrich Herbert, *Fremdarbeiter. Politik und Praxis des 'Ausländer-Einsatzes' in der Kriegswirtschaft des Dritten Reiches* (Berlin/Bonn 1985), esp. pp. 11, 36 and 67 ff. This is among the most important recent studies of the history of Nazi Germany.

[60] In addition to Herbert, see Ian Kershaw, *Popular Opinion and Political Dissent in the Third Reich. Bavaria 1933–1945* (Oxford 1983), Chapters 1 and 7, for the situation of farmers in Bavaria.

destructive, in time. I also agree that 'in the interests of short-term efficiency, the system as a whole was subjected to processes of decay and dissolution'.[61] In its own programmed self-destruction, the Third Reich took a substantial part of the world down in flames with it. The open question is *when* and *why* did these elements in the system actually become determinant of high policy. My own provisional answers remain: in 1938, and on account of internal contradictions that were located not only, but most importantly, in the economy.

A discussion of this kind, however, must be put into a broader historical perspective. Any specific interpretation of a particular turning point or crisis in the history of the Third Reich has to stand the test of being an adequate, or appropriate, part of an overall interpretation. If the view put forward of a small part of the story does not fit in with any plausible picture of the whole, then that view of the part is likely to be wrong, however well documented it may appear to be. How do these vital criteria apply to my argument concerning the domestic component in the Nazi drive to war in 1938–9? A variety of different long-term perspectives could be chosen with a view to testing the hypotheses in this sense: the questions at issue are many and complex, and deserve a much fuller discussion than I have space for here. I can conclude only with some schematic remarks on four elements of a longer historical perspective, of an overall interpretation.

The first concerns the development of class relations over the whole period between 1933 and 1945. On the surface my interpretation of 1938–9 does not fit in very well with what we know of such general developments. Until 1936 mass unemployment continued to exercise the heaviest social and political discipline. In the picture I have drawn, the German working class, although deprived of its collective rights and independent organizations, then reappears in the late 1930s as a fairly vigorous historical actor, able to cause the regime perplexity and weakness of purpose, and able to secure changes in state policy. More recent research has shown that this did not continue to be the case to the same degree through the war years.[62] The power of command of the regime over the industrial workers became greater, not less, and even toward the end of the war, movements of discontent and opposition tended to be isolated and exceptional.[63] Thus the events of 1938–9 were not a good guide to the future. The main reasons for this reassertion of

---

[61] Herbst, 'Die Krise des nationalsozialistischen Regimes', p. 391.

[62] For an excellent summary see Herbert, *Fremdarbeiter*, p. 17. Salter, 'The Mobilisation of German Labour', covers the whole topic fully, and with great lucidity and subtlety. Werner, *'Bleib übrig!'*, furnishes much more detail, but his study is less well organized and his interpretation less differentiated.

[63] For some of these exceptions, see Werner, *'Bleib übrig!'*, pp. 155–9 (air raids and hours of work in 1941), 193 (wage demands during 1942) and 268–74 (opposition to evacuations from autumn 1943 on).

dictatorial control seem to me to lie in changes that were wrought in, and by, the war itself (and *not*, that is, in the actuation of pre-existing forms of consent).

The Nazi regime never again challenged the working class with a single, open and major attack on its working conditions and living standards, as it had done in September 1939. The closest it came to doing this was in cutting food rations in April 1942, a measure that provoked a rash of memories of 1917–18;[64] but, in general, the further deterioration in the condition of the working class during the war was a gradual and piecemeal process and not the result of massive measures of economic repression.

The years on which I have concentrated thus appear to be exceptional with respect to working-class behaviour and with respect to relations between the class and the regime; they were novel, but, on account of war, they were not a portent of future conflicts or of future governmental weakness. There are good reasons why 1938 and 1939 were *in fact* exceptional. They were the *first* years in which the number of jobs vastly exceeded the number of available workers, with all the new opportunities this offered to workers, and with all the new challenges and disruptions it caused the employers and to the state. For the same reason, they were the *first* years in which the state had to try to regulate, comprehensively, the whole huge and complex area of the labour market, wages and working conditions. These were exceptionally difficult administrative tasks. They pitted a dictatorial machine lacking in personnel and experience against a most uncooperative population.[65] These were also the years of transition from peace to war, to a war that was not popular. For all these reasons the years 1938–9 formed a unique conjuncture, a special period of transition in which everything was at stake. In my original work I did not sufficiently emphasize their peculiarity as two critical years of transition. To call them such does not, I think, diminish the validity of the interpretation, but rather gives these problems their precise place in a long-term chronology.

On two other counts, however, the picture of a domestic crisis helping to propel Germany into war in 1939 does fit in more simply with long-term perspectives on the history of the Third Reich. I have argued that war became necessary in order for rearmament to be continued at a high level. Following from this, and subsequently in time, war became in every sense an end in itself for the regime. This seems to me to be the

---

[64] Ibid., pp. 194–7, gives a good account of the problems over food rations during 1942.

[65] On the administrative weakness of the machinery of the Trustees of Labour see Rüdiger Hachtmann, 'Von der Klassenharmonie zum regulierten Klassenkampf', *Soziale Bewegungen, Jahrbuch 1: Arbeiterbewegung und Faschismus* (Frankfurt/New York 1984), pp. 163 f. Schweitzer, 'Plans and Markets: Nazi Style', contains hints in a similar direction for 1938.

overriding fact about the Nazi conduct of the Second World War, including its resistance to the bitter end. It was not just a matter of Hitler extolling the virtues of martial combat. In a material sense, in the invasion of the Soviet Union the *means* (armed force) and the *goal* (living space) were collapsed into each other and, in the barbaric German policies of occupation, became indistinguishable from one another. It was clear in advance that the German armies would have to live off the land.[66] This war of racial destruction and economic imperialism became an end in itself, and that is one reason why Nazi Germany lost the war in Russia. If we try to imagine some kind of German victory, it was only to be a prelude to further military expansion in the Middle East and North Africa. And so on. If, for Nazism, wars basically served the prosecution of further wars, this decisive logic first broke through in Hitler's policy-making in 1938–9, when the limits of rearmament within Germany's existing boundaries and within its existing 'constitution' were reached. Hitler's basic choice in 1938–9 was, perhaps, to get war started, *so that it could be continued* – whatever the immediate strategic risks, and whatever basic strategic goals he may have had. It is not my intention in any way to belittle detailed investigations of the development of Hitler's strategy, but there may be some risk of overlooking the fact that this was based on a categorical and continuing option for *war as such*, an option that made a perverse kind of sense in domestic and economic terms at the time at which it first became manifestly clear. After that, conquests were to provide the space and the resources for further conquests. To put it another way, a Third Reich 'at peace' is an unimaginable contradiction in terms.[67]

Plunder provides the last long-term perspective that tends to validate this approach to Nazi policy-making in 1938–9 – above all, the plunder of people. This was not a long-nurtured goal of policy, but rather an ineluctable necessity, given Nazi economic policy and aims. Some 8 million foreigners worked in Germany during the war, most of them as prisoners of war or deportees. This points to a basic fact that was already becoming visible in 1938: there were simply not enough German people to permit the fulfilment of Nazi ambitions, hence the need to conquer other people. But foreign workers were also used during the war in a very precise way: to keep to a minimum the sacrifices imposed upon German

---

[66] See Hillgruber, *Hitlers Strategie*, pp. 264 ff.; O. Bartov, *The Eastern Front, 1941–1945. German Troops and the Barbarization of Warfare* (London 1985).

[67] I do not wish with this argument to fall back toward earlier interpretations by Rauschning or Bullock of Hitler as a cynical nihilist. It is possible to accept fully that he had an ideological commitment to the destruction of the Soviet Union and to the conquest of living space there, while maintaining the strongest possible doubts that the Nazi war would have ended, or even been greatly reduced in intensity, in the case of military victory in Russia.

women. This protection of many German women from long hours in munitions factories, etc., was not only direct protection of the women themselves; quite as important, it was a protection of the regime's reputation among men, among the women's husbands and fathers, who were themselves mostly soldiers or armaments workers (and whose morale, or prejudices, the regime had to respect). The conscription of German women into industrial wage labour in large numbers would have been intensely unpopular among men; the regime knew this, and there is much evidence for that fact.[68] But on two occasions when this step had to be seriously considered the German armed forces conquered new populations that could be brought to work in Germany. This was the case with the French in the summer of 1940, and with the Russians in the winter of 1941–2. In each case the regime had been just about to take the bitter risk of conscripting German women, and then stopped, because conquered labour could be used to fill the gaps. The level of mobilization of German women for war work remained low through to 1945.[69] In this vital sphere the policies of guns and butter, so distinctive of the later 1930s, were continued throughout the war by means of the conquest and plunder of foreign workers. War, that is, was essential to the maintenance of this very important piece of civilian economy in wartime Nazi Germany.

Finally, there is perhaps a basic dilemma of perception. At the level of one's deepest historical intuitions there must remain a great sense of incompatibility between the Third Reich that, on the one hand, we know to have mobilized such terrifying destructive energies, to have unfolded such sustained and violent bureaucratic and military power, to have resisted until the very end of the war; and, on the other hand, the Third Reich depicted above: a regime whose leadership was increasingly entrapped in economic and political contradictions largely of its own making and that sought escape or resolution or maintenance of its distinctive identity through a series of sudden lurches in policy and through ever more explosive risk-taking. Instinctively we feel the crises and confusions, the desperate improvisations and the brutal irrationalities

---

[68] For some particularly striking evidence see Niethammer (ed.), 'Die Jahre weiss man nicht', pp. 126 f., 267, and 270.

[69] See Mason, 'Women in Germany, 1925–1940. Family, Welfare and Work', p. 200 above; Herbert, Fremdarbeiter, pp. 96 ff., 142 and 175. Overy, '"Blitzkriegswirtschaft?"' pp. 425 ff., is mistaken on this general issue; if the mobilization of female labour in Germany really were as thorough as he presents it, the repeated, agonized debates in the political leadership about whether to conscript women or not become incomprehensible. The problem was the shortage of women for factory labour. Overy obtains his high figure for *economically active* women (*Erwerbspersonen*) by including all those who worked as family assistants, often for no wage, on farms, in shops, etc. It is true that their contribution to the war economy, especially in agriculture, should not be underestimated, but the problem that the regime repeatedly faced, and ducked, was that of finding sufficient women for factory labour.

that so consistently characterized affairs at the apex of the politico-economic system, to be out of key with the evidence of the sweeping march of conquest and genocide and with the tenacious defence of the Greater German Reich in 1944–5. How can the latter possibly have been the outcome of policy-making procedures that were demonstrably so incoherent and crisis-ridden, of a political and economic system so riven with conflict and contradiction? Something *seems* not to add up.

I believe that one must insist on the truth and the compatibility of both of these faces of Nazi Germany. The historiographical problem is less that of reconciling the two realities, which may be attempted, for example, by emphasizing the manner in which Hitler himself personified both elements simultaneously. The problem is rather that of working out, in all spheres and at all levels, a set of dynamic and dialectical relationships between the strong centripetal pressures at work at the top of the regime and the efficacy of particular sectors of it – of the army, the police/SS, of much of the civil administration, of industry – in the years 1942–4. These relationships may well have been positive rather than negative, at least in the short run. That is, crisis, violent irrationality, and institutional decomposition at the top may in fact have furthered, for a time, the actual effectiveness of the component parts of the dictatorship. Competition among these component parts, their having to act perpetually under conditions of great pressure and often independently of each other, drew out potentials of power that might otherwise have lain dormant. (The price of this was the growing fragmentation of the regime into a series of incompatible racial, economic and strategic projects, a process that was virtually complete by 1942.) These schematic remarks can do no more than suggest in a rough and ready manner how what I have called the basic dilemma of perception may be resolved – or, better, one possible approach to its resolution.

In one sense, the particular example that I have tried to analyse does not illustrate this general argument very well, for the preparation and mobilization for the war of 1939 was in many respects a failure: at every level (diplomatic, economic, domestic–political) the elements of overstrain were too great, and the Third Reich was saved in the crisis of October–November 1939 more by sheer good fortune than by anything else. But this was not true of earlier and later turning points, from the Röhm Purge to the invasion of the Soviet Union, all of which illustrate the strict compatibility between crisis-ridden policy-making and the development and deployment of vast political and military power. The example of 1938–9 remains of value, however, not only because of its intrinsic historical importance, but also on account of the multiplicity and clarity of those elements in the situation which made Hitler's option for war such an explosive gamble. Violent lurches of this kind were no less essential parts of the history of Nazi Germany than such manifestations of power as the extermination of the European Jews or the occupation of Italy in September 1943.

Analyses need to emphasize both elements in the system, and to explore their interdependence in a concrete manner. Versions that give exclusive emphasis to the Nazi regime's growing output of military and economic power inevitably create the impression that the steps that led in this direction were relatively smooth.[70] These steps were, on the contrary, highly discontinuous, decisionistic, risk-laden, increasingly blind to economic and strategic realities, and thus increasingly violent. It is a central part of my argument that such policy-making was not only wilful, but also emerged with a high degree of necessity from the economic and political system of Nazi Germany itself. It is no paradox, still less a contradiction, that policy-making of this kind could unleash phases, or sectoral blocks, of great power, especially of destructive power; in ways that still need to be understood in detail, the two in fact went hand in hand. What the system, and the policy-making that it engendered, could *not* do was construct a coherent, imperial, and stable Third Reich. That possibility had already begun to fall apart in 1938–9 – an observation that in no way belittles the immense efforts necessary on the part of the Allied Powers finally to defeat Nazi Germany.

[70] This point constitutes my greatest disagreement with the recent work of Richard Overy on these questions. See Overy, 'Hitler's War and the German Economy. A Reinterpretation', *Economic History Review*, 2nd ser., no. 35 (1982), pp. 272–91; 'Germany, "Domestic Crisis" and War'; and '"Blitzkriegswirtschaft?"'

10

WHATEVER HAPPENED TO 'FASCISM'?

I WANT to argue in the notes which follow that an attempt to 're-evaluate' the Third Reich in the late 1980s ought to have space for a slightly longer historiographical perspective than was evident in most of the papers and much of the discussion at the Philadelphia conference. Many different points could be raised in this context. I want to confine myself to one because it seems the most difficult and the most problematic: that is, the disappearance of theories, or articulated concepts of fascism from research and writing about the Third Reich in the course of the past twelve years or so. If it is used at all, the term now appears in the new literature (outside East Germany) in a loosely descriptive sense, devoid of theoretical baggage.[1]

I believe that this amounts to an enormous change, both in the conceptualization of National Socialism and in the directions of new research. This change should not be passed over in silence as though fascism theory just melted away, but calls for some kind of stocktaking, towards which these remarks constitute a first fragmentary contribution. My own position on the issues involved is sufficiently muddled for me to try to write about them without having axes to grind: while I felt that the fascism debates of the 1960s and 1970s brought enduring gains to the analysis of Nazism (see below), I never took a fully active part in them; I could never rid myself of basic conceptual doubts and confusions concerning *capital*, I always felt that a comparative dimension was missing from the writing on German fascism, and I thus usually

This short essay is based on comments made by Mason in the concluding session of the conference 'Reevaluating the Third Reich', held at the University of Pennsylvania in April 1988. The final text was written by Mason and the footnotes have been completed as far as possible from short-hand references in this text. The papers from the conference have been published in Thomas Childers and Jane Caplan (eds.), *Reevaluating the Third Reich* (New York 1993).

[1] See, for example, Lutz Niethammer (ed.), *Lebensgeschichte und Sozialkultur im Ruhrgebiet 1930 bis 1980* (Berlin 1983–5), 3 vols.

preferred to use the terms National Socialism or Third Reich. This was true even of the notion of the 'primacy of politics', in itself a very blunt instrument for a theoretical analysis of fascism.[2]

The consensus that theories of fascism were possible and essential was once very wide. A full survey of the literature would be out of place here, but liberal and 'apolitical' scholars were broadly represented in the discussions for a time. These discussions now seem closely linked with the *marxisant* writings of Kühnl, Kitchen, and the circle of *Das Argument*,[3] but it is as well to recall that those who edited and contributed to the *Reader's Guide to Fascism* and to the massive *Who were the Fascists?*[4] also had a strong commitment to this type of approach, although they had intellectually and politically little in common with marxist students of these problems. *The Nature of Fascism*,[5] to take the title of another eclectic book, offers further evidence, if it were needed, of the appeal which the concept once had. In the late 1980s, however, such certainties (and my own old uncertainties) seem obsolete: most of the interesting new work is concerned specifically with Germany, Nazism and the Third Reich, especially with the relationship between institutional structures and policy-making on the one hand, and with biological politics (racism and eugenics) on the other. The most extreme peculiarities of German Nazism have thus slowly and silently come to dominate our moral, political and professional concerns. When referred to at all at the Philadelphia conference, fascism seemed to have become old hat. This amounts not to an organic development of a line of historical enquiry; it is much more like a fundamental change of paradigm.

I want to consider first of all what elements of the fascism debate deserve to be retrieved and to be maintained in constant intellectual life and circulation. It seems then in place to speculate about why the debate faded away. Lastly, it is necessary to point out how the discussion is being revived, or rather recast in a totally new form.

1. The first enduring achievement of the fascism debate was the retrieval of a mass of contemporary (1920s and 1930s) marxist and neo-marxist writings on the subject. Whether our present concerns are with the movements and the regimes, or with the left resistance to them, these works are too important simply to fall out of fashion. Second, the

---

[2] Tim Mason, 'The Primacy of Politics. Politics and Economics in National Socialist Germany', pp. 53–76 above.

[3] Reinhard Kühnl, *Formen burgerlicher Herrschaft. Liberalismus–Faschismus* (Reinbek 1971); idem. (ed.), *Texte zur Faschismusdiscussion. Positionen und Kontroversen* (Reinbek 1974); idem., 'Probleme einer Theorie über den internationalen Faschismus', *Politische Vierteljahresschrift*, vol. 16 (1975); Martin Kitchen, *Fascism* (London 1976); *Das Argument*, a marxist periodical published in West Berlin since the 1960s: for the 1960s debates on fascism see especially issues 30, 32, 33, 41, 43 (1964–7).

[4] Walter Laqueur (ed.), *Fascism. A Reader's Guide.* (Harmondsworth 1976); S. U. Larsen, B. Hagtvet and J. P. Myklebust (eds.), *Who Were the Fascists? Social Roots of European Fascism* (Bergen 1980).   [5] S. J. Woolf (ed.), *The Nature of Fascism* (London 1968).

debate put class relations and class–state relations firmly at the centre of the stage. Many historians never believed that they belonged there anyway, and have been provoked to write long, fruitful monographs to prove their case; and at least some erstwhile theorists of fascism have come to doubt whether centre-stage is the right place for these issues. But I would argue very strongly that the themes should not be marginalized in the course of a hunt for novel research topics. One outstanding example of the ways in which the old conceptual apparatus can be fruitfully and discreetly married to new empirical research into the history of society and of ideologies, is Ulrich Herbert's book *Fremdarbeiter*.[6] Class–class and class–state relations also call for constant critical inclusion into studies where they do not appear to be of primary importance, to be the engine of history – studies of gender roles, case studies in local history, etc. The present wave of doubts about and within marxism has many justifications, but none of them should lead to a wholesale abandonment of the basic *questions*, however many of the fascist answers may need to be radically revised or abandoned.

2. The decline of the fascist paradigm is not easy to chart. I can see little explicit evidence that the sustained, sharp and comprehensive attacks on it by liberal and conservative scholars such as H. A. Winkler, H. A. Turner, and K. D. Bracher have had much persuasive effect – the debate was perhaps too confrontational for there to be space for 'conversions'.[7] At a purely intellectual level, it seems to me rather that fascism theory ran into three dead-ends in respect of the progress of empirical research within its own conceptual framework. The first dead-end was self-inflicted, in the sense that theorists of fascism did very little solid empirical work on their own home ground, on the political economy of the period 1928–45; the territory which was theorized as being crucial was largely left to the research of other scholars, while secondary issues, such as fascist aesthetics and *faschistische Öffentlichkeit* (the fascist public sphere), aroused at least as much interest on the left. The second dead-end was Nazi racism, which was not studied systematically; this issue has always threatened to shatter generic concepts of fascism, and its highly uncertain treatment goes a long way towards explaining why German writings on fascism received so little attention on the left in Italy. This leads on to the third dead-end, the weakness of the whole discussion in terms of comparative empirical work. A debate on these themes which did not

---

[6] Ulrich Herbert, *Fremdarbeiter. Politik und Praxis des 'Ausländer-Einsatzes' in der Kriegswirtschaft des Dritten Reiches* (Berlin 1985). See also the broad survey of foreign labour by Ulrich Herbert, *A History of Foreign Labor in Germany 1880–1950* (Ann Arbor, MI 1990).

[7] See especially H. A. Winkler, *Revolution, Staat, Faschismus. Zur Revision des historischen Materialismus* (Göttingen 1978); Henry A. Turner Jr (ed.), *Reappraisals of Fascism* (New York 1975); Karl Dietrich Bracher, *Zeitgeschichtliche Kontroversen. Um Faschismus, Totalitarismus, Demokratie* (Munich 1976); and idem, *The Age of Ideologies* (London 1984).

refer continuously to Italy, France, Romania, or even Britain was bound to start revolving around itself in ever decreasing concentric circles.

These intellectual constraints and limitations were clearly not trivial, but neither were they necessarily terminal – the work *could* gradually have expanded its basis and have continued to develop. Thus I tend to believe that the decisive reasons for the decline of the fascism paradigm lay elsewhere – that is, in broader changes in the political culture. The first to note here is the slow decline and fragmentation of the movements of 1968. Fascism was very much a concept of these movements, especially so in Germany where young people faced a parental generation, now in power, which had not resisted the Nazis and had not talked openly with their children about the Third Reich.[8] There is a precise sense in which the German 1968 was a tragically belated (and thus to a degree misconceived) anti-fascist movement, not just contesting the parental generation *per se* but learning from and making good its terrible political errors. Fascism, as I recall from many discussions in Berlin in the 1960s, was not just an epoch which ended in 1945, but was also something which the Christian Democrats and the right wing of the Social Democrats were *then* trying to reinstate in a less barbaric form – *die formierte Gesellschaft* (planned society) of Ludwig Ehrhard and Rüdiger Altmann, the militarized police forces of West Berlin, etc. In the event, however, the SPD took control of the national government, there was a marked liberalization, and the 1968 movement went off in forty different directions, one of them terroristic. It was partly on account of this national sea-change (which 1968 itself did a lot to bring about) that the generic concept of fascism lost its intellectual force among students and younger scholars on the left.

The second major change which must be considered in this context is the development of feminism. This political–cultural movement of the left has also helped to undermine the classical paradigm of fascism. Outside the works of Wilhelm Reich, there was little room in fascism theory for such themes as gender and reproduction, and even Reich had little to say about the vast field of reactionary eugenics. Feminist inspirations and struggles have opened up very large new areas of research into the historical reality of Nazism and German society in the twentieth century, themes which have burst the seams of older concepts of fascism both in an empirical and in a theoretical sense.[9]

---

[8] [A textual note here refers to 'Jones', but I have been unable to trace the reference.]

[9] Feminist publications are now too numerous to mention in full, but important representative works in English include Renate Bridenthal et al. (eds.), *When Biology Became Destiny. Women in Weimar and Nazi Germany* (New York 1984); and Claudia Koonz, *Mothers in the Fatherland* (New York 1987). In German, see especially Gisela Bock, *Zwangssterilisation im Nationalsozialismus. Studien zur Rassenpolitik und Frauenpolitik* (Opladen 1986). Notes in the original text mention two other works which have had great impact on study of the social and ideological aspects of fascism: Klaus Theweleit, *Male Fantasies*

The third political cultural change which has worked in the same direction has been the steadily growing public awareness of Nazi genocide, above all the genocide of the Jews. This huge fact has come to dominate public perceptions of the history of Nazi Germany to an ever greater extent with the passing of the years, and in some measure scholarly research has followed this shift in public opinion.

At this point it may be helpful to try to relate the decline of fascism theory to the vexed question of attempts to 'historicize' the Third Reich; this effort may be doubly helpful in the sense that the meaning of 'historicization' only becomes clear in the course of the practical use of the term. Most theorists of fascism in the 1960s and 1970s understood Nazism *also* as a repository of possible lessons, warnings and injunctions about economic and political developments in the near future; the Third Reich was 'relevant'. This is far from the concerns of those scholars who now wish to 'historicize' it; the latter do not wish to deny its moral, cultural and political *implications* for the present, but they do assert that Nazism belongs definitively to the past. 'Historicization' has been presented as a novel idea, and threatens to become one in which methodological ruminations and moral sensibilities take command in a manner which can only lead to muddle.[10] The decline of that type of historical curiosity specifically associated with fascism theory seems to me to be one example of 'historicization' which *has actually taken place*, and a very important one.

However, this should in no way be understood as the happy triumph of the ivory tower over the seductions of politically committed history. Feminist history is politically committed, but the sustained and growing contribution to research and understanding which it has made, has, I would argue, in fact done a great deal to historicize Nazism, by immensely broadening out notions of what it is that requires to be described and explained. If we now have some concrete notions of German-society-and-Nazism, this is due as much to feminist work as it is to the proliferation of local case studies. And German society is the proper object of historicizing reflection and analysis. It is no paradox that this should be in part the outcome of a particular militancy in the present – historiographical progress normally occurs in this way. Normally, but not always: for the third political–cultural change noted above, the growing public preoccupation with genocide, may fuel the passions for research, but may also make critical distance more difficult, not less. Fascism theory suffered both from a lack of critical distance and from a

(Minneapolis, MN 1989), 2 vols.; and Detlev Peukert, *Inside Nazi Germany. Conformity, Opposition and Racism in Everyday Life* (London 1985).

[10] See Ian Kershaw, *The Nazi Dictatorship. Problems and Perspectives of Interpretation*, 3rd edn (London 1993), Chapter 9.

lack of comprehensive vision, both of them qualities essential to a historicized understanding of Nazism. Theorists of fascism failed to comprehend anti-Semitism, but it is no answer to read the whole of German history in terms of genocide, for that too contains elements of the 'contemporaneity of the past' which can get in the way of critical moral discussion.[11]

This partial digression points towards the next observation, which is that no new paradigms have been put forward to take the place of theories of fascism. Those who wish to historicize Nazism may believe that we can do very well without *any* paradigms of that kind. To judge, however, from the conference papers and from other new literature, there is something like a new consensus concerning the focus of research on Nazism. The most interesting new research takes it as axiomatic that the Third Reich was unique (in the radical sense of that word), and concentrates our attention on the broad gamut of Nazi biological politics (also unique), and upon the institutions invented to implement them, often at the lowest administrative level (which also have a first appearance of uniqueness). It is thus impossible to conclude this section of these remarks without pointing to a paradox: the above position is the same as that put forward in outline, but insistently, by Karl Dietrich Bracher since 1970. Bracher has repeatedly argued that the Third Reich was unique, revolutionary, totalitarian, on account of the absolute pre-eminence which it gave to biological politics.[12] I doubt very much that Bracher's direct influence has been great, since in the debate between functionalists and intentionalists he has aligned himself firmly with the latter, even on the issue of the Reichstag fire, whereas most of the new research feels itself much more indebted to various functionalist approaches. I can only note, not resolve, this paradox. It really does deserve to be noted, however, for it is a sign of how much things are in flux.

3. There are obviously no clear or simple ways out of these dilemmas. The Third Reich will go on being re-evaluated, and new and old schools of interpretation will continue to shift in relation to each other. One limited but concrete way forward may lie in the making of systematic comparisons – above all with Fascist Italy; that type of work, that is, which the exponents of fascism theory largely failed to do fifteen years or so ago. One of the most remarkable features of that barren cultural episode which carries the name 'Historikerstreit' is that the question of comparability was raised, to the best of my knowledge, only in respect of

[11] Saul Friedländer, 'Some Reflections on the Historicization of National Socialism', *German Politics and Society*, vol. 13 (February 1988), pp. 9–21; see also the exchange of letters between Friedländer and Martin Broszat, reprinted as 'A Controversy about the Historicization of National Socialism', *New German Critique*, no. 44 (spring/summer 1988), pp. 85–126.
[12] Karl Dietrich Bracher and Leo Valiani, *Fascismo et nazionalsocialismo* (Bologna 1986).

Stalin's Russia, Pol Pot, etc., and *not* in respect of Fascist Italy, which did, after all, provide Nazi Germany with a certain model and a loyal ally in war. Comparison (which is different from homologization) is an essential part of the historian's work, but like must be compared with like, and it is a distorting deviation to compare Nazi Germany with Stalinist Russia, a society which was at a completely different stage of cultural and political development and was pursuing radically different political goals. This negative part of the argument has been well stated, by Jürgen Kocka among others, but the positive side of the argument has gone by default – that is, the argument in favour of systematic comparison with Fascist Italy.[13]

The question of fascism has re-emerged in this new form. The old theories offer little by way of starting points, except perhaps for the political economy of 1922 and of 1932–3 (i.e. the Italian Fascist and the Nazi seizures of power respectively). These theories tended to make Nazism look like Italian Fascism, without knowing what Italian Fascism actually looked like. Today, comparisons must commence with specific analytical questions which are capable in principle of empirical answers. The aim cannot be to reconstruct a 'theory of fascism' through the painstaking accumulation of comparative building blocks, for there are fundamental cognitive and methodological objects to the notion that theory can be constructed in this way. The goal must rather be to establish specific similarities and contrasts between the two regimes, and to establish the reasons for them, maintaining the while a strict agnosticism with respect to the radical uniqueness of the one or the other. The themes available for such work are legion.

This may be illustrated first by two examples taken from the Philadelphia conference. Was there a strong eugenics movement in Fascist Italy? Yes, it was highly vocal and highly professional, but it ran up against the opposition of the Vatican (stronger in Italy than Galen in Germany!), and it lacked executive/administrative power.[14] Did denunciations play such an important role in enhancing the power of the various Fascist police forces as they did for the Gestapo? Almost certainly not, and this greatly diminished the repressive power of the Fascist dictatorship, which was unable, for example, to pre-empt the great strike wave which began in Turin in March 1943; but why this was the case calls for a lot of difficult research and analysis in both German and Italian cultural and social history. Why should denunciation have been dishonourable in Italy, but not in Germany? There is no single answer, but the importance of the

---

[13] Jürgen Kocka, 'Hitler sollte nicht durch Stalin und Pol Pot verdrängt werden', in *'Historikerstreit'. Die Dokumentation der Kontroverse um die Einzigartigkeit der national-sozialistischen Judenvernichtung* (Munich/Zürich 1987), pp. 132–42.

[14] See MacGregor Knox, 'Conquest, Foreign and Domestic, in Fascist Italy and Nazi Germany', *Journal of Modern History*, vol. 56 (March 1987), pp. 1–57.

question is obvious.[15]

Such an approach to the question of Fascism/Nazism is not entirely new. Wolfgang Schieder has recently compared the stages of the seizure of power by the two regimes, coming to the conclusion that they were fundamentally similar.[16] Macgregor Knox has compared the relationship between the domestic and foreign policies of the two regimes, coming to the conclusion that both regimes used foreign policy to revolutionize domestic affairs (one may argue that the relationship between the two spheres of state activity was in fact the opposite, but the author's method is impeccable, his conclusions consistently stimulating).[17] Paolo Pombeni has executed a beautiful systematic comparison between the two parties, concluding that their functions and structure were basically similar.[18] Charles Maier has compared the Nazi and the Fascist economies to the effect that the similarities outweighted the differences.[19] At a lower level of empirical research, I have tried to examine a contrast: the capacity of the Italian working class to launch a widespread strike in March 1943, of a kind which never came about in Germany.[20] I conclude that the difference had to do above all with the much greater administrative capacity of the Nazi regime, both in killing and providing welfare, than that of the Fascist state.

These essays indicate that the discussion can enter a new phase. Any less cautious formulation would be out of place. The question of Italian participation in genocide – against the Jews, in Africa, in the Balkans – remains hotly debated. Most Italian historians and publicists think that this issue marked off Italian Fascism from German Nazism in a decisive manner. But the problem is not resolved by counting corpses. What matters is the genocidal potential of the regime, and how one interprets in this light the various instances of mass murder which were committed in the name of fascism. There is no doubt that the persecution of the Jews was carried out in Italy with less efficiency and enthusiasm than in any other country except Denmark. But the overall question remains open, in the sense that much research and analysis remains to be done. The fact

---

[15] Robert Gellately, 'The Gestapo and German Society. Political Denunciation in the Gestapo Case Files', *Journal of Modern History*, no. 60 (Decmeber 1988), pp. 654–94; Tim Mason, 'Arbeiter ohne Gewerkschaften. Masserwiderstand in NS-Deutschland und in faschistischen Italien', *Journal für Geschichte* (November 1985), pp. 28–36.

[16] I have not been able to locate this reference to a recent publication by Wolfgang Schieder, but see his collection *Faschismus als soziale Bewegung. Deutschland und Italien im Vergleich* (Göttingen 1983).

[17] Knox, 'Conquest, Foreign and Domestic'.

[18] Paolo Pombeni, *Demagogia e tirannide. Uno studie sulla forma partito del fascismo* (Bologna 1984).

[19] Charles Maier, 'The Economics of Fascism and Nazism', in idem. (ed.), *In Search of Stability* (Cambridge 1987), pp. 70–120.

[20] Mason, 'Arbeiter ohne Gewerkschaften'.

that most Italians of all political colours are resistant to a positive comparison between 'their' Fascism and German Nazism is a political–historical fact of great significance; it may also be an obstacle to historical work.

None of these remarks imply that the old concept of fascism can, or should be revived. On the contrary, they point to a different programme of work, which (alone, I believe) can identify just how peculiar (or typical) was the German road to organized inhumanity. If we can now do without much of the original contents of the concept of fascism, we cannot do without comparison. 'Historicization' may easily become a recipe for provincialism. And the moral absolutes of Habermas, however politically and didactically impeccable, also carry a shadow of provincialism, as long as they fail to recognize that fascism was a continental phenomenon, and that Nazism was a peculiar part of something much larger.[21] Pol Pot, the rat torture and the fate of the Armenians are all extraneous to any serious discussion of Nazism; Mussolini's Italy is not.

[21] The reference here is to Habermas' contributions to the 'Historikerstreit'; see 'Historikerstreit', pp. 62–76, 95–7, 243–55, 383–7.

BIBLIOGRAPHY OF PUBLICATIONS BY TIMOTHY MASON

BOOKS AND ARTICLES

'Some Origins of the Second World War', *Past and Present*, no. 29 (December 1964), pp. 67–87. Reprinted in Esmonde Robertson (ed.), *The Origins of the Second World War*, London 1971, pp. 105–35.

'Labour in the Third Reich 1933–39', *Past and Present*, no. 33 (April 1966), pp. 112–41.

'Der Primat der Politik. Politik und Wirtschaft im Nationalsozialismus, *Das Argument. Berliner Hefte für Probleme der Gesellschaft*, no. 41 (December 1966), pp. 73–94. English translation: 'The Primacy of Politics – Politics and Economics in National Socialist Germany', in S. J. Woolf (ed.), *The Nature of Fascism*, London 1968, pp. 165–95; reprinted in Henry A. Turner, Jr (ed.), *Nazism and the Third Reich*, New York 1972, pp. 175–200.

'Der antifaschistische Widerstand der Arbeiterbewegung im Spiegel der SED-Historiographie', *Das Argument*, no. 43 (July 1967), pp. 144–53.

'Primat der Industrie? Eine Erwiderung', *Das Argument*, no. 47 (July 1968), pp. 193–209.

'The Legacy of 1918 for National Socialism', in A. J. Nicholls and E. Matthias (eds.), *German Democracy and the Triumph of Hitler*, London 1971, pp. 15–39. Reprinted as Chapter 1 of *Sozialpolitik im Dritten Reich. Arbeiterklasse und Volksgemeinschaft*.

'National Socialist Policies Towards the German Working Class, 1925 to 1939', D. Phil., Oxford 1971.

'Zur politischen Relevanz historischer Theorien', *Aus Politik und Zeitgeschichte*, no. 20, (1972) pp. 33–42.

'Zur Entstehung des Gesetzes zur Ordnung der nationalen Arbeit vom 20. Januar 1934. Ein Versuch über das Verhältnis "archaischer" und "moderne" Momente in der neuesten deutschen Geschichte', in Hans Mommsen, Dietmar Petzina and Bernd Weisbrod (eds.), *Industrielles System und politische Entwicklung in der Weimarer Republik*, Düsseldorf 1974, pp. 322–51.

Arbeiterklasse und Volksgemeinschaft. Dokumente und Materialien zur deutschen Arbeiterpolitik 1936–1939, Opladen 1975.

'Innere Krise und Angriffskrieg 1938/1939', in F. Forstmeier and H.-E. Volkmann (eds.), *Wirtschaft und Rüstung am Vorabend des Zweiten Weltkriegs*, Düsseldorf 1975, pp. 158–88.

'Zur Funktion des Angriffskrieges 1939', in G. Ziebura (ed.), *Grundfragen der Deutschen Aussenpolitik seit 1871*, Darmstadt 1975, pp. 376–413.

'Women in Germany, 1925–1940. Family, Welfare and Work. Part I', *History Workshop Journal*, no. 1 (spring 1976), pp. 74–113.

'Women in Germany, 1925–1940. Family, Welfare and Work. Part II', *History Workshop Journal*, no. 2 (autumn 1976), pp. 5–32.

'Zur Lage der Frauen in Deutschland 1930 bis 1940. Wohlfahrt, Arbeit und Familie', in G. Dill et al., (eds.), *Gesellschaft. Beiträge zur Marxschen Theorie* vol. 6 Frankfurt 1976, pp. 118–93 (version of 'Women in Germany 1925–1940' Parts I and II).

'Class Conflict and Scientific Management in American Industry', *History Workshop Journal*, no. 3 (spring 1977), pp. 81–2.

Sozialpolitik im Dritten Reich. Arbeiterklasse und Volksgemeinschaft, Opladen 1977. Italian translation: *La politica sociale del Terzo Reich*, Bari 1980; English translation: *Social Policy in the Third Reich. The Working Class and the 'National Commmunity'*, Oxford/Providence 1993.

'National Socialism and the German Working Class, 1925–May 1933', *New German Critique*, no. 11 (spring 1977), pp. 49–93 (translation of Chapter 2 of *Sozialpolitik im Dritten Reich. Arbeiterklasse und Volksgemeinschaft*).

'L'oppozisione operaio nella Germania nazista', *Movimento operaio e socialista*, no. 1 (1980), pp. 91–108.

'Intention and Explanation. A Current Controversy about the interpretation of National Socialism', in Gerhard Hirschfeld and Lothar Kettenacker (eds.), *Der 'Führerstaat'. Mythos und Realität/The 'Führer State'. Myth and Reality*, Stuttgart 1981, pp. 23–42. Italian translation: 'Interpretazioni del Nazionalsocialismo', *Italia Contemporanea*, no. 139 (June 1980), pp. 3–18.

'Open Questions on Nazism', in Raphael Samuel (ed.), *People's History and Socialist Theory*, London 1981, pp. 205–10.

'Arbeiteropposition im nationalsozialistischen Deutschland', in Detlev Peukert and Jürgen Reulecke (eds.), *Die Reihen fast geschlossen. Beiträge zur Geschichte des Alltags unterm Nationalsozialismus*, Wuppertal 1981, pp. 293–313.

'The Workers' Opposition in Nazi Germany', *History Workshop Journal*, no. 11 (spring 1981), pp. 120–37.

'Die Bändigung der Arbeiterklasse im nationalsozialistischen Deutschland. Eine Einleitung', in Carola Sachse et al., *Angst, Belohnung, Zucht und Ordnung. Herrschaftsmechanismen im Nationalsozialismus*, Opladen 1982, pp. 11–53.

'Comrade and Lover. Rosa Luxemburg's Letters to Leo Jogiches', *History Workshop Journal*, no. 13 (spring 1982), pp. 94–109. Italian translation: 'Lettere d'Amore di Rosa Luxemburg', *Quaderni Piacentini*, no. 6 (1982), pp. 177–98.

'Injustice and Resistance. Barrington Moore and the Reaction of German Workers to Nazism', in R. J. Bullen et al. (eds.), *Ideas into Politics. Aspects of European History 1880–1950*, London 1984, pp. 106–18.

'Massenwiderstand ohne Organisation. Streiks im faschistischen Italien und NS-Deutschland', *Gewerkschaftliche Monatshefte*, vol. 32, no. 9 (1984), pp. 518–32; reprinted in Ernst Breit (ed.), *Aufstieg des Nationalsozialismus, Untergang der Republik, Zerschlagung der Gewerkschaften*, Cologne 1984, pp. 197–212.

'Arbeiter ohne Gewerkschaften. Massenwiderstand im NS-Deutschland und im faschistischen Italien', *Journal für Geschichte* (November 1985), pp. 28–36.

'History Workshop', *Passato e Presente*, 8 (1985), pp. 175–86.

'Il nazismo come professione', *Rinascita*, no. 18 (18 May 1985), pp. 18–19.

'Il fascismo "Made in Italy". La mostra sull'economia italiana fra le due guerre', *Italia Contemporanea*, no. 158 (1985), pp. 5–32. English translation: 'The Great Economic History Show', *History Workshop Journal*, no. 21 (spring 1986), pp. 3–35.

'The Third Reich and the German Left. Persecution and Resistance', in Hedley Bull (ed.), *The Challenge of the Third Reich. The Adam von Trott Memorial Lectures*, Oxford 1986, pp. 95–115. Italian translation: 'Il Terzo Reich e la sinistra tedesca. Persecuzione e resistenza', Centro Piero Gobetti, *Annali* (1989), pp. 129–54.

'Moderno, modernità e modernizzazione: un montaggio', *Movimento operaio e socialista*, vol. I, no. 2 (1987), pp. 45–61. English translation: 'Italy and Modernization', *History Workshop Journal*, no. 25 (spring 1988), pp. 127–47.

'Gli scioperi di Torino del Marzo '43', in F. F. Tosi, G. Grasso and M. Legnani (eds.), *L'Italia nella seconda guerra mondiale e nella Resistenza*, Milan 1988, pp. 399–422.

'Debate. Germany, "Domestic Crisis" and War in 1939. Comment 2', *Past and Present*, no. 122 (February 1989), pp. 205–21.

'Whatever Happened to "Fascism"?', *Radical History Review*, no. 49 (winter 1991), pp. 89–98; reprinted in Childers and Caplan (eds.), *Reevaluating the Third Reich*, pp. 253–62.

'The Domestic Dynamics of Nazi Conquests. A Response to Critics', in Thomas Childers and Jane Caplan (eds.), *Reevaluating the Third Reich*, New York 1993, pp. 161–89.

BOOK REVIEWS

Maser, Werner, *Hitlers Mein Kampf* (*Das Argument*, no. 41 (December 1966), pp. 522–3).

Heinz Boberach (ed.), *Meldungen aus dem Reich* (*Das Argument*, no. 41, (December 1966), pp. 523–5).

Margret Boveri, *Wir lügen alle* (*Das Argument*, no. 41 (December 1966), pp. 527–9).

'The Coming of the Nazis' (*Times Literary Supplement*, 1 February 1974, pp. 93–6).

Noakes, Jeremy and Pridham, Geoffrey (eds.), *Documents on Nazism 1919–1945* (*Times Higher Education Supplement*, 20 December 1974, p. 20).

Ludwig, Karl–Heinz, *Technik und Ingenieure im Dritten Reich* (*Times Literary Supplement*, 5 November 1976, p. 1402).

Lee, Joseph, *The Modernisation of Irish Society 1848–1918* (*History Workshop*

Journal, no. 1 (spring 1976), pp. 261–3).

'The Nat Soc Years' (*Times Literary Supplement*, 18 January 1977, p. 104).

Feldman, Gerald D., *Iron and Steel in the German Inflation 1916–1923* (*Journal of Modern History*, vol. 50, (1978) pp. 786–9).

Carsten, F. L., *Fascist Movements in Austria* (*Slavonic and East European Review*, vol. 57 (1978), pp. 314–16).

'The Writing of History as Literary and Moral Art' (*Times Higher Education Supplement*, 1 December 1978, pp. 14–15).

Beyerchen, Alan, *Scientists under Hitler. Politics and the Physics Community in the Third Reich* (*Times Higher Education Supplement*, 7 April 1978), p. viii).

'Zur Frauenarbeit im Dritten Reich' (*Archiv für Sozialgeschichte*, vol. 19 (1979), pp. 579–84).

Stone, Norman, *Hitler* and James J. Barnes and Patience Barnes, *Hitler's Mein Kampf in Britain and America: A Publishing History* (*New Statesman* 26 September 1980, p. 30).

Abraham, David, *The Collapse of the Weimar Republic* (*American Historical Review*, vol. 87 (October 1982), pp. 1122–3; and letter in *American Historical Review*, vol. 88 (October 1983), pp. 1143–4).

'Resistance in the Ruhr' (*Times Literary Supplement*, 7 May 1982, pp. 513–14).

Hobsbawm, E. J. and Ranger, T., (eds.), *L'invenzione della tradizione* (*Passato e Presente*, no. 14/15 (1987), pp. 11–20).

'Storiografia della cultura operaio', (*Italia Contemporanea*, no. 167 (June 1987), pp. 103–9).

Claudia Koonz, *Mothers in the Fatherland* (History Workshop Journal, vol. 26, (autumn 1988) pp. 200–3).

OTHER

Consulting editor to Michael Freeman, *An Atlas of Nazi Germany*, London 1987.

BIBLIOGRAPHY OF WORKS CITED

Readers are referred to the Bibliography of publications by Tim Mason for works by this author.

Books are listed in the editions cited in the texts; titles of English translations and of subsequently published doctoral dissertations, and dates of new editions, have been added in brackets following the main entry.

Adorno, Theodor W. and Dirks, Walter (eds.), *Betriebsklima. Eine industriesoziologische Untersuchung aus dem Ruhrgebiet*, Frankfurter Beiträge zur Soziologie, vol. III, Frankfurt am Main 1955.

Akten zur deutschen auswärtigen Politik 1918–1945 (ADAP), ser. D: 1937–45, Baden-Baden 1950.

Alasia, Gianni, Carcano, Giancarlo, Giovana, Mario, et al., *Un giorno del '43. La classe operaia sciopera*, Turin 1983.

Arbeitswissenschatfliches Institut der DAF, *Jahrbuch 1940/1*, vol. I.

Aretz, Jürgen, *Katholische Arbeiterbewegung und Nationalsozialismus*, Mainz 1978 (Mainz 1982).

Backhaus, H.-G., Bahr, H.-D., Brandt, G., Eberle, F., Euchner, W., Helberger, C., Hennig, E., Hirsch, J., Mohl, E. T., Müller, W., Negt, O., Reichelt, H., Schäfer, G. and Schmidt, A. (eds), *Gesellschaft. Beiträge zur Marxschen Theorie*, vol. VI, Frankfurt am Main 1976.

Bairati, Piero, *Vittorio Valletta*, Turin 1983.

Baldwin, Peter (ed.), *Reworking the Past. Hitler, the Holocaust, and the Historians' Debate*, Boston, MA 1990.

Baritz, Loren, *The Servants of Power. A History of the Use of Social Science in American Industry*, 2nd edn, New York 1965 (Westport, CT 1974).

Bartov, Omer, *The Eastern Front, 1941–1945. German Troops and the Barbarization of Warfare*, London 1985.

Bauer, Otto, Marcuse, Herbert and Rosenberg, Arthur, *Faschismus und Kapitalismus. Theorien über die sozialen Ursprünge und die Funktion des Faschismus*, ed. Wolfgang Abendroth, Frankfurt am Main 1967.

Baumann, Zygmunt, *Modernity and the Holocaust*, Oxford 1989.

Bäumer, Peter C., 'Das Deutsche Institut für technische Arbeitsschulung (DINTA)', *Schriften des Vereins für Sozialpolitik*, vol. 181, Munich/Leipzig

1930.
Baumgart, Winfried, 'Zur Ansprache Hitlers vor den Führern der Wehrmacht am 22. August 1939', *Vierteljahrschefte für Zeitgeschichte*, vol. 16, no. 2 (April 1968), pp. 120–49.

Bergmann, Klaus, *Agrarromantik und Grossstadtfeindschaft*, Meisenheim am Glan 1970.

Berlin, Isaiah, *Four Essays on Liberty*, London 1969 (Oxford 1982).

Bertolo, G., E. Brunetta et al., *Operai e Contadini nella crisi italiana del 1943/44*, Milan 1974.

Bilanz des Zweiten Weltkrieges. Erkenntnisse und Verpflichtungen für die Zukunft, Oldenburg/Hamburg 1953.

Blaich, Fritz, 'Wirtschaft und Rüstung in Deutschland', Wolfgang Benz and Hermann Graml (eds.), *Sommer 1939. Die Grossmächte und der europäische Krieg*, Stuttgart 1979.

Blake, Judith, 'Coercive Pronatalism and American Population Policy', in Rose Laub Coser (ed.), *The Family. Its Structures and Functions*, 2nd edn, London 1974, pp. 276–317.

Blanke, B., Reiche, R. and Werth, J., 'Die Faschismus-Theorie der DDR', *Das Argument*, no. 33 (May 1965), pp. 35–48.

Bloch, Ernest, *Vom Hasard zur Katastrophe. Politische Aufsätze aus den Jahren 1934–1939*, Frankfurt am Main 1972.

'Die Frau im Dritten Reich', (February 1937), in idem, *Politische Messungen, Pestzeit, Vormärz*, Frankfurt am Main, 1970 (Frankfurt am Main 1985).

Boberach, Heinz (ed.), *Meldungen aus dem Reich*, Neuwied/Berlin 1965 (Pawlak 1984).

Bock, Gisela, *Zwangssterilisation im Nationalsozialismus. Studien zur Rassenpolitik und Frauenpolitik*, Opladen 1986.

Bracher, Karl Dietrich, *Die Auflösung der Weimarer Republik*, 3rd edn, Villingen 1960 (Düsseldorf 1984).

Zeitgeschichtliche Kontroversen um Faschismus, Totalitarismus, Demokratie, Munich 1976.

The Age of Ideologies, London 1984.

'Tradition and revolution im Nationalsozialismus', in Manfred Funke (ed.), *Hitler, Deutschland und die Mächte*, Düsseldorf 1977, pp. 17–29.

'The Role of Hitler. Perspectives of Interpretation', in Walter Laqueur (ed.), *Fascism. A Reader's Guide*, Harmondsworth 1979, pp. 193–212.

Bracher, Karl Dietrich, Sauer, Wolfgang and Schulz, Gerhard, *Die national-sozialistische Machtergreifung. Studien zur Errichtung des totalitären Her-rschaftssystems in Deutschland 1933–1934*, Cologne/Opladen 1960 (Frankfurt am Main 1983).

Bracher, Karl Dietrich and Valiani, Leo, *Fascismo e nazionalsocialismo*, Bologna 1986.

Brady, Robert A., *The Rationalization Movement in German Industry*, Berkeley, CA. 1933 (New York 1974).

The Spirit and Structure of German Fascism, London 1937 (New York 1971).

Bramsted, Ernest K., *Goebbels and National Socialist Propaganda 1925–1945*,

London 1965.

Bremme, Gabriele, *Die politische Rolle der Frau in Deutschland. Eine Untersuchung über der Einfluss der Frauen bei Wahlen und ihre Teilnahme in Partei und Parlament*, Göttingen 1956.

Bretschneider, Heike, *Der Widerstand gegen den Nationalsozialismus in München 1933 bis 1945*, Munich 1968.

Bridenthal, Renate, 'Beyond *Kinder, Küche, Kirche.* Weimar Women at Work', *Central European History*, vol. 6, no. 2 (1973), pp. 148–66.

Bridenthal, Renate, Grossmann, Atina and Kaplan, Marion (eds.), *When Biology Became Destiny. Women in Weimar and Nazi Germany*, New York 1984.

Briefs, Goetz, *The Proletariat. A Challenge to Western Civilization*, New York/London 1937 (New York 1975).

Broszat, Martin, *Der Staat Hitlers. Grundlegung und Entwicklung seiner innerer Verfassung*, Frankfurt am Main 1969 (*The Hitler State. The Foundation and Development of the Internal Structure of the Third Reich*, London 1981).

'Soziale Motivation und Führer-Bindung des Nationalsozialismus', *Vierteljahrshefte für Zeitgeschichte*, vol. 18, no. 4 (1970), pp. 392–409.

Broszat, Marin, et al. (eds.), *Bayern in der NS-Zeit*, 6 vols., Munich/Vienna, 1977–83.

Bry, Gerhard, *Wages in Germany, 1871–1945*, Princeton, NJ 1960.

Bullock, Alan, *The Life and Times of Ernest Bevin*, vol. II: *Minister of Labour 1940–1945*, London 1967.

Bürgdorfer, Friderich, *Volk ohne Jugend. Geburtenschwund und Überalterung des deutschen Volkskörpers*, Zeitschrift für Geopolitik, 2nd edn, Appendix 9, Berlin 1934.

Burleigh, Michael and Wippermann, Wolfgang, *The Racial State: Germany 1933–1945*, Cambridge 1991.

Calder, Angus, *The People's War. Britain 1939–1945*, rev. edn, London 1971 (London 1986).

Caplan, Jane, 'Theories of Fascism: Nicos Poulantzas as Historian', *History Workshop Journal*, no. 3 (spring 1977), pp. 83–100.

'The Civil Servant in the Third Reich', D. Phil. thesis, Oxford 1974 (*Government Without Administration. State and Civil Service in Weimar and Nazi Germany*, Oxford 1988).

'The Historiography of National Socialism', Michael Bentley, ed., *The Writing of History. An International Guide to Classical and Current Historiography* (London, forthcoming).

Carroll, Berenice A., *Design for Total War. Arms and Economics in the Third Reich*, The Hague/Paris 1968.

Chakotin, Sergei, *The Rape of the Masses*, New York 1940 (New York 1971).

Chilston, Viscount, 'The Rearmament of Britain, France and Germany down to the Munich Agreement of 30 September 1938', *Survey of International Affairs*, no. 3 (1938).

Clocchiati, Amerigo, *Cammina frut*, Milan 1972.

Cohn, Norman, *Warrant for Genocide*, London 1967 (Chico, CA 1981).

Coser, Rose Laub (ed.), *The Family. Its Structures and Functions*, 2nd edn.,

London 1974.

Czichon, Eberhard, 'Das Primat der Industrie im Kartell der nationalsozialistischen Macht', *Das Argument*, no. 47 (July 1968), pp. 168–92.

Dahrendorf, Ralf, *Gesellschaft und Demokratie in Deutschland*, Munich 1965 (*Society and Democracy in Germany*, London 1968).

Davin, Anna, 'Imperialism and Motherhood', *History Workshop Journal*, no. 5 (Spring 1978), pp. 9–65.

De Grazia, Victoria, *The Culture of Consent. The Mass Organization of Leisure in Fascist Italy*, Cambridge/New York 1981.

Deakin, Frederick W., *The Last Days of Mussolini*, Harmondsworth 1967.

Deist, Wilhelm, Messerschmidt, Manfred, Volkmann, Hans-Erich and Wette, Wolfram, *Das deutsche Reich und der Zweite Weltkrieg*, vol. I: *Ursachen und Voraussetzungen der deutschen Kriegspolitik*, Militärgeschichtliches Forschungsamt, Stuttgart 1979 (Frankfurt am Main 1989).

Dellavalle, Claudio, *Operai, industriali e Partito comunista nel Biellese 1940/1945*, Istituto Nazionale per la Storia del Movimento di Liberazione in Italia, Milan 1978.

'Gli scioperi del marzo–aprile 1943', *L'impegno. Rivista di storia contemporanea*, March 1983.

Deutsch, Harold H., *The Conspiracy against Hitler in the Twilight War*, Minneapolis, MN 1968.

Deutsche Sozialpolitik. Bericht der Deutschen Arbeitsfront, Zentralbüro, Sozialamt, 30 June 1936 to 31 August 1937, and 1 January to 31 December 1938, 2 vols., Berlin 1937, 1939.

Deutschlandberichte der Sozialdemokratischen Partei Deutschlands (Sopade), 1934–40, Frankfurt am Main 1980.

Dicks, Henry V., *Licensed Mass Murder. A Sociopsychological Study of Some SS-Killers*, London 1972.

Diels, Rudolf, *Lucifer ante Portas. Zwischen Severing und Heydrich*, Stuttgart 1950.

Dmitrov, Georgi, *Report to the 7th Congress Communist International*, London n.d. (1935).

Documents on German Foreign Policy, ser. D, vol. I, Washington, DC 1949.

Domarus, Max (ed.), *Hitler. Reden und Proklamationen*, 2 vols., Würzburg 1962 (Munich 1965; *Hitler: Speeches and Proclamations, 1932–1945. The Chronicle of a Dictatorship*, London 1990).

Dominik, Hans, *Das Schaltwerk der Siemens-Schuckertwerke AG Berlin*, Berlin 1929.

Dülffer, Jost, 'Bonapartism, Fascism and National Socialism', *Journal of Contemporary History*, vol. 11, no. 4 (October 1976), pp. 109–28.

'Der Beginn des Krieges 1939. Hitler, die innere Krise und das Mächtesystem', *Geschichte und Gesellschaft*, vol. 2, no. 4 (1976), pp. 443–70.

Eiber, L., *Arbeiter unter der nationalsozialistischen Herrschaft*, Munich 1979.

Eichholtz, Dietrich *Geschichte der deutschen Kriegswirtschaft 1939–1945*, 2nd edn, vol. I, East Berlin 1971 (E. Berlin 1984).

'Probleme einer Wirtschaftsgeschichte des Faschismus in Deutschland', *Jahrbuch für Wirtschaftsgeschichte*, 1963, Part III.

'Die IG-Farben-"Friedensplanung"', *Jahrbuch für Wirtschaftsgeschichte*, 1966, Part III, pp. 271–332.

Eicholtz, Dietrich and Gossweiler, Kurt, 'Noch einmal. Politik und Wirtschaft 1933–1945', *Das Argument*, no. 47 (July 1968), pp. 210–27.

Eley, Geoff, 'Nazism, Politics and the Image of the Past', *Past and Present*, no. 121 (November 1988), pp. 171–208.

'Wie denken wir über Politik? Alltagsgeschichte und die Kategorie des Politischen', Berliner Geschichtswerkstatt (ed.), *Alltagsgeschichte, Subjektivität und Geschichte. Zur Theorie und Praxis von Alltagsgeschichte*, Münster forthcoming.

Engels, Friedrich, 'The Role of Force in History' (1887), Karl Marx/Friedrich Engels, *Collected Works*, vol. XXVI, London 1990, pp. 455–510.

Erbe, R. *Die Nazionalsozialistische Wirtschaftspolitik*, Zürich 1958.

Esenweine-Rothe, Ingeborg, *Die Wirtschaftsverbände von 1933 bis 1945*, Berlin 1965.

Evans, Richard J., *The Feminist Movement in Germany 1894–1933*, London 1976.

In Hitler's Shadow. West German Historians and the Attempt to Escape from the Nazi Past, New York 1989.

'German Women and the Triumph of Hitler', *Journal of Modern History*, vol. 48, no. 1, (March 1976), supplement, pp. 123–75.

Federau, Fritz, *Der Zweite Weltkrieg. Seine Finanzierung in Deutschland*, Tübingen 1962.

Fest, Joachim C., *Hitler. Eine Biographie*, Frankfurt am Main/Vienna 1973 (*Hitler. A Biography*, London 1974).

Finzi, Roberto, *L'unità operaia contro il fascismo. Gli scioperi del marzo '43*, Bologna 1974.

Forever in the Shadow of Hitler? Original Documents of the Historikerstreit, trans. James Knowlton and Truett Cates, Atlantic Highlands, NJ 1993.

Frauengruppe Faschismusforschung, *Mutterkreuz und Arbeitsbuch. Zur Geschichte der Frauen in der Weimarer Republik und im Nationalsozialismus*, Frankfurt am Main 1981.

Friedlander, Saul, *Memory, History, and the Extermination of the Jews of Europe*, Bloomington, IN 1993.

'Some Reflections on the Historicization of National Socialism', *German Politics and Society*, vol. 13 (February 1988), pp. 9–21.

Friedlander, Saul (ed.), *Probing the Limits of Representation. Nazism and the 'Final Solution'*, Cambridge, MA 1992.

Friedlander, Saul and Broszat, Martin, 'A Controversy about the Historicization of National Socalism', *New German Critique*, no. 44 (spring/summer 1988), pp. 85–126.

Gackenholz, H., 'Reichskanzlei den 5 November 1937', *Forschungen zu Staat und Verfassung. Festgabe für Fritz Hartung*, Berlin 1958.

Gedye, G. E. R., *Fallen Bastions*, London 1939 (New York 1972).

Geer, J. S., *Der Markt der geschlossenen Nachfrage*, Berlin 1961.

Gellately, Robert, 'The Gestapo and German Society. Political Denunciation in the Gestapo Case Files', *Journal of Modern History*, no. 60 (December 1988), pp. 654–94.

Gersdorff, Ursula von (ed.), *Frauen im Kriegsdienst*, Stuttgart 1969.
Geyer, Michael, 'Rüstungsbeschleunigung und Inflation. Zur Inflationsdenkschrift des Oberkommandos der Wehrmacht vom November 1981', *Militärgeschichtliche Mitteilungen*, no. 2 (1981), pp. 121–86.
Glass, D. V., *Population Policies and Movements in Europe*, Oxford 1940 (1967).
Gobbi, Romolo, *Operaia e resistenza*, Turin 1973.
Goeb, Alexander, *Er war sechzehn als man ihn hängte*, Reinbek 1981.
Gouldner, Alvin W., *The Coming Crisis of Western Sociology*, London 1971.
Griepenburg, R. and Tjaden, K. H., 'Faschismus und Bonapartismus', *Das Argument*, no. 41 (December 1966), pp. 461–72.
Grünfeld, Judith. 'Rationalization and the Employment and Wages of Women in Germany', *International Labour Review*, vol. 29, no. 5 (May 1934), pp. 605–32.
Guillebaud, C. W., *The Social Policy of Nazi Germany*, Cambridge 1941 (New York 1971).
Hachtmann, Rüdiger, 'Von der Klassenharmonie zum regulierten Klassenkampf', *Soziale Bewegungen, Jahrbuch 1: Arbeiterbewegung und Faschismus*, Frankfurt am Main/New York 1984.
Harmsen, Hans and Lohse, Franz (eds.), *Bevölkerungsfragen. Bericht des Internationalen Kongresses fur Bevölkerungswissenschaft*, Munich 1936.
Harrison, Brian, 'For Church, Queen and Country. The Girls' Friendly Society 1874–1920', *Past and Present*, no. 61 (November 1973), pp. 107–38.
Hartman, Geoffrey (ed.), *Holocaust Remembrance. The Shapes of Memory*, Oxford 1993.
Harvey, Elizabeth, *Youth and the Welfare State in Weimar Germany*, Oxford 1993.
Hassell, Ulrich von, *Vom anderen Deutschland*, 3rd edn., Zürich 1947.
Hausen, Karin, 'Familie als Gegenstand historischer Sozialwissenschaft', *Geschichte und Gesellschaft*, vol. 1, no. 2/3 (1975), pp. 171–209.
'Mütter zwischen Geschäftsinteressen und kultischer Verehrung', in Gerhard Huck (ed.), *Sozialgeschichte der Freizeit*, Wuppertal 1980, pp. 249–80. ('Mother's Day in the Weimar Republic', in R. Bridenthal, A. Grossmann and M. Kaplan (eds.), *When Biology Became Destiny*, New York 1984.).
Havens, Thomas R. H., 'Women and War in Japan, 1937–1945', *American Historical Review*, vol. 80, no. 4 (October 1975), pp. 913–34.
Heberle, Rudolf, *From Democracy to Nazism*, Baton Rouge 1945 (New York 1970).
Herbert, Ulrich, *Fremdarbeiter. Politik und Praxis des 'Ausländer-Einsatzes' in der Kriegswirtschaft des Dritten Reiches*, Berlin/Bonn 1985.
A History of Foreign Labor in Germany 1880–1950, Ann Arbor, MI 1990.
Herbst, Ludolf, *Der Totale Krieg und die Ordnung der Wirtschaft*, Stuttgart 1982.
'Die Krise des nationalsozialistischen Regimes am Vorabend des Zweiten Weltkrieges und die forcierte Aufrüstung', *Vierteljahrshefte für Zeitgeschichte*, vol. 26, no. 3 (July 1978), pp. 347–92.
'Die Mobilmachung der Wirtschaft 1938/39 als Problem des nationalsozialistischen Herrschaftssystems', in Wolfgang Benz and Hermann Graml (eds.), *Sommer 1939. Die Grossmächte und der europäische Krieg*, Stuttgart 1979.
Hetzer, Gerhard, 'Die Industriestadt Augsburg', in Martin Broszat, Elke Fröhlich and Anton Grossmann (eds.), *Bayern in der NS-Zeit*, vol. III,

Munich/Vienna 1981, pp. 1–233.

Hildebrand, Klaus, *Vom Reich zum Weltreich*, Munich 1969.

'Weltmacht oder Untergang? Hitlers Deutschland 1941–1945', in Oswald Hauser (ed.), *Weltpolitik II, 1939–1945. 14 Vorträge*, Göttingen 1975.

'Hitlers Programm und seine Realisierung 1939–1942', in Manfred Funke (ed.), *Hitler, Deutschland und die Mächte*, Düsseldorf 1977, pp. 63–93.

'Nationalsozialismus ohne Hitler?', *Geschichte in Wissenschaft und Unterricht*, vol. 31 (1980), pp. 289–305.

'Monokratie oder Polykratie? Hitlers Herrschaft und das Dritte Reich', in Gerhard Hirschfeld and Lothar Kettenacker (eds.), *The 'Führer State'. Myth and Reality. Studies on the Politics and Structure of the Third Reich*, Stuttgart 1981, pp. 73–97.

Hillgruber, Andreas, *Hitlers Strategie. Politik und Kriegführung 1940–41*, Frankfurt am Main 1965 (Munich 1982).

'Forschungsstand und Literatur zum Ausbruch des zweiten Weltkrieges', in Wolfgang Benz and Hermann Graml (eds.), *Sommer 1939. Die Grossmächte und der europäische Krieg*, Stuttgart 1979.

Hillman, H. 'The Comparative Strength of the Great Powers', in A. Toynbee and F. T. Ashton-Gwatkin (eds.), *Survey of International Affairs. The World in March 1939*, London 1952.

Hinsley, F. H., review of A. J. P. Taylor, *The Origins of the Second World War*, *The Historical Journal*, vol. 4, no. 2 (1961), pp. 222–9.

'Historikerstreit', *Die Dokumentation der Kontroverse um die Einzigartigkeit der nationalsozialistischen Judenvernichtung*, Munich/Zürich 1987.

Historisches Archiv der Stadt Köln, *Widerstand und Verfolgung in Köln 1933–1945*, Cologne 1974.

Hitler, Adolf, 'Warum musste ein 8. November kommen?', *Deutschlands Erneuerung*, vol. 4 (1924), pp. 199–207.

Hitlers Zweites Buch, ed. Gerhard Weinberg, Stuttgart 1961 (*Hitler's Secret Book*, New York 1983).

Mein Kampf, Munich 1941 (*My Struggle*, London 1981).

Hoch, Anton, und Gruchman, Lothar, *Georg Elser. Der Attentäter aus dem Volke*, Frankfurt am Main 1980.

Hoess, Rudolf, *Commandant of Auschwitz*, London 1959.

Hofer, Walter, *Die Entfesselung des zweiten Weltkrieges*, rev. edn, Frankfurt am Main 1960 (Düsseldorf 1984).

Hoffmann, Peter, *Hitler's Personal Security*, London 1979.

Hoffmann, Walter Gustav, *Das Wachstum der deutschen Wirtschaft seit der Mitte des 19. Jahrhunderts*, Berlin/Heidelberg 1965.

Höhne, Heinz, *Der Ordern unter dem Totenkopf*, Hamburg 1966 (*The Order of the Death's Head*, London 1981).

Homze, Edward L., *Foreign Labor in Nazi Germany*, Princeton, NJ 1967.

Horbach, M., *Out of the Night*, London 1967.

Horkheimer, Max, Fromm, Erich and Marcuse, Hebert, et al., *Studien über Autorität und Familie*, Paris 1936.

Horn, Daniel, 'Youth Resistance in the Third Reich', *Journal of Social History*, vol. 7, no. 1 (autumn 1973), pp. 26–50.

Huck, Alfred, Nipperdey, Hans Carl and Dietz, Rolf, *Gesetz zur Ordnung der nationalen Arbeit*, 3rd edn, Munich/Berlin 1939.

Huck, Gerhard (ed.), *Sozialgeschichte der Freizit*, Wuppertal 1980.

Jacobsen, Hans-Adolf, *Fall 'Gelb'*, Wiesbaden 1957.

Jacobsen, Hans-Adolf (ed.), *Dokumente zur Vorgeschichte des Westfeldzuges, 1939–1940*, vol. I, Göttingen 1956.

Janssen, Gregor, *Das Ministerium Speer. Deutschlands Rüstung im Krieg*, Berlin/Frankfurt/Vienna 1968.

Jay, Martin, *The Dialectical Imagination*, Boston/Toronto 1973.

Jessop, Bob, *The Capitalist State. Marxist Theories and Methods*, New York 1982.

Johnson, Richard, 'Thompson, Genovese, and Socialist–Humanist History', *History Workshop Journal*, no. 6 (autumn 1978), pp. 79–100.

Kahn-Freund, Otto, 'Das soziale Ideal des Reichsarbeitsgerichts', in Thilo Ramm (ed.), *Arbeitsrecht und Politik. Quellentexte 1918–1933*, Neuwied 1966.

Kaiser, David, *Economic Diplomacy and the Origins of the Second World War*, Princeton, NJ 1980.

'Germany, "Domestic Crisis" and War in 1939. Comment 1', *Past and Present*, no. 122 (February 1989), pp. 200–5.

Kater, Michael, 'Krise des Frauenstudiums in der Weimarer Republik', *Vierteljahresschrift für Sozial- und Wirtschaftsgeschichte*, vol. 59 (1972), pp. 207–55.

Kele, Max H., *Nazis and Workers. National Socialist Appeals to German Labor 1919–1933*, Chapel Hill, NC 1972.

Kershaw, Ian, *Der Hitler-Mythos. Volksmeinung und Propaganda im Dritten Reich*, Stuttgart 1980 (*The Hitler Myth. Image and Reality in the Third Reich*, Oxford 1987).

Popular Opinion and Political Dissent in the Third Reich. Bavaria 1933–1945, Oxford 1983.

The Nazi Dictatorship. Problems and Perspectives of Interpretation, London 1985 (3rd edn, London 1993).

'The Nazi State: An Exceptional State?', *New Left Review*, no. 176 (July/August 1989), pp. 47–67.

Kirkpatrick, Clifford, *Nazi Germany. Its Women and Family Life*, Indianapolis/New York 1938.

Kitchen, Martin, *Fascism*, London 1976.

'August Thalheimer's Theory of Fascism', *Journal of the History of Ideas*, vol. 34, no. 1 (1973), pp. 67–78.

Klein, Burton H., *Germany's Economic Preparations for War*, Cambridge, MA 1959.

'Germany's Preparation for War. A Re-examination', *American Economic Review*, vol. 38 (March 1948), pp. 56–77.

Klemperer, V., *LTI. Notizbuch eines Philogen*, Berlin 1947 (Leipzig 1987).

Klessmann, Christoph, *Polnische Bergarbeiter im Ruhrgebiet 1870–1945*, Göttingen 1978.

Knodel, John E., *The Decline of Fertility in Germany 1871–1939*, Princeton, NJ 1974.

Knox, Macgregor, 'Conquest, Foreign and Domestic, in Fascist Italy and Nazi

Germany', *Journal of Modern History*, vol. 56 (March 1984), pp. 1–57.

Kocka, Jürgen, *Die Angestellten in der deutschen Geschichte 1850–1980*, Göttingen 1981.

Köhler, Jochen, *Klettern in der Grossstadt*, Berlin 1981.

Köllman, Wolfgang, 'Bevölkerungsentwicklung in der Weimarer Republik', in Hans Mommsen, Dietmar Petzina and Bernd Weisbrod (eds.), *Industrielles System und politische Entwicklung in der Weimarer Republik*, Düsseldorf 1974, pp. 76–84.

König, René, *Die Zeit ohne Eigenschaften*, ed. K. Reinisch, Stuttgart 1961.

Koonz, Claudia, *Mothers in the Fatherland. Women, the Family and Nazi Politics*, London 1987.

Kroll, Gerhard, *Von der Weltwirtschaftskrise zur Staatskonjunktur*, Berlin 1958.

Kuczynski, Robert R., *The Measurement of Population Growth. Methods and Results*, London 1935 (New York 1969).

Kuczynski, Robert R., *Childless Marriages*, London, n.d. (1939?); reprint of three articles from *The Sociological Review*, vol. 30 (1938).

Kühnl, Reinhard, *Formen bürgerlicher Herrschaft. Liberalismus–Faschismus*, Reinbek 1971.

'Probleme einer Theorie über den internationalen Faschismus', *Politische Vierteljahresschrift*, vol. 16 (1975).

Kühnl, Reinhard (ed.), *Texte zur Faschismusdiskussion. Positionen und Kontroversen*, Reinbek, 1974.

Kühr, Herbert, *Parteien und Wähler im Stadt- und Landkreis Essen in der Zeit der Weimarer Republik*, Düsseldorf 1973.

Lacapra, Dominick, *Representing the Holocaust. History, Theory, Trauma*, Bloomington, IN 1994.

Laqueur, Walter (ed.), *Fascism. A Reader's Guide. Analyses, Interpretations, Bibliographies*, Harmondsworth 1976.

Larsen, Stein Ugelvik, Hagtvet, Bernt and Myklebust, Jan Petter (eds.), *Who Were the Fascists? Social Roots of European Fascism*, Bergen 1980.

Lasch, Christopher, 'The Family and History', *New York Review of Books*, vol. 22, no. 18–20 (November–December 1975).

Leber, Annedore, *Das Gewissen steht auf*, Berlin/Frankfurt am Main 1956 (Mainz 1984).

Leppert-Fögen, Annette, *Die deklassierte Klasse. Studien zur Geschichte und Ideologie des Kleinbürgertums*, Frankfurt am Main 1974.

Lipstadt, Deborah, *Denying the Holocaust. The Growing Assault on Truth and Memory*, New York 1993.

Lochner, Louis P., *Tycoons and Tyrants*, Chicago 1954.

Loewenberg, Peter, 'The Psychohistorical Origins of the Nazi Youth Cohort', *American Historical Review*, vol. 76, no. 5 (December 1971), pp. 1457–502.

Lubasz, Heinz, *New York Review of Books*, vol 11, no. 11 (19 December 1968), p. 33.

Lüdtke, Alf, 'Faschismus-Potentiale und faschistische Herrschaft oder Theorie-Defizite und antifaschistische Strategie', in H.-G. Backhaus et al. (eds.), *Gesellschaft. Beiträge zur Marxschen Theorie*, vol. VI, Frankfurt am Main 1976, pp. 194–241.

'"Formierung der Massen": oder Mitmachen und Hinnehmen?' "Alltagsgeschichte" und Faschismusanalyse', in Heide Gerstenberger and Dorothea Schmidt (eds.), *Normalität oder Normalisierung? Geschichtswerkstätten und Faschismusanalyse*, Munster 1987, pp. 15–34.

'"Ehre der Arbeit?" Industriearbeiter und Macht der Symbole. Zur Reichsweite symbolischer Orientierungen im Nationalsozialismus', in Klaus Tenfelde (ed.), *Arbeiter im 20. Jahrhundert*, Stuttgart 1991, pp. 343–92.

Lüdtke, Alf (ed.), *Alltagsgeschichte. Zur Rekonstruktion historischer Erfahrungen und Lebensweisen*, Frankfurt am Main 1989.

Lukes, Steven, *Individualism*, Oxford 1973 (1984).

Luraghi, Raimondo, *Il movimento operaio torinese durante la Resistenza*, Turin 1958.

Lyotard, Jean François, *The Differend. Phrases in Dispute*, Minneapolis, MN 1988.

McIntyre, Jill, 'Women and the Professions in Germany, 1930–1940', in Anthony Nicholls and Erich Matthias (eds.), *German Democracy and the Triumph of Hitler*, London 1971, pp. 175–213.

Maier, Charles, 'Between Taylorism and Technocracy', *Journal of Contemporary History*, vol. 5, no. 2 (1970), pp. 27–61.

'The Economics of Fascism and Nazism', in idem (ed.), *In Search of Stability*, Cambridge 1987, pp. 70–120.

The Unmasterable Past. History, Holocaust and German National Identity, Cambridge, MA 1988.

Mann, Reinhard, *Protest und Kontrolle im Dritten Reich*, Frankfurt am Main/New York 1987.

Mansfeld, Werner, *Die Ordnung der nationalen Arbeit. Handausgabe mit Erläuterungen*, Berlin 1941.

'Lohnpolitik im Kriege', *Monatshefte für NS-Sozialpolitik*, vol. 6 (1939), pp. 383–6.

Mansfeld, Werner, Pohl, W., Steinmann, G. and Krause, A. B., *Die Ordnung der nationalen Arbeit. Kommentar*, Berlin/Leipzig/Mannheim/Munich 1934.

Martel, Gorden (ed.), *The Origins of the Second World War Reconsidered. The A. J. P. Taylor debate after Twenty-Five Years*, London 1986.

Maschmann, Melita, *Fazit*, Stuttgart 1963 (Munich 1980; *Account Rendered*, London 1965).

Mass Observation, *People in Production. An Enquiry into British War Production*, Harmondsworth 1942.

Massola, Umberto, *Marzo 1943 ore 10*, with Preface by Luigi Longo, Rome 1950. *Critica marxista*, nos. 5 and 6, 1971; 1976.

Gli scioperi del '43. Marzo–aprile: le fabbriche contro il fascismo, Rome 1973.

Massola, Umberto and Girolamo Li Causi, *Gli scioperi del 1943–44*, Rome 1945.

Meinck, G., *Hitler und die deutsche Aufrüstung 1933–37*, Wiesbaden 1959.

Merkl, Peter H., *Political Violence under the Swastika. 581 Early Nazis*, Princeton, NJ 1975 (Berkeley, CA 1986).

Middleton, Chris, 'Sexual Inequality and Stratification Theory', in Frank Parkin (ed.), *The Social Analysis of Class Structure*, London 1974.

Milward, Alan, *The German Economy at War*, London 1965.

War, Economy and Society, 1939–1945, London 1977.

Mitchell, B. R. and Deane, Phyllis, *Abstract of British Historical Statistics*, 2nd edn, Cambridge 1971.

Mommsen, Hans, *Beamtentum im Dritten Reich*, Stuttgart 1966.

'National Socialism. Continuity and Change', in Walter Laqueur (ed.), *Fascism. A Reader's Guide*, Harmondsworth 1976, pp. 151–92.

'Ausnahmezustand als Herrschaftstechnik des NS-Regimes', in Manfred Funke (ed.), *Hitler, Deutschland und die Mächte*, Düsseldorf 1977, pp. 30–45.

'Nationalsozialismus als vorgetäuschte Modernisierung', in Walter H. Pehle (ed.), *Der historische Ort des Nationalsozialismus*, Frankfurt am Main 1990, pp. 31–46.

Moore, Barrington Jr, *Injustice. The Social Bases of Obedience and Revolt*, London 1978.

Mowat, Charles L., *The Charity Organization Society 1869–1913*, London 1961.

Murphy, Richard C., *Polish In-Migrants in Bottrop 1891–1933*, Ph.D. thesis, Iowa 1977 (*Guestworkers in the German Reich. A Polish Community in Wilhelmine Germany* (Boulder, CO 1983).

Neumann, Franz, *Behemoth. The Structure and Practice of National Socialism*, London 1942 (New York 1972).

New Left Review, nos. 83 (January–February 1974), and 89 (January–February 1975).

Niethammer, Lutz, 'Wie wohnten die Arbeiter im Kaiserreich?', *Archiv für Sozialgeschichte*, vol. 16 (1976), pp. 61–134.

Niethammer, Lutz (ed.), *Lebensgeschichte und Sozialkultur im Ruhrgebiet 1930 bis 1960*, vol. I: *'Die Jahre weiss man nicht, wo man die heute hinsetzen soll.' Faschismuserfahrungen im Ruhrgebiet*; vol. II: *'Hinterher merkt man, dass es richtig war, dass es schiefgegangen ist.' Nachkriegserfahrungen im Ruhrgebiet*; vol. III: *'Wir kriegen jetzt andere Zeiten.' Auf der Suche nach der Erfahrung des Volkes in nachfaschistischen Länder*, Berlin/Bonn, 1983–5.

Niethammer, Lutz, Borsdorf, Ulrich and Brandt, Peter (eds.), *Arbeiterinitiative 1945*, Wuppertal 1980.

Noakes, Jeremy, *The Nazi Party in Lower Saxony 1921–1933*, London 1971.

Noakes, Jeremy and Pridham, Geoffrey (eds.), *Documents on Nazism 1919–1945*, London 1974 (*Nazism 1919–1945. A Documentary History* (Exeter 1983–8), 3 vols).

Nolan, Mary, *Visions of Modernity. American Business and the Modernization of Germany*, New York 1994.

'Class Struggles in the Third Reich', in *Radical History Review*, vol. 4, no. 2/3 (1977).

Nolte, Ernst, *Theorien über den Faschismus*, Cologne/Berlin 1967.

Overy, Richard, *War and Economy in the Third Reich*, Oxford 1994.

'Hitler's War and the German Economy. A Reinterpretation', *Economic History Review*, 2nd ser., vol. 35, no. 2 (1982), pp. 272–91.

'Germany, "Domestic Crisis" and War in 1939', *Past and Present*, no. 116 (August 1987), pp. 138–68.

'"Blitzkriegswirtschaft"? Finanz, Lebensstandard und Arbeitseinsatz in Deutschland 1939–1945', *Vierteljahrshefte für Zeitgeschichte*, vol. 36, no. 3

(July 1988), pp. 379–435.

Parsons, Talcott, 'Democracy and Social Structure in Pre-Nazi Germany', in idem, *Essays in Sociological Theory*, Glencoe 1954 (New York 1966).

Pavone, Claudio, *Una guerra civile. Saggio storico sulla moralità nella Resistenza*, Turin 1991.

Paxton, Robert O., *Vichy France. Old Guard and New Order, 1940–1944*, New York 1972 (New York 1982).

Pelcovits, Nathan A., 'The Social Honor Courts of Nazi Germany', *Political Science Quarterly*, vol. 53, no. 3 (September 1938), 350–71.

Peterson, Edward Norman, *Hjalmar Schacht. For and Against Hitler*, Boston, MA 1954.

Petzina, Dietmar, *Der nationalsozialistische Vierjahresplan*, diss., Mannheim 1965.
Autarkiepolitik im Dritten Reich. Der nationalsozialistische Vierjahresplan, Stuttgart 1968.
'Die Mobilisierung deutscher Arbeitskräfte vor und während des Zweiten Weltkrieges', *Vierteljahrshefte für Zeitgeschichte*, vol. 18, no. 4 (October 1970), pp. 443–55.

Peukert, Detlev, *Ruhrarbeiter gegen den Faschismus*, Frankfurt am Main 1976.
Die KPD im Widerstand. Verfolgung und Untergrundarbeit an Rhein und Ruhr 1933–1945, Wuppertal 1980.
Inside Nazi Germany. Conformity, Opposition and Racism in Everyday Life, London 1987.
'Der deutsche Arbeiterwiderstand 1933–1945', *Aus Politik und Zeitgeschichte. Beilage zur Wochenschrift 'Das Parlament'*, 14 July 1979.
'Edelweisspiraten, Meuten, Swing', in Gerhard Huck (ed.), *Sozialgeschichte der Freizeit*, Wuppertal 1980, pp. 307–27.
The Weimar Republic. The Crisis of Classical Modernity, London 1991.
'The Genesis of the "Final Solution" from the Spirit of Science', in Thomas Childers and Jane Caplan (eds.), *Reevaluating the Third Reich*, New York 1993, pp. 234–52.

Peukert, Detlev and Reulecke, Jürgen (eds.), *Die Reihen fast geschlossen. Beiträge zur Geschichte des Alltags unterm Nationalsozialismus*, Wuppertal 1981.

Picker, Henry and Schramm, Percy Ernst (eds.), *Hitlers Tischgespräche im Führerhauptquartier 1941/42*, 2nd edn. Stuttgart 1965 (Frankfurt am Main 1989).

Pombeni, Paolo, *Demagogia e tirannide. Uno studie sulla forma partito de fascismo*, Bologna 1984.

Poor, Harold, 'City versus Country. Urban Change and Development in the Weimar Republic', in Hans Mommsen, Dietmar Petzina and Bernd Weisbrod (eds.), *Industrielles System und politische Entwicklung in der Weimarer Republik*, Düsseldorf 1974, pp. 111–27.

Postan, M. M., *British War Production*, History of the Second World War, UK Civil Series, London 1952.

Poulantzas, Nicos, *Political Power and Social Classes*, London 1973.
Fascism and Dictatorship. The Third International and the Problem of Fascism, London 1974.

Preller, Ludwig, *Sozialpolitik in der Weimarer Republik*, Stuttgart 1949 (Düsseldorf 1978).

Prinz, Michael, *Vom neuen Mittelstand zum Volksgenossen*, Munich 1986.

Prinz, Michael and Zitelmann, Rainer (eds.), *Nationalsozialismus und Modernisierung*, Darmstadt 1991.

Radkau, Joachim, 'Entscheidungsprozesse und Entscheidungsdefizite in der deutschen Aussenwirtschaftspolitik 1933–1940', *Geschichte und Gesellschaft*, vol. 2, no. 1 (1976), pp. 33–65.

Ramm, Thilo, 'Nationalsozialismus und Arbeitsrecht', *Kritische Justiz*, no. 2 (1969), pp. 108–20.

Ramm, Thilo (ed.), *Arbeitsrecht und Politik. Quellentexte 1918–1933*, Neuwied 1966.

Recker, Marie-Luise, *Nationalsozialistische Sozialpolitik im Zweiten Weltkrieg*, Munich 1985.

Reich, Wilhelm, *The Mass Psychology of Fascism* (1933), Harmondsworth 1975.

Reulecke, Jürgen, 'Veränderungen des Arbeitskräftepotentials im Dritten Reich 1900–1933', in Hans Mommsen, Dietmar Petzina and Bernd Weisbrod (eds.), *Industrielles System und politische Entwicklung in der Weimarer Republik*, Düsseldorf 1974, pp. 84–95.

Reynolds, P. A., 'Hitler's War?', *History*, vol. 46 (1961), pp. 212–17.

Richards, Eric, 'Women in the British Economy since about 1700. An Interpretation', *History*, vol. 59 (October 1974), pp. 337–57.

Robertson, Esmonde M., *Hitler's Pre-War Policy and Military Plans 1933–1939*, London 1963.

Robertson, Esmonde M. (ed.), *The Origins of the Second World War*, London 1973.

Robinson, Paul A., *The Sexual Radicals*, London 1970.

Rohe, Karl, *Das Reichsbanner Schwarz–Rot–Gold*, Düsseldorf 1966.

Rosenberg, Arthur, *A History of the German Republic*, London 1936 (New York 1965).

Rosenhaft, Eve, 'Working-class Life and Working-class Politics', in Richard Bessel and E. J. Feuchtwanger (eds.), *Social Change and Political Development in Weimar Germany*, London 1981, pp. 207–40.

Rowbotham, Sheila, *Woman's Consciousness, Man's World*, Harmondsworth 1973.

Rowntree, B. Seebohm, *The Human Factor in Business*, 3rd edn, London 1938 (New York 1979).

Sachse, Carola, Siegel, Tilla, Spode, Hasso, Spohn, Wolfgang, *Angst, Belohnung, Zucht und Ordnung. Herrschaftsmechanismen im Nationalsozialismus*, Opladen 1982.

Salter, Stephen, 'The Mobilisation of German Labour, 1939–1945', D.Phil. thesis, Oxford 1983.

Sauer, Wolfgang, Schulz, Gerhard and Bracher, Karl Dietrich, *Die nationalsozialistische Machtergreifung*, Cologne/Opladen 1960.

Schacht, Hjalmar, *Account Settled*, London 1949.

Schieder, Wolfgang, *Faschismus als soziale Bewegung. Deutschland und Italien im Vergleich*, Göttingen 1983.

Schlicker, Wolfgang, 'Arbeitsdienstbestrebungen des deutschen Monopolkapitals in der Weimarer Republik unter besonderer Berücksichtigung des Deutschen

Instituts für technische Arbeitsschulung', *Jahrbuch für Wirtschaftsgeschichte*, 1971, Part III.

Schmidt, Hans Dieter, et al., *Frauenfeindlichkeit. Sozialpsychologische Aspekte der Misogynie*, Munich 1973.

Schoenbaum, David, *Hitler's Social Revolution. Class and Status in Nazi Germany 1933–1939*, New York 1966 (New York 1980).

Schumacher, Martin, *Mittelstandsfront und Republik. Die Wirtschaftspartei-Reichspartei des deutschen Mittelstandes 1919–1933*, Düsseldorf 1972.

Schumann, Hans-Gerd, *Nationalsozialismus und Gewerkschaftsbewegung*, Hanover/Frankfurt am Main 1958.

Schutz der werktätigen Frau, Reichsarbeitsministerium, Berlin 1941.

Schweitzer, Arthur, *Big Business in the Third Reich*, Bloomington, IN 1964.

'The Foreign Exchange Crisis of 1936', *Zeitschrift für die gesamte Staatswissenschaft*, vol. 118, no. 2 (1962), pp. 243–77.

'Plans and Markets: Nazi Style', *Kyklos: International Review for Social Sciences*, vol. 30 (1977), pp. 88–115.

Schwenger, Rudolf, 'Die betriebliche Sozialpolitik im Ruhrkohlenbergbau', *Schriften des Vereins für Sozialpolitik*, vol. 186, no. 1 (1932).

'Die betriebliche Sozialpolitik in der westdeustchen Grosseisenindustrie', *Schriften des Vereins für Sozialpolitik*, vol. 186, no. 2 (1934).

Seeber, Eva, *Zwangsarbeiter in der faschistischen Kriegswirtschaft*, East Berlin 1964.

Sender, Toni, *The Autobiography of a German Rebel*, London 1940.

Senise, Carmine, *Quando ero capo della polizia*, Rome 1946.

Siebert, Wolfgang, *Das Recht der Arbeit*, Berlin/Leipzig/Vienna 1941.

Simpson, A. E., 'The Struggle for Control of the German Economy 1936–37', *Journal of Modern History*, vol. 31 (1959), pp. 37–45.

Smelser, Neil J., *Social Change in the Industrial Revolution. An Application of Theory to the Lancashire Cotton Industry, 1770–1840*, London 1959.

Speer, Albert, *Erinnerungen*, Berlin 1969 (*Inside the Third Reich*, London 1970).

Spriano, Paolo, *Storia del Partito communista italiana*, vol. IV, Turin 1976.

Statistical Digest of the War, History of the Second World War, UK Civil Series, London 1951.

Statistisches Handbuch von Deutschland 1928–1944, Munich 1949.

Stephenson, Jill, 'Girls' Higher Education in Germany in the 1930s', *Journal of Contemporary History*, vol. 10, no. 1 (January 1975), pp. 41–69.

'Women in Nazi Society 1930–1940', Ph.D. thesis, Edinburgh 1974 (*Women in Nazi Society*, London 1975).

The Nazi Organization of Women, London 1981.

Steubel, H., 'Die Finanzierung der Aufrüstung im Dritten Reich', *Europa Archiv* (June 1951).

Sullerot, Evelyne, 'Condition de la femme', in Alfred Sauvy (ed.), *Historie économique de la France entre les deux guerres*, vol. III, Paris 1972, pp. 418–34.

Syrup, Friedrich, *Hundert Jahre staatlicher Sozialpolitik*, ed. Julius Scheuble; rev. Otto Neuloh, Stuttgart 1957.

Sywottek, Arnold, *Deutsche Volksdemokratie. Studien zur politischen Konzeption der KPD 1935–1946*, Düsseldorf 1971.

Taylor, A. J. P., *The Origins of the Second World War*, 5th impression, London 1963.

Theweleit, Klaus, *Männerfantasien*, Frankfurt am Main 1977, 2 vols. (*Male Fantasies*, Minneapolis, MN 1989).

Thomas, Georg, *Geschichte der deutschen Wehr- und Rüstungswirtschaft (1918–1943/ 45)*, ed. Wolfgang Birkenfeld, Boppard am Rhein 1966.

Thomas, Katherine, *Women in Nazi Germany*, London 1943.

Thönnessen, Werner, *The Emancipation of Women. The Rise and Fall of the Women's Movement in German Social Democracy, 1863–1933*, London 1973.

Titmuss, Richard, *Essays on the Welfare State*, London 1958, 6th edn 1966 (London 1976).

Titmuss, Richard and Kathleen, *Parents Revolt. A Study of the Declining Birth-Rate in Acquisitive Societies*, London 1942 (New York 1985).

Treue, Wilhelm (ed. and introd.), 'Hitlers Denkschrift zum Vierjahresplan 1936', *Vierteljahrshefte für Zeitgeschichte*, vol. 3, no. 3 (July 1955), pp. 184–210.

Treue, Wilhelm (ed.), 'Rede Hitlers vor der deutschen Presse (10. November 1938)', *Vierteljahrshefte für Zeitgeschichte*, vol. 6, no. 2 (April 1958), pp. 175–91.

Trial of the Major War Criminals Before the International Military Tribunal Nuremberg, 14 November 1945–1 October 1946, 42 vols., Nuremberg 1947–9.

Tröger, Annemarie, 'The Creation of a Female Assembly-Line Proletariat', in Renate Bridenthal et al. (eds.), *When Biology Became Destiny*, New York 1984, pp. 236–70.

Trotsky, Leon, *The Struggle Against Fascism in Germany* (1930–40), New York 1971.

Turner, Henry Ashby, Jr, *Stresemann and the Politics of the Weimar Republic*, Princeton, NJ 1963 (Westport, CT 1979).

Turner, Henry Ashby, Jr (ed.), *Nazism and the Third Reich*, New York 1972. *Faschismus und Kapitalismus in Deutschland*, Göttingen 1972 (Göttingen 1980).

Turner, Henry Ashby, Jr. (ed.), *Reappraisals of Fascism*, New York 1975.

Vaccarino, Giorgio, 'Gli scioperi del marzo 1943. Contributo per una storia del movimento operaio a Torino', in *Aspetti della Resistenza in Piemonte*, Istituto storico della Resistenza in Piemonte, Turin 1950.

Problemi della Resistenza italiana, Modena 1966.

Vidal-Naquet, Pierre, *Assassins of Memory. Essays on the Denial of the Holocaust*, New York 1992.

Vierhaus, Rudolf, 'Auswirkungen der Krise um 1930 in Deutschland. Beiträge zu einer historisch-psychologischen Analyse', in Wolfgang Conze and Hans Raupach (eds.), *Die Staats- und Wirtschaftskrise des Deutschen Reiches*, Stuttgart 1967, pp. 155–75.

Voigt, G., 'Zur Sprache des Faschismus', *Das Argument*, no. 43 (July 1967), pp. 154–65.

Volkmann, Hans-Erich, 'Aussenhandel und Aufrüstung in Deutschland 1933 bis 1939', in F. Forstmeier and H.-E. Volkmann (eds.), *Wirtschaft und Rüstung am Vorabend des zweiten Weltkrieges*, Düsseldorf, 1975, pp. 81–131.

'Die NS-Wirtschaft in Vorbereitung des Krieges', in Wilhelm Deist, Manfred Messerschmidt, Hans-Erich Volkmann and Wolfram Wette, *Das deutsche Reich und der Zweite Weltkrieg*, Stuttgart 1979, vol. I: *Ursachen und Voraussetzungen der deutschen Kriegspolitik*, pp. 175–368.

Vollmer, Bernhard, *Volksopposition im Polizeistaat*, Stuttgart 1957.

Wagner, Elisabeth (ed.), *Der Generalquartiermeister. Briefe und Tagebuchaufzeichnungen des Generalquartiermeisters des Heeres General der Artillerie Eduard Wagner*, Munich/Vienna 1963.

Werner, Wolfgang Franz, *'Bleib übrig!' Deutsche Arbeiter in der nationalsozialistischen Kriegswirtschaft*, Düsseldorf 1983.

Werth, Alexander, *The Destiny of France*, London 1937.

Willmot, Louise, 'National Socialist Youth Organisations for Girls', D.Phil. thesis, Oxford 1979.

Winkler, Dörte, *Frauenarbeit im 'Dritten Reich'*, Hamburg 1977.

Winkler, Heinrich August, *Mittelstand, Demokratie und Nationalsozialismus. Die politische Entwicklung von Handwerk und Kleinhandel in der Weimarer Republik*, Cologne 1972.

Revolution, Staat, Faschismus. Zur Revision des historischen Materialismus, Göttingen 1978.

'Der entbehrliche Stand. Zur Mittelstandspolitik im "Dritten Reich"', *Archiv für Sozialgeschichte*, vol. 17 (1977), pp. 1–40.

Winkler, Lutz, *Studie zur gesellschaftlichen Funktion faschistischer Sprache*, Frankfurt am Main 1970.

Wisotzky, Klaus, 'Der Ruhrbergbau am Vorabend des Zweiten Weltkriegs', *Vierteljahrshefte für Zeitgeschichte*, vol. 30, no. 3 (July 1982), pp. 418–61.

Wolin, Sheldon, *Politics and Vision*, New York 1960.

Woolf, Stuart J. (ed.), *The Nature of Fascism*, London 1968.

Wunderlich, Frieda, *Farm Labor in Germany 1810–1945. Its Historical Development within the Framework of Agricultural and Social Policy*, Princeton, NJ 1961.

Wynn, Margaret, *Family Policy*, 2nd edn, Harmondsworth 1972.

Young, James, *Writing and Rewriting the Holocaust. Narrative and the Consequences of Interpretation*, Bloomington, IN 1988.

Youngson, A. J., *The British Economy, 1920–57*, London 1960.

Ziebura, Gilbert (ed.), *Grundfragen der deutschen Aussenpolitik seit 1871*, Darmstadt 1975.

Zorn, Gerda and Meyer, Gertrud (eds.), *Frauen gegen Hitler. Berichte aus dem Widerstand 1933–1945*, Frankfurt am Main 1974 (West Berlin 1984).

Zumpe, Lotte, 'Ein Beitrag zur Wirtschafts- und Sozialgeschichte des deutschen Faschismus', *Jahrbuch für Wirtschaftgeschichte*, 1979, Part IV.

INDEX